P9-DXO-282

Also by Barack Obama

The Audacity of Hope

Dreams from My Father

Dreams from My Father

A Story of Race and Inheritance

Barack Obama

CROWN PUBLISHERS
NEW YORK

Published in the United States by Crown Publishers, an imprint of the Crown
Publishing Group, a division of Random House, Inc., New York.

www.crownpublishing.com

Crown is a trademark and the Crown colophon is a registered trademark of
Random House, Inc.

Originally published in hardcover in 1995 by Times Books, an imprint of the
Crown Publishing Group, a division of Random House, Inc. and in paperback
by Kodansha America, Inc., in 1996. Subsequently published in paperback with
preface and keynote address in 2004 by Three Rivers Press, an imprint of the
Crown Publishing Group, a division of Random House, Inc. This edition
appears without keynote address.

Grateful acknowledgment is made to Russell & Volkening as agents for Ntozake
Shange for permission to reprint an excerpt from *For Colored Girls Who Have
Considered Suicide When the Rainbow Is Enuf* by Ntozake Shange, copyright © 1975,
renewed 2003 by Ntozake Shange.

Printed in the United States of America

Library of Congress Cataloging-in-Publication Data
Obama, Barack.
Dreams from my father : a story of race and inheritance /
Barack Obama.
1. Obama, Barack. 2. African Americans—Biography. 3. Racially mixed people—
United States—Biography. 4. Racism—United States. 5. United States—Race
relations. I. Title.
E185.97.O23A3 2004
973'.0405967625013'092—dc22   2004012412

ISBN 978-0-307-38341-9

11 12 13 14 15 16 17 18 19 20

First Edition

"For we are strangers before them,
and sojourners, as were all our fathers.

1 CHRONICLES 29:15

PREFACE TO THE 2004 EDITION

· ·

ALMOST A DECADE HAS passed since this book was first published. As I mention in the original introduction, the opportunity to write the book came while I was in law school, the result of my election as the first African-American president of the *Harvard Law Review*. In the wake of some modest publicity, I received an advance from a publisher and went to work with the belief that the story of my family, and my efforts to understand that story, might speak in some way to the fissures of race that have characterized the American experience, as well as the fluid state of identity—the leaps through time, the collision of cultures—that mark our modern life.

Like most first-time authors, I was filled with hope and despair upon the book's publication—hope that the book might succeed beyond my youthful dreams, despair that I had failed to say anything worth saying. The reality fell somewhere in between. The reviews were mildly favorable. People actually showed up at the readings my publisher arranged. The sales were underwhelming. And, after a few months, I went on with the business of my life, certain that my career as an author would be short-lived, but glad to have survived the process with my dignity more or less intact.

I had little time for reflection over the next ten years. I ran a voter registration project in the 1992 election cycle, began a civil rights practice, and started teaching constitutional law at the University of Chicago. My wife and I bought a house, were blessed with two gorgeous, healthy, and mischievous daughters, and struggled to pay the bills. When a seat in the state legislature opened up in 1996, some friends persuaded me to run for the office, and I won. I had been warned, before taking office, that state politics lacks the glamour of its Washington counterpart; one labors largely in obscurity, mostly on topics that mean a great deal to some but that the average man or woman on the street can safely ignore (the regulation of mobile homes, say, or the tax consequences of farm equipment depreciation). Nonetheless, I found the work satisfying, mostly because the scale of state politics allows for concrete results—an expansion of health insurance for poor children, or a reform of laws that send innocent men to death row—within a meaningful time frame. And too, because within the capitol building of a big, industrial state, one sees every day the face of a nation in constant conversation: inner-city mothers and corn and bean farmers, immigrant day laborers alongside suburban investment bankers—all jostling to be heard, all ready to tell their stories.

A few months ago, I won the Democratic nomination for a seat as the U.S. senator from Illinois. It was a difficult race, in a crowded field of well-funded, skilled, and prominent candidates; without organizational backing or personal wealth, a black man with a funny name, I was considered a long shot. And so, when I won a majority of the votes in the Democratic primary, winning in white areas as well as black, in the suburbs as well as Chicago, the reaction that followed echoed the response to my election to the *Law Review*. Mainstream commentators expressed surprise and genuine hope that my victory signaled a broader change in our racial politics. Within the black community, there was a sense of pride regarding my accomplishment, a pride mingled with frustration that fifty years after *Brown* v. *Board of Education* and forty years after the passage of the Voting Rights Act, we should still be celebrating the possibility (and only the possibility, for I have a tough general election coming up) that I might be the sole African American—and only the third since Reconstruction—to serve in the Senate. My family, friends, and I were mildly bewildered by the attention, and constantly aware of the gulf between the hard sheen of media reports and the messy, mundane realities of life as it is truly lived.

Just as that spate of publicity prompted my publisher's interest a decade ago, so has this fresh round of news clippings encouraged the book's re-publication. For the first time in many years, I've pulled out a copy and read a few chapters to see how much my voice may have changed over time. I confess to wincing every so often at a poorly chosen word, a mangled sentence, an expression of emotion that seems indulgent or overly practiced. I have the urge to cut the book by fifty pages or so, possessed as I am with a keener appreciation for brevity. I cannot honestly say, however, that the voice in this book is not mine—that I would tell the story much differently today than I did ten years ago, even if certain passages have proven to be inconvenient politically, the grist for pundit commentary and opposition research.

What has changed, of course, dramatically, decisively, is the context in which the book might now be read. I began writing against a backdrop of Silicon Valley and a booming stock market; the collapse of the Berlin Wall; Mandela—in slow, sturdy steps—emerging from prison to lead a country; the signing of peace accords in Oslo. Domestically, our cultural debates—around guns and abortion and rap lyrics—seemed so fierce precisely because Bill Clinton's Third Way, a scaled-back welfare state without grand ambition but without sharp edges, seemed to describe a broad, underlying consensus on bread-and-butter issues, a consensus to which even George W. Bush's first campaign, with its "compassionate conservatism," would have to give a nod. Internationally, writers announced the end of history, the ascendance of free markets and liberal democracy, the replacement of old hatreds and wars between nations with virtual communities and battles for market share.

And then, on September 11, 2001, the world fractured.

It's beyond my skill as a writer to capture that day, and the days that would follow—the planes, like specters, vanishing into steel and glass; the slow-motion cascade of the towers crumbling into themselves; the ash-covered figures wandering the streets; the anguish and the fear. Nor do I pretend to understand the stark nihilism that drove the terrorists that day and that drives their brethren still. My powers of empathy, my ability to reach into another's heart, cannot penetrate the blank stares of those who would murder innocents with abstract, serene satisfaction.

What I do know is that history returned that day with a vengeance; that, in fact, as Faulkner reminds us, the past is never dead and buried—it isn't even past. This collective history, this past, directly touches my own. Not merely because the bombs of Al Qaeda have marked, with an eerie precision, some of the landscapes of my life—the buildings and roads and faces of Nairobi, Bali, Manhattan; not merely because, as a consequence of 9/11, my name is an irresistible target of mocking websites from overzealous Republican operatives. But also because the underlying struggle—between worlds of plenty and worlds of want; between the modern and the ancient; between those who embrace our teeming, colliding, irksome diversity, while still insisting on a set of values that binds us together, and those who would seek, under whatever flag or slogan or sacred text, a certainty and simplification that justifies cruelty toward those not like us—is the struggle set forth, on a miniature scale, in this book.

I know, I have seen, the desperation and disorder of the powerless: how it twists the lives of children on the streets of Jakarta or Nairobi in much the same way as it does the lives of children on Chicago's

South Side, how narrow the path is for them between humiliation and untrammeled fury, how easily they slip into violence and despair. I know that the response of the powerful to this disorder—alternating as it does between a dull complacency and, when the disorder spills out of its proscribed confines, a steady, unthinking application of force, of longer prison sentences and more sophisticated military hardware—is inadequate to the task. I know that the hardening of lines, the embrace of fundamentalism and tribe, dooms us all.

And so what was a more interior, intimate effort on my part, to understand this struggle and to find my place in it, has converged with a broader public debate, a debate in which I am professionally engaged, one that will shape our lives and the lives of our children for many years to come.

The policy implications of all this are a topic for another book. Let me end instead on a more personal note. Most of the characters in this book remain a part of my life, albeit in varying degrees—a function of work, children, geography, and turns of fate.

The exception is my mother, whom we lost, with a brutal swiftness, to cancer a few months after this book was published.

She had spent the previous ten years doing what she loved. She traveled the world, working in the distant villages of Asia and Africa, helping women buy a sewing machine or a milk cow or an education that might give them a foothold in the world's economy. She gathered friends from high and low, took long walks, stared at the moon, and foraged through the local markets of Delhi or Marrakesh for some trifle, a scarf or stone carving that would make her laugh or please the eye. She wrote reports, read novels, pestered her children, and dreamed of grandchildren.

We saw each other frequently, our bond unbroken. During the writing of this book, she would read the drafts, correcting stories that I had misunderstood, careful not to comment on my characterizations of her but quick to explain or defend the less flattering aspects of my father's character. She managed her illness with grace and good humor, and she helped my sister and me push on with our lives, despite our dread, our denials, our sudden constrictions of the heart.

I think sometimes that had I known she would not survive her illness, I might have written a different book—less a meditation on the absent parent, more a celebration of the one who was the single constant in my life. In my daughters I see her every day, her joy, her capacity for wonder. I won't try to describe how deeply I mourn her passing still. I know that she was the kindest, most generous spirit I have ever known, and that what is best in me I owe to her.

INTRODUCTION

....

I ORIGINALLY INTENDED A VERY different book. The opportunity to write it first arose while I was still in law school, after my election as the first black president of the *Harvard Law Review*, a legal periodical largely unknown outside the profession. A burst of publicity followed that election, including several newspaper articles that testified less to my modest accomplishments than to Harvard Law School's peculiar place in the American mythology, as well as America's hunger for any optimistic sign from the racial front—a morsel of proof that, after all, some progress has been made. A few publishers called, and I, imagining myself to have something original to say about the current state of race relations, agreed to take off a year after graduation and put my thoughts to paper.

In that last year of law school, I began to organize in my mind, with a frightening confidence, just how the book would proceed. There would be an essay on the limits of civil rights litigation in bringing about racial equality, thoughts on the meaning of community and the restoration of public life through grassroots organizing, musings on affirmative action and Afrocentrism—the list of topics filled an entire page. I'd include personal anecdotes, to be sure, and analyze the sources of certain recurring emotions. But all in all it was an intellectual journey that I imagined for myself, complete with maps and restpoints and a strict itinerary: the first section completed by March, the second submitted for revision in August. . . .

When I actually sat down and began to write, though, I found my mind pulled toward rockier shores. First longings leapt up to brush my heart. Distant voices appeared, and ebbed, and then appeared again. I remembered the stories that my mother and her parents told me as a child, the stories of a family trying to explain itself. I recalled my first year as a community organizer in Chicago and my awkward steps toward manhood. I listened to my grandmother, sitting under a mango tree as she braided my sister's hair, describing the father I had never truly known.

Compared to this flood of memories, all my well-ordered theories seemed insubstantial and premature. Still, I strongly resisted the idea of offering up my past in a book, a past that left me feeling exposed, even slightly ashamed. Not because that past is particularly painful or perverse but because it speaks to those aspects of myself that resist conscious choice and that—on the surface, at least—contradict the world I now occupy. After all, I'm thirty-three now; I work as a lawyer active in the social and political life of Chicago, a town that's accustomed to its racial wounds and prides itself on a certain lack of sentiment. If I've been able to fight off cynicism, I nevertheless like to think of myself as wise to the world, careful not to expect too much.

And yet what strikes me most when I think about the story of my family is a running strain of innocence, an innocence that seems unimaginable, even by the measures of childhood. My wife's cousin, only six years old, has already lost such innocence: A few weeks ago he reported to his parents that some of his first grade classmates had refused to play with him because of his dark, unblemished skin. Obviously his parents, born and raised in Chicago and Gary, lost their own innocence long ago, and although they aren't bitter—the two of them being as strong and proud and resourceful as any parents I know—one hears the pain in their voices as they begin to have second thoughts about having moved out of the city into a mostly white suburb, a move they made to protect their son from the possibility of being caught in a gang shooting and the certainty of attending an underfunded school.

They know too much, we have all seen too much, to take my parents' brief union—a black man and white woman, an African and an American—at face value. As a result, some people have a hard time taking me at face value. When people who don't know me well, black or white, discover my background (and it is usually a discovery, for I ceased to advertise my mother's race at the age of twelve or thirteen, when I began to suspect that by doing so I was ingratiating myself to whites), I see the split-second adjustments they have to make, the searching of my eyes for some telltale sign. They no longer know who I am. Privately, they guess at my troubled heart, I suppose—the mixed blood, the divided soul, the ghostly image of the tragic mulatto trapped between two worlds. And if I were to explain that no, the tragedy is not mine, or at least not mine alone, it is yours, sons and daughters of Plymouth Rock and Ellis Island, it is yours, children of Africa, it is the tragedy of both my wife's six-year-old cousin and his white first grade classmates, so that you need not guess at what troubles me, it's on the nightly news for all to see, and that if we could acknowledge at least that much then the tragic cycle begins to break down . . . well, I suspect that I sound incurably naive, wedded to lost hopes, like those Communists who peddle their newspapers on the fringes of various college towns. Or worse, I sound like I'm trying to hide from myself.

I don't fault people their suspicions. I learned long ago to distrust my childhood and the stories that shaped it. It was only many years later, after I had sat at my father's grave and spoken to him through Africa's red soil, that I could circle back and evaluate these early stories for myself. Or, more accurately, it was only then that I understood that I had spent much of my life trying to rewrite these stories, plugging up holes in the narrative, accommodating unwelcome details, projecting individual choices against the blind sweep of history, all in the hope of extracting some granite slab of truth upon which my unborn children can firmly stand.

At some point, then, in spite of a stubborn desire to protect myself from scrutiny, in spite of the periodic impulse to abandon the entire project, what has found its way onto these pages is a record of a personal, interior journey—a boy's search for his father, and through that search a workable meaning for his life as a black American. The result is autobiographical, although whenever someone's asked me over the course of these last three years just what the book is about, I've usually avoided such a description. An autobiography promises feats worthy of record, conversations with famous people, a central role in important events. There is none of that here. At the very least, an autobiography implies a summing up, a certain closure, that hardly suits someone of my years, still busy charting his way through the world. I can't even hold up my experience as being somehow representative of the black American experience ("After all, you don't come from an underprivileged background," a Manhattan publisher helpfully points out to me); indeed, learning to accept that particular truth—that I can embrace my black brothers and sisters, whether in this country or in Africa, and affirm a common destiny without pretending to speak to, or for, all our various struggles—is part of what this book's about.

Finally, there are the dangers inherent in any autobiographical work: the temptation to color events in ways favorable to the writer, the tendency to overestimate the interest one's experiences hold for others, selective lapses of memory. Such hazards are only magnified when the writer lacks the wisdom of age; the distance that can cure one of certain vanities. I can't say that I've avoided all, or any, of these hazards successfully. Although much of this book is based on contemporaneous journals or the oral histories of my family, the dialogue is necessarily an approximation of what was actually said or relayed to me. For the sake of compression, some of the characters that appear are composites of people I've known, and some events appear out of precise chronology. With the exception of my family and a handful of public figures, the names of most characters have been changed for the sake of their privacy.

Whatever the label that attaches to this book—autobiography, memoir, family history, or something else—what I've tried to do is write an honest account of a particular province of my life. When I've strayed, I've been able to look to my agent, Jane Dystel, for her faith and tenacity; to my editor, Henry Ferris, for his gentle but firm correctives; to Ruth Fecych and the staff at Times Books, for their enthusiasm and attention in shepherding the manuscript through its various stages; to my friends, especially Robert Fisher, for their generous readings; and to my wonderful wife, Michelle, for her wit, grace, candor, and unerring ability to encourage my best impulses.

It is to my family, though—my mother, my grandparents, my siblings, stretched across oceans and continents—that I owe the deepest gratitude and to whom I dedicate this book. Without their constant love and support, without their willingness to let me sing their song and their toleration of the occasional wrong note, I could never have hoped to finish. If nothing else, I hope that the love and respect I feel for them shines through on every page.

PART ONE

Origins

CHAPTER ONE

· ·

A FEW MONTHS AFTER MY twenty-first birthday, a stranger called to give me the news. I was living in New York at the time, on Ninety-fourth between Second and First, part of that unnamed, shifting border between East Harlem and the rest of Manhattan. It was an uninviting block, treeless and barren, lined with soot-colored walk-ups that cast heavy shadows for most of the day. The apartment was small, with slanting floors and irregular heat and a buzzer downstairs that didn't work, so that visitors had to call ahead from a pay phone at the corner gas station, where a black Doberman the size of a wolf paced through the night in vigilant patrol, its jaws clamped around an empty beer bottle.

None of this concerned me much, for I didn't get many visitors. I was impatient in those days, busy with work and unrealized plans, and prone to see other people as unnecessary distractions. It wasn't that I didn't appreciate company exactly. I enjoyed exchanging Spanish pleasantries with my mostly Puerto Rican neighbors, and on my way back from classes I'd usually stop to talk to the boys who hung out on the stoop all summer long about the Knicks or the gunshots they'd heard the night before. When the weather was good, my roommate and I might sit out on the fire escape to smoke cigarettes and study the dusk washing blue over the city, or watch white people from the better neighborhoods nearby walk their dogs down our block to let the animals shit on our curbs—"Scoop the poop, you bastards!" my roommate would shout with impressive rage, and we'd laugh at the faces of both master and beast, grim and unapologetic as they hunkered down to do the deed.

I enjoyed such moments—but only in brief. If the talk began to wander, or cross the border into familiarity, I would soon find reason to excuse myself. I had grown too comfortable in my solitude, the safest place I knew.

I remember there was an old man living next door who seemed to share my disposition. He lived alone, a gaunt, stooped figure who wore a heavy black overcoat and a misshapen fedora on those rare occasions when he left his apartment. Once in a while I'd run into him on his way back from the store, and I would offer to carry his groceries up the long flight of stairs. He would look at me and shrug, and we would begin our ascent, stopping at each landing so that he could catch his breath. When we finally arrived at his apartment, I'd carefully set the bags down on the floor and he would offer a courtly nod of acknowledgment before shuffling inside and closing the latch. Not a single word would pass between us, and not once did he ever thank me for my efforts.

The old man's silence impressed me; I thought him a kindred spirit. Later, my roommate would find him crumpled up on the third-floor landing, his eyes wide open, his limbs stiff and curled up like a baby's. A crowd gathered; a few of the women crossed themselves, and the smaller children whispered with excitement. Eventually the paramedics arrived to take away the body and the police let themselves into the old man's apartment. It was neat, almost empty— a chair, a desk, the faded portrait of a woman with heavy eyebrows and a gentle smile set atop the mantelpiece. Somebody opened the refrigerator and found close to a thousand dollars in small bills rolled up inside wads of old newspaper and carefully arranged behind mayonnaise and pickle jars.

The loneliness of the scene affected me, and for the briefest moment I wished that I had learned the old man's name. Then, almost immediately, I regretted my desire, along with its companion grief. I felt as if an understanding had been broken between us—as if, in that barren room, the old man was whispering an untold history, telling me things I preferred not to hear.

It must have been a month or so later, on a cold, dreary November morning, the sun faint behind a gauze of clouds, that the other call came. I was in the middle of making myself breakfast, with coffee on the stove and two eggs in the skillet, when my roommate handed me the phone. The line was thick with static.

"Barry? Barry, is this you?"

"Yes. . . . Who's this?"

"Yes, Barry . . . this is your Aunt Jane. In Nairobi. Can you hear me?"

"I'm sorry—who did you say you were?"

"Aunt Jane. Listen, Barry, your father is dead. He is killed in a car accident. Hello? Can you hear me? I say, your father is dead. Barry, please call your uncle in Boston and tell him. I can't talk now, okay, Barry. I will try to call you again. . . ."

That was all. The line cut off, and I sat down on the couch, smelling eggs burn in the kitchen, staring at cracks in the plaster, trying to measure my loss.

At the time of his death, my father remained a myth to me, both more and less than a man. He had left Hawaii back in 1963, when I was only two years old, so that as a child I knew him only through the stories that my mother and grandparents told. They all had their favorites, each one seamless, burnished smooth from repeated use. I can still picture Gramps leaning back in his old stuffed chair after dinner, sipping whiskey and cleaning his teeth with the cellophane from his cigarette pack, recounting the time that my father almost threw a man off the Pali Lookout because of a pipe. . . .

"See, your mom and dad decided to take this friend of his sight-seeing around the island. So they drove up to the Lookout, and Barack was probably on the wrong side of the road the whole way over there—"

"Your father was a terrible driver," my mother explains to me. "He'd end up on the left-hand side, the way the British drive, and if you said something he'd just huff about silly American rules—"

"Well, this particular time they arrived in one piece, and they got out and stood at the railing to admire the view. And Barack, he was puffing away on this pipe that I'd given him for his birthday, point-ing out all the sights with the stem, like a sea captain—"

"Your father was really proud of this pipe," my mother interrupts again. "He'd smoke it all night while he studied, and sometimes—"

"Look, Ann, do you want to tell the story or are you going to let me finish?"

"Sorry, Dad. Go ahead."

"Anyway, this poor fella—he was another African student, wasn't he? Fresh off the boat. This poor kid must've been impressed with the way Barack was holding forth with this pipe, 'cause he asked if he could give it a try. Your dad thought about it for a minute, and finally agreed, and as soon as the fella took his first puff, he started coughing up a fit. Coughed so hard that the pipe slipped out of his hand and dropped over the railing, a hundred feet down the face of the cliff."

Gramps stops to take another nip from his flask before continu-ing. "Well, now, your dad was gracious enough to wait until his friend stopped coughing before he told him to climb over the railing and bring the pipe back. The man took one peek down this ninety-degree incline and told Barack that he'd buy him a replacement—"

"Quite sensibly," Toot says from the kitchen. (We call my grandmother Tutu, Toot for short; it means "grandparent" in Hawaiian, for she decided on the day I was born that she was still too young to be called Granny.) Gramps scowls but decides to ignore her.

"—but Barack was adamant about getting *his* pipe back, because it was a gift and couldn't be replaced. So the fella took another look, and shook his head again, and that's when your dad picked him clear off the ground and started dangling him over the railing!"

Gramps lets out a hoot and gives his knee a jovial slap. As he laughs, I imagine myself looking up at my father, dark against the brilliant sun, the transgressor's arms flailing about as he's held aloft. A fearsome vision of justice.

"He wasn't really holding him over the railing, Dad," my mother says, looking to me with concern, but Gramps takes another sip of whiskey and plows forward.

"At this point, other people were starting to stare, and your mother was begging Barack to stop. I guess Barack's friend was just holding his breath and saying his prayers. Anyway, after a couple of minutes, your dad set the man back down on his feet, patted him on the back, and suggested, calm as you please, that they all go find themselves a beer. And don't you know, that's how your dad acted for the rest of the tour—like nothing happened. Of course, your mother was still pretty upset when they got home. In fact, she was barely talking to your dad. Barack wasn't helping matters any, either, 'cause when your mother tried to tell us what had happened he just shook his head and started to laugh. 'Relax, Anna,' he said to her—your dad had this deep baritone, see, and this British accent." My grandfather tucks his chin into his neck at this point, to capture the full effect. " 'Relax, Anna,' he said. 'I only wanted to teach the chap a lesson about the proper care of other people's property!' "

Gramps would start to laugh again until he started to cough, and Toot would mutter under her breath that she supposed it was a good thing

that my father had realized that dropping the pipe had just been an accident because who knows what might have happened otherwise, and my
mother would roll her eyes at me and say they were exaggerating.

"Your father can be a bit domineering," my mother would admit
with a hint of a smile. "But it's just that he is basically a very honest
person. That makes him uncompromising sometimes."

She preferred a gentler portrait of my father. She would tell the
story of when he arrived to accept his Phi Beta Kappa key in his
favorite outfit—jeans and an old knit shirt with a leopard-print pattern. "Nobody told him it was this big honor, so he walked in and
found everyone standing around this elegant room dressed in tuxedos. The only time I ever saw him embarrassed."

And Gramps, suddenly thoughtful, would start nodding to himself
"It's a fact, Bar," he would say. "Your dad could handle just about any
situation, and that made everybody like him. Remember the time he
had to sing at the International Music Festival? He'd agreed to sing
some African songs, but when he arrived it turned out to be this big
to-do, and the woman who performed just before him was a semi-
professional singer, a Hawaiian gal with a full band to back her up.
Anyone else would have stopped right there, you know, and explained
that there had been a mistake. But not Barack. He got up and started
singing in front of this big crowd—which is no easy feat, let me tell
you—and he wasn't great, but he was so sure of himself that before
you knew it he was getting as much applause as anybody."

My grandfather would shake his head and get out of his chair to
flip on the TV set. "Now there's something you can learn from your
dad," he would tell me. "*Confidence.* The secret to a man's success."

That's how all the stories went—compact, apocryphal, told in rapid
succession in the course of one evening, then packed away for months,
sometimes years, in my family's memory. Like the few photographs
of my father that remained in the house, old black-and-white studio

prints that I might run across while rummaging through the closets in search of Christmas ornaments or an old snorkle set. At the point where my own memories begin, my mother had already begun a courtship with the man who would become her second husband, and I sensed without explanation why the photographs had to be stored away. But once in a while, sitting on the floor with my mother, the smell of dust and mothballs rising from the crumbling album, I would stare at my father's likeness—the dark laughing face, the prominent forehead and thick glasses that made him appear older than his years—and listen as the events of his life tumbled into a single narrative.

He was an African, I would learn, a Kenyan of the Luo tribe, born on the shores of Lake Victoria in a place called Alego. The village was poor, but his father—my other grandfather, Hussein Onyango Obama—had been a prominent farmer, an elder of the tribe, a medicine man with healing powers. My father grew up herding his father's goats and attending the local school, set up by the British colonial administration, where he had shown great promise. He eventually won a scholarship to study in Nairobi; and then, on the eve of Kenyan independence, he had been selected by Kenyan leaders and American sponsors to attend a university in the United States, joining the first large wave of Africans to be sent forth to master Western technology and bring it back to forge a new, modern Africa.

In 1959, at the age of twenty-three, he arrived at the University of Hawaii as that institution's first African student. He studied econometrics, worked with unsurpassed concentration, and graduated in three years at the top of his class. His friends were legion, and he helped organize the International Students Association, of which he became the first president. In a Russian language course, he met an awkward, shy American girl, only eighteen, and they fell in love. The girl's parents, wary at first, were won over by his charm and intellect; the young couple married, and she bore them a son, to whom he bequeathed his name. He won another scholarship—this time to pursue his Ph.D. at Harvard—but not the money to take his new family with him. A separation occurred, and he returned to Africa to fulfill his promise to the continent. The mother and child stayed behind, but the bond of love survived the distances. . . .

There the album would close, and I would wander off content, swaddled in a tale that placed me in the center of a vast and orderly universe. Even in the abridged version that my mother and grandparents offered, there were many things I didn't understand. But I rarely asked for the details that might resolve the meaning of "Ph.D." or "colonialism," or locate Alego on a map. Instead, the path of my father's life occupied the same terrain as a book my mother once bought for me, a book called *Origins,* a collection of creation tales from around the world, stories of Genesis and the tree where man was born, Prometheus and the gift of fire, the tortoise of Hindu legend that floated in space, supporting the weight of the world on its back. Later, when I became more familiar with the narrower path to happiness to be found in television and the movies, I'd become troubled by questions. What supported the tortoise? Why did an omnipotent God let a snake cause such grief? Why didn't my father return? But at the age of five or six I was satisfied to leave these distant mysteries intact, each story self-contained and as true as the next, to be carried off into peaceful dreams.

That my father looked nothing like the people around me—that he was black as pitch, my mother white as milk—barely registered in my mind.

In fact, I can recall only one story that dealt explicitly with the subject of race; as I got older, it would be repeated more often, as if it captured the essence of the morality tale that my father's life had become. According to the story, after long hours of study, my father had joined my grandfather and several other friends at a local Waikiki bar. Everyone was in a festive mood, eating and drinking to the sounds of a slack-key guitar, when a white man abruptly announced to the bartender, loudly enough for everyone to hear, that he shouldn't have to drink good liquor "next to a nigger." The room fell quiet and people turned to my father, expecting a fight. Instead, my father stood up, walked over to the man, smiled, and proceeded to lecture him about the folly of bigotry, the promise of the American dream, and the universal rights of man. "This fella felt so bad when Barack was finished," Gramps would say, "that he reached into his pocket and gave Barack a hundred dollars on the spot. Paid for all our drinks and puu-puus for the rest of the night—and your dad's rent for the rest of the month."

By the time I was a teenager, I'd grown skeptical of this story's veracity and had set it aside with the rest. Until I received a phone call, many years later, from a Japanese-American man who said he had been my father's classmate in Hawaii and now taught at a midwestern university. He was very gracious, a bit embarrassed by his own impulsiveness; he explained that he had seen an interview of me in his local paper and that the sight of my father's name had brought back a rush of memories. Then, during the course of our conversation, he repeated the same story that my grandfather had told, about the white man who had tried to purchase my father's forgiveness. "I'll never forget that," the man said to me over the phone; and in his voice I heard the same note that I'd heard from Gramps so many years before, that note of disbelief—and hope.

Miscegenation. The word is humpbacked, ugly, portending a monstrous outcome: like *antebellum* or *octoroon*, it evokes images of another era, a distant world of horsewhips and flames, dead magnolias and crumbling porticos. And yet it wasn't until 1967—the year I celebrated my sixth birthday and Jimi Hendrix performed at Monterey, three years after Dr. King received the Nobel Peace Prize, a time when America had already begun to weary of black demands for equality, the problem of discrimination presumably solved—that the Supreme Court of the United States would get around to telling the state of Virginia that its ban on interracial marriages violated the Constitution. In 1960, the year that my parents were married, *miscegenation* still described a felony in over half the states in the Union. In many parts of the South, my father could have been strung up from a tree for merely looking at my mother the wrong way; in the most sophisticated of northern cities, the hostile stares, the whispers, might have driven a woman in my mother's predicament into a back-alley abortion—or at the very least to a distant convent that could arrange for adoption. Their very image together would have been considered lurid and perverse, a handy retort to the handful of softheaded liberals who supported a civil rights agenda.

Sure—but would you let your daughter marry one?

The fact that my grandparents had answered yes to this question, no matter how grudgingly, remains an enduring puzzle to me. There was nothing in their background to predict such a response, no New England transcendentalists or wild-eyed socialists in their family tree. True, Kansas had fought on the Union side of the Civil War; Gramps liked to remind me that various strands of the family contained ardent abolitionists. If asked, Toot would turn her head in profile to show off her beaked nose, which, along with a pair of jet-black eyes, was offered as proof of Cherokee blood.

But an old, sepia-toned photograph on the bookshelf spoke most eloquently of their roots. It showed Toot's grandparents, of Scottish and English stock, standing in front of a ramshackle homestead, unsmiling and dressed in coarse wool, their eyes squinting at the sun-baked, flinty life that stretched out before them. Theirs were the faces of American Gothic, the WASP bloodline's poorer cousins, and in their eyes one could see truths that I would have to learn later as facts: that Kansas had entered the Union free only after a violent precursor to the Civil War, the battle in which John Brown's sword tasted first blood; that while one of my great-great-grandfathers, Christopher Columbus Clark, had been a decorated Union soldier, his wife's mother was rumored to have been a second cousin of Jefferson Davis, president of the Confederacy; that although another distant ancestor had indeed been a full-blooded Cherokee, such lineage was a source of considerable shame to Toot's mother, who blanched whenever someone mentioned the subject and hoped to carry the secret to her grave.

That was the world in which my grandparents had been raised, the dab-smack, landlocked center of the country, a place where decency and endurance and the pioneer spirit were joined at the hip with conformity and suspicion and the potential for unblinking cruelty. They had grown up less than twenty miles away from each other—my grandmother in Augusta, my grandfather in El Dorado, towns too small to warrant boldface on a road map—and the childhoods they liked to recall for my benefit portrayed small-town, Depression-era America in all its innocent glory: Fourth of July parades and the picture shows on the side of a barn; fireflies in a jar and the taste of vine-ripe tomatoes, sweet as apples; dust storms and hailstorms and classrooms filled with farm boys who got sewn into their woolen underwear at the beginning of winter and stank like pigs as the months wore on.

Even the trauma of bank failures and farm foreclosures seemed romantic when spun through the loom of my grandparents' memories, a time when hardship, the great leveler that had brought people closer together, was shared by all. So you had to listen carefully to recognize the subtle hierarchies and unspoken codes that had policed their early lives, the distinctions of people who don't have a lot and live in the middle of nowhere. It had to do with something called respectability—there were respectable people and not-so-respectable people—and although you didn't have to be rich to be respectable, you sure had to work harder at it if you weren't.

Toot's family was respectable. Her father held a steady job all through the Depression, managing an oil lease for Standard Oil. Her mother had taught normal school before the children were born. The family kept their house spotless and ordered Great Books through the mail; they read the Bible but generally shunned the tent revival circuit, preferring a straight-backed form of Methodism that valued reason over passion and temperance over both.

My grandfather's station was more troublesome. Nobody was sure why—the grandparents who had raised him and his older brother weren't very well off, but they were decent, God-fearing Baptists, supporting themselves with work in the oil rigs around Wichita. Somehow, though, Gramps had turned out a bit wild. Some of the neighbors pointed to his mother's suicide: it was Stanley, after all, then only eight years old, who had found her body. Other, less charitable, souls would simply shake their heads: The boy takes after his philandering father, they would opine, the undoubtable cause of the mother's unfortunate demise.

Whatever the reason, Gramps's reputation was apparently well deserved. By the age of fifteen he'd been thrown out of high school for punching the principal in the nose. For the next three years he lived off odd jobs, hopping rail cars to Chicago, then California, then back again, dabbling in moonshine, cards, and women. As he liked to tell it, he knew his way around Wichita, where both his and Toot's families had moved by that time, and Toot doesn't contradict him; certainly, Toot's parents believed the stories that they'd heard about the young man and strongly disapproved of the budding courtship. The first time Toot brought Gramps over to her house to meet the family, her father took one look at my grandfather's black, slicked-back hair and his perpetual wise-guy grin and offered his unvarnished assessment.

"He looks like a wop."

My grandmother didn't care. To her, a home economics major fresh out of high school and tired of respectability, my grandfather must have cut a dashing figure. I sometimes imagine them in every American town in those years before the war, him in baggy pants and a starched undershirt, brim hat cocked back on his head, offering a cigarette to this smart-talking girl with too much red lipstick and hair dyed blond and legs nice enough to model hosiery for the local department store. He's telling her about the big cities, the endless highway, his imminent escape from the empty, dust-ridden plains, where big plans mean a job as a bank manager and entertainment means an ice-cream soda and a Sunday matinee, where fear and lack of imagination choke your dreams so that you already know on the day that you're born just where you'll die and who it is that'll bury you. He won't end up like that, my grandfather insists; he has dreams, he has plans; he will infect my grandmother with the great peripatetic itch that had brought both their forebears across the Atlantic and half of a continent so many years before.

They eloped just in time for the bombing of Pearl Harbor, and my grandfather enlisted. And at this point the story quickens in my mind like one of those old movies that show a wall calendar's pages peeled back faster and faster by invisible hands, the headlines of Hitler and Churchill and Roosevelt and Normandy spinning wildly to the drone of bombing attacks, the voice of Edward R. Murrow and the BBC. I watch as my mother is born at the army base where Gramps is stationed; my grandmother is Rosie the Riveter, working on a bomber assembly line; my grandfather sloshes around in the mud of France, part of Patton's army.

Gramps returned from the war never having seen real combat, and the family headed to California, where he enrolled at Berkeley under the GI bill. But the classroom couldn't contain his ambitions, his restlessness, and so the family moved again, first back to Kansas, then through a series of small Texas towns, then finally to Seattle, where they stayed long enough for my mother to finish high school. Gramps worked as a furniture salesman; they bought a house and found themselves bridge partners. They were pleased that my mother proved bright in school, although when she was offered early admission into the University of Chicago, my grandfather forbade her to go, deciding that she was still too young to be living on her own.

And that's where the story might have stopped: a home, a family, a respectable life. Except something must have still been gnawing at my grandfather's heart. I can imagine him standing at the edge of the Pacific, his hair prematurely gray, his tall, lanky frame bulkier now, looking out at the horizon until he could see it curve and still smelling, deep in his nostrils, the oil rigs and corn husks and hard-bitten lives that he thought he had left far behind. So that when the manager of the furniture company where he worked happened to mention that a new store was about to open in Honolulu, that business prospects seemed limitless there, what with statehood right around the corner, he would rush home that same day and talk my grandmother into selling their house and packing up yet again, to embark on the final leg of their journey, west, toward the setting sun. . . .

He would always be like that, my grandfather, always searching for that new start, always running away from the familiar. By the time the family arrived in Hawaii, his character would have been fully formed, I think—the generosity and eagerness to please, the awkward mix of sophistication and provincialism, the rawness of emotion that could make him at once tactless and easily bruised. His was an American character, one typical of men of his generation, men who embraced the notion of freedom and individualism and the open road without always knowing its price, and whose enthusiasms could as easily lead to the cowardice of McCarthyism as to the heroics of World War II. Men who were both dangerous and promising precisely because of their fundamental innocence; men prone, in the end, to disappointment.

In 1960, though, my grandfather had not yet been tested; the disappointments would come later, and even then they would come slowly, without the violence that might have changed him, for better or worse. In the back of his mind he had come to consider himself as something of a freethinker—bohemian, even. He wrote poetry on occasion, listened to jazz, counted a number of Jews he'd met in the furniture business as his closest friends. In his only skirmish into organized religion, he would enroll the family in the local Unitarian Universalist congregation; he liked the idea that Unitarians drew on the scriptures of all the great religions ("It's like you get five religions in one," he would say). Toot would eventually dissuade him of his views on the church ("For Christ's sake, Stanley, religion's not supposed to be like buying breakfast cereal!"), but if my grandmother was more skeptical by nature, and disagreed with Gramps on some of his more outlandish notions, her own stubborn independence, her own insistence on thinking something through for herself, generally brought them into rough alignment.

All this marked them as vaguely liberal, although their ideas would never congeal into anything like a firm ideology; in this, too, they were American. And so, when my mother came home one day and mentioned a friend she had met at the University of Hawaii, an African student named Barack, their first impulse was to invite him over for dinner. The poor kid's probably lonely, Gramps would have thought, so far away from home. Better take a look at him, Toot would have said to herself. When my father arrived at the door, Gramps might have been immediately struck by the African's resemblance to Nat King Cole, one of his favorite singers; I imagine him asking my father if he can sing, not understanding the mortified look on my mother's face. Gramps is probably too busy telling one of his jokes or arguing with Toot over how to cook the steaks to notice my mother reach out and squeeze the smooth, sinewy hand beside hers. Toot notices, but she's polite enough to bite her lip and offer dessert; her instincts warn her against making a scene. When the evening is over, they'll both remark on how intelligent the young man seems, so dignified, with the measured gestures, the graceful draping of one leg over another—and how about that accent!

But would they let their daughter *marry* one?

We don't know yet; the story to this point doesn't explain enough. The truth is that, like most white Americans at the time, they had never really given black people much thought. Jim Crow had made its way north into Kansas well before my grandparents were born, but at least around Wichita it appeared in its more informal, genteel form, without much of the violence that pervaded the Deep South. The same unspoken codes that governed life among whites kept contact between the races to a minimum; when black people appear at all in the Kansas of my grandparents' memories, the images are fleeting— black men who come around the oil fields once in a while, searching for work as hired hands; black women taking in the white folks' laundry or helping clean white homes. Blacks are there but not there, like Sam the piano player or Beulah the maid or Amos and Andy on the radio—shadowy, silent presences that elicit neither passion nor fear.

It wasn't until my family moved to Texas, after the war, that questions of race began to intrude on their lives. During his first week on the job there, Gramps received some friendly advice from his fellow furniture salesmen about serving black and Mexican customers: "If the coloreds want to look at the merchandise, they need to come after hours and arrange for their own delivery." Later, at the bank where she worked, Toot made the acquaintance of the janitor, a tall and dignified black World War II vet she remembers only as Mr. Reed. While the two of them chatted in the hallway one day, a secretary in the office stormed up and hissed that Toot should never, ever, "call no nigger 'Mister.' " Not long afterward, Toot would find Mr. Reed in a corner of the building weeping quietly to himself. When she asked him what was wrong, he straightened his back, dried his eyes, and responded with a question of his own.

"What have we ever done to be treated so mean?"

My grandmother didn't have an answer that day, but the question lingered in her mind, one that she and Gramps would sometimes discuss once my mother had gone to bed. They decided that Toot would keep calling Mr. Reed "Mister," although she understood, with a mixture of relief and sadness, the careful distance that the janitor now maintained whenever they passed each other in the halls. Gramps began to decline invitations from his coworkers to go out for a beer, telling them he had to get home to keep the wife happy. They grew inward, skittish, filled with vague apprehension, as if they were permanent strangers in town.

This bad new air hit my mother the hardest. She was eleven or twelve by this time, an only child just growing out of a bad case of asthma. The illness, along with the numerous moves, had made her something of a loner—cheerful and easy-tempered but prone to bury her head in a book or wander off on solitary walks—and Toot began to worry that this latest move had only made her daughter's eccentricities more pronounced. My mother made few friends at her new school. She was teased mercilessly for her name, Stanley Ann (one of Gramps's less judicious ideas—he had wanted a son). Stanley Steamer, they called her. Stan the Man. When Toot got home from work, she would usually find my mother alone in the front yard, swinging her legs off the porch or lying in the grass, pulled into some solitary world of her own.

Except for one day. There was that one hot, windless day when Toot came home to find a crowd of children gathered outside the picket fence that surrounded their house. As Toot drew closer, she could make out the sounds of mirthless laughter, the contortions of rage and disgust on the children's faces. The children were chanting, in a high-pitched, alternating rhythm:

"Nigger lover!"

"Dirty Yankee!"

"Nigger lover!"

The children scattered when they saw Toot, but not before one of the boys had sent the stone in his hand sailing over the fence. Toot's eyes followed the stone's trajectory as it came to rest at the foot of a tree. And there she saw the cause for all the excitement: my mother and a black girl of about the same age lying side by side on their stomachs in the grass, their skirts gathered up above their knees, their toes dug into the ground, their heads propped up on their hands in front of one of my mother's books. From a distance the two girls seemed perfectly serene beneath the leafy shade. It was only when Toot opened the gate that she realized the black girl was shaking and my mother's eyes shone with tears. The girls remained motionless, paralyzed in their fear, until Toot finally leaned down and put her hands on both their heads.

"If you two are going to play," she said, "then for goodness sake, go on inside. Come on. Both of you." She picked up my mother and reached for the other girl's hand, but before she could say anything more, the girl was in a full sprint, her long legs like a whippet's as she vanished down the street.

Gramps was beside himself when he heard what had happened. He interrogated my mother, wrote down names. The next day he took the morning off from work to visit the school principal. He personally called the parents of some of the offending children to give them a piece of his mind. And from every adult that he spoke to, he received the same response:

"You best talk to your daughter, Mr. Dunham. White girls don't play with coloreds in this town."

It's hard to know how much weight to give to these episodes, what permanent allegiances were made or broken, or whether they stand out only in the light of subsequent events. Whenever he spoke to me about it, Gramps would insist that the family left Texas in part because of their discomfort with such racism. Toot would be more circumspect; once, when we were alone, she told me that they had moved from Texas only because Gramps wasn't doing particularly well on his job, and because a friend in Seattle had promised him something better. According to her, the word *racism* wasn't even in their vocabulary back then. "Your grandfather and I just figured we should treat people decently, Bar. That's all."

She's wise that way, my grandmother, suspicious of overwrought sentiments or overblown claims, content with common sense. Which is why I tend to trust her account of events; it corresponds to what I know about my grandfather, his tendency to rewrite his history to conform with the image he wished for himself.

And yet I don't entirely dismiss Gramps's recollection of events as a convenient bit of puffery, another act of white revisionism. I can't, precisely because I know how strongly Gramps believed in his fictions, how badly he wanted them to be true, even if he didn't always know how to make them so. After Texas I suspect that black people became a part of these fictions of his, the narrative that worked its way through his dreams. The condition of the black race, their pain, their wounds, would in his mind become merged with his own: the absent father and the hint of scandal, a mother who had gone away, the cruelty of other children, the realization that he was no fair-haired boy—that he looked like a "wop." Racism was part of that past, his instincts told him, part of convention and respectability and status, the smirks and whispers and gossip that had kept him on the outside looking in.

Those instincts count for something, I think; for many white people of my grandparents' generation and background, the instincts ran in an opposite direction, the direction of the mob. And although Gramps's relationship with my mother was already strained by the time they reached Hawaii—she would never quite forgive his instability and often-violent temper and would grow ashamed of his crude, ham-fisted manners—it was this desire of his to obliterate the past, this confidence in the possibility of remaking the world from whole cloth, that proved to be his most lasting patrimony. Whether Gramps realized it or not, the sight of his daughter with a black man offered at some deep unexplored level a window into his own heart.

Not that such self-knowledge, even if accessible, would have made my mother's engagement any easier for him to swallow. In fact, how and when the marriage occurred remains a bit murky, a bill of particulars that I've never quite had the courage to explore. There's no record of a real wedding, a cake, a ring, a giving away of the bride. No families were in attendance; it's not even clear that people back in Kansas were fully informed. Just a small civil ceremony, a justice of the peace. The whole thing seems so fragile in retrospect, so haphazard. And perhaps that's how my grandparents intended it to be, a trial that would pass, just a matter of time, so long as they maintained a stiff upper lip and didn't do anything drastic.

If so, they miscalculated not only my mother's quiet determination but also the sway of their own emotions. First the baby arrived, eight pounds, two ounces, with ten toes and ten fingers and hungry for food. What in the heck were they supposed to do?

Then time and place began to conspire, transforming potential misfortune into something tolerable, even a source of pride. Sharing a few beers with my father, Gramps might listen to his new son-in-law sound off about politics or the economy, about far-off places like Whitehall or the Kremlin, and imagine himself seeing into the future. He would begin to read the newspapers more carefully, finding early reports of America's newfound integrationist creed, and decide in his mind that the world was shrinking, sympathies changing; that the family from Wichita had in fact moved to the forefront of Kennedy's New Frontier and Dr. King's magnificent dream. How could America send men into space and still keep its black citizens in bondage? One of my earliest memories is of sitting on my grandfather's shoulders as the astronauts from one of the Apollo missions arrived at Hickam Air Force Base after a successful splashdown. I remember the astronauts, in aviator glasses, as being far away, barely visible through the portal of an isolation chamber. But Gramps would always swear that one of the astronauts waved just at me and that I waved back. It was part of the story he told himself. With his black son-in-law and his brown grandson, Gramps had entered the space age.

And what better port for setting off on this new adventure than Hawaii, the Union's newest member? Even now, with the state's population quadrupled, with Waikiki jammed wall to wall with fast-food emporiums and pornographic video stores and subdivisions marching relentlessly into every fold of green hill, I can retrace the first steps I took as a child and be stunned by the beauty of the islands. The trembling blue plane of the Pacific. The moss-covered cliffs and the cool rush of Manoa Falls, with its ginger blossoms and high canopies filled with the sound of invisible birds. The North Shore's thunderous waves, crumbling as if in a slow-motion reel. The shadows off Pali's peaks; the sultry, scented air.

Hawaii! To my family, newly arrived in 1959, it must have seemed as if the earth itself, weary of stampeding armies and bitter civilization, had forced up this chain of emerald rock where pioneers from across the globe could populate the land with children bronzed by the sun. The ugly conquest of the native Hawaiians through aborted treaties and crippling disease brought by the missionaries; the carving up of rich volcanic soil by American companies for sugarcane and pineapple plantations; the indenturing system that kept Japanese, Chinese, and Filipino immigrants stooped sunup to sunset in these same fields; the internment of Japanese-Americans during the war— all this was recent history. And yet, by the time my family arrived, it had somehow vanished from collective memory, like morning mist that the sun burned away. There were too many races, with power among them too diffuse, to impose the mainland's rigid caste system;

and so few blacks that the most ardent segregationist could enjoy a vacation secure in the knowledge that race mixing in Hawaii had little to do with the established order back home.

Thus the legend was made of Hawaii as the one true melting pot, an experiment in racial harmony. My grandparents—especially Gramps, who came into contact with a range of people through his furniture business—threw themselves into the cause of mutual understanding. An old copy of Dale Carnegie's *How to Win Friends and Influence People* still sits on his bookshelf. And growing up, I would hear in him the breezy, chatty style that he must have decided would help him with his customers. He would whip out pictures of the family and offer his life story to the nearest stranger; he would pump the hand of the mailman or make off-color jokes to our waitresses at restaurants.

Such antics used to make me cringe, but people more forgiving than a grandson appreciated his curiosity, so that while he never gained much influence, he made himself a wide circle of friends. A Japanese-American man who called himself Freddy and ran a small market near our house would save us the choicest cuts of aku for sashimi and give me rice candy with edible wrappers. Every so often, the Hawaiians who worked at my grandfather's store as deliverymen would invite us over for poi and roast pig, which Gramps gobbled down heartily (Toot would smoke cigarettes until she could get home and fix herself some scrambled eggs). Sometimes I would accompany Gramps to Ali'i Park, where he liked to play checkers with the old Filipino men who smoked cheap cigars and spat up betel-nut juice as if it were blood. And I still remember how, one early morning, hours before the sun rose, a Portuguese man to whom my grandfather had given a good deal on a sofa set took us out to spear fish off Kailua Bay. A gas lantern hung from the cabin on the small fishing boat as I watched the men dive into inky-black waters, the beams of their flashlights glowing beneath the surface until they emerged with a large fish, iridescent and flopping at the end of one pole. Gramps told me its Hawaiian name, humu-humu-nuku-nuku-apuaa, which we repeated to each other the entire way home.

In such surroundings, my racial stock caused my grandparents few problems, and they quickly adopted the scornful attitude local residents took toward visitors who expressed such hang-ups. Sometimes when Gramps saw tourists watching me play in the sand, he would come up beside them and whisper, with appropriate reverence, that I was the great-grandson of King Kamehameha, Hawaii's first monarch. "I'm sure that your picture's in a thousand scrapbooks, Bar," he liked to tell me with a grin, "from Idaho to Maine." That particular story is ambiguous, I think; I see in it a strategy to avoid hard issues. And yet Gramps would just as readily tell another story, the one about the tourist who saw me swimming one day and, not knowing who she was talking to, commented that "swimming must just come naturally to these Hawaiians." To which he responded that that would be hard to figure, since "that boy happens to be my grandson, his mother is from Kansas, his father is from the interior of Kenya, and there isn't an ocean for miles in either damn place." For my grandfather, race wasn't something you really needed to worry about anymore; if ignorance still held fast in certain locales, it was safe to assume that the rest of the world would be catching up soon.

In the end I suppose that's what all the stories of my father were really about. They said less about the man himself than about the changes that had taken place in the people around him, the halting process by which my grandparents' racial attitudes had changed. The stories gave voice to a spirit that would grip the nation for that fleeting period between Kennedy's election and the passage of the Voting Rights Act: the seeming triumph of universalism over parochialism and narrow-mindedness, a bright new world where differences of race or culture would instruct and amuse and perhaps even ennoble. A useful fiction, one that haunts me no less than it haunted my family, evoking as it does some lost Eden that extends beyond mere childhood.

There was only one problem: my father was missing. He had left paradise, and nothing that my mother or grandparents told me could obviate that single, unassailable fact. Their stories didn't tell me why he had left. They couldn't describe what it might have been like had he stayed. Like the janitor, Mr. Reed, or the black girl who churned up dust as she raced down a Texas road, my father became a prop in someone else's narrative. An attractive prop—the alien figure with the heart of gold, the mysterious stranger who saves the town and wins the girl—but a prop nonetheless.

I don't really blame my mother or grandparents for this. My father may have preferred the image they created for him—indeed, he may have been complicit in its creation. In an article published in the *Honolulu Star-Bulletin* upon his graduation, he appears guarded and responsible, the model student, ambassador for his continent. He mildly scolds the university for herding visiting students into dormitories and forcing them to attend programs designed to promote cultural understanding—a distraction, he says, from the practical training he seeks. Although he hasn't experienced any problems himself, he detects self-segregation and overt discrimination taking place between the various ethnic groups and expresses wry amusement at the fact that "Caucasians" in Hawaii are occasionally at the receiving end of prejudice. But if his assessment is relatively clear-eyed, he is careful to end on a happy note: One thing other nations can learn from Hawaii, he says, is the willingness of races to work together toward common development, something he has found whites elsewhere too often unwilling to do.

I discovered this article, folded away among my birth certificate and old vaccination forms, when I was in high school. It's a short piece, with a photograph of him. No mention is made of my mother or me, and I'm left to wonder whether the omission was intentional on my father's part, in anticipation of his long departure. Perhaps the reporter failed to ask personal questions, intimidated by my father's imperious manner; or perhaps it was an editorial decision, not part of the simple story that they were looking for. I wonder, too, whether the omission caused a fight between my parents.

I would not have known at the time, for I was too young to realize that I was supposed to have a live-in father, just as I was too young to know that I needed a race. For an improbably short span it seems that my father fell under the same spell as my mother and her parents; and for the first six years of my life, even as that spell was broken and the worlds that they thought they'd left behind reclaimed each of them, I occupied the place where their dreams had been.

CHAPTER TWO

....

T HE ROAD TO THE embassy was choked with traffic: cars, motorcycles, tricycle rickshaws, buses and jitneys filled to twice their capacity, a procession of wheels and limbs all fighting for space in the midafternoon heat. We nudged forward a few feet, stopped, found an opening, stopped again. Our taxi driver shooed away a group of boys who were hawking gum and loose cigarettes, then barely avoided a motor scooter carrying an entire family on its back—father, mother, son, and daughter all leaning as one into a turn, their mouths wrapped with handkerchiefs to blunt the exhaust, a family of bandits. Along the side of the road, wizened brown women in faded brown sarongs stacked straw baskets high with ripening fruit, and a pair of mechanics squatted before their open-air garage, lazily brushing away flies as they took an engine apart. Behind them, the brown earth dipped into a smoldering dump where a pair of round-headed tots frantically chased a scrawny black hen. The children slipped in the mud and corn husks and banana leaves, squealing with pleasure, until they disappeared down the dirt road beyond.

Things eased up once we hit the highway, and the taxi dropped us off in front of the embassy, where a pair of smartly dressed Marines nodded in greeting. Inside the courtyard, the clamor of the street was

replaced by the steady rhythm of gardening clippers. My mother's boss
was a portly black man with closely cropped hair sprinkled gray at the
temples. An American flag draped down in rich folds from the pole
beside his desk. He reached out and offered a firm handshake: "How
are you, young man?" He smelled of after-shave and his starched collar
cut hard into his neck. I stood at attention as I answered his questions
about the progress of my studies. The air in the office was cool and dry,
like the air of mountain peaks: the pure and heady breeze of privilege.

Our audience over, my mother sat me down in the library while
she went off to do some work. I finished my comic books and the
homework my mother had made me bring before climbing out of my
chair to browse through the stacks. Most of the books held little
interest for a nine-year-old boy—World Bank reports, geological
surveys, five-year development plans. But in one corner I found a collection of *Life* magazines neatly displayed in clear plastic binders. I
thumbed through the glossy advertisements—Goodyear Tires and
Dodge Fever, Zenith TV ("Why not the best?") and Campbell's Soup
("Mm-mm good!"), men in white turtlenecks pouring Seagram's over
ice as women in red miniskirts looked on admiringly—and felt
vaguely reassured. When I came upon a news photograph, I tried to
guess the subject of the story before reading the caption. The photograph of French children dashing over cobblestoned streets: that was
a happy scene, a game of hide-and-go-seek after a day of schoolbooks
and chores; their laughter spoke of freedom. The photograph of a
Japanese woman cradling a young, naked girl in a shallow tub: that
was sad; the girl was sick, her legs twisted, her head fallen back
against the mother's breast, the mother's face tight with grief, perhaps she blamed herself. . . .

Eventually I came across a photograph of an older man in dark
glasses and a raincoat walking down an empty road. I couldn't guess
what this picture was about; there seemed nothing unusual about the
subject. On the next page was another photograph, this one a close-up

of the same man's hands. They had a strange, unnatural pallor, as if blood had been drawn from the flesh. Turning back to the first picture, I now saw that the man's crinkly hair, his heavy lips and broad, fleshy nose, all had this same uneven, ghostly hue.

He must be terribly sick, I thought. A radiation victim, maybe, or an albino—I had seen one of those on the street a few days before, and my mother had explained about such things. Except when I read the words that went with the picture, that wasn't it at all. The man had received a chemical treatment, the article explained, to lighten his complexion. He had paid for it with his own money. He expressed some regret about trying to pass himself off as a white man, was sorry about how badly things had turned out. But the results were irreversible. There were thousands of people like him, black men and women back in America who'd undergone the same treatment in response to advertisements that promised happiness as a white person.

I felt my face and neck get hot. My stomach knotted; the type began to blur on the page. Did my mother know about this? What about her boss—why was he so calm, reading through his reports a few feet down the hall? I had a desperate urge to jump out of my seat, to show them what I had learned, to demand some explanation or assurance. But something held me back. As in a dream, I had no voice for my newfound fear. By the time my mother came to take me home, my face wore a smile and the magazines were back in their proper place. The room, the air, was quiet as before.

We had lived in Indonesia for over three years by that time, the result of my mother's marriage to an Indonesian named Lolo, another student she had met at the University of Hawaii. His name meant "crazy" in Hawaiian, which tickled Gramps to no end, but the meaning didn't suit the man, for Lolo possessed the good manners and easy grace of his people. He was short and brown, handsome, with thick black hair and features that could have as easily been Mexican or Samoan as Indonesian; his tennis game was good, his smile uncommonly even, and his temperament imperturbable. For two years, from the time I was four until I was six, he endured endless hours of chess with Gramps and long wrestling sessions with me. When my mother sat me down one day to tell me that Lolo had proposed and wanted us to move with him to a faraway place, I wasn't surprised and expressed no objections. I did ask her if she loved him—I had been around long enough to know such things were important. My mother's chin trembled, as it still does when she's fighting back tears, and she pulled me into a long hug that made me feel very brave, although I wasn't sure why.

Lolo left Hawaii quite suddenly after that, and my mother and I spent months in preparation—passports, visas, plane tickets, hotel reservations, an endless series of shots. While we packed, my grandfather pulled out an atlas and ticked off the names in Indonesia's island chain: Java, Borneo, Sumatra, Bali. He remembered some of the names, he said, from reading Joseph Conrad as a boy. The Spice Islands, they were called back then, enchanted names, shrouded in mystery. "Says here they still got tigers over there," he said. "And orangutangs." He looked up from the book and his eyes widened. "Says here they even got *headhunters!*" Meanwhile, Toot called the State Department to find out if the country was stable. Whoever she spoke to there informed her that the situation was under control. Still, she insisted that we pack several trunks full of foodstuffs: Tang, powdered milk, cans of sardines. "You never know what these people will eat," she said firmly. My mother sighed, but Toot tossed in several boxes of candy to win me over to her side.

Finally, we boarded a Pan Am jet for our flight around the globe. I wore a long-sleeved white shirt and a gray clip-on tie, and the stewardesses plied me with puzzles and extra peanuts and a set of metal pilot's wings that I wore over my breast pocket. On a three-day stopover in Japan, we walked through bone-chilling rains to see the great bronze Buddha at Kamakura and ate green tea ice cream on a ferry that passed through high mountain lakes. In the evenings my mother studied flash cards. Walking off the plane in Djakarta, the tarmac rippling with heat, the sun bright as a furnace, I clutched her hand, determined to protect her from whatever might come.

Lolo was there to greet us, a few pounds heavier, a bushy mustache now hovering over his smile. He hugged my mother, hoisted me up into the air, and told us to follow a small, wiry man who was carrying our luggage straight past the long line at customs and into an awaiting car. The man smiled cheerfully as he lifted the bags into the trunk, and my mother tried to say something to him but the man just laughed and nodded his head. People swirled around us, speaking rapidly in a language I didn't know, smelling unfamiliar. For a long time we watched Lolo talk to a group of brown-uniformed soldiers. The soldiers had guns in their holsters, but they appeared to be in a jovial mood, laughing at something that Lolo had said. When Lolo finally joined us, my mother asked if the soldiers needed to check through our bags.

"Don't worry . . . that's been all taken care of," Lolo said, climbing into the driver's seat. "Those are friends of mine."

The car was borrowed, he told us, but he had bought a brand-new motorcycle—a Japanese make, but good enough for now. The new house was finished; just a few touch-ups remained to be done. I was already enrolled in a nearby school, and the relatives were anxious to meet us. As he and my mother talked, I stuck my head out the back-seat window and stared at the passing landscape, brown and green uninterrupted, villages falling back into forest, the smell of diesel oil and wood smoke. Men and women stepped like cranes through the rice paddies, their faces hidden by their wide straw hats. A boy, wet and slick as an otter, sat on the back of a dumb-faced water buffalo, whipping its haunch with a stick of bamboo. The streets became more congested, small stores and markets and men pulling carts loaded with gravel and timber, then the buildings grew taller, like buildings in Hawaii—Hotel Indonesia, very modern, Lolo said, and the new shopping center, white and gleaming—but only a few were higher than the trees that now cooled the road. When we passed a row of big houses with high hedges and sentry posts, my mother said something I couldn't entirely make out, something about the government and a man named Sukarno.

"Who's Sukarno?" I shouted from the backseat, but Lolo appeared not to hear me. Instead, he touched my arm and motioned ahead of us. "Look," he said, pointing upward. There, standing astride the road, was a towering giant at least ten stories tall, with the body of a man and the face of an ape.

"That's Hanuman," Lolo said as we circled the statue, "the monkey god." I turned around in my seat, mesmerized by the solitary figure, so dark against the sun, poised to leap into the sky as puny traffic swirled around its feet. "He's a great warrior," Lolo said firmly. "Strong as a hundred men. When he fights the demons, he's never defeated."

The house was in a still-developing area on the outskirts of town. The road ran over a narrow bridge that spanned a wide brown river; as we passed, I could see villagers bathing and washing clothes along the steep banks below. The road then turned from tarmac to gravel to dirt as it wound past small stores and whitewashed bungalows until it finally petered out into the narrow footpaths of the kampong. The house itself was modest stucco and red tile, but it was open and airy, with a big mango tree in the small courtyard in front. As we passed through the gate, Lolo announced that he had a surprise for me; but before he could explain we heard a deafening howl from high up in the tree. My mother and I jumped back with a start and saw a big, hairy creature with a small, flat head and long, menacing arms drop onto a low branch.

"A monkey!" I shouted.

"An ape," my mother corrected.

Lolo drew a peanut from his pocket and handed it to the animal's grasping fingers. "His name is Tata," he said. "I brought him all the way from New Guinea for you."

I started to step forward to get a closer look, but Tata threatened to lunge, his dark-ringed eyes fierce and suspicious. I decided to stay where I was.

"Don't worry," Lolo said, handing Tata another peanut. "He's on a leash. Come—there's more."

I looked up at my mother, and she gave me a tentative smile. In the backyard, we found what seemed like a small zoo: chickens and ducks running every which way, a big yellow dog with a baleful howl, two birds of paradise, a white cockatoo, and finally two baby crocodiles, half submerged in a fenced-off pond toward the edge of the compound. Lolo stared down at the reptiles. "There were three," he said, "but the biggest one crawled out through a hole in the fence. Slipped into somebody's rice field and ate one of the man's ducks. We had to hunt it by torchlight."

There wasn't much light left, but we took a short walk down the mud path into the village. Groups of giggling neighborhood children waved from their compounds, and a few barefoot old men came up to shake our hands. We stopped at the common, where one of Lolo's men was grazing a few goats, and a small boy came up beside me holding a dragonfly that hovered at the end of a string. When we returned to the house, the man who had carried our luggage was standing in the backyard with a rust-colored hen tucked under his arm and a long knife in his right hand. He said something to Lolo, who nodded and called over to my mother and me. My mother told me to wait where I was and sent Lolo a questioning glance.

"Don't you think he's a little young?"

Lolo shrugged and looked down at me. "The boy should know where his dinner is coming from. What do you think, Barry?" I

looked at my mother, then turned back to face the man holding the
chicken. Lolo nodded again, and I watched the man set the bird
down, pinning it gently under one knee and pulling its neck out
across a narrow gutter. For a moment the bird struggled, beating its
wings hard against the ground, a few feathers dancing up with the
wind. Then it grew completely still. The man pulled the blade across
the bird's neck in a single smooth motion. Blood shot out in a long,
crimson ribbon. The man stood up, holding the bird far away from
his body, and suddenly tossed it high into the air. It landed with a
thud, then struggled to its feet, its head lolling grotesquely against its
side, its legs pumping wildly in a wide, wobbly circle. I watched as the
circle grew smaller, the blood trickling down to a gurgle, until finally
the bird collapsed, lifeless on the grass.

Lolo rubbed his hand across my head and told me and my mother
to go wash up before dinner. The three of us ate quietly under a dim
yellow bulb—chicken stew and rice, and then a dessert of red, hairy-
skinned fruit so sweet at the center that only a stomachache could
make me stop. Later, lying alone beneath a mosquito net canopy, I
listened to the crickets chirp under the moonlight and remembered
the last twitch of life that I'd witnessed a few hours before. I could
barely believe my good fortune.

"The first thing to remember is how to protect yourself."

Lolo and I faced off in the backyard. A day earlier, I had shown up
at the house with an egg-sized lump on the side of my head. Lolo had
looked up from washing his motorcycle and asked me what had happened, and I told him about my tussle with an older boy who lived
down the road. The boy had run off with my friend's soccer ball, I
said, in the middle of our game. When I chased after him, the boy
picked up a rock. It wasn't fair, I said, my voice choking with aggrieve-
ment. He had cheated.

Lolo had parted my hair with his fingers and silently examined the wound. "It's not bleeding," he said finally, before returning to his chrome.

I thought that had ended the matter. But when he came home from work the next day, he had with him two pairs of boxing gloves. They smelled of new leather, the larger pair black, the smaller pair red, the laces tied together and thrown over his shoulder.

He now finished tying the laces on my gloves and stepped back to examine his handiwork. My hands dangled at my sides like bulbs at the ends of thin stalks. He shook his head and raised the gloves to cover my face.

"There. Keep your hands up." He adjusted my elbows, then crouched into a stance and started to bob. "You want to keep moving, but always stay low—don't give them a target. How does that feel?" I nodded, copying his movements as best I could. After a few minutes, he stopped and held his palm up in front of my nose.

"Okay," he said. "Let's see your swing."

This I could do. I took a step back, wound up, and delivered my best shot. His hand barely wobbled.

"Not bad," Lolo said. He nodded to himself, his expression unchanged. "Not bad at all. Agh, but look where your hands are now. What did I tell you? Get them up. . . ."

I raised my arms, throwing soft jabs at Lolo's palm, glancing up at him every so often and realizing how familiar his face had become after our two years together, as familiar as the earth on which we stood. It had taken me less than six months to learn Indonesia's language, its customs, and its legends. I had survived chicken pox, measles, and the sting of my teachers' bamboo switches. The children of farmers, servants, and low-level bureaucrats had become my best friends, and together we ran the streets morning and night, hustling odd jobs, catching crickets, battling swift kites with razor-sharp lines—the loser watched his kite soar off with the wind, and knew that somewhere other children had formed a long wobbly train, their heads toward the sky, waiting for their prize to land. With Lolo, I learned how to eat small green chill peppers raw with dinner (plenty of rice), and, away from the dinner table, I was introduced to dog meat (tough), snake meat (tougher), and roasted grasshopper (crunchy). Like many Indonesians, Lolo followed a brand of Islam that could make room for the remnants of more ancient animist and Hindu faiths. He explained that a man took on the powers of whatever he ate: One day soon, he promised, he would bring home a piece of tiger meat for us to share.

That's how things were, one long adventure, the bounty of a young boy's life. In letters to my grandparents, I would faithfully record many of these events, confident that more civilizing packages of chocolate and peanut butter would surely follow. But not everything made its way into my letters; some things I found too difficult to explain. I didn't tell Toot and Gramps about the face of the man who had come to our door one day with a gaping hole where his nose should have been: the whistling sound he made as he asked my mother for food. Nor did I mention the time that one of my friends told me in the middle of recess that his baby brother had died the night before of an evil spirit brought in by the wind—the terror that danced in my friend's eyes for the briefest of moments before he let out a strange laugh and punched my arm and broke off into a breathless run. There was the empty look on the faces of farmers the year the rains never came, the stoop in their shoulders as they wandered barefoot through their barren, cracked fields, bending over every so often to crumble earth between their fingers; and their desperation the following year when the rains lasted for over a month, swelling the river and fields until the streets gushed with water and swept as high as my waist and families scrambled to rescue their goats and their hens even as chunks of their huts washed away.

The world was violent, I was learning, unpredictable and often cruel. My grandparents knew nothing about such a world, I decided; there was no point in disturbing them with questions they couldn't answer. Sometimes, when my mother came home from work, I would tell her the things I had seen or heard, and she would stroke my forehead, listening intently, trying her best to explain what she could. I always appreciated the attention—her voice, the touch of her hand, defined all that was secure. But her knowledge of floods and exorcisms and cockfights left much to be desired. Everything was as new to her as it was to me, and I would leave such conversations feeling that my questions had only given her unnecessary cause for concern.

So it was to Lolo that I turned for guidance and instruction. He didn't talk much, but he was easy to be with. With his family and friends he introduced me as his son, but he never pressed things beyond matter-of-fact advice or pretended that our relationship was more than it was. I appreciated this distance; it implied a manly trust. And his knowledge of the world seemed inexhaustible. Not just how to change a flat tire or open in chess. He knew more elusive things, ways of managing the emotions I felt, ways to explain fate's constant mysteries.

Like how to deal with beggars. They seemed to be everywhere, a gallery of ills—men, women, children, in tattered clothing matted with dirt, some without arms, others without feet, victims of scurvy or polio or leprosy walking on their hands or rolling down the crowded sidewalks in jerry-built carts, their legs twisted behind them like contortionists'. At first, I watched my mother give over her money to anyone who stopped at our door or stretched out an arm as we passed on the streets. Later, when it became clear that the tide of pain was endless, she gave more selectively, learning to calibrate the levels of misery. Lolo thought her moral calculations endearing but silly, and whenever he caught me following her example with the few coins in my possession, he would raise his eyebrows and take me aside.

"How much money do you have?" he would ask.

I'd empty my pocket. "Thirty rupiah."

"How many beggars are there on the street?"

I tried to imagine the number that had come by the house in the last week. "You see?" he said, once it was clear I'd lost count. "Better to save your money and make sure you don't end up on the street yourself."

He was the same way about servants. They were mostly young villagers newly arrived in the city, often working for families not much better off than themselves, sending money to their people back in the country or saving enough to start their own businesses. If they had ambition, Lolo was willing to help them get their start, and he would generally tolerate their personal idiosyncrasies: for over a year, he employed a good-natured young man who liked to dress up as a woman on weekends—Lolo loved the man's cooking. But he would fire the servants without compunction if they were clumsy, forgetful, or otherwise cost him money; and he would be baffled when either my mother or I tried to protect them from his judgment.

"Your mother has a soft heart," Lolo would tell me one day after my mother tried to take the blame for knocking a radio off the dresser. "That's a good thing in a woman. But you will be a man someday, and a man needs to have more sense."

It had nothing to do with good or bad, he explained, like or dislike. It was a matter of taking life on its own terms.

I felt a hard knock to the jaw, and looked up at Lolo's sweating face.

"Pay attention. Keep your hands up."

We sparred for another half hour before Lolo decided it was time for a rest. My arms burned; my head flashed with a dull, steady throb. We took a jug full of water and sat down near the crocodile pond.

"Tired?" he asked me.

I slumped forward, barely nodding. He smiled, and rolled up one of his pant legs to scratch his calf. I noticed a series of indented scars that ran from his ankle halfway up his shin.

"What are those?"

"Leech marks," he said. "From when I was in New Guinea. They crawl inside your army boots while you're hiking through the swamps. At night, when you take off your socks, they're stuck there, fat with blood. You sprinkle salt on them and they die, but you still have to dig them out with a hot knife."

I ran my finger over one of the oval grooves. It was smooth and hairless where the skin had been singed. I asked Lolo if it had hurt.

"Of course it hurt," he said, taking a sip from the jug. "Sometimes you can't worry about hurt. Sometimes you worry only about getting where you have to go."

We fell silent, and I watched him out of the corner of my eye. I realized that I had never heard him talk about what he was feeling. I had never seen him really angry or sad. He seemed to inhabit a world of hard surfaces and well-defined thoughts. A queer notion suddenly sprang into my head.

"Have you ever seen a man killed?" I asked him.

He glanced down, surprised by the question.

"Have you?" I asked again.

"Yes," he said.

"Was it bloody?"

"Yes."

I thought for a moment. "Why was the man killed? The one you saw?"

"Because he was weak."

"That's all?"

Lolo shrugged and rolled his pant leg back down. "That's usually enough. Men take advantage of weakness in other men. They're just like countries in that way. The strong man takes the weak man's land. He makes the weak man work in his fields. If the weak man's woman is pretty, the strong man will take her." He paused to take another sip of water, then asked, "Which would you rather be?"

I didn't answer, and Lolo squinted up at the sky. "Better to be strong," he said finally, rising to his feet. "If you can't be strong, be clever and make peace with someone who's strong. But always better to be strong yourself. Always."

My mother watched us from inside the house, propped up at her desk grading papers. What are they talking about? she wondered to herself. Blood and guts, probably; swallowing nails. Cheerful, manly things.

She laughed aloud, then caught herself. That wasn't fair. She really was grateful for Lolo's solicitude toward me. He wouldn't have treated his own son very differently. She knew that she was lucky for Lolo's basic kindness. She set her papers aside and watched me do push-ups. He's growing so fast, she thought. She tried to picture herself on the day of our arrival, a mother of twenty-four with a child in tow, married to a man whose history, whose country, she barely knew. She had known so little then, she realized now, her innocence carried right along with her American passport. Things could have turned out worse. Much worse.

She had expected it to be difficult, this new life of hers. Before leaving Hawaii, she had tried to learn all she could about Indonesia: the population, fifth in the world, with hundreds of tribes and dialects; the history of colonialism, first the Dutch for over three centuries, then the Japanese during the war, seeking control over vast stores of oil, metal, and timber; the fight for independence after the war and the emergence of a freedom fighter named Sukarno as the country's first president. Sukarno had recently been replaced, but all the reports said it had been a bloodless coup, and that the people supported the change. Sukarno had grown corrupt, they said; he was a demagogue, totalitarian, too comfortable with the Communists.

A poor country, underdeveloped, utterly foreign—this much she had known. She was prepared for the dysentery and fevers, the cold water baths and having to squat over a hole in the ground to pee, the electricity's going out every few weeks, the heat and endless mosquitoes. Nothing more than inconveniences, really, and she was tougher than she looked, tougher than even she had known herself to be. And anyway, that was part of what had drawn her to Lolo after Barack had left, the promise of something new and important, helping her husband rebuild a country in a charged and challenging place beyond her parents' reach.

But she wasn't prepared for the loneliness. It was constant, like a shortness of breath. There was nothing definite that she could point to, really. Lolo had welcomed her warmly and gone out of his way to make her feel at home, providing her with whatever creature comforts he could afford. His family had treated her with tact and generosity, and treated her son as one of their own.

Still, something had happened between her and Lolo in the year that they had been apart. In Hawaii he had been so full of life, so eager with his plans. At night when they were alone, he would tell her about growing up as a boy during the war, watching his father and eldest brother leave to join the revolutionary army, hearing the news that both had been killed and everything lost, the Dutch army's setting their house aflame, their flight into the countryside, his mother's selling her gold jewelry a piece at a time in exchange for food. Things would be changing now that the Dutch had been driven out, Lolo had told her; he would return and teach at the university, be a part of that change.

He didn't talk that way anymore. In fact, it seemed as though he barely spoke to her at all, only out of necessity or when spoken to, and even then only of the task at hand, repairing a leak or planning a trip to visit some distant cousin. It was as if he had pulled into some dark hidden place, out of reach, taking with him the brightest part of himself. On some nights, she would hear him up after everyone else had gone to bed, wandering through the house with a bottle of imported whiskey, nursing his secrets. Other nights he would tuck a pistol under his pillow before falling off to sleep. Whenever she asked him what was wrong, he would gently rebuff her, saying he was just tired. It was as if he had come to mistrust words somehow. Words, and the sentiments words carried.

She suspected these problems had something to do with Lolo's job. He was working for the army as a geologist, surveying roads and tunnels, when she arrived. It was mind-numbing work that didn't pay very much; the refrigerator alone cost two months' salary. And now with a wife and child to provide for . . . no wonder he was depressed. She hadn't traveled all this way to be a burden, she decided. She would carry her own weight.

She found herself a job right away teaching English to Indonesian businessmen at the American embassy, part of the U.S. foreign aid package to developing countries. The money helped but didn't relieve her loneliness. The Indonesian businessmen weren't much interested in the niceties of the English language, and several made passes at her. The Americans were mostly older men, careerists in the State Department, the occasional economist or journalist who would mysteriously disappear for months at a time, their affiliation or function in the embassy never quite clear. Some of them were caricatures of the ugly American, prone to making jokes about Indonesians until they found out that she was married to one, and then they would try to play it off—Don't take Jim too seriously, the heat's gotten to him, how's your son by the way, fine, fine boy.

These men knew the country, though, or parts of it anyway, the closets where the skeletons were buried. Over lunch or casual conversation they would share with her things she couldn't learn in the published news reports. They explained how Sukarno had frayed badly the nerves of a U.S. government already obsessed with the march of communism through Indochina, what with his nationalist rhetoric and his politics of nonalignment—he was as bad as Lumumba or Nasser, only worse, given Indonesia's strategic importance. Word was that the CIA had played a part in the coup, although nobody knew for sure. More certain was the fact that after the coup the military had swept the countryside for supposed Communist sympathizers. The death toll was anybody's guess: a few hundred thousand, maybe; half a million. Even the smart guys at the Agency had lost count.

Innuendo, half-whispered asides; that's how she found out that we had arrived in Djakarta less than a year after one of the more brutal and swift campaigns of suppression in modern times. The idea frightened her, the notion that history could be swallowed up so completely, the same way the rich and loamy earth could soak up the rivers of blood that had once coursed through the streets; the way people could continue about their business beneath giant posters of the new president as if nothing had happened, a nation busy developing itself. As her circle of Indonesian friends widened, a few of them would be willing to tell her other stories—about the corruption that pervaded government agencies, the shakedowns by police and the military, entire industries carved out for the president's family and entourage. And with each new story, she would go to Lolo in private and ask him: "Is it true?"

He would never say. The more she asked, the more steadfast he became in his good-natured silence. "Why are you worrying about such talk?" he would ask her. "Why don't you buy a new dress for the party?" She had finally complained to one of Lolo's cousins, a pediatrician who had helped look after Lolo during the war.

"You don't understand," the cousin had told her gently.

"Understand what?"

"The circumstances of Lolo's return. He hadn't planned on coming back from Hawaii so early, you know. During the purge, all students studying abroad had been summoned without explanation, their passports revoked. When Lolo stepped off the plane, he had no idea of what might happen next. We couldn't see him; the army officials took him away and questioned him. They told him that he had just been conscripted and would be going to the jungles of New Guinea for a year. And he was one of the lucky ones. Students studying in Eastern Bloc countries did much worse. Many of them are still in jail. Or vanished.

"You shouldn't be too hard on Lolo," the cousin repeated. "Such times are best forgotten."

My mother had left the cousin's house in a daze. Outside, the sun was high, the air full of dust, but instead of taking a taxi home, she began to walk without direction. She found herself in a wealthy neighborhood where the diplomats and generals lived in sprawling houses with tall wrought-iron gates. She saw a woman in bare feet and a tattered shawl wandering through an open gate and up the driveway, where a group of men were washing a fleet of Mercedes-Benzes and Land Rovers. One of the men shouted at the woman to leave, but the woman stood where she was, a bony arm stretched out before her, her face shrouded in shadow. Another man finally dug in his pocket and threw out a handful of coins. The woman ran after the coins with terrible speed, checking the road suspiciously as she gathered them into her bosom.

Power. The word fixed in my mother's mind like a curse. In America, it had generally remained hidden from view until you dug beneath the surface of things; until you visited an Indian reservation or spoke to a black person whose trust you had earned. But here power was undisguised, indiscriminate, naked, always fresh in the memory. Power had taken Lolo and yanked him back into line just when he thought he'd escaped, making him feel its weight, letting him know that his life wasn't his own. That's how things were; you couldn't change it, you could just live by the rules, so simple once you learned them. And so Lolo had made his peace with power, learned the wisdom of forgetting; just as his brother-in-law had done, making millions as a high official in the national oil company; just as another brother had tried to do, only he had miscalculated and was now reduced to stealing pieces of silverware whenever he came for a visit, selling them later for loose cigarettes.

She remembered what Lolo had told her once when her constant questioning had finally touched a nerve. "Guilt is a luxury only foreigners can afford," he had said. "Like saying whatever pops into your head." She didn't know what it was like to lose everything, to wake up and feel her belly eating itself. She didn't know how crowded and treacherous the path to security could be. Without absolute concentration, one could easily slip, tumble backward.

He was right, of course. She was a foreigner, middle-class and white and protected by her heredity whether she wanted protection or not. She could always leave if things got too messy. That possibility negated anything she might say to Lolo; it was the unbreachable barrier between them. She looked out the window now and saw that Lolo and I had moved on, the grass flattened where the two of us had been. The sight made her shudder slightly, and she rose to her feet, filled with a sudden panic.

Power was taking her son.

Looking back, I'm not sure that Lolo ever fully understood what my mother was going through during these years, why the things he was working so hard to provide for her seemed only to increase the distance between them. He was not a man to ask himself such questions. Instead, he maintained his concentration, and over the period that we lived in Indonesia, he proceeded to climb. With the help of his brother-in-law, he landed a new job in the government relations office of an American oil company. We moved to a house in a better neighborhood; a car replaced the motorcycle; a television and hi-fi replaced the crocodiles and Tata, the ape; Lolo could sign for our dinners at a company club. Sometimes I would overhear him and my mother arguing in their bedroom, usually about her refusal to attend his company dinner parties, where American businessmen from Texas and Louisiana would slap Lolo's back and boast about the palms they had greased to obtain the new offshore drilling rights, while their wives complained to my mother about the quality of Indonesian help. He would ask her how it would look for him to go alone, and remind her that these were her own people, and my mother's voice would rise to almost a shout.

They are *not* my people.

Such arguments were rare, though; my mother and Lolo would remain cordial through the birth of my sister, Maya, through the separation and eventual divorce, up until the last time I saw Lolo, ten years later, when my mother helped him travel to Los Angeles to treat a liver ailment that would kill him at the age of fifty-one. What tension I noticed had mainly to do with the gradual shift in my mother's attitude toward me. She had always encouraged my rapid acculturation in Indonesia: It had made me relatively self-sufficient, undemanding on a tight budget, and extremely well mannered when compared to other American children. She had taught me to disdain the blend of ignorance and arrogance that too often characterized Americans abroad. But she now had learned, just as Lolo had learned, the chasm that separated the life chances of an American from those of an Indonesian. She knew which side of the divide she wanted her child to be on. I was an American, she decided, and my true life lay elsewhere.

Her initial efforts centered on education. Without the money to send me to the International School, where most of Djakarta's foreign children went, she had arranged from the moment of our arrival to supplement my Indonesian schooling with lessons from a U.S. correspondence course.

Her efforts now redoubled. Five days a week, she came into my room at four in the morning, force-fed me breakfast, and proceeded to teach me my English lessons for three hours before I left for school and she went to work. I offered stiff resistance to this regimen, but in response to every strategy I concocted, whether unconvincing ("My stomach hurts") or indisputably true (my eyes kept closing every five minutes), she would patiently repeat her most powerful defense:

"This is no picnic for me either, buster."

Then there were the periodic concerns with my safety, the voice of my grandmother ascendant. I remember coming home after dark one day to find a large search party of neighbors that had been assembled in our yard. My mother didn't look happy, but she was so relieved to see me that it took her several minutes to notice a wet sock, brown with mud, wrapped around my forearm.

"What's that?"

"What?"

"That. Why do you have a sock wrapped around your arm?"

"I cut myself."

"Let's see."

"It's not that bad."

"*Barry.* Let me see it."

I unwrapped the sock, exposing a long gash that ran from my wrist to my elbow. It had missed the vein by an inch, but ran deeper at the muscle, where pinkish flesh pulsed out from under the skin. Hoping to calm her down, I explained what had happened: A friend and I had hitchhiked out to his family's farm, and it started to rain, and on the farm was a terrific place to mudslide, and there was this barbed wire that marked the farm's boundaries, and. . . .

"Lolo!"

My mother laughs at this point when she tells this story, the laughter of a mother forgiving her child those sins that have passed. But her tone alters slightly as she remembers that Lolo suggested we wait until morning to get me stitched up, and that she had to browbeat our only neighbor with a car to drive us to the hospital. She remembers that most of the lights were out at the hospital when we arrived, with no receptionist in sight; she recalls the sound of her frantic footsteps echoing through the hallway until she finally found two young men in boxer shorts playing dominoes in a small room in the back. When she asked them where the doctors were, the men cheerfully replied "We are the doctors" and went on to finish their game before slipping on their trousers and giving me twenty stitches that would leave an ugly scar. And through it all was the pervading sense that her child's life might slip away when she wasn't looking, that everyone else around her would be too busy trying to survive to notice—that, when it counted, she would have plenty of sympathy but no one beside her who believed in fighting against a threatening fate.

It was those sorts of issues, I realize now, less tangible than school transcripts or medical services, that became the focus of her lessons with me. "If you want to grow into a human being," she would say to me, "you're going to need some values."

Honesty—Lolo should not have hidden the refrigerator in the storage room when the tax officials came, even if everyone else, including the tax officials, expected such things. Fairness—the parents of wealthier students should not give television sets to the teachers during Ramadan, and their children could take no pride in the higher marks they might have received. Straight talk—if you didn't like the shirt I bought you for your birthday, you should have just said so instead of keeping it wadded up at the bottom of your closet. Independent judgment—just because the other children tease the poor boy about his haircut doesn't mean you have to do it too.

It was as if, by traveling halfway around the globe, away from the smugness and hypocrisy that familiarity had disclosed, my mother could give voice to the virtues of her midwestern past and offer them up in distilled form. The problem was that she had few reinforcements; whenever she took me aside for such commentary, I would dutifully nod my assent, but she must have known that many of her ideas seemed rather impractical. Lolo had merely explained the poverty, the corruption, the constant scramble for security; he hadn't created it. It remained all around me and bred a relentless skepticism. My mother's confidence in needlepoint virtues depended on a faith I didn't possess, a faith that she would refuse to describe as religious; that, in fact, her experience told her was sacrilegious: a faith that rational, thoughtful people could shape their own destiny. In a land where fatalism remained a necessary tool for enduring hardship, where ultimate truths were kept separate from day-to-day realities, she was a lonely witness for secular humanism, a soldier for New Deal, Peace Corps, position-paper liberalism.

She had only one ally in all this, and that was the distant authority of my father. Increasingly, she would remind me of his story, how he had grown up poor, in a poor country, in a poor continent; how his life had been hard, as hard as anything that Lolo might have known. He hadn't cut corners, though, or played all the angles. He was diligent and honest, no matter what it cost him. He had led his life according to principles that demanded a different kind of toughness, principles that promised a higher form of power. I would follow his example, my mother decided. I had no choice. It was in the genes.

"You have me to thank for your eyebrows . . . your father has these little wispy eyebrows that don't amount to much. But your brains, your character, you got from him."

Her message came to embrace black people generally. She would come home with books on the civil rights movement, the recordings of Mahalia Jackson, the speeches of Dr. King. When she told me stories of schoolchildren in the South who were forced to read books handed down from wealthier white schools but who went on to become doctors and lawyers and scientists, I felt chastened by my reluctance to wake up and study in the mornings. If I told her about the goose-stepping demonstrations my Indonesian Boy Scout troop performed in front of the president, she might mention a different kind of march, a march of children no older than me, a march for freedom. Every black man was Thurgood Marshall or Sidney Poitier; every black woman Fannie Lou Hamer or Lena Horne. To be black was to be the beneficiary of a great inheritance, a special destiny, glorious burdens that only we were strong enough to bear.

Burdens we were to carry with style. More than once, my mother would point out: "Harry Belafonte is the best-looking man on the planet."

It was in this context that I came across the picture in *Life* magazine of the black man who had tried to peel off his skin. I imagine other black children, then and now, undergoing similar moments of revelation. Perhaps it comes sooner for most—the parent's warning not to cross the boundaries of a particular neighborhood, or the frustration of not having hair like Barbie no matter how long you tease and comb, or the tale of a father's or grandfather's humiliation at the hands of an employer or a cop, overheard while you're supposed to be asleep. Maybe it's easier for a child to receive the bad news in small doses, allowing for a system of defenses to build up—although I suspect I was one of the luckier ones, having been given a stretch of childhood free from self-doubt.

I know that seeing that article was violent for me, an ambush attack. My mother had warned me about bigots—they were ignorant, uneducated people one should avoid. If I could not yet consider my own mortality, Lolo had helped me understand the potential of disease to cripple, of accidents to maim, of fortunes to decline. I could correctly identify common greed or cruelty in others, and sometimes even in myself. But that one photograph had told me something else: that there was a hidden enemy out there, one that could reach me without anyone's knowledge, not even my own. When I got home that night from the embassy library, I went into the bathroom and stood in front of the mirror with all my senses and limbs seemingly intact, looking as I had always looked, and wondered if something was wrong with me. The alternative seemed no less frightening—that the adults around me lived in the midst of madness.

The initial flush of anxiety would pass, and I would spend my remaining year in Indonesia much as I had before. I retained a confidence that was not always justified and an irrepressible talent for mischief. But my vision had been permanently altered. On the imported television shows that had started running in the evenings, I began to notice that Cosby never got the girl on *I Spy*, that the black man on *Mission Impossible* spent all his time underground. I noticed that there was nobody like me in the Sears, Roebuck Christmas catalog that Toot and Gramps sent us, and that Santa was a white man.

I kept these observations to myself, deciding that either my mother didn't see them or she was trying to protect me and that I shouldn't expose her efforts as having failed. I still trusted my mother's love—but I now faced the prospect that her account of the world, and my father's place in it, was somehow incomplete.

CHAPTER THREE

· ·

IT TOOK ME A while to recognize them in the crowd. When the sliding doors first parted, all I could make out was the blur of smiling, anxious faces tilted over the guardrail. Eventually I spotted a tall, silver-haired man toward the rear of the crowd, with a short, owlish woman barely visible beside him. The pair began to wave in my direction, but before I could wave back they disappeared behind frosted glass.

I looked to the front of the line, where a Chinese family seemed to be having some problems with the customs officials. They had been a lively bunch during the flight from Hong Kong, the father taking off his shoes and padding up and down the aisles, the children clambering over seats, the mother and grandmother hoarding pillows and blankets and chattering endlessly to one another. Now the family was standing absolutely still, trying to will themselves invisible, their eyes silently following the hands that riffled through their passports and luggage with a menacing calm. The father reminded me of Lolo somehow, and I looked down at the wooden mask I was carrying in my hand. It was a gift from the Indonesian copilot, a friend of my mother's who had led me away as she and Lolo and my new sister, Maya, stood by at the gate. I closed my eyes and pressed the mask to my face. The wood had a nutty, cinnamon smell, and I felt myself drifting back across oceans and over the clouds, into the violet horizon, back to the place where I had once been. . . .

Someone shouted out my name. The mask dropped to my side, and with it my daydream, and I saw my grandparents again standing there, waving almost frantically now. This time I waved back; and then, without thinking, I brought the mask again up to my face, swaying my head in an odd little dance. My grandparents laughed and pointed at me and waved some more until the customs official finally tapped me on the shoulder and asked me if I was an American. I nodded and handed him my passport.

"Go ahead," he said, and told the Chinese family to step to one side.

The sliding doors closed behind me. Toot gathered me into a hug and tossed candy-and-chewing-gum leis around my neck. Gramps threw an arm over my shoulder and said that the mask was a definite improvement. They took me to the new car they had bought, and Gramps showed me how to operate the air-conditioning. We drove along the highway, past fast-food restaurants and economy motels and used-car lots strung with festoons. I told them about the trip and everyone back in Djakarta. Gramps told me what they'd planned for my welcome-back dinner. Toot suggested that I'd need new clothes for school.

Then, suddenly, the conversation stopped. I realized that I was to live with strangers.

The new arrangement hadn't sounded so bad when my mother first explained it to me. It was time for me to attend an American school, she had said; I'd run through all the lessons of my correspondence course. She said that she and Maya would be joining me in Hawaii very soon—a year, tops—and that she'd try to make it there for Christmas. She reminded me of what a great time I'd had living with Gramps and Toot just the previous summer—the ice cream, the cartoons, the days at the beach. "And you won't have to wake up at four in the morning," she said, a point that I found most compelling.

It was only now, as I began to adjust to an indefinite stay and watched my grandparents in the rhythm of their schedules, that I realized how much the two of them had changed. After my mother and I left, they had sold the big, rambling house near the university and now rented a small, two-bedroom apartment in a high-rise on Beretania Street. Gramps had left the furniture business to become a life insurance agent, but as he was unable to convince himself that people needed what he was selling and was sensitive to rejection, the work went badly. Every Sunday night, I would watch him grow more and more irritable as he gathered his briefcase and set up a TV tray in front of his chair, following the lead of every possible distraction, until finally he would chase us out of the living room and try to schedule appointments with prospective clients over the phone. Sometimes I would tiptoe into the kitchen for a soda, and I could hear the desperation creeping out of his voice, the stretch of silence that followed when the people on the other end explained why Thursday wasn't good and Tuesday not much better, and then Gramps's heavy sigh after he had hung up the phone, his hands fumbling through the files in his lap like those of a cardplayer who's deep in the hole.

Eventually, a few people would relent, the pain would pass, and Gramps would wander into my room to tell me stories of his youth or the new joke he had read in *Reader's Digest*. If his calls had gone especially well that night, he might discuss with me some scheme he still harbored—the book of poems he had started to write, the sketch that would soon bloom into a painting, the floor plans for his ideal house, complete with push-button conveniences and terraced landscaping. I saw that the plans grew bolder the further they receded from possibility, but in them I recognized some of his old enthusiasm, and I would usually try to think up encouraging questions that might sustain his good mood. Then, somewhere in the middle of his presentation, we would both notice Toot standing in the hall outside my room, her head tilted in accusation.

"What do you want, Madelyn?"

"Are you finished with your calls, dear?"

"*Yes, Madelyn.* I'm finished with my calls. It's ten o'clock at night!"

"There's no need to holler, Stanley. I just wanted to know if I could go into the kitchen."

"I'm not hollering! Jesus H. Christ, I don't understand why—" But before he could finish, Toot would have retreated into their bedroom, and Gramps would leave my room with a look of dejection and rage.

Such exchanges became familiar to me, for my grandparents' arguments followed a well-worn groove, a groove that originated in the rarely mentioned fact that Toot earned more money than Gramps. She had proved to be a trailblazer of sorts, the first woman vice-president of a local bank, and although Gramps liked to say that he always encouraged her in her career, her job had become a source of delicacy and bitterness between them as his commissions paid fewer and fewer of the family's bills.

Not that Toot had anticipated her success. Without a college education, she had started out as a secretary to help defray the costs of my unexpected birth. But she had a quick mind and sound judgment, and the capacity for sustained work. Slowly she had risen, playing by the rules, until she reached the threshold where competence didn't suffice. There she would stay for twenty years, with scarcely a vacation, watching as her male counterparts kept moving up the corporate ladder, playing a bit loose with information passed on between the ninth hole and the ride to the clubhouse, becoming wealthy men.

More than once, my mother would tell Toot that the bank shouldn't get away with such blatant sexism. But Toot would just pooh-pooh my mother's remarks, saying that everybody could find a reason to complain about something. Toot didn't complain. Every morning, she woke up at five A.M. and changed from the frowsy muu-muus she wore around the apartment into a tailored suit and high-heeled pumps. Her face powdered, her hips girdled, her thinning hair bolstered, she would board the six-thirty bus to arrive at her downtown office before anyone else. From time to time, she would admit a grudging pride in her work and took pleasure in telling us the inside story behind the local financial news. When I got older, though, she would confide in me that she had never stopped dreaming of a house with a white picket fence, days spent baking or playing bridge or volunteering at the local library. I was surprised by this admission, for she rarely mentioned hopes or regrets. It may or may not have been true that she would have preferred the alternative history she imagined for herself, but I came to understand that her career spanned a time when the work of a wife outside the home was nothing to brag about, for her or for Gramps—that it represented only lost years, broken promises. What Toot believed kept her going were the needs of her grandchildren and the stoicism of her ancestors.

"So long as you kids do well, Bar," she would say more than once, "that's all that really matters."

That's how my grandparents had come to live. They still prepared sashimi for the now-infrequent guests to their apartment. Gramps still wore Hawaiian shirts to the office, and Toot still insisted on being called Toot. Otherwise, though, the ambitions they had carried with them to Hawaii had slowly drained away, until regularity—of schedules and pastimes and the weather—became their principal consolation. They would occasionally grumble about how the Japanese had taken over the islands, how the Chinese controlled island finance. During the Watergate hearings, my mother would pry out of them that they had voted for Nixon, the law-and-order candidate, in 1968. We didn't go to the beach or on hikes together anymore; at night, Gramps watched television while Toot sat in her room reading murder mysteries. Their principal excitement now came from new drapes or a stand-alone freezer. It was as if they had bypassed the satisfactions that should come with the middle years, the convergence of maturity with time left, energy with means, a recognition of accomplishment that frees the spirit. At some point in my absence, they had decided to cut their losses and settle for hanging on. They saw no more destinations to hope for.

As the summer drew to a close, I became increasingly restless to start school. My main concern was finding companions my own age; but for my grandparents, my admission into Punahou Academy heralded the start of something grand, an elevation in the family status that they took great pains to let everyone know. Started by missionaries in 1841, Punahou had grown into a prestigious prep school, an incubator for island elites. Its reputation had helped sway my mother in her decision to send me back to the States: It hadn't been easy to get me in, my grandparents told her; there was a long waiting list, and I was considered only because of the intervention of Gramps's boss, who was an alumnus (my first experience with affirmative action, it seems, had little to do with race).

I had gone for several interviews with Punahou's admissions officer the previous summer. She was a brisk, efficient-looking woman who didn't seem fazed that my feet barely reached the floor as she grilled me on my career goals. After the interview, the woman had sent Gramps and me on a tour of the campus, a complex that spread over several acres of lush green fields and shady trees, old masonry schoolhouses and modern structures of glass and steel. There were tennis courts, swimming pools, and photography studios. At one point, we fell behind the guide, and Gramps grabbed me by the arm.

"Hell, Bar," he whispered, "this isn't a school. This is heaven. You might just get me to go back to school with you."

With my admission notice had come a thick packet of information that Toot set aside to pore over one Saturday afternoon. "Welcome to the Punahou family," the letter announced. A locker had been assigned to me; I was enrolled in a meal plan unless a box was checked; there was a list of things to buy—a uniform for physical education, scissors, a ruler, number two pencils, a calculator (optional). Gramps spent the evening reading the entire school catalog, a thick book that listed my expected progression through the next seven years—the college prep courses, the extracurricular activities, the traditions of well-rounded excellence. With each new item, Gramps grew more and more animated; several times he got up, with his thumb saving his place, and headed toward the room where Toot was reading, his voice full of amazement: "Madelyn, get a load of this!"

So it was with a great rush of excitement that Gramps accompanied me on my first day of school. He had insisted that we arrive early, and Castle Hall, the building for the fifth and sixth graders, was not yet opened. A handful of children had already arrived, busy catching up on the summer's news. We sat beside a slender Chinese boy who had a large dental retainer strapped around his neck.

"Hi there," Gramps said to the boy. "This here's Barry. I'm Barry's grandfather. You can call me Gramps." He shook hands with the boy, whose name was Frederick. "Barry's new."

"Me too," Frederick said, and the two of them launched into a lively conversation. I sat, embarrassed, until the doors finally opened and we went up the stairs to our classroom. At the door, Gramps slapped both of us on the back.

"Don't do anything I would do," he said with a grin.

"Your grandfather's funny," Frederick said as we watched Gramps introduce himself to Miss Hefty, our homeroom teacher.

"Yeah. He is."

We sat at a table with four other children, and Miss Hefty, an energetic middle-aged woman with short gray hair, took attendance. When she read my full name, I heard titters break across the room. Frederick leaned over to me.

"I thought your name was Barry."

"Would you prefer if we called you Barry?" Miss Hefty asked. "Barack is such a beautiful name. Your grandfather tells me your father is Kenyan. I used to live in Kenya, you know. Teaching children just your age. It's such a magnificent country. Do you know what tribe your father is from?"

Her question brought on more giggles, and I remained speechless for a moment. When I finally said "Luo," a sandy-haired boy behind me repeated the word in a loud hoot, like the sound of a monkey. The children could no longer contain themselves, and it took a stern reprimand from Miss Hefty before the class would settle down and we could mercifully move on to the next person on the list.

I spent the rest of the day in a daze. A redheaded girl asked to touch my hair and seemed hurt when I refused. A ruddy-faced boy asked me if my father ate people. When I got home, Gramps was in the middle of preparing dinner.

"So how was it? Isn't it terrific that Miss Hefty used to live in Kenya? Makes the first day a little easier, I'll bet."

I went into my room and closed the door.

The novelty of having me in the class quickly wore off for the other kids, although my sense that I didn't belong continued to grow. The clothes that Gramps and I had chosen for me were too old-fashioned; the Indonesian sandals that had served me so well in Djakarta were dowdy. Most of my classmates had been together since kindergarten; they lived in the same neighborhoods, in split-level homes with swimming pools; their fathers coached the same Little League teams; their mothers sponsored the bake sales. Nobody played soccer or badminton or chess, and I had no idea how to throw a football in a spiral or balance on a skateboard.

A ten-year-old's nightmare. Still, in my discomfort that first month, I was no worse off than the other children who were relegated to the category of misfits—the girls who were too tall or too shy, the boy who was mildly hyperactive, the kids whose asthma excused them from PE.

There was one other child in my class, though, who reminded me of a different sort of pain. Her name was Coretta, and before my arrival she had been the only black person in our grade. She was plump and dark and didn't seem to have many friends. From the first day, we avoided each other but watched from a distance, as if direct contact would only remind us more keenly of our isolation.

Finally, during recess one hot, cloudless day, we found ourselves occupying the same corner of the playground. I don't remember what we said to each other, but I remember that suddenly she was chasing me around the jungle gyms and swings. She was laughing brightly, and I teased her and dodged this way and that, until she finally caught me and we fell to the ground breathless. When I looked up, I saw a group of children, faceless before the glare of the sun, pointing down at us.

"Coretta has a boyfriend! Coretta has a boyfriend!"

The chants grew louder as a few more kids circled us.

"She's not my g-girlfriend," I stammered. I looked to Coretta for some assistance, but she just stood there looking down at the ground. "Coretta's got a boyfriend! Why don't you kiss her, mister boyfriend?"

"I'm not her boyfriend!" I shouted. I ran up to Coretta and gave her a slight shove; she staggered back and looked up at me, but still said nothing. "Leave me alone!" I shouted again. And suddenly Coretta was running, faster and faster, until she disappeared from sight. Appreciative laughs rose around me. Then the bell rang, and the teachers appeared to round us back into class.

For the rest of the afternoon, I was haunted by the look on Coretta's face just before she had started to run: her disappointment, and the accusation. I wanted to explain to her somehow that it had been nothing personal; I'd just never had a girlfriend before and saw no particular need to have one now. But I didn't even know if that was true. I knew only that it was too late for explanations, that somehow I'd been tested and found wanting; and whenever I snuck a glance at Coretta's desk, I would see her with her head bent over her work, appearing as if nothing had happened, pulled into herself and asking no favors.

My act of betrayal bought me some room from the other children, and like Coretta, I was mostly left alone. I made a few friends, learned to speak less often in class, and managed to toss a wobbly football around. But from that day forward, a part of me felt trampled on, crushed, and I took refuge in the life that my grandparents led. After school let out, I would walk the five blocks to our apartment; if I had any change in my pockets, I might stop off at a newsstand run by a blind man, who would let me know what new comics had come in. Gramps would be at home to let me into the apartment, and as he lay down for his afternoon nap, I would watch cartoons and sitcom reruns. At four-thirty, I would wake Gramps and we would drive downtown to pick up Toot. My homework would be done in time for dinner, which we ate in front of the television. There I would stay for the rest of the evening, negotiating with Gramps over which programs to watch, sharing the latest snack food he'd discovered at the supermarket. At ten o'clock, I went to my room (Johnny Carson came on at that time, and there was no negotiating around that), and I would fall asleep to the sounds of Top 40 music on the radio.

Nested in the soft, forgiving bosom of America's consumer culture, I felt safe; it was as if I had dropped into a long hibernation. I wonder sometimes how long I might have stayed there had it not been for the telegram Toot found in the mailbox one day.

"Your father's coming to see you," she said. "Next month. Two weeks after your mother gets here. They'll both stay through New Year's."

She carefully folded the paper and slipped it into a drawer in the kitchen. Both she and Gramps fell silent, the way I imagine people react when the doctor tells them they have a serious, but curable, illness. For a moment the air was sucked out of the room, and we stood suspended, alone with our thoughts.

"Well," Toot said finally, "I suppose we better start looking for a place where he can stay."

Gramps took off his glasses and rubbed his eyes.

"Should be one hell of a Christmas."

Over lunch, I explained to a group of boys that my father was a prince.

"My grandfather, see, he's a chief. It's sort of like the king of the tribe, you know . . . like the Indians. So that makes my father a prince. He'll take over when my grandfather dies."

"What about after that?" one of my friends asked as we emptied our trays into the trash bin. "I mean, will you go back and be a prince?"

"Well . . . if I want to, I could. It's sort of complicated, see, 'cause the tribe is full of warriors. Like Obama . . . that means 'Burning Spear.' The men in our tribe all want to be chief, so my father has to settle these feuds before I can come."

As the words tumbled out of my mouth, and I felt the boys readjust to me, more curious and familiar as we bumped into each other in the line back to class, a part of me really began to believe the story. But another part of me knew that what I was telling them was a lie, something I'd constructed from the scraps of information I'd picked up from my mother. After a week of my father in the flesh, I had decided that I preferred his more distant image, an image I could alter on a whim—or ignore when convenient. If my father hadn't exactly disappointed me, he remained something unknown, something volatile and vaguely threatening.

My mother had sensed my apprehension in the days building up to his arrival—I suppose it mirrored her own—and so, in between her efforts to prepare the apartment we'd sublet for him, she would try to assure me that the reunion would go smoothly. She had maintained a correspondence with him throughout the time we had been in Indonesia, she explained, and he knew all about me. Like her, my father had remarried, and I now had five brothers and one sister living in Kenya. He had been in a bad car accident, and this trip was part of his recuperation after a long stay in the hospital.

"You two will become great friends," she decided.

Along with news of my father, she began to stuff me with information about Kenya and its history—it was from a book about Jomo Kenyatta, the first president of Kenya, that I'd pilfered the name Burning Spear. But nothing my mother told me could relieve my doubts, and I retained little of the information she offered. Only once did she really spark my interest, when she told me that my father's tribe, the Luo, were a Nilotic people who had migrated to Kenya from their original home along the banks of the world's greatest river. This seemed promising; Gramps still kept a painting he had once done, a replica of lean, bronze Egyptians on a golden chariot drawn by alabaster steeds. I had visions of ancient Egypt, the great kingdoms I had read about, pyramids and pharaohs, Nefertiti and Cleopatra.

One Saturday I went to the public library near our apartment and, with the help of a raspy-voiced old librarian who appreciated my seriousness, I found a book on East Africa. Only there was no mention of pyramids. In fact, the Luos merited only a short paragraph. *Nilote*, it turned out, described a number of nomadic tribes that had originated in the Sudan along the White Nile, far south of the Egyptian empires. The Luo raised cattle and lived in mud huts and ate corn meal and yams and something called millet. Their traditional costume was a leather thong across the crotch. I left the book open-faced on a table and walked out without thanking the librarian.

The big day finally arrived, and Miss Hefty let me out early from class, wishing me luck. I left the school building feeling like a condemned man. My legs were heavy, and with each approaching step toward my grandparents' apartment, the thump in my chest grew louder. When I entered the elevator, I stood without pressing the button. The door closed, then reopened, and an older Filipino man who lived on the fourth floor got on.

"Your grandfather says your father is coming to visit you today," the man said cheerfully. "You must be very happy."

When—after standing in front of the door and looking out across the Honolulu skyline at a distant ship, and then squinting at the sky to watch sparrows spiral through the air—I could think of no possible means of escape, I rang the doorbell. Toot opened the door.

"There he is! Come on, Bar . . . come meet your father."

And there, in the unlit hallway, I saw him, a tall, dark figure who walked with a slight limp. He crouched down and put his arms around me, and I let my arms hang at my sides. Behind him stood my mother, her chin trembling as usual.

"Well, Barry," my father said. "It is a good thing to see you after so long. Very good."

He led me by the hand into the living room, and we all sat down.

"So, Barry, your grandmama has told me that you are doing very well in school."

I shrugged.

"He's feeling a little shy, I think," Toot offered. She smiled and rubbed my head.

"Well," my father said, "you have no reason to be shy about doing well. Have I told you that your brothers and sister have also excelled in their schooling? It's in the blood, I think," he said with a laugh.

I watched him carefully as the adults began to talk. He was much thinner than I had expected, the bones of his knees cutting the legs of his trousers in sharp angles; I couldn't imagine him lifting anyone off the ground. Beside him, a cane with a blunt ivory head leaned against the wall. He wore a blue blazer, and a white shirt, and a scarlet ascot. His horn-rimmed glasses reflected the light of the lamp so that I couldn't see his eyes very well, but when he took the glasses off to rub the bridge of his nose, I saw that they were slightly yellow, the eyes of someone who's had malaria more than once. There was a fragility about his frame, I thought, a caution when he lit a cigarette or reached for his beer. After an hour or so, my mother suggested that he looked tired and should take a nap, and he agreed. He gathered up his travel

bag, then stopped in mid-stride and began to fish around in it, until he
finally pulled out three wooden figurines—a lion, an elephant, and an
ebony man in tribal dress beating a drum—and handed them to me.

· "Say thank you, Bar," my mother said.

"Thank you," I muttered.

My father and I both looked down at the carvings, lifeless in my
hands. He touched my shoulder.

"They are only small things," he said softly. Then he nodded to
Gramps, and together they gathered up his luggage and went downstairs to the other apartment.

A month. That's how long we would have together, the five of us in
my grandparents' living room most evenings, during the day on drives
around the island or on short walks past the private landmarks of a
family: the lot where my father's apartment had once stood; the
remodeled hospital where I had been born; my grandparents' first
house in Hawaii, before the one on University Avenue, a house I had
never known. There was so much to tell in that single month, so much
explaining to do; and yet when I reach back into my memory for the
words of my father, the small interactions or conversations we might
have had, they seem irretrievably lost. Perhaps they're imprinted too
deeply, his voice the seed of all sorts of tangled arguments that I carry
on with myself, as impenetrable now as the pattern of my genes, so
that all I can perceive is the worn-out shell. My wife offers a simpler
explanation—that boys and their fathers don't always have much to
say to each other unless and until they trust—and this may come
closer to the mark, for I often felt mute before him, and he never
pushed me to speak. I'm left with mostly images that appear and die
off in my mind like distant sounds: his head thrown back in laughter
at one of Gramps's jokes as my mother and I hang Christmas ornaments; his grip on my shoulder as he introduces me to one of his old

friends from college; the narrowing of his eyes, the stroking of his sparse goatee, as he reads his important books.

Images, and his effect on other people. For whenever he spoke—his one leg draped over the other, his large hands outstretched to direct or deflect attention, his voice deep and sure, cajoling and laughing—I would see a sudden change take place in the family. Gramps became more vigorous and thoughtful, my mother more bashful; even Toot, smoked out of the foxhole of her bedroom, would start sparring with him about politics or finance, stabbing the air with her blue-veined hands to make a point. It was as if his presence had summoned the spirit of earlier times and allowed each of them to reprise his or her old role; as if Dr. King had never been shot, and the Kennedys continued to beckon the nation, and war and riot and famine were nothing more than temporary setbacks, and there was nothing to fear but fear itself.

It fascinated me, this strange power of his, and for the first time I began to think of my father as something real and immediate, perhaps even permanent. After a few weeks, though, I could feel the tension around me beginning to build. Gramps complained that my father was sitting in his chair. Toot muttered, while doing the dishes, that she wasn't anybody's servant. My mother's mouth pinched, her eyes avoiding her parents, as we ate dinner. One evening, I turned on the television to watch a cartoon special—*How the Grinch Stole Christmas*—and the whispers broke into shouts.

"Barry, you have watched enough television tonight," my father said. "Go in your room and study now, and let the adults talk."

Toot stood up and turned off the TV. "Why don't you turn the show on in the bedroom, Bar."

"No, Madelyn," my father said, "that's not what I mean. He has been watching that machine constantly, and now it is time for him to study."

My mother tried to explain that it was almost Christmas vacation, that the cartoon was a Christmas favorite, that I had been looking forward to it all week. "It won't last long."

"Anna, this is nonsense. If the boy has done his work for tomorrow, he can begin on his next day's assignments. Or the assignments he will have when he returns from the holidays." He turned to me. "I tell you, Barry, you do not work as hard as you should. Go now, before I get angry at you."

I went to my room and slammed the door, listening as the voices outside grew louder, Gramps insisting that this was his house, Toot saying that my father had no right to come in and bully everyone, including me, after being gone all this time. I heard my father say that they were spoiling me, that I needed a firm hand, and I listened to my mother tell her parents that nothing ever changed with them. We all stood accused, and even after my father left and Toot came in to say that I could watch the last five minutes of my show, I felt as if something had cracked open between all of us, goblins rushing out of some old, sealed-off lair. Watching the green Grinch on the television screen, intent on ruining Christmas, eventually transformed by the faith of the doe-eyed creatures who inhabited Whoville, I saw it for what it was: a lie. I began to count the days until my father would leave and things would return to normal.

The next day, Toot sent me down to the apartment where my father was staying to see if he had any laundry to wash. I knocked, and my father opened the door, shirtless. Inside, I saw my mother ironing some of his clothes. Her hair was tied back in a ponytail, and her eyes were soft and dark, as if she'd been crying. My father asked me to sit down beside him on the bed, but I told him that Toot needed me to help her, and left after relaying the message. Back upstairs, I had begun cleaning my room when my mother came in.

"You shouldn't be mad at your father, Bar. He loves you very much. He's just a little stubborn sometimes."

"Okay," I said without looking up. I could feel her eyes follow me around the room until she finally let out a slow breath and went to the door.

"I know all this stuff is confusing for you," she said. "For me, too. Just try to remember what I said, okay?" She put her hand on the doorknob. "Do you want me to close the door?"

I nodded, but she had been gone for only a minute when she stuck her head back into the room.

"By the way, I forgot to tell you that Miss Hefty has invited your father to come to school on Thursday. She wants him to speak to the class."

I couldn't imagine worse news. I spent that night and all of the next day trying to suppress thoughts of the inevitable: the faces of my classmates when they heard about mud huts, all my lies exposed, the painful jokes afterward. Each time I remembered, my body squirmed as if it had received a jolt to the nerves.

I was still trying to figure out how I'd explain myself when my father walked into our class the next day. Miss Hefty welcomed him eagerly, and as I took my seat I heard several children ask each other what was going on. I became more desperate when our math teacher, a big, no-nonsense Hawaiian named Mr. Eldredge, came into the room, followed by thirty confused children from his homeroom next door.

"We have a special treat for you today," Miss Hefty began. "Barry Obama's father is here, and he's come all the way from Kenya, in Africa, to tell us about his country."

The other kids looked at me as my father stood up, and I held my head stiffly, trying to focus on a vacant point on the blackboard behind him. He had been speaking for some time before I could finally bring myself back to the moment. He was leaning against Miss Hefty's thick oak desk and describing the deep gash in the earth where mankind had first appeared. He spoke of the wild animals that still roamed the plains, the tribes that still required a young boy to kill a lion to prove his manhood. He spoke of the customs of the Luo, how elders received the utmost respect and made laws for all to follow under great-trunked trees. And he told us of Kenya's struggle to be free, how the British had wanted to stay and unjustly rule the people, just as they had in America; how many had been enslaved only because of the color of their skin, just as they had in America; but that Kenyans, like all of us in the room, longed to be free and develop themselves through hard work and sacrifice.

When he finished, Miss Hefty was absolutely beaming with pride. All my classmates applauded heartily, and a few struck up the courage to ask questions, each of which my father appeared to consider carefully before answering. The bell rang for lunch, and Mr. Eldredge came up to me.

"You've got a pretty impressive father."

The ruddy-faced boy who had asked about cannibalism said, "Your dad is pretty cool."

And off to one side, I saw Coretta watch my father say good-bye to some of the children. She seemed too intent to smile; her face showed only a look of simple satisfaction.

Two weeks later he was gone. In that time, we stand together in front of the Christmas tree and pose for pictures, the only ones I have of us together, me holding an orange basketball, his gift to me, him showing off the tie I've bought him ("Ah, people will know that I am very important wearing such a tie"). At a Dave Brubeck concert, I struggle to sit quietly in the dark auditorium beside him, unable to follow the spare equations of sound that the performers make, careful to clap whenever he claps. For brief spells in the day I will lie beside him, the two of us alone in the apartment sublet from a retired old woman whose name I forget, the place full of quilts and doilies and knitted seat covers, and I read my book while he reads his. He remains opaque to me, a present mass; when I mimic his gestures or turns of phrase, I know neither their origins nor their consequences, can't see how they play out over time. But I grow accustomed to his company.

The day of his departure, as my mother and I helped him pack his bags, he unearthed two records, forty-fives, in dull brown dust jackets.

"Barry! Look here—I forgot that I had brought these for you. The sounds of your continent."

It took him a while to puzzle out my grandparents' old stereo, but finally the disk began to turn, and he gingerly placed the needle on the groove. A tinny guitar lick opened, then the sharp horns, the thump of drums, then the guitar again, and then the voices, clean and joyful as they rode up the back beat, urging us on.

"Come, Barry," my father said. "You will learn from the master." And suddenly his slender body was swaying back and forth, the lush sound was rising, his arms were swinging as they cast an invisible net, his feet wove over the floor in off-beats, his bad leg stiff but his rump high, his head back, his hips moving in a tight circle. The rhythm quickened, the horns sounded, and his eyes closed to follow his pleasure, and then one eye opened to peek down at me and his solemn face spread into a silly grin, and my mother smiled, and my grandparents walked in to see what all the commotion was about. I took my first tentative steps with my eyes closed, down, up, my arms swinging, the voices lifting. And I hear him still: As I follow my father into the sound, he lets out a quick shout, bright and high, a shout that leaves much behind and reaches out for more, a shout that cries for laughter.

CHAPTER FOUR

• •

M AN, I'M NOT GOING to any more of these bullshit Punahou parties."

"Yeah, that's what you said the last time."

Ray and I sat down at a table and unwrapped our hamburgers. He was two years older than me, a senior who, as a result of his father's army transfer, had arrived from Los Angeles the previous year. Despite the difference in age, we'd fallen into an easy friendship, due in no small part to the fact that together we made up almost half of Punahou's black high school population. I enjoyed his company; he had a warmth and brash humor that made up for his constant refer-ences to a former L.A. life—the retinue of women who supposedly still called him long-distance every night, his past football exploits, the celebrities he knew. Most of the things he told me I tended to discount, but not everything; it was true, for example, that he was one of the fastest sprinters in the islands, Olympic caliber some said, this despite an improbably large stomach that quivered under his sweat-soaked jersey whenever he ran and left coaches and opposing teams shaking their heads in disbelief. Through Ray I would find out about the black parties that were happening at the university or out on the army bases, counting on him to ease my passage through unfamiliar terrain. In return, I gave him a sounding board for his frustrations.

"I mean it this time," he was saying to me now. "These girls are A-1, USDA-certified racists. All of 'em. White girls. Asian girls—shoot, these Asians worse than the whites. Think we got a disease or something."

"Maybe they're looking at that big butt of yours. Man, I thought you were in training."

"Get your hands out of my fries. You ain't my bitch, nigger . . . buy your own damn fries. Now what was I talking about?"

"Just 'cause a girl don't go out with you doesn't make her racist."

"Don't be thick, all right? I'm not just talking about one time. Look, I ask Monica out, she says no. I say okay . . . your shit's not so hot anyway." Ray stopped to check my reaction, then smiled. "All right, maybe I don't actually say all that. I just tell her okay, Monica, you know, we still tight. Next thing I know, she's hooked up with Steve 'No Neck' Yamaguchi, the two of 'em all holding hands and shit, like a couple of lovebirds. So fine—I figure there're more fish in the sea. I go ask Pamela out. She tells me she ain't going to the dance. I say cool. Get to the dance, guess who's standing there, got her arms around Rick Cook. *'Hi, Ray,'* she says, like she don't know what's going down. Rick Cook! Now you know that guy ain't shit. Sorry-assed motherfucker got nothing on me, right? Nothing."

He stuffed a handful of fries into his mouth. "It ain't just me, by the way. I don't see you doing any better in the booty department."

Because I'm shy, I thought to myself; but I would never admit that to him. Ray pressed the advantage.

"So what happens when we go out to a party with some sisters, huh? What happens? I tell you what happens. Blam! They on us like there's no tomorrow. High school chicks, university chicks—it don't matter. They acting sweet, all smiles. 'Sure you can have my number, baby.' Bet."

"Well . . ."

"Well what? Listen, why don't you get more playing time on the basketball team, huh? At least two guys ahead of you ain't nothing, and you know it, and they know it. I seen you tear 'em up on the playground, no contest. Why wasn't I starting on the football squad this season, no matter how many passes the other guy dropped? Tell me we wouldn't be treated different if we was white. Or Japanese. Or Hawaiian. Or fucking Eskimo."

"That's not what I'm saying."

"So what are you saying?"

"All right, here's what I'm saying. I'm saying, yeah, it's harder to get dates because there aren't any black girls around here. But that don't make the girls that are here all racist. Maybe they just want somebody that looks like their daddy, or their brother, or whatever, and we ain't it. I'm saying yeah, I might not get the breaks on the team that some guys get, but they play like white boys do, and that's the style the coach likes to play, and they're winning the way they play. I don't play that way.

"As for your greasy-mouthed self," I added, reaching for the last of his fries, "I'm saying the coaches may not like you 'cause you're a smart-assed black man, but it might help if you stopped eating all them fries you eat, making you look six months pregnant. That's what I'm saying."

"Man, I don't know why you making excuses for these folks." Ray got up and crumpled his trash into a tight ball. "Let's get out of here. Your shit's getting way too complicated for me."

Ray was right; things had gotten complicated. It had been five years since my father's visit, and on the surface, at least, it had been a placid time marked by the usual rites and rituals that America expects from its children—marginal report cards and calls to the principal's office, part-time jobs at the burger chain, acne and driving tests and turbulent desire. I'd made my share of friends at school, gone on the occasional awkward date; and if I sometimes puzzled over the mysterious realignments of status that took place among my classmates, as some rose and others fell depending on the whims of their bodies or the make of their cars, I took comfort in the knowledge that my own position had steadily improved. Rarely did I meet kids whose families had less than mine and might remind me of good fortune.

My mother did her best to remind me. She had separated from Lolo and returned to Hawaii to pursue a master's degree in anthropology shortly after my own arrival. For three years I lived with her and Maya in a small apartment a block away from Punahou, my mother's student grants supporting the three of us. Sometimes, when I brought friends home after school, my mother would overhear them remark about the lack of food in the fridge or the less-than-perfect housekeeping, and she would pull me aside and let me know that she was a single mother going to school again and raising two kids, so that baking cookies wasn't exactly at the top of her priority list, and while she appreciated the fine education I was receiving at Punahou, she wasn't planning on putting up with any snotty attitudes from me or anyone else, was that understood?

It was understood. Despite my frequent—and sometimes sullen—claims of independence, the two of us remained close, and I did my best to help her out where I could, shopping for groceries, doing the laundry, looking after the knowing, dark-eyed child that my sister had become. But when my mother was ready to return to Indonesia to do her field work, and suggested that I go back with her and Maya to attend the international school there, I immediately said no. I doubted what Indonesia now had to offer and wearied of being new all over again. More than that, I'd arrived at an unspoken pact with my grandparents: I could live with them and they'd leave me alone so long as I kept my trouble out of sight. The arrangement suited my purpose, a purpose that I could barely articulate to myself, much less to them. Away from my mother, away from my grandparents, I was engaged in a fitful interior struggle. I was trying to raise myself to be a black man in America, and beyond the given of my appearance, no one around me seemed to know exactly what that meant.

My father's letters provided few clues. They would arrive sporadically, on a single blue page with gummed-down flaps that obscured any writing at the margins. He would report that everyone was fine, commend me on my progress in school, and insist that my mother, Maya, and I were all welcome to take our rightful place beside him whenever we so desired. From time to time he would include advice, usually in the form of aphorisms I didn't quite understand ("Like water finding its level, you will arrive at a career that suits you"). I would respond promptly on a wide-ruled page, and his letters would find their way into the closet, next to my mother's pictures of him.

Gramps had a number of black male friends, mostly poker and bridge partners, and before I got old enough not to care about hurting his feelings, I would let him drag me along to some of their games. They were old, neatly dressed men with hoarse voices and clothes that smelled of cigars, the kind of men for whom everything has its place and who figure they've seen enough not to have to waste a lot of time talking about it. Whenever they saw me they would give me a jovial slap on the back and ask how my mother was doing; but once it was time to play, they wouldn't say another word except to complain to their partner about a bid.

There was one exception, a poet named Frank who lived in a dilapidated house in a run-down section of Waikiki. He had enjoyed some modest notoriety once, was a contemporary of Richard Wright and Langston Hughes during his years in Chicago—Gramps once showed me some of his work anthologized in a book of black poetry. But by the time I met Frank he must have been pushing eighty, with a big, dewlapped face and an ill-kempt gray Afro that made him look like an old, shaggy-maned lion. He would read us his poetry whenever we stopped by his house, sharing whiskey with Gramps out of an emptied jelly jar. As the night wore on, the two of them would solicit my help in composing dirty limericks. Eventually, the conversation would turn to laments about women.

"They'll drive you to drink, boy," Frank would tell me soberly. "And if you let 'em, they'll drive you into your grave."

I was intrigued by old Frank, with his books and whiskey breath and the hint of hard-earned knowledge behind the hooded eyes. The visits to his house always left me feeling vaguely uncomfortable, though, as if I were witnessing some complicated, unspoken transaction between the two men, a transaction I couldn't fully understand. The same thing I felt whenever Gramps took me downtown to one of his favorite bars, in Honolulu's red-light district.

"Don't tell your grandmother," he would say with a wink, and we'd walk past hard-faced, soft-bodied streetwalkers into a small, dark bar with a jukebox and a couple of pool tables. Nobody seemed to mind that Gramps was the only white man in the place, or that I was the only eleven- or twelve-year-old. Some of the men leaning across the bar would wave at us, and the bartender, a big, light-skinned woman with bare, fleshy arms, would bring a Scotch for Gramps and a Coke for me. If nobody else was playing at the tables, Gramps would spot me a few balls and teach me the game, but usually I would sit at the bar, my legs dangling from the high stool, blowing bubbles into my drink and looking at the pornographic art on the walls—the phosphorescent women on animal skins, the Disney characters in compromising positions. If he was around, a man named Rodney with a wide-brimmed hat would stop by to say hello.

"How's school coming, captain?"

"All right."

"You getting them *A*'s, ain't you?"

"Some."

"That's good. Sally, buy my man here another Coke," Rodney

would say, peeling a twenty off a thick stack he had pulled from his pocket before he fell back into the shadows.

I can still remember the excitement I felt during those evening trips, the enticement of darkness and the click of the cue ball, and the jukebox flashing its red and green lights, and the weary laughter that ran around the room. Yet even then, as young as I was, I had already begun to sense that most of the people in the bar weren't there out of choice, that what my grandfather sought there was the company of people who could help him forget his own troubles, people who he believed would not judge him. Maybe the bar really did help him forget, but I knew with the unerring instincts of a child that he was wrong about not being judged. Our presence there felt forced, and by the time I had reached junior high school I had learned to beg off from Gramps's invitations, knowing that whatever it was I was after, whatever it was that I needed, would have to come from some other source.

TV, movies, the radio; those were the places to start. Pop culture was color-coded, after all, an arcade of images from which you could cop a walk, a talk, a step, a style. I couldn't croon like Marvin Gaye, but I could learn to dance all the *Soul Train* steps. I couldn't pack a gun like Shaft or Superfly, but I could sure enough curse like Richard Pryor.

And I could play basketball, with a consuming passion that would always exceed my limited talent. My father's Christmas gift had come at a time when the University of Hawaii basketball team had slipped into the national rankings on the strength of an all-black starting five that the school had shipped in from the mainland. That same spring, Gramps had taken me to one of their games, and I had watched the players in warm-ups, still boys themselves but to me poised and confident warriors, chuckling to each other about some inside joke, glancing over the heads of fawning fans to wink at the girls on the sidelines, casually flipping layups or tossing high-arcing jumpers until the whistle blew and the centers jumped and the players joined in furious battle.

I decided to become part of that world, and began going down to a playground near my grandparents' apartment after school. From her bedroom window, ten stories up, Toot would watch me on the court until well after dark as I threw the ball with two hands at first, then developed an awkward jump shot, a crossover dribble, absorbed in the same solitary moves hour after hour. By the time I reached high school, I was playing on Punahou's teams, and could take my game to the university courts, where a handful of black men, mostly gym rats and has-beens, would teach me an attitude that didn't just have to do with the sport. That respect came from what you did and not who your daddy was. That you could talk stuff to rattle an opponent, but that you should shut the hell up if you couldn't back it up. That you didn't let anyone sneak up behind you to see emotions—like hurt or fear—you didn't want them to see.

And something else, too, something nobody talked about: a way of being together when the game was tight and the sweat broke and the best players stopped worrying about their points and the worst players got swept up in the moment and the score only mattered because that's how you sustained the trance. In the middle of which you might make a move or a pass that surprised even you, so that even the guy guarding you had to smile, as if to say, "Damn . . ."

My wife will roll her eyes right about now. She grew up with a basketball star for a brother, and when she wants to wind either of us up she will insist that she'd rather see her son play the cello. She's right, of course; I was living out a caricature of black male adolescence, itself a caricature of swaggering American manhood. Yet at a time when boys aren't supposed to want to follow their fathers' tired footsteps, when the imperatives of harvest or work in the factory aren't supposed to dictate identity, so that how to live is bought off the rack or found in magazines, the principal difference between me and most of the man-boys around me—the surfers, the football players, the would-be rock-and-roll guitarists—resided in the limited number of options at my disposal. Each of us chose a costume, armor against uncertainty. At least on the basketball court I could find a community of sorts, with an inner life all its own. It was there that I would make my closest white friends, on turf where blackness couldn't be a disadvantage. And it was there that I would meet Ray and the other blacks close to my age who had begun to trickle into the islands, teenagers whose confusion and anger would help shape my own.

"That's just how white folks will do you," one of them might say when we were alone. Everybody would chuckle and shake their heads, and my mind would run down a ledger of slights: the first boy, in seventh grade, who called me a coon; his tears of surprise—"Why'dya do that?"—when I gave him a bloody nose. The tennis pro who told me during a tournament that I shouldn't touch the schedule of matches pinned up to the bulletin board because my color might rub off; his thin-lipped, red-faced smile—"Can't you take a joke?"—when I threatened to report him. The older woman in my grandparents' apartment building who became agitated when I got on the elevator behind her and ran out to tell the manager that I was following her; her refusal to apologize when she was told that I lived in the building. Our assistant basketball coach, a young, wiry man from New York with a nice jumper, who, after a pick-up game with some talkative black men, had muttered within earshot of me and three of my teammates that we shouldn't have lost to a bunch of niggers; and who, when I told him—with a fury that surprised even me—to shut up, had calmly explained the apparently obvious fact that "there are black people, and there are niggers. Those guys were niggers."

That's just how white folks will do you. It wasn't merely the cruelty involved; I was learning that black people could be mean and then some. It was a particular brand of arrogance, an obtuseness in otherwise sane people that brought forth our bitter laughter. It was as if whites didn't know they were being cruel in the first place. Or at least thought you deserving of their scorn.

White folks. The term itself was uncomfortable in my mouth at first; I felt like a non-native speaker tripping over a difficult phrase. Sometimes I would find myself talking to Ray about *white folks* this or *white folks* that, and I would suddenly remember my mother's smile, and the words that I spoke would seem awkward and false. Or I would be helping Gramps dry the dishes after dinner and Toot would come in to say she was going to sleep, and those same words—*white folks*—would flash in my head like a bright neon sign, and I would suddenly grow quiet, as if I had secrets to keep.

Later, when I was alone, I would try to untangle these difficult thoughts. It was obvious that certain whites could be exempted from the general category of our distrust: Ray was always telling me how cool my grandparents were. The term *white* was simply a shorthand for him, I decided, a tag for what my mother would call a bigot. And although I recognized the risks in his terminology—how easy it was to fall into the same sloppy thinking that my basketball coach had displayed ("There are white folks, and then there are ignorant motherfuckers like you," I had finally told the coach before walking off the court that day)—Ray assured me that we would never talk about whites as whites in front of whites without knowing exactly what we were doing. Without knowing that there might be a price to pay.

But was that right? Was there still a price to pay? That was the complicated part, the thing that Ray and I never could seem to agree on. There were times when I would listen to him tell some blond girl he'd just met about life on L.A.'s mean streets, or hear him explain the scars of racism to some eager young teacher, and I could swear that just beneath the sober expression Ray was winking at me, letting me in on the score. Our rage at the white world needed no object, he seemed to be telling me, no independent confirmation; it could be switched on and off at our pleasure. Sometimes, after one of his performances, I would question his judgment, if not his sincerity. We weren't living in the Jim Crow South, I would remind him. We weren't consigned to some heatless housing project in Harlem or the

Bronx. We were in goddamned Hawaii. We said what we pleased, ate where we pleased; we sat at the front of the proverbial bus. None of our white friends, guys like Jeff or Scott from the basketball team, treated us any differently than they treated each other. They loved us, and we loved them back. Shit, seemed like half of 'em wanted to be black themselves—or at least Doctor J.

Well, that's true, Ray would admit.

Maybe we could afford to give the bad-assed nigger pose a rest. Save it for when we really needed it.

And Ray would shake his head. A pose, huh? Speak for your own self.

And I would know that Ray had flashed his trump card, one that, to his credit, he rarely played. I was different, after all, potentially suspect; I had no idea who my own self was. Unwilling to risk exposure, I would quickly retreat to safer ground.

Perhaps if we had been living in New York or L.A., I would have been quicker to pick up the rules of the high-stake game we were playing. As it was, I learned to slip back and forth between my black and white worlds, understanding that each possessed its own language and customs and structures of meaning, convinced that with a bit of translation on my part the two worlds would eventually cohere. Still, the feeling that something wasn't quite right stayed with me, a warning that sounded whenever a white girl mentioned in the middle of conversation how much she liked Stevie Wonder; or when a woman in the supermarket asked me if I played basketball; or when the school principal told me I was cool. I did like Stevie Wonder, I did love basketball, and I tried my best to be cool at all times. So why did such comments always set me on edge? There was a trick there somewhere, although what the trick was, who was doing the tricking, and who was being tricked, eluded my conscious grasp.

One day in early spring Ray and I met up after class and began walking in the direction of the stone bench that circled a big banyan tree on

Punahou's campus. It was called the Senior Bench, but it served mainly as a gathering place for the high school's popular crowd, the jocks and cheerleaders and partygoing set, with their jesters, attendants, and ladies-in-waiting jostling for position up and down the circular steps. One of the seniors, a stout defensive tackle named Kurt, was there, and he shouted loudly as soon as he saw us.

"Hey, Ray! Mah main man! Wha's happenin'!"

Ray went up and slapped Kurt's outstretched palm. But when Kurt repeated the gesture to me, I waved him off.

"What's his problem?" I overheard Kurt say to Ray as I walked away. A few minutes later, Ray caught up with me and asked me what was wrong.

"Man, those folks are just making fun of us," I said.

"What're you talking about?"

"All that 'Yo baby, give me five' bullshit."

"So who's mister sensitive all of a sudden? Kurt don't mean nothing by it."

"If that's what you think, then hey—"

Ray's face suddenly glistened with anger. "Look," he said, "I'm just getting along, all right? Just like I see you getting along, talking your game with the teachers when you need them to do you a favor. All that stuff about 'Yes, Miss Snooty Bitch, I just find this novel so engaging, if I can just have one more day for that paper, I'll kiss your white ass.' It's their world, all right? They own it, and we in it. So just get the fuck outta my face."

By the following day, the heat of our argument had dissipated, and Ray suggested that I invite our friends Jeff and Scott to a party Ray was throwing out at his house that weekend. I hesitated for a moment—we had never brought white friends along to a black party—but Ray insisted, and I couldn't find a good reason to object. Neither could Jeff or Scott; they both agreed to come so long as I was willing to drive. And so that Saturday night, after one of our games, the three of us piled into Gramps's old Ford Granada and rattled our way out to Schofield Barracks, maybe thirty miles out of town.

When we arrived the party was well on its way, and we steered ourselves toward the refreshments. The presence of Jeff and Scott seemed to make no waves; Ray introduced them around the room, they made some small talk, they took a couple of the girls out on the dance floor. But I could see right away that the scene had taken my white friends by surprise. They kept smiling a lot. They huddled together in a corner. They nodded self-consciously to the beat of the music and said "Excuse me" every few minutes. After maybe an hour, they asked me if I'd be willing to take them home.

"What's the matter?" Ray shouted over the music when I went to let him know we were leaving. "Things just starting to heat up."

"They're not into it, I guess."

Our eyes met, and for a long stretch we just stood there, the noise and laughter pulsing around us. There were no traces of satisfaction in Ray's eyes, no hints of disappointment; just a steady gaze, as unblinking as a snake's. Finally he put out his hand, and I grabbed hold of it, our eyes still fixed on each other. "Later, then," he said, his hand slipping free from mine, and I watched him walk away through the crowd, asking about the girl he'd been talking to just a few minutes before.

Outside the air had turned cool. The street was absolutely empty, quiet except for the fading tremor of Ray's stereo, the blue lights flickering in the windows of bungalows that ran up and down the tidy lane, the shadows of trees stretching across a baseball field. In the car, Jeff put an arm on my shoulder, looking at once contrite and relieved. "You know, man," he said, "that really taught me something. I mean, I can see how it must be tough for you and Ray sometimes, at school parties . . . being the only black guys and all."

I snorted. "Yeah. Right." A part of me wanted to punch him right there. We started down the road toward town, and in the silence, my mind began to rework Ray's words that day with Kurt, all the discus-

sions we had had before that, the events of that night. And by the
time I had dropped my friends off, I had begun to see a new map of
the world, one that was frightening in its simplicity, suffocating in its
implications. We were always playing on the white man's court, Ray
had told me, by the white man's rules. If the principal, or the coach,
or a teacher, or Kurt, wanted to spit in your face, he could, because
he had power and you didn't. If he decided not to, if he treated you
like a man or came to your defense, it was because he knew that the
words you spoke, the clothes you wore, the books you read, your
ambitions and desires, were already his. Whatever he decided to do,
it was his decision to make, not yours, and because of that fundamental power he held over you, because it preceded and would outlast his individual motives and inclinations, any distinction between
good and bad whites held negligible meaning. In fact, you couldn't
even be sure that everything you had assumed to be an expression of
your black, unfettered self—the humor, the song, the behind-the-
back pass—had been freely chosen by you. At best, these things were
a refuge; at worst, a trap. Following this maddening logic, the only
thing you could choose as your own was withdrawal into a smaller
and smaller coil of rage, until being black meant only the knowledge
of your own powerlessness, of your own defeat. And the final irony:
Should you refuse this defeat and lash out at your captors, they would
have a name for that, too, a name that could cage you just as good.
Paranoid. Militant. Violent. Nigger.

Over the next few months, I looked to corroborate this nightmare
vision. I gathered up books from the library—Baldwin, Ellison,
Hughes, Wright, DuBois. At night I would close the door to my
room, telling my grandparents I had homework to do, and there I
would sit and wrestle with words, locked in suddenly desperate argument, trying to reconcile the world as I'd found it with the terms of
my birth. But there was no escape to be had. In every page of every

book, in Bigger Thomas and invisible men, I kept finding the same anguish, the same doubt; a self-contempt that neither irony nor intellect seemed able to deflect. Even DuBois's learning and Baldwin's love and Langston's humor eventually succumbed to its corrosive force, each man finally forced to doubt art's redemptive power, each man finally forced to withdraw, one to Africa, one to Europe, one deeper into the bowels of Harlem, but all of them in the same weary flight, all of them exhausted, bitter men, the devil at their heels.

Only Malcolm X's autobiography seemed to offer something different. His repeated acts of self-creation spoke to me; the blunt poetry of his words, his unadorned insistence on respect, promised a new and uncompromising order, martial in its discipline, forged through sheer force of will. All the other stuff, the talk of blue-eyed devils and apocalypse, was incidental to that program, I decided, religious baggage that Malcolm himself seemed to have safely abandoned toward the end of his life. And yet, even as I imagined myself following Malcolm's call, one line in the book stayed me. He spoke of a wish he'd once had, the wish that the white blood that ran through him, there by an act of violence, might somehow be expunged. I knew that, for Malcolm, that wish would never be incidental. I knew as well that traveling down the road to self-respect my own white blood would never recede into mere abstraction. I was left to wonder what else I would be severing if and when I left my mother and my grandparents at some uncharted border.

And, too: If Malcolm's discovery toward the end of his life, that some whites might live beside him as brothers in Islam, seemed to offer some hope of eventual reconciliation, that hope appeared in a distant future, in a far-off land. In the meantime, I looked to see where the people would come from who were willing to work toward this future and populate this new world. After a basketball game at the university gym one day, Ray and I happened to strike up a conversation with a tall, gaunt man named Malik who played with us now and again. Malik mentioned that he was a follower of the Nation of Islam but that since Malcolm had died and he had moved to Hawaii he no longer went to mosque or political meetings, although he still sought comfort in solitary prayer. One of the guys sitting nearby must have overheard us, for he leaned over with a sagacious expression on his face.

"You all talking about Malcolm, huh? Malcolm tells it like it is, no doubt about it."

"Yeah," another guy said. "But I tell you what—you won't see me moving to no African jungle anytime soon. Or some goddamned desert somewhere, sitting on a carpet with a bunch of Arabs. No sir. And you won't see me stop eating no ribs."

"Gotta have them ribs."

"And pussy, too. Don't Malcolm talk about no pussy? Now you know that ain't gonna work."

I noticed Ray laughing and looked at him sternly. "What are you laughing at?" I said to him. "You've never read Malcolm. You don't even know what he says."

Ray grabbed the basketball out of my hand and headed for the opposite rim. "I don't need no books to tell me how to be black," he shouted over his head. I started to answer, then turned to Malik, expecting some words of support. But the Muslim said nothing, his bony face set in a faraway smile.

I decided to keep my own counsel after that, learning to disguise my feverish mood. A few weeks later, though, I awoke to the sound of an argument in the kitchen—my grandmother's voice barely audible, followed by my grandfather's deep growl. I opened my door to see Toot entering their bedroom to get dressed for work. I asked her what was wrong.

"Nothing. Your grandfather just doesn't want to drive me to work this morning, that's all."

When I entered the kitchen, Gramps was muttering under his breath. He poured himself a cup of coffee as I told him that I would be willing to give Toot a ride to work if he was tired. It was a bold offer, for I didn't like to wake up early. He scowled at my suggestion.

"That's not the point. She just wants me to feel bad."

"I'm sure that's not it, Gramps."

"Of course it is." He sipped from his coffee. "She's been catching the bus ever since she started at the bank. She said it was more convenient. And now, just because she gets pestered a little, she wants to change everything."

Toot's diminutive figure hovered in the hall, peering at us from behind her bifocals.

"That's not true, Stanley."

I took her into the other room and asked her what had happened.

"A man asked me for money yesterday. While I was waiting for the bus."

"That's all?"

Her lips pursed with irritation. "He was very aggressive, Barry. Very aggressive. I gave him a dollar and he kept asking. If the bus hadn't come, I think he might have hit me over the head."

I returned to the kitchen. Gramps was rinsing his cup, his back turned to me. "Listen," I said, "why don't you just let me give her a ride. She seems pretty upset."

"By a panhandler?"

"Yeah, I know—but it's probably a little scary for her, seeing some big man block her way. It's really no big deal."

He turned around and I saw now that he was shaking. " It *is* a big deal. It's a big deal to me. She's been bothered by men before. You know why she's so scared this time? I'll tell you why. Before you came in, she told me the fella was *black*." He whispered the word. "That's the real reason why she's bothered. And I just don't think that's right."

The words were like a fist in my stomach, and I wobbled to regain my composure. In my steadiest voice, I told him that such an attitude bothered me, too, but assured him that Toot's fears would pass and that we should give her a ride in the meantime. Gramps slumped into a chair in the living room and said he was sorry he had told me. Before my eyes, he grew small and old and very sad. I put my hand on his shoulder and told him that it was all right, I understood.

We remained like that for several minutes, in painful silence. Finally he insisted that he drive Toot after all, and struggled up from his seat to get dressed. After they left, I sat on the edge of my bed and thought about my grandparents. They had sacrificed again and again for me. They had poured all their lingering hopes into my success. Never had they given me reason to doubt their love; I doubted if they ever would. And yet I knew that men who might easily have been my brothers could still inspire their rawest fears.

That night, I drove into Waikiki, past the bright-lit hotels and down toward the Ala-Wai Canal. It took me a while to recognize the house, with its wobbly porch and low-pitched roof. Inside, the light was on, and I could see Frank sitting in his overstuffed chair, a book of poetry in his lap, his reading glasses slipping down his nose. I sat in the car, watching him for a time, then finally got out and tapped on the door. The old man barely looked up as he rose to undo the latch. It had been three years since I'd seen him.

"Want a drink?" he asked me. I nodded and watched him pull down a bottle of whiskey and two plastic cups from the kitchen cupboard. He looked the same, his mustache a little whiter, dangling like dead ivy over his heavy upper lip, his cut-off leans with a few more holes and tied at the waist with a length of rope.

"How's your grandpa?"

"He's all right."

"So what are you doing here?"

I wasn't sure. I told Frank some of what had happened. He nodded and poured us each a shot. "Funny cat, your grandfather," he said. "You know we grew up maybe fifty miles apart?"

I shook my head.

"We sure did. Both of us lived near Wichita. We didn't know each other, of course. I was long gone by the time he was old enough to remember anything. I might have seen some of his people, though. Might've passed 'em on the street. If I did, I would've had to step off the sidewalk to give 'em room. Your grandpa ever tell you about things like that?"

I threw the whiskey down my throat, shaking my head again.

"Naw," Frank said, "I don't suppose he would have. Stan doesn't like to talk about that part of Kansas much. Makes him uncomfortable. He told me once about a black girl they hired to look after your mother. A preacher's daughter, I think it was. Told me how she became a regular part of the family. That's how he remembers it, you understand—this girl coming in to look after somebody else's children, her mother coming to do somebody else's laundry. A regular part of the family."

I reached for the bottle, this time pouring my own. Frank wasn't watching me; his eyes were closed now, his head leaning against the back of his chair, his big wrinkled face like a carving of stone. "You can't blame Stan for what he is," Frank said quietly. "He's basically a good man. But he doesn't *know* me. Any more than he knew that girl that looked after your mother. He *can't* know me, not the way I know him. Maybe some of these Hawaiians can, or the Indians on the reservation. They've seen their fathers humiliated. Their mothers desecrated. But your grandfather will never know what that feels like. That's why he can come over here and drink my whiskey and fall asleep in that chair you're sitting in right now. Sleep like a baby. See, that's something I can never do in his house. *Never.* Doesn't matter how tired I get, I still have to watch myself. I have to be vigilant, for my own survival."

Frank opened his eyes. "What I'm trying to tell you is, your grandma's right to be scared. She's at least as right as Stanley is. She understands that black people have a reason to hate. That's just how it is. For your sake, I wish it were otherwise. But it's not. So you might as well get used to it."

Frank closed his eyes again. His breathing slowed until he seemed to be asleep. I thought about waking him, then decided against it and walked back to the car. The earth shook under my feet, ready to crack open at any moment. I stopped, trying to steady myself, and knew for the first time that I was utterly alone.

CHAPTER FIVE

········· ·········· ···

T HREE O'CLOCK IN THE morning. The moon-washed
streets empty, the growl of a car picking up speed down a distant road. The revelers would be tucked away by now, paired off or
alone, in deep, beer-heavy sleep, Hasan at his new lady's place—don't
stay up, he had said with a wink. And now just the two of us to wait
for the sunrise, me and Billie Holiday, her voice warbling through
the darkened room, reaching toward me like a lover.

> *I'm a fool . . . to want you.*
> *Such a fool . . . to want you.*

I poured myself a drink and let my eyes skip across the room:
bowls of pretzel crumbs, overflowing ashtrays, empty bottles like a
skyline against the wall. Great party. That's what everybody had said:
Count on Barry and Hasan to rock the house. Everybody except
Regina. Regina hadn't enjoyed herself. What was it that she'd said
before she left? *You always think it's about you.* And then that stuff
about her grandmother. Like I was somehow responsible for the fate
of the entire black race. As if it was me who had kept her grandma on
her knees all her life. To hell with Regina. To hell with her high-

horse, holier-than-thou, you-let-me-down look in her eyes. She didn't know me. She didn't understand where I was coming from.

I fell back on the couch and lit a cigarette, watching the match burn down until it tickled my fingertips, then feeling the prick on the skin as I pinched the flame dead. *What's the trick?* the man asks. *The trick is not caring that it hurts.* I tried to remember where I'd heard the line, but it was lost to me now, like a forgotten face. No matter. Billie knew the same trick; it was in that torn-up, trembling voice of hers. And I had learned it, too; that's what my last two years in high school had been about, after Ray went off to junior college somewhere and I had set the books aside; after I had stopped writing to my father and he'd stopped writing back. I had grown tired of trying to untangle a mess that wasn't of my making.

I had learned not to care.

I blew a few smoke rings, remembering those years. Pot had helped, and booze; maybe a little blow when you could afford it. Not smack, though—Micky, my potential initiator, had been just a little too eager for me to go through with that. Said he could do it blindfolded, but he was shaking like a faulty engine when he said it. Maybe he was just cold; we were standing in a meat freezer in the back of the deli where he worked, and it couldn't have been more than twenty degrees in there. But he didn't look like he was shaking from the cold. Looked more like he was sweating, his face shiny and tight. He had pulled out the needle and the tubing, and I'd looked at him standing there, surrounded by big slabs of salami and roast beef, and right then an image popped into my head of an air bubble, shiny and round like a pearl, rolling quietly through a vein and stopping my heart. . . .

Junkie. Pothead. That's where I'd been headed: the final, fatal role of the young would-be black man. Except the highs hadn't been about that, me trying to prove what a down brother I was. Not by then, anyway. I got high for just the opposite effect, something that could push questions of who I was out of my mind, something that could flatten out the landscape of my heart, blur the edges of my memory. I had discovered that it didn't make any difference whether you smoked reefer in the white classmate's sparkling new van, or in the dorm room of some brother you'd met down at the gym, or on the beach with a couple of Hawaiian kids who had dropped out of school and now spent most of their time looking for an excuse to brawl. Nobody asked you whether your father was a fat-cat executive who cheated on his wife or some laid-off joe who slapped you around whenever he bothered to come home. You might just be bored, or alone. Everybody was welcome into the club of disaffection. And if the high didn't solve whatever it was that was getting you down, it could at least help you laugh at the world's ongoing folly and see through all the hypocrisy and bullshit and cheap moralism.

That's how it had seemed to me then, anyway. It had taken a couple of years before I saw how fates were beginning to play themselves out, the difference that color and money made after all, in who survived, how soft or hard the landing when you finally fell. Of course, either way, you needed some luck. That's what Pablo had lacked, mostly, not having his driver's license that day, a cop with nothing better to do than to check the trunk of his car. Or Bruce, not finding his way back from too many bad acid trips and winding up in a funny farm. Or Duke, not walking away from the car wreck. . . .

I had tried to explain some of this to my mother once, the role of luck in the world, the spin of the wheel. It was at the start of my senior year in high school; she was back in Hawaii, her field work completed, and one day she had marched into my room, wanting to know the details of Pablo's arrest. I had given her a reassuring smile and patted her hand and told her not to worry, I wouldn't do anything stupid. It was usually an effective tactic, another one of those tricks I had learned: People were satisfied so long as you were courteous and smiled and made no sudden moves. They were more than satisfied;

they were relieved—such a pleasant surprise to find a well-mannered young black man who didn't seem angry all the time.

Except my mother hadn't looked satisfied. She had just sat there, studying my eyes, her face as grim as a hearse.

"Don't you think you're being a little casual about your future?" she said.

"What do you mean?"

"You know exactly what I mean. One of your friends was just arrested for drug possession. Your grades are slipping. You haven't even started on your college applications. Whenever I try to talk to you about it you act like I'm just this great big bother."

I didn't need to hear all this. It wasn't like I was flunking out. I started to tell her how I'd been thinking about maybe not going away for college, how I could stay in Hawaii and take some classes and work part-time. She cut me off before I could finish. I could get into any school in the country, she said, if I just put in a little effort. "Remember what that's like? Effort? Damn it, Bar, you can't just sit around like some good-time Charlie, waiting for luck to see you through."

"A good-time what?"

"A good-time Charlie. A loafer."

I looked at her sitting there, so earnest, so certain of her son's destiny. The idea that my survival depended on luck remained a heresy to her; she insisted on assigning responsibility somewhere—to herself, to Gramps and Toot, to me. I suddenly felt like puncturing that certainty of hers, letting her know that her experiment with me had failed. Instead of shouting, I laughed. "A good-time Charlie, huh? Well, why not? Maybe that's what I want out of life. I mean, look at Gramps. He didn't even go to college."

The comparison caught my mother by surprise. Her face went slack, her eyes wavered. It suddenly dawned on me, her greatest fear. "Is that what you're worried about?" I asked. "That I'll end up like Gramps?"

She shook her head quickly. "You're already much better educated than your grandfather," she said. But the certainty had finally drained from her voice. Instead of pushing the point, I stood up and left the room.

Billie had stopped singing. The silence felt oppressive, and I suddenly felt very sober. I rose from the couch, flipped the record, drank what was left in my glass, poured myself another. Upstairs, I could hear someone flushing a toilet, walking across a room. Another insomniac, probably, listening to his life tick away. That was the problem with booze and drugs, wasn't it? At some point they couldn't stop that ticking sound, the sound of certain emptiness. And that, I suppose, is what I'd been trying to tell my mother that day: that her faith in justice and rationality was misplaced, that we couldn't overcome after all, that all the education and good intentions in the world couldn't help plug up the holes in the universe or give you the power to change its blind, mindless course.

Still, I'd felt bad after that particular episode; it was the one trick my mother always had up her sleeve, that way she had of making me feel guilty. She made no bones about it, either. "You can't help it," she told me once. "Slipped it into your baby food. Don't worry, though," she added, smiling like the Cheshire cat. "A healthy, dose of guilt never hurt anybody. It's what civilization was built on, guilt. A highly underrated emotion."

We could joke about it by then, for her worst fears hadn't come to pass. I had graduated without mishap, was accepted into several respectable schools, and settled on Occidental College in Los Angeles mainly because I'd met a girl from Brentwood while she was vacationing in Hawaii with her family. But I was still just going through the motions, as indifferent toward college as toward most everything else. Even Frank thought I had a bad attitude, although he was less than clear about how I should change it.

What had Frank called college? *An advanced degree in compromise.* I thought back to the last time I had seen the old poet, a few days before I left Hawaii. We had made small talk for a while; he complained about his feet, the corns and bone spurs that he insisted were a direct result of trying to force African feet into European shoes. Finally he had asked me what it was that I expected to get out of college. I told him I didn't know. He shook his big, hoary head.

"Well," he said, "that's the problem, isn't it? You *don't know.* You're just like the rest of these young cats out here. All you know is that college is the next thing you're supposed to do. And the people who are old enough to know better, who fought all those years for your right to go to college—they're just so happy to see you in there that they won't tell you the truth. The real price of admission."

"And what's that?"

"Leaving your race at the door," he said. "Leaving your people behind." He studied me over the top of his reading glasses. "Understand something, boy. You're not going to college to get educated. You're going there to get *trained.* They'll train you to want what you don't need. They'll train you to manipulate words so they don't mean anything anymore. They'll train you to forget what it is that you already know. They'll train you so good, you'll start believing what they tell you about equal opportunity and the American way and all that shit. They'll give you a corner office and invite you to fancy dinners, and tell you you're a credit to your race. Until you want to actually start running things, and then they'll yank on your chain and let you know that you may be a well-trained, well-paid nigger, but you're a nigger just the same."

"So what is it you're telling me—that I shouldn't be going to college?"

Frank's shoulders slumped, and he fell back in his chair with a sigh. "No. I didn't say that. You've got to go. I'm just telling you to keep your eyes open. Stay awake."

It made me smile, thinking back on Frank and his old Black Power, dashiki self. In some ways he was as incurable as my mother, as certain in his faith, living in the same sixties time warp that Hawaii had created. Keep your eyes open, he had warned. It wasn't as easy as it sounded. Not in sunny L.A. Not as you strolled through Occidental's campus, a few miles from Pasadena, tree-lined and Spanish-tiled. The students were friendly, the teachers encouraging. In the fall of 1979, Carter, gas lines, and breast-beating were all on their way out. Reagan was on his way in, morning in America. When you left campus, you drove on the freeway to Venice Beach or over to Westwood, passing East L.A. or South Central without even knowing it, just more palm trees peeking out like dandelions over the high concrete walls. L.A. wasn't all that different from Hawaii, not the part you saw. Just bigger, and easier to find a barber who knew how to cut your hair.

Anyway, most of the other black students at Oxy didn't seem all that worried about compromise. There were enough of us on campus to constitute a tribe, and when it came to hanging out many of us chose to function like a tribe, staying close together, traveling in packs. Freshman year, when I was still living in the dorms, there'd be the same sort of bull sessions that I'd had with Ray and other blacks back in Hawaii, the same grumblings, the same list of complaints. Otherwise, our worries seemed indistinguishable from those of the white kids around us. Surviving classes. Finding a well-paying gig after graduation. Trying to get laid. I had stumbled upon one of the well-kept secrets about black people: that most of us weren't interested in revolt; that most of us were tired of thinking about race all the time; that if we preferred to keep to ourselves it was mainly because that was the easiest way to stop thinking about it, easier than spending all your time mad or trying to guess whatever it was that white folks were thinking about you.

So why couldn't I let it go?

I don't know. I didn't have the luxury, I suppose, the certainty of

the tribe. Grow up in Compton and survival becomes a revolutionary act. You get to college and your family is still back there rooting
for you. They're happy to see you escape; there's no question of
betrayal. But I hadn't grown up in Compton, or Watts. I had nothing to escape from except my own inner doubt. I was more like the
black students who had grown up in the suburbs, kids whose parents
had already paid the price of escape. You could spot them right away
by the way they talked, the people they sat with in the cafeteria.
When pressed, they would sputter and explain that they refused to be
categorized. They weren't defined by the color of their skin, they
would tell you. They were individuals.

That's how Joyce liked to talk. She was a good-looking woman,
Joyce was, with her green eyes and honey skin and pouty lips. We
lived in the same dorm my freshman year, and all the brothers were
after her. One day I asked her if she was going to the Black Students'
Association meeting. She looked at me funny, then started shaking
her head like a baby who doesn't want what it sees on the spoon.

"I'm not black," Joyce said. "I'm *multiracial*." Then she started
telling me about her father, who *happened* to be Italian and was the
sweetest man in the world; and her mother, who *happened* to be part
African and part French and part Native American and part something
else. "Why should I have to choose between them?" she asked me. Her
voice cracked, and I thought she was going to cry. "It's not white people
who are making me choose. Maybe it used to be that way, but now
they're willing to treat me like a person. No—it's *black people* who always
have to make everything racial. *They're* the ones making me choose.
They're the ones who are telling me that I can't be who I am. . . ."

They, they, they. That was the problem with people like Joyce.
They talked about the richness of their multicultural heritage and it
sounded real good, until you noticed that they avoided black people.
It wasn't a matter of conscious choice, necessarily, just a matter of
gravitational pull, the way integration always worked, a one-way

street. The minority assimilated into the dominant culture, not the other way around. Only white culture could be neutral and objective. Only white culture could be nonracial, willing to adopt the occasional exotic into its ranks. Only white culture had individuals. And we, the half-breeds and the college-degreed, take a survey of the situation and think to ourselves, Why should we get lumped in with the losers if we don't have to? We become only so grateful to lose ourselves in the crowd, America's happy, faceless marketplace; and we're never so outraged as when a cabbie drives past us or the woman in the elevator clutches her purse, not so much because we're bothered by the fact that such indignities are what less fortunate coloreds have to put up with every single day of their lives—although that's what we tell ourselves—but because we're wearing a Brooks Brothers suit and speak impeccable English and yet have somehow been mistaken for an ordinary nigger.

Don't you know who I am? I'm an *individual!*

I sat up, lit another cigarette, emptied the bottle into my glass. I knew I was being too hard on poor Joyce. The truth was that I understood her, her and all the other black kids who felt the way she did. In their mannerisms, their speech, their mixed-up hearts, I kept recognizing pieces of myself. And that's exactly what scared me. Their confusion made me question my own racial credentials all over again, Ray's trump card still lurking in the back of my mind. I needed to put distance between them and myself, to convince myself that I wasn't compromised—that I was indeed still awake.

To avoid being mistaken for a sellout, I chose my friends carefully. The more politically active black students. The foreign students. The Chicanos. The Marxist professors and structural feminists and punk-rock performance poets. We smoked cigarettes and wore leather jackets. At night, in the dorms, we discussed neocolonialism, Franz Fanon, Eurocentrism, and patriarchy. When we ground out our cigarettes in the hallway carpet or set our stereos so loud that the walls began to shake, we were resisting bourgeois society's stifling constraints. We weren't indifferent or careless or insecure. We were alienated.

But this strategy alone couldn't provide the distance I wanted, from Joyce or my past. After all, there were thousands of so-called campus radicals, most of them white and tenured and happily tolerated. No, it remained necessary to prove which side you were on, to show your loyalty to the black masses, to strike out and name names.

I thought back to that time when I was still living in the dorms, the three of us in Reggie's room—Reggie, Marcus, and myself—the patter of rain against the windowpane. We were drinking a few beers and Marcus was telling us about his run-in with the L.A.P.D. "They had no reason to stop me," he was saying. "No reason 'cept I was walking in a white neighborhood. Made me spread-eagle against the car. One of 'em pulled out his piece. I didn't let 'em scare me, though. That's what gets these storm troopers off, seeing fear in a black man. . . ."

I watched Marcus as he spoke, lean and dark and straight-backed, his long legs braced apart, comfortable in a white T-shirt and blue denim overalls. Marcus was the most conscious of brothers. He could tell you about his grandfather the Garveyite; about his mother in St. Louis who had raised her kids alone while working as a nurse; about his older sister who had been a founding member of the local Panther party; about his friends in the joint. His lineage was pure, his loyalties clear, and for that reason he always made me feel a little off-balance, like a younger brother who, no matter what he does, will always be one step behind. And that's just how I was feeling at that moment, listening to Marcus pronounce on his authentic black experience, when Tim walked into the room.

"Hey, guys," Tim had said, waving cheerfully. He turned to me. "Listen, Barry—do you have that assignment for Econ?"

Tim was not a conscious brother. Tim wore argyle sweaters and pressed jeans and talked like Beaver Cleaver. He planned to major in business. His white girlfriend was probably waiting for him up in his room, listening to country music. He was happy as a clam, and I wanted nothing more than for him to go away. I got up, walked with him down the hall to my room, gave him the assignment he needed. As soon as I got back to Reggie's room, I somehow felt obliged to explain.

"Tim's a trip, ain't he," I said, shaking my head. "Should change his name from Tim to Tom."

Reggie laughed, but Marcus didn't. Marcus said, "Why you say that, man?"

The question caught me by surprise. "I don't know. The dude's just goofy, that's all."

Marcus took a sip of his beer and looked me straight in the eye. "Tim seems all right to me," he said. "He's going about his business. Don't bother nobody. Seems to me we should be worrying about whether our own stuff's together instead of passing judgment on how other folks are supposed to act."

A year later, and I still burned with the memory, the anger and resentment I'd felt at that moment, Marcus calling me out in front of Reggie like that. But he'd been right to do it, hadn't he? He had caught me in a lie. Two lies, really—the lie I had told about Tim and the lie I was telling about myself. In fact, that whole first year seemed like one long lie, me spending all my energy running around in circles, trying to cover my tracks.

Except with Regina. That's probably what had drawn me to Regina, the way she made me feel like I didn't have to lie. Even that first time we met, the day she walked into the coffee shop and found Marcus giving me grief about my choice of reading material. Marcus had waved her over to our table, rising slightly to pull out a chair.

"Sister Regina," Marcus said. "You know Barack, don't you? I'm trying to tell Brother Barack here about this racist tract he's reading." He held up a copy of *Heart of Darkness*, evidence for the court. I reached over to snatch it out of his hands.

"Man, stop waving that thing around."

"See there," Marcus said. "Makes you embarrassed, don't it—just being seen with a book like this. I'm telling you, man, this stuff will poison your mind." He looked at his watch. "Damn, I'm late for class." He leaned over and pecked Regina on the cheek. "Talk to this brother, will you? I think he can still be saved."

Regina smiled and shook her head as we watched Marcus stride out the door. "Marcus is in one of his preaching moods, I see."

I tossed the book into my backpack. "Actually, he's right," I said. "It is a racist book. The way Conrad sees it, Africa's the cesspool of the world, black folks are savages, and any contact with them breeds infection."

Regina blew on her coffee. "So why are you reading it?"

"Because it's assigned." I paused, not sure if I should go on. "And because—"

"Because . . ."

"And because the book teaches me things," I said. "About white people, I mean. See, the book's not really about Africa. Or black people. It's about the man who wrote it. The European. The American. A particular way of looking at the world. If you can keep your distance, it's all there, in what's said and what's left unsaid. So I read the book to help me understand just what it is that makes white people so afraid. Their demons. The way ideas get twisted around. It helps me understand how people learn to hate."

"And that's important to you."

My life depends on it, I thought to myself. But I didn't tell Regina that. I just smiled and said, "That's the only way to cure an illness, right? Diagnose it."

She smiled back and sipped her coffee. I had seen her around before, usually sitting in the library with a book in hand, a big, dark woman who wore stockings and dresses that looked homemade, along with tinted, oversized glasses and a scarf always covering her head. I knew she was a junior, helped organize black student events, didn't go out much. She stirred her coffee idly and asked, "What did Marcus call you just now? Some African name, wasn't it?"

"Barack."

"I thought your name was Barry."

"Barack's my given name. My father's name. He was Kenyan."

"Does it mean something?"

"It means 'Blessed.' In Arabic. My grandfather was a Muslim."

Regina repeated the name to herself, testing out the sound. "Barack. It's beautiful." She leaned forward across the table. "So why does everybody call you Barry?"

"Habit, I guess. My father used it when he arrived in the States. I don't know whether that was his idea or somebody else's. He probably used Barry because it was easier to pronounce. You know—helped him fit in. Then it got passed on to me. So I could fit in."

"Do you mind if I call you Barack?"

I smiled. "Not as long as you say it right."

She tilted her head impatiently, her mouth set in mock offense, her eyes ready to surrender to laughter. We ended up spending the afternoon together, talking and drinking coffee. She told me about her childhood in Chicago, the absent father and struggling mother, the South Side six-flat that never seemed warm enough in winter and got so hot in the summer that people went out by the lake to sleep. She told me about the neighbors on her block, about walking past the taverns and pool halls on the way to church on Sunday. She told me about evenings in the kitchen with uncles and cousins and grandparents, the stew of voices bubbling up in laughter. Her voice evoked a vision of black life in all its possibility, a vision that filled me with longing—a longing for place, and a fixed and definite history. As we were getting up to leave, I told Regina I envied her.

"For what?"

"I don't know. For your memories, I guess."

Regina looked at me and started to laugh, a round, full sound from deep in her belly.

"What's so funny?"

"Oh, Barack," she said, catching her breath, "isn't life something? And here I was all this time wishing I'd grown up in Hawaii."

Strange how a single conversation can change you. Or maybe it only seems that way in retrospect. A year passes and you know you feel differently, but you're not sure what or why or how, so your mind casts back for something that might give that difference shape: a word, a glance, a touch. I know that after what seemed like a long absence, I had felt my voice returning to me that afternoon with Regina. It remained shaky afterward, subject to distortion. But entering sophomore year I could feel it growing stronger, sturdier, that constant, honest portion of myself, a bridge between my future and my past.

It was around that time that I got involved in the divestment campaign. It had started as something of a lark, I suppose, part of the radical pose my friends and I sought to maintain, a subconscious end run around issues closer to home. But as the months passed and I found myself drawn into a larger role—contacting representatives of the African National Congress to speak on campus, drafting letters to the faculty, printing up flyers, arguing strategy—I noticed that people had begun to listen to my opinions. It was a discovery that made me hungry for words. Not words to hide behind but words that could carry a message, support an idea. When we started planning the rally for the trustees' meeting, and somebody suggested that I open the thing, I quickly agreed. I figured I was ready, and could reach people where it counted. I thought my voice wouldn't fail me.

Let's see, now. What was it that I had been thinking in those days leading up to the rally? The agenda had been carefully arranged beforehand—I was only supposed to make a few opening remarks, in the middle of which a couple of white students would come onstage dressed in their paramilitary uniforms to drag me away. A bit of street theater, a way to dramatize the situation for activists in South Africa. I knew the score, had helped plan the script. Only, when I sat down to prepare a few notes for what I might say, something had happened. In my mind it somehow became more than just a two-minute speech, more than a way to prove my political orthodoxy. I started to remember my father's visit to Miss Hefty's class; the look on Coretta's face that day; the power of my father's words to transform. If I could just find the right words, I had thought to myself. With the right words everything could change—South Africa, the lives of ghetto kids just a few miles away, my own tenuous place in the world.

I was still in that trancelike state when I mounted the stage. For I don't know how long, I just stood there, the sun in my eyes, the crowd of a few hundred restless after lunch. A couple of students were throwing a Frisbee on the lawn; others were standing off to the side, ready to break off to the library at any moment. Without waiting for a cue, I stepped up to the microphone.

"There's a struggle going on," I said. My voice barely carried beyond the first few rows. A few people looked up, and I waited for the crowd to quiet.

"I say, there's a struggle going on!"

The Frisbee players stopped.

"It's happening an ocean away. But it's a struggle that touches each and every one of us. Whether we know it or not. Whether we want it or not. A struggle that demands we choose sides. Not between black and white. Not between rich and poor. No—it's a harder choice than that. It's a choice between dignity and servitude. Between fairness and injustice. Between commitment and indifference. A choice between right and wrong . . ."

I stopped. The crowd was quiet now, watching me. Somebody started to clap. "Go on with it, Barack," somebody else shouted. "Tell it like it is." Then the others started in, clapping, cheering, and I knew that I had them, that the connection had been made. I took hold of the mike, ready to plunge on, when I felt someone's hands grabbing me from behind. It was just as we'd planned it, Andy and Jonathan looking grim-faced behind their dark glasses. They started yanking me off the stage, and I was supposed to act like I was trying to break free, except a part of me wasn't acting, I really wanted to stay up there, to hear my voice bouncing off the crowd and returning back to me in applause. I had so much left to say.

But my part was over. I stood on the side as Marcus stepped up to the mike in his white T-shirt and denims, lean and dark and straight-backed and righteous. He explained to the audience what they had just witnessed, why the administration's waffling on the issue of South Africa was unacceptable. Then Regina got up and testified, about the pride her family had felt in seeing her at college and the shame she now felt knowing that she was a part of an institution that paid for its privilege with the profits of oppression. I should have been proud of the two of them; they were eloquent, you could tell the crowd was moved. But I wasn't really listening anymore. I was on the outside again, watching, judging, skeptical. Through my eyes, we suddenly appeared like the sleek and well-fed amateurs we were, with our black chiffon armbands and hand-painted signs and earnest young faces. The Frisbee players had returned to their game. When the trustees began to arrive for their meeting, a few of them paused behind the glass walls of the administration building to watch us, and I noticed the old white men chuckling to themselves, one old geezer even waving in our direction. The whole thing was a farce, I thought to myself—the rally, the banners, everything. A pleasant afternoon diversion, a school play without the parents. And me and my one-minute oration—the biggest farce of all.

At the party that night, Regina came up to me and offered her congratulations. I asked what for.

"For that wonderful speech you gave."

I popped open a beer. "It was short, anyway."

Regina ignored my sarcasm. "That's what made it so effective," she said. "You spoke from the heart, Barack. It made people want to hear more. When they pulled you away, it was as if—"

"Listen, Regina," I said, cutting her off, "you are a very sweet lady. And I'm happy you enjoyed my little performance today. But that's the last time you will ever hear another speech out of me. I'm going to leave the preaching to you. And to Marcus. Me, I've decided I've got no business speaking for black folks."

"And why is that?"

I sipped on my beer, my eyes wandering over the dancers in front of us. "Because I've got nothing to say, Regina. I don't believe we made any difference by what we did today. I don't believe that what happens to a kid in Soweto makes much difference to the people we were talking to. Pretty words don't make it so. So why do I pretend otherwise? I'll tell you why. Because it makes *me* feel important. Because *I* like the applause. It gives me a nice, cheap thrill. That's all."

"You don't really believe that."

"That's what I believe."

She stared at me, puzzled, trying to figure out whether I was pulling her leg. "Well, you could have fooled me," she said finally, trying to match my tone. "Seemed to me like I heard a man speak who believed in something. A black man who cared. But hey, I guess I'm stupid."

I took another swig of beer and waved at someone coming through the door. "Not stupid, Regina. Naive."

She took a step back, her hands on her hips. "Naive? *You're* calling *me* naive? Uh-uh. I don't think so. If anybody's naive, it's you. You're the one who seems to think he can run away from himself. You're the one who thinks he can avoid what he feels." She stuck a finger in my chest. "You wanna know what your real problem is? You always think everything's about you. You're just like Reggie and Marcus and Steve and all the other brothers out here. The rally is about you. The speech is about you. The hurt is always your hurt. Well, let me tell you something, Mr. Obama. It's not just about you. It's never just about you. It's about people who need your help. Children who are depending on you. They're not interested in your irony or your sophistication or your ego getting bruised. And neither am I."

Just as she was finishing, Reggie wandered out of the kitchen, drunker than I was. He came over and threw his arm around my shoulder. "Obama! Great party, man!" He threw Regina a sloppy grin. "Let me tell you, Regina, Obama and me go way back. Should have seen our parties last year, back at the dorms. Man, you remember that time we stayed up the whole weekend? Forty hours, no sleep. Started Saturday morning and didn't stop till Monday."

I tried to change the subject, but Reggie was on a roll. "I'm telling you, Regina, it was wild. When the maids show up Monday morning, we were all still sitting in the hallway, looking like zombies. Bottles everywhere. Cigarette butts. Newspapers. That spot where Jimmy threw up . . ." Reggie turned to me and started to laugh, spilling more beer on the rug. "You remember, don't you, man? Shit was so bad, those little old Mexican ladies started to cry. 'Dios Mio,' one of 'em says, and the other one starts patting her on the back. Oh shit, we were crazy. . . ."

I smiled weakly, feeling Regina stare me down like the bum that I was. When she finally spoke it was as if Reggie weren't there.

"You think that's funny?" she said to me. Her voice was shaking, barely a whisper. "Is that what's real to you, Barack—making a mess for somebody else to clean up? That could have been my grandmother, you know. She had to clean up behind people for most of her life. I'll bet the people she worked for thought it was funny, too."

She grabbed her purse off the coffee table and headed for the door. I thought about running after her, but I noticed a few people staring at me and I didn't want a scene. Reggie pulled on my arm, looking hurt and confused, like a lost child.

"What's her problem?" he said.

"Nothing," I said. I took the beer out of Reggie's hand and set it on top of the bookshelf. "She just believes in things that aren't really there."

I rose from the couch and opened my front door, the pent-up smoke trailing me out of the room like a spirit. Up above, the moon had slipped out of sight, only its glow still visible along the rim of high clouds. The sky had begun to lighten; the air tasted of dew.

Look at yourself before you pass judgment. Don't make someone else clean up your mess. It's not about you. They were such simple points, homilies I had heard a thousand times before, in all their variations, from TV sitcoms and philosophy books, from my grandparents and from my mother. I had stopped listening at a certain point, I now realized, so wrapped up had I been in my own perceived injuries, so eager was I to escape the imagined traps that white authority had set for me. To that white world, I had been willing to cede the values of my childhood, as if those values were somehow irreversibly soiled by the endless falsehoods that white spoke about black.

Except now I was hearing the same thing from black people I respected, people with more excuses for bitterness than I might ever claim for myself. Who told you that being honest was a white thing? they asked me. Who sold you this bill of goods, that your situation exempted you from being thoughtful or diligent or kind, or that morality had a color? You've lost your way, brother. Your ideas about yourself—about who you are and who you might become—have grown stunted and narrow and small.

I sat down on the doorstep and rubbed the knot in the back of my neck. How had that happened? I started to ask myself, but before the question had even formed in my mind, I already knew the answer. Fear. The same fear that had caused me to push Coretta away back in grammar school. The same fear that had caused me to ridicule Tim in front of Marcus and Reggie. The constant, crippling fear that I didn't belong somehow, that unless I dodged and hid and pretended to be something I wasn't I would forever remain an outsider, with the rest of the world, black and white, always standing in judgment.

So Regina was right; it had been just about me. My fear. My needs. And now? I imagined Regina's grandmother somewhere, her back bent, the flesh of her arms shaking as she scrubbed an endless floor. Slowly, the old woman lifted her head to look straight at me, and in her sagging face I saw that what bound us together went beyond anger or despair or pity.

What was she asking of me, then? Determination, mostly. The determination to push against whatever power kept her stooped instead of standing straight. The determination to resist the easy or the expedient. You might be locked into a world not of your own making, her eyes said, but you still have a claim on how it is shaped. You still have responsibilities.

The old woman's face dissolved from my mind, only to be replaced by a series of others. The copper-skinned face of the Mexican maid, straining as she carries out the garbage. The face of Lolo's mother drawn with grief as she watches the Dutch burn down her house. The tight-lipped, chalk-colored face of Toot as she boards the six-thirty A.M. bus that will take her to work. Only a lack of imagination, a failure of nerve, had made me think that I had to choose between them. They all asked the same thing of me, these grandmothers of mine.

My identity might begin with the fact of my race, but it didn't, couldn't, end there.

At least that's what I would choose to believe.

For a few minutes more I sat still in my doorway, watching the sun glide into place, thinking about the call to Regina I'd be making that day. Behind me, Billie was on her last song. I picked up the refrain, humming a few bars. Her voice sounded different to me now. Beneath the layers of hurt, beneath the ragged laughter, I heard a willingness to endure. Endure—and make music that wasn't there before.

CHAPTER SIX

· ·

I SPENT MY FIRST NIGHT in Manhattan curled up in an alley-way. It wasn't intentional; while still in L.A., I had heard that a friend of a friend would be vacating her apartment in Spanish Harlem, near Columbia, and that given New York's real estate market I'd better grab it while I could. An agreement was reached; I wired ahead with the date of my August arrival; and after dragging my luggage through the airport, the subways, Times Square, and across 109th from Broadway to Amsterdam, I finally stood at the door, a few minutes past ten P.M.

I pressed the buzzer repeatedly, but no one answered. The street was empty, the buildings on either side boarded up, a bulk of rectangular shadows. Eventually, a young Puerto Rican woman emerged from the building, throwing a nervous look my way before heading down the street. I rushed to catch the door before it slammed shut, and, pulling my luggage behind me, proceeded upstairs to knock, and then bang, on the apartment door. Again, no answer, just a sound down the hall of a deadbolt thrown into place.

New York. Just like I pictured it. I checked my wallet—not enough money for a motel. I knew one person in New York, a guy named Sadik whom I'd met in L.A., but he'd told me that he worked all night at a bar somewhere. With nothing to do but wait, I carried my luggage back downstairs and sat on the stoop. After a while, I reached into my back pocket, pulling out the letter I'd been carrying since leaving L.A.

Dear Son,

It was such a pleasant surprise to hear from you after so long. I am fine and doing all those things which you know are expected of me in this country. I just came back from London where I was attending to Government business, negotiating finances, etc. In fact it is because of too much travel that I rarely write to you. In any case, I think I shall do better from now on.

You will be pleased to know that all your brothers and sisters here are fine, and send their greetings. Like me, they approve of your decision to come home after graduation. When you come, we shall, together, decide on how long you may wish to stay. Barry, even if it is only for a few days, the important thing is that you know your people, and also that you know where you belong.

Please look after yourself, and say hallo to your mum, Tutu, and Stanley. I hope to hear from you soon.

Love,
Dad

I folded the letter along its seams and stuffed it back into my pocket. It hadn't been easy to write him; our correspondence had all but died over the past four years. In fact, I had gone through several drafts, crossing out lines, struggling for the appropriate tone, resisting the impulse to explain too much. "Dear Father." "Dear Dad." "Dear Dr. Obama." And now he had answered me, cheerful and calm. Know where you belong, he advised. He made it sound simple, like calling directory assistance.

"Information—what city, please?"

"Uh . . . I'm not sure. I was hoping you could tell me. The name's Obama. Where do I belong?"

Maybe it really was that simple for him. I imagined my father sitting at his desk in Nairobi, a big man in government, with clerks and secretaries bringing him papers to sign, a minister calling him for advice, a loving wife and children waiting at home, his own father's village only a day's drive away. The image made me vaguely angry, and I tried to set it aside, concentrating instead on the sound of salsa coming from an open window somewhere down the block. The same thoughts kept returning to me, though, as persistent as the beat of my heart.

Where did I belong? My conversation with Regina that night after the rally might have triggered a change in me, left me warm with good intentions. But I was like a drunk coming out of a long, painful binge, and I had soon felt my newfound resolve slipping away, without object or direction. Two years from graduation, I had no idea what I was going to do with my life, or even where I would live. Hawaii lay behind me like a childhood dream; I could no longer imagine settling there. Whatever my father might say, I knew it was too late to ever truly claim Africa as my home. And if I had come to understand myself as a black American, and was understood as such, that understanding remained unanchored to place. What I needed was a community, I realized, a community that cut deeper than the common despair that black friends and I shared when reading the latest crime statistics, or the high fives I might exchange on a basketball court. A place where I could put down stakes and test my commitments.

And so, when I heard about a transfer program that Occidental had arranged with Columbia University, I'd been quick to apply. I figured that if there weren't any more black students at Columbia than there were at Oxy, I'd at least be in the heart of a true city, with black neighborhoods in close proximity. As it was, there wasn't much in L.A. to hold me back. Most of my friends were graduating that year: Hasan off to work with his family in London, Regina on her way to Andalusia to study Spanish Gypsies.

And Marcus? I wasn't sure what had happened to Marcus. He should have had one more year left, but something had gotten to him midway through his junior year, something that I recognized, even if I couldn't quite name it. I thought back to one evening, sitting with him in the library, before he'd decided to drop out of school. An Iranian student, an older balding man with a glass eye, was sitting across the table from us, and he had noticed Marcus reading a book on the economics of slavery. Although the drift of his eye gave the Iranian a menacing look, he was a friendly and curious man, and eventually he leaned over the table and asked Marcus a question about the book.

"Tell me, please," the man said. "How do you think such a thing as slavery was permitted to last for so many years?"

"White people don't see us as human beings," Marcus said. "Simple as that. Most of 'em still don't."

"Yes, I see. But what I mean to ask is, why didn't black people fight?"

"They did fight. Nat Turner, Denmark Vescey—"

"Slave rebellions," the Iranian interrupted. "Yes, I have read something about them. These were very brave men. But they were so few, you see. Had I been a slave, watching these people do what they did to my wife, my children . . . well, I would have preferred death. This is what I don't understand—why so many men did not fight at all. Until death, you see?"

I looked at Marcus, waiting for him to answer. But he remained silent, his face not angry as much as withdrawn, eyes fastened to a spot on the table. His lack of response confused me, but after a pause I took up the attack, asking the Iranian if he knew the names of the untold thousands who had leaped into shark-infested waters before their prison ships had ever reached American ports; asking if, once the ships had landed, he would have still preferred death had he known that revolt might only visit more suffering on women and children. Was the collaboration of some slaves any different than the silence of some Iranians who stood by and did nothing as Savak thugs murdered and tortured opponents of the Shah? How could we judge other men until we had stood in their shoes?

This last remark seemed to catch the man off guard, and Marcus finally rejoined the conversation, repeating one of Malcolm X's old saws about the difference between house Negroes and field Negroes. But he spoke as if he weren't convinced of his own words, and after a few minutes he abruptly stood up and walked toward the door.

We never did talk about that conversation, Marcus and I. Maybe it didn't explain anything; there were more than enough reasons for someone like Marcus to feel restless in a place like Occidental. I know that in the months that followed, I began to notice changes in him, as if he were haunted by specters that had seeped through the cracks of our safe, sunny world. Initially, he became more demonstrative in his racial pride: He took to wearing African prints to class and started lobbying the administration for an all-black dormitory. Later, he grew uncommunicative. He began to skip classes, hitting the reefer more heavily. He let his beard grow out, let his hair work its way into dreadlocks.

Finally he told me that he was going to take a leave from school for a while. "Need a break from this shit," he said. We were walking through a park in Compton, hanging out at an all-day festival there. It was a beautiful afternoon, everybody in shorts, children screeching as they ran through the grass, but Marcus seemed distracted and barely spoke. Only when we passed a group of bongo players did he seem to come to life. We sat beside them under a tree, transfixed by the sound, watching the dark, barely cupped hands dance low off the hide. After a while I started to get bored and wandered off to talk to a pretty young woman selling meat pies. When I returned, Marcus was still there, except he was playing now, his long legs crossed, borrowed bongos nestling in his lap. Through the haze of smoke that surrounded him, his face was expressionless; his eyes were narrow, as if he were trying to shut out the sun. For almost an hour I watched him play without rhythm or nuance, just pounding the hell out of those drums, beating back untold memories. And right then I realized that Marcus needed my help as much as I needed his, that I wasn't the only one searching for answers.

I looked down now at the abandoned New York street. Did Marcus know where he belonged? Did any of us? Where were the fathers, the uncles and grandfathers, who could help explain this gash in our hearts? Where were the healers who might help us rescue meaning from defeat? They were gone, vanished, swallowed up by time. Only their cloudy images remained, and their once-a-year letters full of dime store advice. . . .

It was well past midnight by the time I crawled through a fence that led to an alleyway. I found a dry spot, propped my luggage beneath me, and fell asleep, the sound of drums softly shaping my dreams. In the morning, I woke up to find a white hen pecking at the garbage near my feet. Across the street, a homeless man was washing himself at an open hydrant and didn't object when I joined him. There was still no one home at the apartment, but Sadik answered his phone when I called him and told me to catch a cab to his place on the Upper East Side.

He greeted me on the street, a short, well-built Pakistani who had come to New York from London two years earlier and found his caustic wit and unabashed desire to make money perfectly pitched to the city's mood. He had overstayed his tourist visa and now made a living in New York's high-turnover, illegal immigrant workforce, waiting on tables. As we entered the apartment I saw a woman in her underwear sitting at the kitchen table, a mirror and a razor blade pushed off to one side.

"Sophie," Sadik started to say, "this is Barry—"

"Barack," I corrected, dropping my bags on the floor. The woman waved vaguely, then told Sadik that she'd be gone by the time he got back. I followed Sadik back downstairs and into a Greek coffee shop across the street. I apologized again about having called so early.

"Don't worry about it," Sadik said. "She seemed much prettier last night." He studied the menu, then set it aside. "So tell me, Bar— sorry. *Barack*. Tell me, Barack. What brings you to our fair city?"

I tried to explain. I had spent the summer brooding over a mis-spent youth, I said—the state of the world and the state of my soul. "I want to make amends," I said. "Make myself of some use."

Sadik broke open the yolk of an egg with his fork. "Well, amigo . . . you can talk all you want about saving the world, but this city tends to eat away at such noble sentiments. Look out there." He gestured to the crowd along First Avenue. "Everybody looking out for number one. Survival of the fittest. Tooth and claw. Elbow the other guy out of the way. That, my friend, is New York. But . . ." He shrugged and mopped up some egg with his toast. "Who knows? Maybe you'll be the exception. In which case I will doff my hat to you."

Sadik tipped his coffee cup toward me in mock salute, his eyes searching for any immediate signs of change. And in the coming months he would continue to observe me as I traveled, like a large lab rat, through the byways of Manhattan. He would suppress a grin when the seat I had offered to a middle-aged woman on the subway was snatched up by a burly young man. At Bloomingdale's, he would lead me past human mannequins who spritzed perfume into the air and watch my reaction as I checked over the eye-popping price tags on winter coats. He would offer me lodging again when I gave up the apartment on 109th for lack of heat, and accompany me to Housing Court when it turned out that the sublessors of my second apartment had failed to pay the rent and run off with my deposit.

"Tooth and claw, Barack. Stop worrying about the rest of these bums out here and figure out how you're going to make some money out of this fancy degree you'll be getting."

When Sadik lost his own lease, we moved in together. And after a few months of closer scrutiny, he began to realize that the city had indeed had an effect on me, although not the one he'd expected. I stopped getting high. I ran three miles a day and fasted on Sundays. For the first time in years, I applied myself to my studies and started keeping a journal of daily reflections and very bad poetry. Whenever Sadik tried to talk me into hitting a bar, I'd beg off with some tepid excuse, too much work or not enough cash. One day, before leaving the apartment in search of better company, he turned to me and offered his most scathing indictment.

"You're becoming a bore."

I knew he was right, although I wasn't sure myself what exactly had happened. In a way, I was confirming Sadik's estimation of the city's allure, I suppose; its consequent power to corrupt. With the Wall Street boom, Manhattan was humming, new developments cropping up everywhere; men and women barely out of their twenties already enjoying ridiculous wealth, the fashion merchants fast on their heels. The beauty, the filth, the noise, and the excess, all of it dazzled my senses; there seemed no constraints on originality of lifestyles or the manufacture of desire—a more expensive restaurant, a finer suit of clothes, a more exclusive nightspot, a more beautiful woman, a more potent high. Uncertain of my ability to steer a course of moderation, fearful of falling into old habits, I took on the temperament if not the convictions of a street corner preacher, prepared to see temptation everywhere, ready to overrun a fragile will.

My reaction was more than just an attempt to curb an excessive appetite, though, or a response to sensory overload. Beneath the hum, the motion, I was seeing the steady fracturing of the world taking place. I had seen worse poverty in Indonesia and glimpsed the violent mood of inner-city kids in L.A.; I had grown accustomed, everywhere, to suspicion between the races. But whether because of New York's density or because of its scale, it was only now that I began to grasp the almost mathematical precision with which America's race and class problems joined; the depth, the ferocity, of resulting tribal wars; the bile that flowed freely not just out on the streets but in the stalls of Columbia's bathrooms as well, where, no matter how many times the administration tried to paint them over, the walls remained scratched with blunt correspondence between niggers and kikes.

It was as if all middle ground had collapsed, utterly. And nowhere, it seemed, was that collapse more apparent than in the black community I had so lovingly imagined and within which I had hoped to find refuge. I might meet a black friend at his Midtown law firm, and before heading to lunch at the MoMA, I would look out across the city toward the East River from his high-rise office, imagining a satisfactory life for myself—a vocation, a family, a home. Until I noticed that the only other blacks in the office were messengers or clerks, the only other blacks in the museum the blue-jacketed security guards who counted the hours before they could catch their train home to Brooklyn or Queens.

I might wander through Harlem—to play on courts I'd once read about or to hear Jesse Jackson make a speech on 125th; or, on a rare Sunday morning, to sit in the back pews of Abyssinian Baptist Church, lifted by the gospel choir's sweet, sorrowful song—and catch a fleeting glimpse of that thing which I sought. But I had no guide that might show me how to join this troubled world, and when I looked for an apartment there, I found Sugar Hill's elegant brownstones occupied and out of reach, the few decent rental buildings with ten-year-long waiting lists, so that all that remained were the rows and rows of uninhabitable tenements, in front of which young men counted out their rolls of large bills, and winos slouched and stumbled and wept softly to themselves.

I took all this as a personal affront, a mockery of my tender ambitions—although, when I brought up the subject with people who had lived in New York for a while, I was told there was nothing original about my observations. The city was out of control, they said, the polarization a natural phenomenon, like monsoons or continental drift. Political discussions, the kind that at Occidental had once seemed so intense and purposeful, came to take on the flavor of the socialist conferences I sometimes attended at Cooper Union or the African cultural fairs that took place in Harlem and Brooklyn during the summers—a few of the many diversions New York had to offer, like going to a foreign film or ice-skating at Rockefeller Center. With a bit of money, I was free to live like most middle-class blacks in Manhattan, free to choose a motif around which to organize my life, free to patch together a collage of styles, friends, watering holes, political affiliations. I sensed, though, that at some stage—maybe when you had children and decided that you could stay in the city only at the cost of a private school, or when you began takings cabs at night to avoid the subways, or when you decided that you needed a doorman in your apartment building—your choice was irrevocable, the divide was now impassable, and you would find yourself on the side of the line that you'd never intended to be on.

Unwilling to make that choice, I spent a year walking from one end of Manhattan to the other. Like a tourist, I watched the range of human possibility on display, trying to trace out my future in the lives of the people I saw, looking for some opening through which I could reenter.

It was in this humorless mood that my mother and sister found me when they came to visit during my first summer in New York.

"He's so skinny," Maya said to my mother.

"He only has two towels!" my mother shouted as she inspected the bathroom. "And three plates!" They both began to giggle.

They stayed with Sadik and me for a few nights, then moved to a condominium on Park Avenue that a friend of my mother's had offered them while she was away. That summer I had found a job clearing a construction site on the Upper West Side, so my mother and sister spent most of their days exploring the city on their own. When we met for dinner, they would give me a detailed report of their adventures: eating strawberries and cream at the Plaza, taking the ferry to the Statue of Liberty, visiting the Cézannes at the Met. I would eat in silence until they were finished and then begin a long discourse on the problems of the city and the politics of the dispossessed. I scolded Maya for spending one evening watching TV instead of reading the novels I'd bought for her. I instructed my mother on the various ways that foreign donors and international development organizations like the one she was working for bred dependence in the Third World. When the two of them withdrew to the kitchen, I would overhear Maya complaining to my mother.

"Barry's okay, isn't he? I mean, I hope he doesn't lose his cool and become one of those freaks you see on the streets around here."

One evening, while thumbing through *The Village Voice*, my mother's eyes lit on an advertisement for a movie, *Black Orpheus*, that was showing downtown. My mother insisted that we go see it that night; she said that it was the first foreign film she had ever seen.

"I was only sixteen then," she told us as we entered the elevator. "I'd just been accepted to the University of Chicago—Gramps hadn't told me yet that he wouldn't let me go—and I was there for the summer, working as an au pair. It was the first time that I'd ever been really on my own. Gosh, I felt like such an adult. And when I saw this film, I thought it was the most beautiful thing I had ever seen."

We took a cab to the revival theater where the movie was playing. The film, a groundbreaker of sorts due to its mostly black, Brazilian cast, had been made in the fifties. The story line was simple: the myth of the ill-fated lovers Orpheus and Eurydice set in the favelas of Rio during Carnival. In Technicolor splendor, set against scenic green hills, the black and brown Brazilians sang and danced and strummed guitars like carefree birds in colorful plumage. About halfway through the movie, I decided that I'd seen enough, and turned to my mother to see if she might be ready to go. But her face, lit by the blue glow of the screen, was set in a wistful gaze. At that moment, I felt as if I were being given a window into her heart, the unreflective heart of her youth. I suddenly realized that the depiction of childlike blacks I was now seeing on the screen, the reverse image of Conrad's dark savages, was what my mother had carried with her to Hawaii all those years before, a reflection of the simple fantasies that had been forbidden to a white middle-class girl from Kansas, the promise of another life: warm, sensual, exotic, different.

I turned away, embarrassed for her, irritated with the people around me. Sitting there in the dark, I was reminded of a conversation I'd had a few years earlier with a friend of my mother's, an English-man who had worked for an international aid organization through-out Africa and Asia. He had told me that of all the different peoples he had met in his travels, the Dik of Sudan were the strangest.

"Usually, after a month or two, you make contact," he had said. "Even where you don't speak the language, there's a smile or a joke, you know—some semblance of recognition. But at the end of a year with the Dik, they remained utterly alien to me. They laughed at the things that drove me to despair. What I thought was funny seemed to leave them stone cold."

I had spared him the information that the Dik were Nilotes, distant cousins of mine. I had tried to imagine this pale Englishman in a parched desert somewhere, his back turned away from a circle of naked tribesmen, his eyes searching an empty sky, bitter in his solitude. And the same thought had occurred to me then that I carried with me now as I left the movie theater with my mother and sister: The emotions between the races could never be pure; even love was tarnished by the desire to find in the other some element that was missing in ourselves. Whether we sought out our demons or salvation, the other race would always remain just that: menacing, alien, and apart.

"Kind of corny, huh," Maya said as my mother went to the bath-room.

"What?"

"The movie. It was kind of corny. Just Mom's style."

For the next several days, I tried to avoid situations where my mother and I might be forced to talk. Then, a few days before they were about to leave, I stopped by while Maya was taking a nap. My mother noticed a letter addressed to my father in my hand. I asked her if she had an international postage stamp.

"You guys arranging a visit?"

I told her briefly of my plans as she dug out a stamp from the bottom of her purse. Actually she came up with two stamps; they had melted together in the summer heat. She gave me a sheepish grin and put water on to boil so we could steam them apart.

"Well, I think it'll be wonderful for you two to finally get to know each other," she said from the kitchen. "He was probably a bit tough for a ten-year-old to take, but now that you're older . . ."

I shrugged. "Who knows?"

She stuck her head out of the kitchen. "I hope you don't feel resentful towards him."

"Why would I?"

"I don't know." She returned to the living room and we sat there for a while, listening to the sounds of traffic below. The teapot whistled, and I stamped my envelope. Then, without any prompting, my mother began to retell an old story, in a distant voice, as if she were telling it to herself.

"It wasn't your father's fault that he left, you know. I divorced him. When the two of us got married, your grandparents weren't happy with the idea. But they said okay—they probably couldn't have stopped us anyway, and they eventually came around to the idea that it was the right thing to do. Then Barack's father—your grandfather Hussein—wrote Gramps this long, nasty letter saying that he didn't approve of the marriage. He didn't want the Obama blood sullied by a white woman, he said. Well, you can imagine how Gramps reacted to that. And then there was a problem with your father's first wife . . . he had told me they were separated, but it was a village wedding, so there was no legal document that could show a divorce. . . ."

Her chin had begun to tremble, and she bit down on her lip, steadying herself. She said, "Your father wrote back, saying he was going ahead with it. Then you were born, and we agreed that the three of us would return to Kenya after he finished his studies. But your grandfather Hussein was still writing to your father, threatening to have his student visa revoked. By this time Toot had become hysterical—she had read about the Mau-Mau rebellion in Kenya a few years earlier, which the Western press really played up—and she was sure that I would have my head chopped off and you would be taken away.

"Even then, it might have worked out. When your father graduated from UH, he received two scholarship offers. One was to the New School, here in New York. The other one was to Harvard. The New School agreed to pay for everything—room and board, a job on campus, enough to support all three of us. Harvard just agreed to pay tuition. But Barack was such a stubborn bastard, he had to go to Harvard. How can I refuse the best education? he told me. That's all he could think about, proving that he was the best. . . ."

She sighed, running her hands through her hair. "We were so young, you know. I was younger than you are now. He was only a few years older than that. Later, when he came to visit us in Hawaii that time, he wanted us to come live with him. But I was still married to Lolo then, and his third wife had just left him, and I just didn't think . . ."

She stopped and laughed to herself. "Did I ever tell you that he was late for our first date? He asked me to meet him in front of the university library at one. When I got there he hadn't arrived, but I figured I'd give him a few minutes. It was a nice day, so I laid out on one of the benches, and before I knew it I had fallen asleep. Well, an hour later—an hour!—he shows up with a couple of his friends. I woke up and the three of them were standing over me, and I heard your father saying, serious as can be, 'You see, gentlemen. I told you that she was a fine girl, and that she would wait for me.' "

My mother laughed once more, and once again I saw her as the child she had been. Except this time I saw something else: In her smiling, slightly puzzled face, I saw what all children must see at some point if they are to grow up—their parents' lives revealed to them as separate and apart, reaching out beyond the point of their union or the birth of a child, lives unfurling back to grandparents, great-grandparents, an infinite number of chance meetings, misunderstandings, projected hopes, limited circumstances. My mother was that girl with the movie of beautiful black people in her head, flattered by my father's attention, confused and alone, trying to break out of the grip of her own parents' lives. The innocence she carried that day, waiting for my father, had been tinged with misconceptions, her own needs. But it was a guileless need, one without self-consciousness, and perhaps that's how any love begins, impulses and cloudy images that allow us to break across our solitude, and then, if we're lucky, are finally transformed into something firmer. What I heard from my mother that day, speaking about my father, was something that I suspect most Americans will never hear from the lips of those of another race, and so cannot be expected to believe might exist between black and white: the love of someone who knows your life in the round, a love that will survive disappointment. She saw my father as everyone hopes at least one other person might see him; she had tried to help the child who never knew him see him in the same way. And it was the look on her face that day that I would remember when a few months later I called to tell her that my father had died and heard her cry out over the distance.

After I spoke to my mother, I phoned my father's brother in Boston and we had a brief, awkward conversation. I didn't go to the funeral,

so I wrote my father's family in Nairobi a letter expressing my con-
dolences. I asked them to write back, and wondered how they were
faring. But I felt no pain, only the vague sense of an opportunity lost,
and I saw no reason to pretend otherwise. My plans to travel to
Kenya were placed on indefinite hold.

Another year would pass before I would meet him one night, in a
cold cell, in a chamber of my dreams. I dreamed I was traveling by
bus with friends whose names I've forgotten, men and women with
different journeys to make. We rolled across deep fields of grass and
hills that bucked against an orange sky.

An old white man, heavyset, sat beside me, and I read in a book
that he held in his hands that our treatment of the old tested our
souls. He told me he was a union man, off to meet his daughter.

We stopped at an old hotel, a grand hotel with chandeliers. There
was a piano in the lobby and a lounge filled with cushions of soft
satin, and I took one of the cushions and placed it on the piano
bench, and the old white man sat down, retarded now, or senile, and
when I looked again he was a small black girl, her feet barely reaching the pedals. She smiled and started to play, and then a waitress
came in, a young Hispanic woman, and the waitress frowned at us,
but under the frown was a laugh, and she raised a finger to her lips as
if we were sharing a secret.

I dozed for the rest of the trip, and woke up to find everyone gone.
The bus came to a halt, and I got off and sat down on the curb. Inside
a building made of rough stone, a lawyer spoke to a judge. The judge
suggested that perhaps my father had spent enough time in his jail,
that perhaps it was time to release him. But the lawyer objected vig-
orously, citing precedent and various statutes, the need to maintain
order. The judge shrugged and got up from the bench.

I stood before the cell, opened the padlock, and set it carefully on
a window ledge. My father was before me, with only a cloth wrapped
around his waist; he was very thin, with his large head and slender

frame, his hairless arms and chest. He looked pale, his black eyes luminous against an ashen face, but he smiled and gestured for the tall, mute guard to please stand aside.

"Look at you," he said. "So tall—and so thin. Gray hairs, even!" And I saw that it was true, and I walked up to him and we embraced. I began to weep, and felt ashamed, but could not stop myself.

"Barack. I always wanted to tell you how much I love you," he said. He seemed small in my arms now, the size of a boy.

He sat at the corner of his cot and set his head on his clasped hands and stared away from me, into the wall. An implacable sadness spread across his face. I tried to joke with him; I told him that if I was thin it was only because I took after him. But he couldn't be budged, and when I whispered to him that we might leave together, he shook his head and told me it would be best if I left.

I awoke still weeping, my first real tears for him—and for me, his jailor, his judge, his son. I turned on the light and dug out his old letters. I remembered his only visit—the basketball he had given me and how he had taught me to dance. And I realized, perhaps for the first time, how even in his absence his strong image had given me some bulwark on which to grow up, an image to live up to, or disappoint.

I stepped to the window and looked outside, listening to the first sounds of morning—the growl of the garbage trucks, footsteps in the apartment next door. I needed to search for him, I thought to myself, and talk with him again.

PART TWO

Chicago

CHAPTER SEVEN

....

In 1983, I DECIDED to become a community organizer.

There wasn't much detail to the idea; I didn't know anyone making a living that way. When classmates in college asked me just what it was that a community organizer did, I couldn't answer them directly. Instead, I'd pronounce on the need for change. Change in the White House, where Reagan and his minions were carrying on their dirty deeds. Change in the Congress, compliant and corrupt. Change in the mood of the country, manic and self-absorbed. Change won't come from the top, I would say. Change will come from a mobilized grass roots.

That's what I'll do, I'll organize black folks. At the grass roots. For change.

And my friends, black and white, would heartily commend me for my ideals before heading toward the post office to mail in their graduate school applications.

I couldn't really blame them for being skeptical. Now, with the benefit of hindsight, I can construct a certain logic to my decision, show how becoming an organizer was a part of that larger narrative, starting with my father and his father before him, my mother and her parents, my memories of Indonesia with its beggars and farmers and the loss of Lolo to power, on through Ray and Frank, Marcus and Regina; my move to New York; my father's death. I can see that my choices were never truly mine alone—and that that is how it should be, that to assert otherwise is to chase after a sorry sort of freedom.

But such recognition came only later. At the time, about to graduate from college, I was operating mainly on impulse, like a salmon swimming blindly upstream toward the site of his own conception. In classes and seminars, I would dress up these impulses in the slogans and theories that I'd discovered in books, thinking—falsely—that the slogans meant something, that they somehow made what I felt more amenable to proof. But at night, lying in bed, I would let the slogans drift away, to be replaced with a series of images, romantic images, of a past I had never known.

They were of the civil rights movement, mostly, the grainy black-and-white footage that appears every February during Black History Month, the same images that my mother had offered me as a child. A pair of college students, hair short, backs straight, placing their orders at a lunch counter teetering on the edge of riot. SNCC workers standing on a porch in some Mississippi backwater trying to convince a family of sharecroppers to register to vote. A county jail bursting with children, their hands clasped together, singing freedom songs.

Such images became a form of prayer for me, bolstering my spirits, channeling my emotions in a way that words never could. They told me (although even this much understanding may have come later, is also a construct, containing its own falsehoods) that I wasn't alone in my particular struggles, and that communities had never been a given in this country, at least not for blacks. Communities had to be created, fought for, tended like gardens. They expanded or contracted with the dreams of men—and in the civil rights movement those dreams had been large. In the sit-ins, the marches, the jailhouse songs, I saw the African-American community becoming more than just the place where you'd been born or the house where you'd been raised. Through organizing, through shared sacrifice, membership had been earned. And because membership was earned—because this community I imagined was still in the making, built on the promise that the larger American community, black, white, and brown, could somehow redefine itself—I believed that it might, over time, admit the uniqueness of my own life.

That was my idea of organizing. It was a promise of redemption.

And so, in the months leading up to graduation, I wrote to every civil rights organization I could think of, to any black elected official in the country with a progressive agenda, to neighborhood councils and tenant rights groups. When no one wrote back, I wasn't discouraged. I decided to find more conventional work for a year, to pay off my student loans and maybe even save a little bit. I would need the money later, I told myself. Organizers didn't make any money; their poverty was proof of their integrity.

Eventually a consulting house to multinational corporations agreed to hire me as a research assistant. Like a spy behind enemy lines, I arrived every day at my mid-Manhattan office and sat at my computer terminal, checking the Reuters machine that blinked bright emerald messages from across the globe. As far as I could tell I was the only black man in the company, a source of shame for me but a source of considerable pride for the company's secretarial pool. They treated me like a son, those black ladies; they told me how they expected me to run the company one day. Sometimes, over lunch, I would tell them about all my wonderful organizing plans, and they would smile and say, "That's good, Barack," but the look in their eyes told me they were secretly disappointed. Only Ike, the gruff black security guard in the lobby, was willing to come right out and tell me I'd be making a mistake.

"Organizing? That's some kinda politics, ain't it? Why you wanna do something like that?"

I tried to explain my political views, the importance of mobilizing the poor and giving back to the community. But Ike just shook his head. "Mr. Barack," he said, "I hope you don't mind if I give you a little bit of advice. You don't have to take it, now, but I'm gonna give it to you anyhow. Forget about this organizing business and do something that's gonna make you some money. Not greedy, you understand. But enough. I'm telling you this 'cause I can see potential in you. Young man like you, got a nice voice—hell, you could be one a them announcers on TV. Or sales . . . got a nephew about your age making some real money there. That's what we need, see. Not more folks running around here, all rhymes and jive. You can't help folks that ain't gonna make it nohow, and they won't appreciate you trying. Folks that wanna make it, they gonna find a way to do it on they own. How old are you anyway?"

"Twenty-two."

"See there. Don't waste your youth, Mr. Barack. Wake up one morning, an old man like me, and all you gonna be is tired, with nothing to show for it."

I didn't pay Ike much attention at the time; I thought he sounded too much like my grandparents. Nevertheless, as the months passed, I felt the idea of becoming an organizer slipping away from me. The company promoted me to the position of financial writer. I had my own office, my own secretary, money in the bank. Sometimes, coming out of an interview with Japanese financiers or German bond traders, I would catch my reflection in the elevator doors—see myself in a suit and tie, a briefcase in my hand—and for a split second I would imagine myself as a captain of industry, barking out orders, closing the deal, before I remembered who it was that I had told myself I wanted to be and felt pangs of guilt for my lack of resolve.

Then one day, as I sat down at my computer to write an article on interest-rate swaps, something unexpected happened. Auma called.

I had never met this half sister; we had written only intermittently.

I knew that she had left Kenya to study in Germany, and in our letters we had mentioned the possibility of my going there for a visit, or perhaps her coming to the States. But the plans had always been left vague—neither of us had any money, we would say; maybe next year. Our correspondence maintained a cordial distance.

Now, suddenly, I heard her voice for the first time. It was soft and dark, tinged with a colonial accent. For a few moments I couldn't understand the words, only the sound, a sound that seemed to have always been there, misplaced but not forgotten. She was coming to the States, she said, on a trip with several friends. Could she come to see me in New York?

"Of course," I said. "You can stay with me; I can't wait." And she laughed, and I laughed, and then the line grew quiet with static and the sound of our breath. "Well," she said, "I can't stay on the phone too long, it's so expensive. Here's the flight information"; and we hung up quickly after that, as if our contact was a treat to be doled out in small measures.

I spent the next few weeks rushing around in preparation: new sheets for the sofa bed, extra plates and towels, a scrubbing for the tub. But two days before she was scheduled to arrive, Auma called again, the voice thicker now, barely a whisper.

"I can't come after all," she said. "One of our brothers, David . . . he's been killed. In a motorcycle accident. I don't know any more than that." She began to cry. "Oh, Barack. Why do these things happen to us?"

I tried to comfort her as best I could. I asked her if I could do anything for her. I told her there would be other times for us to see each other. Eventually her voice quieted; she had to go book a flight home, she said.

"Okay, then, Barack. See you. 'Bye."

After she hung up, I left my office, telling my secretary I'd be gone for the day. For hours I wandered the streets of Manhattan, the sound of Auma's voice playing over and over in my mind. A continent away, a woman cries. On a dark and dusty road, a boy skids out of control, tumbling against hard earth, wheels spinning to silence. Who were these people, I asked myself, these strangers who carried my blood? What might save this woman from her sorrow? What wild, unspoken dreams had this boy possessed?

Who was I, who shed no tears at the loss of his own?

I still wonder sometimes how that first contact with Auma altered my life. Not so much the contact itself (that meant everything, would mean everything) or the news that she gave me of David's death (that, too, is an absolute; I would never know him, and that says enough), but rather the timing of her call, the particular sequence of events, the raised expectations and then the dashed hopes, coming at a time when the idea of becoming an organizer was still just that, an idea in my head, a vague tug at my heart.

Maybe it made no difference. Maybe by this time I was already committed to organizing and Auma's voice simply served to remind me that I still had wounds to heal, and could not heal myself. Or maybe, if David hadn't died when he did, and Auma had come to New York as originally planned, and I had learned from her then what I would only learn later, about Kenya, and about our father . . . well, maybe it would have relieved certain pressures that had built up inside me, showing me a different idea of community, allowing my ambitions to travel a narrower, more personal course, so that in the end I might have taken my friend Ike's advice and given myself over to stocks and bonds and the pull of respectability.

I don't know. What's certain is that a few months after Auma's call I turned in my resignation at the consulting firm and began looking in earnest for an organizing job. Once again, most of my letters went unanswered, but after a month or so I was called in for an interview by the director of a prominent civil rights organization in the city. He was a tall, handsome black man, dressed in a crisp white shirt, a paisley tie, and red suspenders. His office was furnished with Italian chairs and African sculpture, a bar service built into the exposed brick. Through a tall window, sunlight streamed down on a bust of Dr. King.

"I like it," the director said after looking over my résumé. "Particularly the corporate experience. That's the real business of a civil rights organization these days. Protest and pickets won't cut it anymore. To get the job done, we've got to forge links between business, government, and the inner city." He clasped his broad hands together, then showed me a glossy annual report opened to a page that listed the organization's board of directors. There was one black minister and ten white corporate executives. "You see?" the director said. "Public-private partnerships. The key to the future. And that's where young people like yourself come in. Educated. Self-assured. Comfortable in boardrooms. Why, just last week I was discussing the problem with the secretary of HUD at a White House dinner. Terrific guy, Jack. He'd be interested in meeting a young man like you. Of course I'm a registered Democrat, but we have to learn to work with whoever's in power. . . ."

On the spot he offered me the job, which involved organizing conferences on drugs, unemployment, housing. Facilitating dialogue, he called it. I declined his generous offer, deciding I needed a job closer to the streets. I spent three months working for a Ralph Nader offshoot up in Harlem, trying to convince the minority students at City College about the importance of recycling. Then a week passing out flyers for an assemblyman's race in Brooklyn—the candidate lost and I never did get paid.

In six months I was broke, unemployed, eating soup from a can. In search of some inspiration, I went to hear Kwame Touré, formerly Stokely Carmichael of SNCC and Black Power fame, speak at Columbia. At the entrance to the auditorium, two women, one black, one Asian, were selling Marxist literature and arguing with each other about Trotsky's place in history. Inside, Touré was proposing a program

to establish economic ties between Africa and Harlem that would cir-
cumvent white capitalist imperialism. At the end of his remarks, a thin
young woman with glasses asked if such a program was practical given
the state of African economies and the immediate needs facing black
Americans. Touré cut her off in midsentence. "It's only the brainwash-
ing that you've received that makes it impractical, sister," he said. His
eyes glowed inward as he spoke, the eyes of a madman or a saint. The
woman remained standing for several minutes while she was upbraided
for her bourgeois attitudes. People began to file out. Outside the auditorium, the two Marxists were now shouting at the top of their lungs.

"Stalinist pig!"

"Reformist bitch!"

It was like a bad dream. I wandered down Broadway, imagining
myself standing at the edge of the Lincoln Memorial and looking out
over an empty pavilion, debris scattering in the wind. The movement
had died years ago, shattered into a thousand fragments. Every path
to change was well trodden, every strategy exhausted. And with each
defeat, even those with the best of intentions could end up further and
further removed from the struggles of those they purported to serve.

Or just plain crazy. I suddenly realized that I was talking to myself
in the middle of the street. People on their way home from work
were cutting a small arc around me, and I thought I recognized a
couple of Columbia classmates in the crowd, their suit jackets thrown
over their shoulders, carefully avoiding my glance.

I had all but given up on organizing when I received a call from Marty
Kaufman. He explained that he'd started an organizing drive in
Chicago and was looking to hire a trainee. He'd be in New York the fol-
lowing week and suggested that we meet at a coffee shop on Lexington.

His appearance didn't inspire much confidence. He was a white
man of medium height wearing a rumpled suit over a pudgy frame.
His face was heavy with two-day-old whiskers; behind a pair of thick,

wire-rimmed glasses, his eyes seemed set in a perpetual squint. As he rose from the booth to shake my hand, he spilled some tea on his shirt.

"So," Marty said, dabbing the stain with a paper napkin. "Why does somebody from Hawaii want to be an organizer?"

I sat down and told him a little bit about myself.

"Hmmph." He nodded, taking notes on a dog-eared legal pad. "You must be angry about something."

"What do you mean by that?"

He shrugged. "I don't know what exactly. But something. Don't get me wrong—anger's a requirement for the job. The only reason anybody decides to become an organizer. Well-adjusted people find more relaxing work."

He ordered more hot water and told me about himself. He was Jewish, in his late thirties, had been reared in New York. He had started organizing in the sixties with the student protests, and ended up staying with it for fifteen years. Farmers in Nebraska. Blacks in Philadelphia. Mexicans in Chicago. Now he was trying to pull urban blacks and suburban whites together around a plan to save manufacturing jobs in metropolitan Chicago. He needed somebody to work with him, he said. Somebody black.

"Most of our work is with churches," he said. "If poor and working-class people want to build real power, they have to have some sort of institutional base. With the unions in the shape they're in, the churches are the only game in town. That's where the people are, and that's where the values are, even if they've been buried under a lot of bullshit. Churches won't work with you, though, just out of the goodness of their hearts. They'll talk a good game—a sermon on Sunday, maybe, or a special offering for the homeless. But if push comes to shove, they won't really move unless you can show them how it'll help them pay their heating bill."

He poured himself more hot water. "What do you know about Chicago anyway?"

I thought a moment. "Hog butcher to the world," I said finally.

Marty shook his head. "The butcheries closed a while ago."

"The Cubs never win."

"True."

"America's most segregated city," I said. "A black man, Harold Washington, was just elected mayor, and white people don't like it."

"So you've been following Harold's career," Marty said. "I'm surprised you haven't gone to work for him."

"I tried. His office didn't write back."

Marty smiled and took off his glasses, cleaning them with the end of his tie. "Well, that's the thing to do, isn't it, if you're young and black and interested in social issues? Find a political campaign to work for. A powerful patron—somebody who can help you with your own career. And Harold's powerful, no doubt about it. Lots of charisma. He has almost monolithic support in the black community. About half the Hispanics, a handful of white liberals. You're right about one thing, though. The whole atmosphere in the city is polarized. A big media circus. Not much is getting done."

I leaned back in my seat. "And whose fault is that?"

Marty put his glasses back on and met my stare. "It's not a question of fault," he said. "It's a question of whether any politician, even somebody with Harold's talent, can do much to break the cycle. A polarized city isn't necessarily a bad thing for a politician. Black or white."

He offered to start me off at ten thousand dollars the first year, with a two-thousand-dollar travel allowance to buy a car; the salary would go up if things worked out. After he was gone, I took the long way home, along the East River promenade, and tried to figure out what to make of the man. He was smart, I decided. He seemed committed to his work. Still, there was something about him that made me wary. A little too sure of himself, maybe. And white—he'd said himself that that was a problem.

The old fluted park lamps flickered to life; a long brown barge rolled through the gray waters toward the sea. I sat down on a bench, considering my options, and noticed a black woman and her young son approach. The boy yanked the woman up to the railing, and they stood side by side, his arm wrapped around her leg, a single silhouette against the twilight. Eventually the boy's head craned upward with what looked like a question. The woman shrugged her shoulders and the boy took a few steps toward me.

"Excuse me, mister," he shouted. "You know why sometimes the river runs that way and then sometimes it goes this way?"

The woman smiled and shook her head, and I said it probably had to do with the tides. The answer seemed to satisfy the boy, and he went back to his mother. As I watched the two of them disappear into dusk, I realized I had never noticed which way the river ran.

A week later, I loaded up my car and drove to Chicago.

CHAPTER EIGHT

∙∙

I HAD BEEN TO CHICAGO once before. It was during the summer after my father's visit to Hawaii, before my eleventh birthday, when Toot had decided it was time I saw the mainland of the United States. Perhaps the two things were connected, her decision and my father's visit—his presence (once again) disturbing the world she and Gramps had made for themselves, triggering in her a desire to reclaim antecedents, her own memories, and pass them on to her grandchildren.

We traveled for over a month, Toot and my mother and Maya and I—Gramps had lost his taste for traveling by this time and chose to stay behind. We flew to Seattle, then went down the coast to California and Disneyland, east to the Grand Canyon, across the Great Plains to Kansas City, then up to the Great Lakes before heading back west through Yellowstone Park. We took Greyhound buses, mostly, and stayed at Howard Johnson's, and watched the Watergate hearings every night before going to bed.

We were in Chicago for three days, in a motel in the South Loop. It must have been sometime in July, but for some reason I remember the days as cold and gray. The motel had an indoor swimming pool, which impressed me; there were no indoor pools in Hawaii. Standing beneath the el tracks, I closed my eyes as a train passed and shouted as loud as I could. At the Field Museum, I saw two shrunken heads that were kept on display. They were wrinkled but well preserved, each the size of my palm, their eyes and mouths sewn shut, just as I would have expected. They appeared to be of European extraction: The man had a small goatee, like a conquistador; the female had flowing red hair. I stared at them for a long time (until my mother pulled me away), feeling—with the morbid glee of a young boy—as if I had stumbled upon some sort of cosmic joke. Not so much the fact that the heads had been shrunk—that I could understand; it was the same idea as eating tiger meat with Lolo, a form of magic, a taking of control. Rather, the fact that these little European faces were here in a glass case, where strangers, perhaps even descendants, might observe the details of their gruesome fate. That no one seemed to think that odd. It was a different sort of magic, these harsh museum lights, the neat labels, the seeming indifference of the visitors who passed; another effort at control.

Fourteen years later, the city appeared much prettier. It was another July, and the sun sparkled through the deep green trees. The boats were out of their moorings, their distant sails like the wings of doves across Lake Michigan. Marty had told me that he would be busy those first few days, and so I was left on my own. I had bought a map, and I followed Martin Luther King Drive from its northernmost to its southernmost point, then went back up Cottage Grove, down byways and alleys, past the apartment buildings and vacant lots, convenience stores and bungalow homes. And as I drove, I remembered. I remembered the whistle of the Illinois Central, bearing the weight of the thousands who had come up from the South so many years before; the black men and women and children, dirty from the soot of the railcars, clutching their makeshift luggage, all making their way to Canaan Land. I imagined Frank in a baggy suit and wide lapels, standing in front of the old Regal Theatre, waiting to see

Duke or Ella emerge from a gig. The mailman I saw was Richard Wright, delivering mail before his first book sold; the little girl with the glasses and pigtails was Regina, skipping rope. I made a chain between my life and the faces I saw, borrowing other people's memories. In this way I tried to take possession of the city, make it my own. Yet another sort of magic.

On the third day I passed Smitty's Barbershop, a fifteen-by-thirty-foot storefront on the edge of Hyde Park with four barber's chairs and a card table for LaTisha, the part-time manicurist. The door was propped open when I walked in, the barbershop smells of hair cream and antiseptic mingling with the sound of men's laughter and the hum of slow fans. Smitty turned out to be an older black man, gray-haired, slender and stooped. His chair was open and so I took a seat, soon joining in the familiar barbershop banter of sports and women and yesterday's headlines, conversation at once intimate and anonymous, among men who've agreed to leave their troubles outside.

Somebody had just finished telling a story about his neighbor—the man had been caught in bed with his wife's cousin and chased at the point of a kitchen knife, buck naked, out into the street—when the talk turned to politics.

"Vrdolyak and the rest of them crackers don't know when to quit," the man with the newspaper said, shaking his head in disgust. "When Old Man Daley was mayor, didn't nobody say nothing about him putting all them Irish up in City Hall. But the minute Harold tries to hire some black people, just to even things out, they call it reverse racism—"

"Man, that's how it always is. Whenever a black man gets into power, they gonna try and change the rules on him."

"Worse part is, newspapers acting like it was black folks that started this whole mess."

"What you expect from the white man's paper?"

"You right. Harold knows what he's doing, though. Just biding his time till the next election."

That's how black people talked about Chicago's mayor, with a familiarity and affection normally reserved for a relative. His picture was everywhere: on the walls of shoe repair shops and beauty parlors; still glued to lampposts from the last campaign; even in the windows of the Korean dry cleaners and Arab grocery stores, displayed prominently, like some protective totem. From the barbershop wall, that portrait looked down on me now: the handsome, grizzled face, the bushy eyebrows and mustache, the twinkle in the eyes. Smitty noticed me looking at the picture and asked if I'd been in Chicago during the election. I told him I hadn't. He nodded his head.

"Had to be here before Harold to understand what he means to this city," Smitty said. "Before Harold, seemed like we'd always be second-class citizens."

"Plantation politics," the man with the newspaper said.

"That's just what it was, too," Smitty said. "A plantation. Black people in the worst jobs. The worst housing. Police brutality rampant. But when the so-called black committeemen came around election time, we'd all line up and vote the straight Democratic ticket. Sell our soul for a Christmas turkey. White folks spitting in our faces, and we'd reward 'em with the vote."

Clumps of hair fell into my lap as I listened to the men recall Harold's rise. He had run for mayor once before, shortly after the elder Daley died, but the candidacy had faltered—a source of shame, the men told me, the lack of unity within the black community, the doubts that had to be overcome. But Harold had tried again, and this time the people were ready. They had stuck with him when the press played up the income taxes he'd failed to pay ("Like the white cats don't cheat on every damn thing every minute of their lives"). They had rallied behind him when white Democratic committeemen,

Vrdolyak and others, announced their support for the Republican candidate, saying that the city would go to hell if it had a black mayor. They had turned out in record numbers on election night, ministers and gang-bangers, young and old.

And their faith had been rewarded. Smitty said, "The night Harold won, let me tell you, people just ran the streets. It was like the day Joe Louis knocked out Schmeling. Same feeling. People weren't just proud of Harold. They were proud of themselves. I stayed inside, but my wife and I, we couldn't get to bed until three, we were so excited. When I woke up the next morning, it seemed like the most beautiful day of my life. . . ."

Smitty's voice had fallen to a whisper, and everyone in the room began to smile. From a distance, reading the newspapers back in New York, I had shared in their pride, the same sort of pride that made me root for any pro football team that fielded a black quarterback. But something was different about what I was now hearing; there was a fervor in Smitty's voice that seemed to go beyond politics. "Had to be here to understand," he had said. He'd meant here in Chicago; but he could also have meant here in my shoes, an older black man who still burns from a lifetime of insults, of foiled ambitions, of ambitions abandoned before they've been tried. I asked myself if I could truly understand that. I assumed, took for granted, that I could. Seeing me, these men had made the same assumption. Would they feel the same way if they knew more about me? I wondered. I tried to imagine what would happen if Gramps walked into the barbershop at that moment, how the talk would stop, how the spell would be broken; the different assumptions at work.

Smitty handed me the mirror to check his handiwork, then pulled off my smock and brushed off the back of my shirt. "Thanks for the history lesson," I said, standing up.

"Hey, that part's free. Haircut's ten dollars. What's your name, anyway?"

"Barack."

"Barack, huh. You a Muslim?"

"Grandfather was."

He took the money and shook my hand. "Well, Barack, you should come back a little sooner next time. Your hair was looking awful raggedy when you walked in."

Late that afternoon, Marty picked me up in front of my new address and we headed south on the Skyway. After several miles, we took an exit leading into the southeast side, past rows of small houses made of gray clapboard or brick, until we arrived at a massive old factory that stretched out over several blocks.

"The old Wisconsin Steel plant."

We sat there in silence, studying the building. It expressed some of the robust, brutal spirit of Chicago's industrial past, metal beams and concrete rammed together, without much attention to comfort or detail. Only now it was empty and rust-stained, like an abandoned wreck. On the other side of the chain-link fence, a spotted, mangy cat ran through the weeds.

"All kinds of people used to work in the plant," Marty said as he wheeled the car around and started back down the road. "Blacks. Whites. Hispanics. All working the same jobs. All living the same kind of lives. But outside the plant, most of them didn't want anything to do with each other. And these are the church people I'm talking about. Brothers and sisters in Christ."

We came to a stoplight, and I noticed a group of young white men in their undershirts, drinking beer on a stoop. A Vrdolyak poster hung in one of the windows, and several of the men began to glare in my direction. I turned to Marty.

"So what makes you think they can work together now?"

"They don't have any choice. Not if they want their jobs back."

As we reentered the highway, Marty began to tell me more about the organization he'd built. The idea had first come to him two years earlier, he said, when he'd read reports of the plant closings and lay-offs then sweeping across South Chicago and the southern suburbs. With the help of a sympathetic Catholic auxiliary bishop, he'd gone to meet with pastors and church members in the area, and heard both blacks and whites talk about their shame of unemployment, their fear of losing a house or of being cheated out of a pension—their common sense of having been betrayed.

Eventually over twenty suburban churches had agreed to form an organization, which they named the Calumet Community Religious Conference, or CCRC. Another eight churches had joined the city arm of the organization, called Developing Communities Project, or DCP. Things hadn't moved quite as fast as Marty had hoped; the unions hadn't yet signed on, and the political war in the city council had proven to be a major distraction. Still, CCRC had recently won its first significant victory: a $500,000 computerized job placement program that the Illinois legislature had agreed to fund. We were on our way to a rally to celebrate this new job bank, Marty explained, the opening shot in a long-term campaign.

"It's going to take a while to rebuild manufacturing out here," he said. "Ten years, minimum. But once we get the unions involved, we'll have a base to negotiate from. In the meantime, we just need to stop the hemorrhage and give people some short-term victories. Something to show people how much power they have once they stop fighting each other and start going after the real enemy."

"And who's that?"

Marty shrugged. "The investment bankers. The politicians. The fat cat lobbyists."

Marty nodded to himself, squinting at the road ahead. Looking at him, I began to suspect that he wasn't as cynical as he liked to make out, that the plant we'd just left carried a larger meaning for him. Somewhere in his life, I thought, he, too, had been betrayed.

It was twilight by the time we crossed the city line and pulled into the parking lot of a large suburban school, where crowds of people were already making their way into the auditorium. They appeared as Marty had described them: laid-off steelworkers, secretaries, and truck drivers, men and women who smoked a lot and didn't watch their weight, shopped at Sears or Kmart, drove late-model cars from Detroit and ate at Red Lobster on special occasions. A barrel-chested black man in a cleric's collar greeted us at the door and Marty introduced him as Deacon Wilbur Milton, copresident of the organization. With his short, reddish beard and round cheeks, the man reminded me of Santa Claus.

"Welcome," Will said, pumping my hand. "We been wondering when we'd actually get to meet you. Thought maybe Marty just made you up."

Marty peeked inside the auditorium. "How's turnout looking?"

"Good so far. Everybody seems to be making their quota. Governor's people just called to say he's on his way."

Marty and Will began walking toward the stage, their heads buried in the evening's agenda. I started to follow them, but found my path blocked by three black women of indeterminate age. One of them, a pretty woman with orange-tinted hair, introduced herself as Angela, then leaned over to me and whispered, "You're Barack, aren't you?"

I nodded.

"You don't know how glad we are to see you."

"You really don't," the older woman next to Angela said. I offered the woman my hand, and she smiled to show off a gold front tooth. "I'm sorry," she said, taking my hand, "I'm Shirley." She gestured toward the last woman, dark and heavyset. "This is Mona. Don't he look clean-cut, Mona?"

"Sure does," Mona said with a laugh.

"Don't get me wrong," Angela said, her voice still lowered a pitch. "I've got nothing against Marty. But the fact is, there's only so far you can—"

"Hey, Angela!" We looked up to see Marty waving at us from the stage. "You guys can talk to Barack all you want later. Right now I need all of you up here with me."

The women exchanged knowing looks before Angela turned back to me.

"I guess we better get going," she said. "But we really do have to talk. Soon."

"Sure do," said Mona before the three of them walked away, Angela and Shirley busy chatting away in the front, Mona leisurely bringing up the rear.

The auditorium was almost filled by this time, two thousand people in all, maybe a third of them blacks bused in from the city. At seven o'clock, a choir sang two gospel songs, Will took a roll call of all the churches represented, and a white Lutheran from the suburbs explained the history and mission of CCRC. A procession of speakers then mounted the stage: a black legislator and a white legislator, a Baptist minister and Cardinal Bernardin, and finally the governor, who offered his solemn pledge of support for the new job bank and recited evidence of his tireless efforts on behalf of the working men and women of Illinois.

To my mind the whole thing came off a bit flat, like a political convention or a TV wrestling match. Still, the crowd seemed to be enjoying itself. Some people hoisted bright banners bearing the name of their church. Others broke into boisterous cheers as a friend or relative was recognized from the stage. Seeing all these black and white faces together in one place, I, too, found myself feeling cheered, recognizing in myself the same vision driving Marty, his confidence in the populist impulse and working-class solidarity; his faith that if you could just clear away the politicians and media and bureaucrats and give everybody a seat at the table, then ordinary people could find common ground.

When the rally was over, Marty mentioned that he had to give some people a ride home, so instead of riding with him I decided to take one of the buses heading back to the city. As it turned out, there was an empty seat next to Will on the bus, and in the glow of the freeway lights, he began to tell me a little about himself.

He had grown up in Chicago, he said, and served in Vietnam. After the war, he had found a job as an executive trainee at Continental Illinois Bank and had risen fast, enjoying the trappings of the work—the car, the suits, the downtown office. Then the bank had reorganized and Will was laid off, leaving him shaken and badly in debt. It was the turning point in his life, he said, God's way of telling him to get his values straight. Rather than look for another job in banking, he turned to Christ. He joined St. Catherine's parish in West Pullman and took a job as the janitor there. The decision had put some strain on his marriage—his wife was "still adjusting," he said—but according to Will, the ascetic lifestyle suited his new mission: to spread the Good News and puncture some of the hypocrisy he saw in the church.

"A lot of black folks in the church get mixed up in middle-class attitudes," Will said. "Think that as long as they follow the letter of Scripture, they don't need to follow the spirit. Instead of reaching out to people who are hurting, they make them feel unwelcome. They look at people funny unless they're wearing the right clothes to mass, talk proper and all that. They figure they're comfortable, so why put themselves out. Well, Christ ain't about comfort, is he? He preached a social gospel. Took his message to the weak. The downtrodden. And that's exactly what I tell some of these middle-class Negroes whenever I stand up on Sunday. Tell 'em what they don't wanna hear."

"Do they listen?"

"No." Will chuckled. "But that don't stop me. It's like this collar I wear. That really gets some of 'em mad. 'Collars are for priests,' they tell me. But see, just 'cause I'm married and can't be ordained don't mean I don't have a calling. Ain't nothing in the Bible talking about collars. So I go ahead and wear a collar to let people know where I'm coming from.

"In fact, I wore a collar when some of us went to meet with Cardinal Bernardin about a month back. Everyone was real uptight about it. Then they got upset when I called the Cardinal 'Joe' instead of 'Your Holiness.' But you know, Bernardin was cool. He's a spiritual man. I could tell we understood each other. It's these rules again that keep us apart—rules of men, not rules of God. See, Barack, I'm in the Catholic church, but I was raised a Baptist. Could've joined a Methodist church, Pentecostal, whatever, just as easy. St. Catherine's is just where God happened to send me. And He cares more about whether I'm about the business of helping others than whether I'm straight on my catechisms."

I nodded, deciding not to ask what a catechism was. In Indonesia, I had spent two years at a Muslim school, two years at a Catholic school. In the Muslim school, the teacher wrote to tell my mother that I made faces during Koranic studies. My mother wasn't overly concerned. "Be respectful," she'd said. In the Catholic school, when it came time to pray, I would pretend to close my eyes, then peek around the room. Nothing happened. No angels descended. Just a parched old nun and thirty brown children, muttering words. Sometimes the nun would catch me, and her stern look would force my lids back shut. But that didn't change how I felt inside. I felt that way now, listening to Will; my silence was like closing my eyes.

The bus came to a stop in the church parking lot, and Will walked to the front of the bus. He thanked everybody for coming and urged them to stay involved. "It's a long road we're traveling," he said, "but tonight showed me what we can do when we put our minds to it. That good feeling you got right now, we got to keep it going till we got this neighborhood back on its feet."

A few people smiled and offered an amen. But as I stepped off the bus, I heard a woman behind me whispering to her friend, "I don't need to hear about the neighborhood, girl. Where these jobs they talking about?"

The day after the rally, Marty decided it was time for me to do some real work, and he handed me a long list of people to interview. Find out their self-interest, he said. That's why people become involved in organizing—because they think they'll get something out of it. Once I found an issue enough people cared about, I could take them into action. With enough actions, I could start to build power.

Issues, action, power, self-interest. I liked these concepts. They bespoke a certain hardheadedness, a worldly lack of sentiment; politics, not religion. For the next three weeks, I worked day and night, setting up and conducting my interviews. It was harder than I'd expected. There was the internal resistance I felt whenever I picked up the phone to set up the interviews, as images of Gramps's insurance sales calls crept into my mind: the impatience that waited at the other end of the line, the empty feeling of messages left unreturned. Most of my appointments were in the evening, home visits, and the people were tired after a full day's work. Sometimes I would arrive only to find that the person had forgotten our appointment, and I'd have to remind him or her of who I was as I was eyed suspiciously from behind a half-opened door.

Still, these were minor difficulties. Once they were overcome, I found that people didn't mind a chance to air their opinions about a do-nothing alderman or the neighbor who refused to mow his lawn. The more interviews I did, the more I began to hear certain recurring themes. I learned, for example, that most of the people in the area had been raised farther north or on Chicago's West Side, in the cramped black enclaves that restrictive covenants had created for most of the city's history. The people I talked to had some fond memories of that self-contained world, but they also remembered the absence of heat and light and space to breathe—that, and the sight of their parents grinding out life in physical labor.

A few had followed their parents into the steel mills or onto the assembly line. But many more had found jobs as mail carriers, bus drivers, teachers, and social workers, taking advantage of the more rigorous enforcement of antidiscrimination laws in the public sector. Such jobs had benefits and provided enough security to think about taking on a mortgage. With the passage of fair housing laws, they began to buy homes, one at a time, in Roseland and other white neighborhoods. Not because they were necessarily interested in mingling with whites, they insisted, but because the houses there were affordable, with small yards for their children; because the schools were better and the stores cheaper, and maybe just because they could.

Often, as I listened to these stories, I would find myself reminded of the stories that Gramps and Toot and my mother had told—stories of hardship and migration, the drive for something better. But there was an inescapable difference between what I was now hearing and what I remembered, as if the images of my childhood had been run in reverse. In these new stories, For Sale signs cropped up like dandelions under a summer sun. Stones flew through windows and the strained voices of anxious parents could be heard calling children indoors from innocent games. Entire blocks turned over in less than six months; entire neighborhoods in less than five years.

In these stories, wherever black and white met, the result was sure to be anger and grief.

The area had never fully recovered from this racial upheaval. The stores and banks had left with their white customers, causing main thoroughfares to decompose. City services had declined. Still, when the blacks who'd now lived in their homes for ten or fifteen years looked back on the way things had turned out, they did so with some measure of satisfaction. On the strength of two incomes, they had paid off house notes and car notes, maybe college educations for the sons or daughters whose graduation pictures filled every mantelpiece. They had kept their homes up and kept their children off the streets; they had formed block clubs to make sure that others did too.

It was when they spoke of the future that a certain disquiet entered their voices. They would mention a cousin or sibling who came by every so often asking for money; or an adult child, unemployed, who still lived at home. Even the success of those children who'd made it through college and into the white-collar world harbored within it an element of loss—the better these children did, the more likely they were to move away. In their place, younger, less stable families moved in, the second wave of migrants from poorer neighborhoods, new-comers who couldn't always afford to keep up with their mortgage payments or invest in periodic maintenance. Car thefts were up; the leafy parks were empty. People began to spend more time inside; they invested in elaborate wrought-iron doors; they wondered if they could afford to sell at a loss and retire to a warmer climate, perhaps move back to the South.

So despite the deserved sense of accomplishment these men and women felt, despite the irrefutable evidence of their own progress, our conversations were marked by another, more ominous strain. The boarded-up homes, the decaying storefronts, the aging church rolls, kids from unknown families who swaggered down the streets— loud congregations of teenage boys, teenage girls feeding potato chips to crying toddlers, the discarded wrappers tumbling down the block—all of it whispered painful truths, told them the progress they'd found was ephemeral, rooted in thin soil; that it might not even last their lifetimes.

And it was this dual sense, of individual advancement and collec-tive decline, that I thought accounted for some of the attitudes agi-tating Will when we'd spoken the night of the rally. I heard it in the excessive pride some of the men took in the well-stocked bars they'd built in their basements, with the lava lamps and the mirrored walls.

In the protective plastic that the women kept over their spotless car-
pets and sofas. In all of it, one saw a determined effort to shore up the
belief that things had in fact changed, if only some people would start
acting right. "I try to avoid driving through Roseland when I can," a
woman from neighboring Washington Heights explained to me one
evening. "People down there are just rougher. You can see it in the
way they keep up their homes. You didn't see things like that when
the white folks still lived there."

Distinctions between neighborhoods, then blocks, then finally
neighbors within a block; attempts to cordon off, control the decay.
One thing I noticed, though. The woman so concerned with the
cruder habits of her neighbors had a picture of Harold in her kitchen,
right next to the sampler of the Twenty-third Psalm. So did the
young man who lived in the crumbling apartment a few blocks away
and was trying to make ends meet by mixing records at dance parties.
As it had for the men in Smitty's barbershop, the election had given
both these people a new idea of themselves. Or maybe it was an old
idea, born of a simpler time. Harold was something they still held in
common: Like my idea of organizing, he held out an offer of collective redemption.

I tossed my third-week report onto Marty's desk and took a seat as he
read it through.

"Not bad," he said when he was finished.

"Not bad?"

"Yeah, not bad. You're starting to listen. But it's still too abstract . . .
like you're taking a survey or something. If you want to organize
people, you need to steer away from the peripheral stuff and go
towards people's centers. The stuff that makes them tick. Otherwise,
you'll never form the relationships you need to get them involved."

The man was starting to get on my nerves. I asked him if he ever
worried about becoming too calculating, if the idea of probing

people's psyches and gaining their trust just to build an organization ever felt manipulative. He sighed.

"I'm not a poet, Barack. I'm an organizer."

What did that mean? I left the office in a foul mood. Later, I had to admit that Marty was right. I still had no idea how I might translate what I was hearing into action. In fact, it wasn't until I came to the end of my interviews that an opportunity seemed to present itself.

It was during a meeting with Ruby Styles, a stocky woman who worked as an office manager on the north side of the city. We had been talking about her teenage son, Kyle, a bright but diffident boy who was starting to have trouble at school, when she mentioned a rise in local gang activity. One of Kyle's friends had been shot just last week, she said, right in front of his house. The boy was all right, but now Ruby was worried about her own son's safety.

My ears perked up; this sounded like self-interest. Over the next few days, I had Ruby introduce me to other parents who shared her fears and felt frustrated over the lackluster police response. When I suggested that we invite the district commander to a neighborhood meeting so the community could air its concerns, everyone agreed; and as we talked about publicity one of the women mentioned that there was a Baptist church on the block where the boy had been shot, and that the pastor there, a Reverend Reynolds, might be willing to make an announcement to his congregation.

It took me a week of phone calls, but when I finally reached Reverend Reynolds, his response seemed promising. He was the president of the local ministerial alliance, he said—"churches coming together to preach the social gospel." He said that the group would be holding its regular meeting the very next day and that he would be happy to put me on the agenda.

I hung up the phone full of excitement, and arrived at Reverend Reynolds's church early the next morning. A pair of young women dressed in white gowns and gloves met me in the foyer and showed me to a large conference room where ten or twelve older black men stood talking in a loose circle. A particularly distinguished-looking gentleman came up to greet me. "You must be Brother Obama," he said, taking my hand. "Reverend Reynolds. You're just in time— we're about to start."

We all sat around a long table, and Reverend Reynolds led us in prayer before offering me the floor. Suppressing my nerves, I told the ministers about the increased gang activity and the meeting we had planned, and passed out flyers for them to distribute in their congregations. "With your leadership," I said, warming up to my subject, "this can be a first step towards cooperation on all kinds of issues. Fixing the schools. Bringing jobs back into the neighborhood . . ."

Just as I passed out the last flyers, a tall, pecan-colored man entered the room. He wore a blue, double-breasted suit and a large gold cross against his scarlet tie. His hair was straightened and swept back in a pompadour.

"Brother Smalls, you just missed an excellent presentation," Reverend Reynolds said. "This young man, Brother Obama, has a plan to organize a meeting about the recent gang shooting."

Reverend Smalls poured himself a cup of coffee and perused the flyer. "What's the name of your organization?" he asked me.

"Developing Communities Project."

"Developing Communities . . ." His brow knotted. "I think I remember some white man coming around talking about some Developing something or other. Funny-looking guy. Jewish name. You connected to the Catholics?"

I told him that some of the Catholic churches in the area were involved.

"That's right, I remember now." Reverend Smalls sipped his coffee and leaned back in his chair. "I told that white man he might as well pack up and get on out of here. We don't need nothing like this around here."

"I—"

"Listen . . . what's your name again? Obamba? Listen, Obamba, you may mean well. I'm sure you do. But the last thing we need is to join up with a bunch of white money and Catholic churches and Jewish organizers to solve our problems. They're not interested in us. Shoot, the archdiocese in this city is run by stone-cold racists. Always has been. White folks come in here thinking they know what's best for us, hiring a buncha high-talking college-educated brothers like yourself who don't know no better, and all they want to do is take over. It's all a political thing, and that's not what this group here is about."

I stammered that the church had always taken the lead in addressing community issues, but Reverend Smalls just shook his head. "You don't understand," he said. "Things have changed with the new mayor. I've known the district police commander since he was a beat cop. The aldermen in this area are all committed to black empowerment. Why we need to be protesting and carrying on at our own people? Anybody sitting around this table got a direct line to City Hall. Fred, didn't you just talk to the alderman about getting that permit for your parking lot?"

The rest of the room had grown quiet. Reverend Reynolds cleared his throat. "The man's new around here, Charles. He's just trying to help."

Reverend Smalls smiled and patted me on the shoulder. "Don't misunderstand me now. Like I said, I know you mean well. We need some young blood to help out with the cause. All I'm saying is that right now you're on the wrong side of the battle."

I sat there, roasting like a pig on a spit, as the pastors went on to discuss a joint Thanksgiving service in the park across the street. When the meeting was over, Reverend Reynolds and a few of the others thanked me for coming.

"Don't take Charles too seriously," one of them advised. "He can be a little strong sometimes." But I noticed that none of them left with my flyers; and later in the week, when I tried to call some of the ministers back, their secretaries kept telling me they were gone for the day.

We went forward with our police meeting, which proved a small disaster. Only thirteen people showed up, scattered across rows of empty chairs. The district commander canceled on us, sending a community relations officer instead. Every few minutes an older couple walked in looking for the Bingo game. I spent most of the evening directing this wayward traffic upstairs, while Ruby sat glumly onstage, listening to the policeman lecture about the need for parental discipline.

About halfway through the meeting, Marty arrived.

After it was over, he came up and put a hand on my shoulder.

"Feels like shit, huh?"

It did. He helped me clean up, then took me out for coffee and pointed out some of my mistakes. The problem of gangs was too general to make an impression on people—issues had to be made concrete, specific, and winnable. I should have prepared Ruby more carefully—and set out fewer chairs. Most important, I needed to spend more time getting to know the leaders in the community; flyers couldn't pull people out on a rainy night.

"That reminds me," he said as we stood up to go. "Whatever happened to those pastors you were supposed to be meeting with?"

I told him about Reverend Smalls. He started to laugh. "Guess it's a good thing I didn't tag along, huh?"

I wasn't amused. "Why didn't you warn me about Smalls?"

"I did warn you," Marty said, opening the door to his car. "I told you Chicago's polarized and that politicians use it to their own advantage. That's all Smalls is—a politician who happens to wear a collar. Anyway, it's not the end of the world. You should just be glad you learned your lesson early."

Yes, but which lesson? Watching Marty drive away, I thought back to the day of the rally: the sound of Smitty's voice in the barbershop; the rows of black and white faces in the school auditorium, there because of the factory's desolation and Marty's own sense of betrayal; the cardinal, a small, pale, unassuming man in a black robe and glasses, smiling onstage as Will swallowed him up in a big bear hug; Will, so certain that the two men understood each other.

Each image carried its own lesson, each was subject to differing interpretations. For there were many churches, many faiths. There were times, perhaps, when those faiths seemed to converge—the crowd in front of the Lincoln Memorial, the Freedom Riders at the lunch counter. But such moments were partial, fragmentary. With our eyes closed, we uttered the same words, but in our hearts we each prayed to our own masters; we each remained locked in our own memories; we all clung to our own foolish magic.

A man like Smalls understood that, I thought. He understood that the men in the barbershop didn't want the victory of Harold's election—their victory—qualified. They wouldn't want to hear that their problems were more complicated than a group of devious white aldermen, or that their redemption was incomplete. Both Marty and Smalls knew that in politics, like religion, power lay in certainty— and that one man's certainty always threatened another's.

I realized then, standing in an empty McDonald's parking lot in the South Side of Chicago, that I was a heretic. Or worse—for even a heretic must believe in something, if nothing more than the truth of his own doubt.

CHAPTER NINE

....

THE ALTGELD GARDENS PUBLIC housing project sat at Chicago's southernmost edge: two thousand apartments arranged in a series of two-story brick buildings with army-green doors and grimy mock shutters. Everybody in the area referred to Altgeld as "the Gardens" for short, although it wasn't until later that I considered the irony of the name, its evocation of something fresh and well tended—a sanctified earth.

True, there was a grove of trees just south of the project, and running south and west of that was the Calumet River, where you could sometimes see men flick fishing lines lazily into darkening waters. But the fish that swam those waters were often strangely discolored, with cataract eyes and lumps behind their gills. People ate their catch only if they had to.

To the east, on the other side of the expressway, was the Lake Calumet landfill, the largest in the Midwest.

And to the north, directly across the street, was the Metropolitan Sanitary District's sewage treatment plant. The people of Altgeld couldn't see the plant or the open-air vats that went on for close to a mile; as part of a recent beautification effort, the district maintained a long wall of earth in front of the facility, dotted with hastily planted saplings that refused to grow month after month, like hairs swept across a bald man's head. But officials could do nothing to hide the smell—a heavy, putrid odor that varied in strength depending on the temperature and the wind's direction, and seeped through windows no matter how tightly they were shut.

The stench, the toxins, the empty, uninhabited landscape. For close to a century, the few square miles surrounding Altgeld had taken in the offal of scores of factories, the price people had paid for their high-wage jobs. Now that the jobs were gone, and those people that could had already left, it seemed only natural to use the land as a dump.

A dump—and a place to house poor blacks. Altgeld may have been unique in its physical isolation, but it shared with the city's other projects a common history: the dreams of reformers to build decent housing for the poor; the politics that had concentrated such housing away from white neighborhoods, and prevented working families from living there; the use of the Chicago Housing Authority—the CHA—as a patronage trough; the subsequent mismanagement and neglect. It wasn't as bad as Chicago's high-rise projects yet, the Robert Taylors and Cabrini Greens, with their ink-black stairwells and urine-stained lobbies and random shootings. Altgeld's occupancy rate held steady at ninety percent, and if you went inside the apartments, you would more often than not find them well-kept, with small touches—a patterned cloth thrown over torn upholstery, an old calendar left hanging on the wall for its tropical beach scenes—that expressed the lingering idea of home.

Still, everything about the Gardens seemed in a perpetual state of disrepair. Ceilings crumbled. Pipes burst. Toilets backed up. Muddy tire tracks branded the small, brown lawns strewn with empty flower planters—broken, tilted, half buried. The CHA maintenance crews had stopped even pretending that repairs would happen any time soon. So that most children in Altgeld grew up without ever having seen a garden. Children who could see only that things were used up, and that there was a certain pleasure in speeding up the decay.

I took the turn into Altgeld at 131st and came to a stop in front of Our Lady of the Gardens Church, a flat brick building toward the rear of the development. I was there to meet some of our key leaders, to talk about the problems in our organizing effort, and how we might get things back on track. But as I cut off the engine and started reaching for my briefcase, something stopped me short. The view, perhaps; the choking gray sky. I closed my eyes and leaned my head against the car seat, feeling like the first mate on a sinking ship.

Over two months had passed since the botched police meeting, and things had gone badly. There had been no marches, no sit-ins, no freedom songs. Just a series of miscues and misunderstandings, tedium and stress. Part of the problem was our base, which—in the city, at least—had never been large: eight Catholic parishes flung across several neighborhoods, all with black congregations but all led by white priests. They were isolated men, these priests, mostly of Polish or Irish descent, men who had entered the seminary in the sixties intending to serve the poor and heal racial wounds but who lacked the zeal of their missionary forefathers; kinder men, perhaps better men, but also softer for their modernity. They had seen their sermons of brotherhood and goodwill trampled under the stampede of white flight, their efforts at recruiting new members met with suspicion by the dark faces—mostly Baptist, Methodist, Pentecostal—now surrounding their churches. Marty had convinced them that organizing would break this isolation, that it would not only stop the neighborhoods' decline but also reenergize their own parishes and rekindle their spirits. That hope had been fragile, though, and by the time I met with them they had already resigned themselves to their disappointments.

"The truth is," one of the priests told me, "most of us out here are looking to get a transfer. The only reason I'm still around is that nobody's willing to replace me."

Morale was even worse among the laity, black folks like Angela, Shirley, and Mona, the three women I'd met at the rally. They were spirited, good-humored women, those three, women who—without husbands to help—somehow managed to raise sons and daughters, juggle an assortment of part-time jobs and small business schemes, and organize Girl Scout troops, fashion shows, and summer camps for the parade of children that wandered through the church every day. Since none of the three actually lived in Altgeld—they all owned small houses just west of the project—I had asked them once what motivated them to do what they did. Before I could finish the question, they had all rolled their eyes as if on cue.

"Watch out, girl," Angela told Shirley, causing Mona to chuckle merrily. "Barack's about to interview you. He's got that look."

And Shirley said, "We're just a bunch of bored middle-aged women, Barack, with nothing better to do with our time. But"—and here Shirley threw a hand onto her bony hip and raised her cigarette to her lips like a movie star—"if Mr. Right comes along, then watch out! It's good-bye Altgeld, hello Monte Carlo!"

I hadn't heard any jokes from them lately, though. All I'd heard were complaints. The women complained that Marty didn't care about Altgeld. They complained that Marty was arrogant and didn't listen to their suggestions.

Most of all, they complained about the new job bank that we had announced with such fanfare the night of the rally, but that had turned out to be a bust. As Marty had planned it, a state university out in the suburbs had been assigned to run the program—it was a matter of efficiency, he explained, since the university had the computers already in place. Unfortunately, two months after it was supposed to have started, no one had found work through the program. The computers didn't work right; the data entry was plagued with errors; people were sent to interview for jobs that didn't exist. Marty was livid, and at least once a week he would have to drive out to the university, cursing under his breath as he tried to pry answers out of officials who seemed more concerned with next year's funding cycle. But the women from Altgeld weren't interested in Marty's frustrations. All they knew was that $500,000 had gone somewhere, and it wasn't in their neighborhood. For them, the job bank became yet more evidence that Marty had used them to push a secret agenda, that somehow whites in the suburbs were getting the jobs they'd been promised.

"Marty's just looking out for his own," they grumbled.

I had tried my best to mediate the conflict, defending Marty against charges of racism, suggesting to him that he cultivate more tact. Marty told me I was wasting my time. According to him, the only reason Angela and the other leaders in the city were sore was because he'd refused to hire them to run the program. "That's what ruins a lot of so-called community organizations out here. They start taking government money. They hire big, do-nothing staffs. Pretty soon, they've become big patronage operations, with clients to be serviced. Not leaders. *Clients*. To be *serviced*." He spit the words out, as if they were unclean. "Jesus, it makes you sick just thinking about it."

And then, seeing the still-fretful look on my face, he added, "If you're going to do this work, Barack, you've got to stop worrying about whether people like you. They won't."

Patronage, politics, hurt feelings, racial grievances—they were all of a piece to Marty, distractions from his larger purpose, corruptions of a noble cause. He was still trying to bring the union in then, convinced that they would replenish our ranks, deliver our ship to shore. One day in late September, he had asked Angela and me to join him at a meeting with union officials from LTV Steel, one of the few remaining steel operations in the city. It had taken Marty over a month to set up the meeting, and he was brimming with energy that day, talking at a rapid clip about the company, the union, and new phases in the organizing campaign.

Eventually the president of the local—a young, handsome Irishman who'd been recently elected on a promise of reform—entered the hall, along with two husky black men, the union treasurer and vice-president. After the introductions, we all sat down and Marty made his pitch. The corporation was preparing to get out of the steelmaking business, he said, and wage concessions would only prolong the agony. If the union wanted to preserve jobs, it had to take some new, bold steps. Sit down with the churches and develop a plan for a worker buyout. Negotiate with the city for concessionary utility and tax rates during the transition. Pressure the banks to provide loans that could be used to invest in the new technology needed to make the plant competitive again.

Throughout the monologue, the union officials shifted uneasily in their chairs. Finally the president stood up and told Marty that his ideas merited further study but that right now the union had to focus on making an immediate decision about management's offer. In the parking lot afterward, Marty looked stunned.

"They're not interested," he told me, shaking his head. "Like a bunch of lemmings running towards a cliff."

I had felt bad for Marty. I had felt worse for Angela. She hadn't said a word throughout the entire meeting, but as I pulled out of the union parking lot to drive her home, she had turned to me and said, "I didn't understand a word Marty was saying."

And I suppose it was then that I understood the difficulty of what Marty had tried to pull off, and the depth of his miscalculation. It wasn't so much that Angela had missed some of the details of Marty's presentation; as we continued to talk, it had become apparent that she understood Marty's proposal at least as well as I did. No, the real meaning of her remark was this: She had come to doubt the relevance to her own situation of keeping the LTV plant open. Organizing with the unions might help the few blacks who remained in the plants keep their jobs; it wouldn't dent the rolls of the chronically unemployed any time soon. A job bank might help workers who already had skills and experience find something else; it wouldn't teach the black teenage dropout how to read or compute.

In other words, it was different for black folks. It was different now, just as it had been different for Angela's grandparents, who'd been barred from the unions, then spat on as scabs; for her parents, who had been kept out of the best patronage jobs that the Machine had to offer in the days before *patronage* became a dirty word. In his eagerness to do battle with the downtown power brokers, the investment bankers in their fancy suits, Marty wanted to wish such differences away as part of an unfortunate past. But for someone like Angela, the past *was* the present; it determined her world with a force infinitely more real than any notions of class solidarity. It explained why more blacks hadn't been able to move out into the suburbs while the going was still good, why more blacks hadn't climbed up the ladder into the American dream. It explained why the unemployment in black neighborhoods was more widespread and longstanding, more desperate; and why Angela had no patience with those who wanted to treat black people and white people exactly the same.

It explained Altgeld.

I looked at my watch: ten past two. Time to face the music. I got out of my car and rang the church doorbell. Angela answered, and led me into a room where the other leaders were waiting: Shirley, Mona, Will, and Mary, a quiet, dark-haired white woman who taught elementary school at St. Catherine's. I apologized for being late and poured myself some coffee.

"So," I said, taking a seat on the windowsill. "Why all the long faces?"

"We're quitting," Angela said.

"Who's quitting?"

Angela shrugged. "Well . . . I am, I guess. I can't speak for everybody else."

I looked around the room. The other leaders averted their eyes, like a jury that's delivered an unfavorable verdict.

"I'm sorry, Barack," Angela continued. "It has nothing to do with you. The truth is, we're just tired. We've all been at this for two years, and we've got nothing to show for it."

"I understand you're frustrated, Angela. We're all a little frustrated. But you need to give it more time. We—"

"We don't have more time," Shirley broke in. "We can't keep on making promises to our people, and then have nothing happen. We need something *now*."

I fidgeted with my coffee cup, trying to think of something else to say. Words jumbled up in my head, and for a moment I was gripped with panic. Then the panic gave way to anger. Anger at Marty for talking me into coming to Chicago. Anger at the leaders for being short-sighted. Anger at myself for believing I could have ever bridged the gap between them. I suddenly remembered what Frank had told me that night back in Hawaii, after I had heard that Toot was scared of a black man.

That's the way it is, he had said. You might as well get used to it.

In this peevish mood, I looked out the window and saw a group of young boys gathered across the street. They were tossing stones at the boarded-up window of a vacant apartment, their hoods pulled over their heads like miniature monks. One of the boys reached up and started yanking at a loose piece of plywood nailed across the apartment door, then stumbled and fell, causing the others to laugh. A part of me suddenly felt like joining them, tearing apart the whole dying landscape, piece by piece. Instead, I turned back toward Angela.

"Let me ask you something," I said, pointing out the window. "What do you suppose is going to happen to those boys out there?"

"Barack . . ."

"No, I'm just asking you a question. You say you're tired, the same way most folks out here are tired. So I'm just trying to figure out what's going to happen to those boys. Who's going to make sure they get a fair shot? The alderman? The social workers? The gangs?"

I could hear my voice rising, but I didn't let up. "You know, I didn't come here 'cause I needed a job. I came here 'cause Marty said there were some people who were serious about doing something to change their neighborhoods. I don't care what's happened in the past. I know that I'm here, and committed to working with you. If there's a problem, then we'll fix it. If you don't think anything's happened after working with me, then I'll be the first one to tell you to quit. But if you all are planning to quit now, then I want you to answer my question."

I stopped there, trying to read each of their faces. They seemed surprised at my outburst, though none of them was as surprised as me. I knew I was on precarious ground; I wasn't close enough to any of them to be sure my play wouldn't backfire. At that particular moment, though, I had no other hand to play. The boys outside moved on down the street. Shirley went to get herself more coffee. After what seemed like ten minutes, Will finally spoke up.

"I don't know about the rest of you, but I think we've talked about this same old mess long enough. Marty knows we got problems. That's why he hired Barack. Ain't that right, Barack?"

I nodded cautiously.

"Things still bad out here. Ain't nothing gone away. So what *I* wanna know," he said, turning to me, "is what we gonna do from here on out."

I told him the truth. "I don't know, Will. You tell me."

Will smiled, and I sensed that the immediate crisis had passed. Angela agreed to give it another few months. I agreed to concentrate more time on Altgeld. We spent the next half hour talking strategy and handing out assignments. On our way out, Mona came up and took me by the arm.

"You handled that meeting pretty good, Barack. Seems like you know what you're doing."

"I don't, Mona. I don't have a clue."

She laughed. "Well, I promise I won't tell nobody."

"I appreciate that, Mona. I sure do appreciate that."

That evening, I called Marty and told him some of what had happened. He wasn't surprised: several of the suburban churches were already starting to drop out. He gave me a few suggestions for approaching the job issue in Altgeld, then advised me to pick up the pace of my interviews.

"You're going to need to find some new leaders, Barack. I mean, Will's a terrific guy and all that, but do you really want to depend on him to keep the organization afloat?"

I understood Marty's point. As much as I liked Will, as much as I appreciated his support, I had to admit that some of his ideas were . . . well, eccentric. He liked to smoke reefer at the end of a day's work ("If God didn't want us to smoke the stuff, he wouldn't have put it on this here earth"). He would walk out of any meeting that he decided was boring. Whenever I took him along to interview members of his church, he'd start arguing with them about their incorrect reading of Scripture, their choice of lawn fertilizer, or the constitutionality of the income tax (he felt that tax violated the Bill of Rights, and conscientiously refused to pay).

"Maybe if you listened to other people a little more," I had told him once, "they'd be more responsive."

Will had shaken his head. "I *do* listen. That's the problem. Everything they say is wrong."

Now, after the meeting in Altgeld, Will had a new idea. "These mixed-up Negroes inside St. Catherine's ain't never gonna do nothing," he said. "If we wanna get something done, we gonna have to take it to the streets!" He pointed out that many of the people who lived

in the immediate vicinity of St. Catherine's were jobless and struggling; those were the people we should be targeting, he said. And
because they might not feel comfortable attending a meeting hosted
by a foreign church, we should conduct a series of street corner meetings around West Pullman, allowing them to gather on neutral turf.

I was skeptical at first, but unwilling as I was to discourage any initiative, I helped Will and Mary prepare a flyer, for distribution along
the block closest to the church. A week later, the three of us stood out
on the corner in the late autumn wind. The street remained empty at
first, the shades drawn down the rows of brick bungalows. Then,
slowly, people began to emerge, one or two at a time, women in hair
nets, men in flannel shirts or windbreakers, shuffling through the
brittle gold leaves, edging toward the growing circle. When the gathering numbered twenty or so, Will explained that St. Catherine's was
part of a larger organizing effort and that "we want you to talk to
your neighbors about all the things y'all complain about when you're
sitting at the kitchen table."

"Well, all I can say is, it's about time," one woman said.

For almost an hour, people talked about potholes and sewers, stop
signs and abandoned lots. As the afternoon fell to dusk, Will
announced that we'd be moving the meetings to St. Catherine's basement starting the following month. Walking back to the church, I
heard the crowd still behind us, a murmur in the fading light. Will
turned to me and smiled.

"Told you."

We repeated these street corner meetings on three, four, five
blocks—Will at the center with his priest's collar and Chicago Cubs
jacket, Mary with her sign-in sheets circling the edges of the crowd.
By the time we moved the meetings indoors, we had a group of close
to thirty people, prepared to work for little more than a cup of coffee.

It was before such a meeting that I found Mary alone in the

church hall, making a pot of coffee. The evening's agenda was neatly printed on a sheet of butcher's paper taped to the wall; the chairs were all set up. Mary waved at me while searching a cupboard for sugar and creamer, and told me Will was running a little late.

"Need any help?" I asked her.

"Can you reach this?"

I pulled down the sugar from the top shelf. "Anything else?"

"No. I think we're all set."

I took a seat and watched Mary finish arranging the cups. She was a hard person to know, Mary was; she didn't like to talk much, about herself or her past. I knew that she was the only white person from the city who worked with us, one of maybe five white people left in West Pullman. I knew that she had two daughters, one ten and one twelve; the younger one had a disability that made walking difficult and required regular therapy.

And I knew that the father was absent, although Mary never mentioned him. Only in bits and pieces, over the course of many months, would I learn that she had grown up in a small Indiana town, part of a big, working-class Irish family. Somehow she had met a black man there; they had dated secretly, were married; her family refused to speak to her again, and the newlyweds moved to West Pullman, where they bought a small house. Then the man left, and Mary found herself beached in a world she knew little of, without anything but the house and two manila-hued daughters, unable to return to the world she had known.

Sometimes I would stop by Mary's house just to say hello, drawn perhaps by the loneliness I sensed there, and the easy parallels between my own mother and Mary; and between myself and Mary's daughters, such sweet and pretty girls whose lives were so much more difficult than mine had ever been, with grandparents who shunned them, black classmates who teased them, all the poison in the air. Not that the family had no support; after Mary's husband left, the neighbors had shown her and her children solicitude, helping them fix a leaky roof, inviting them to barbecues and birthday parties, commending Mary on all her good works. Still, there were limits to how far the neighbors could accept the family, unspoken boundaries to the friendships that Mary could make with the women—specially the married ones—that she met. Her only real friends were her daughters—and now Will, whose own fall, and idiosyncratic faith, gave them something private to share.

With nothing left to do for the meeting, Mary sat down and watched me scribble some last-minute notes to myself.

"Do you mind if I ask you something, Barack?"

"No, go ahead."

"Why are you here? Doing this work, I mean."

"For the glamour."

"No, I'm serious. You said yourself you don't need this job. And you're not very religious, are you?"

"Well . . ."

"So why do you do it? That's why Will and I do this, you know. Because it's part of our faith. But with you, I don't—"

At that moment, the door opened and Mr. Green walked in. He was an older man in a hunting jacket and a cap whose earflaps hung stiffly against his chin.

"How you doing, Mr. Green."

"Fine, just fine. Getting chilly, though. . . ."

Mrs. Turner and Mr. Albert quickly followed, then the rest of the group, all bundled up against the hint of an early winter. They unbuttoned their coats, prepared coffee for themselves, and engaged in the small, unhurried talk that helped warm up the room. Finally Will walked in wearing cut-off jeans and a red T-shirt with "Deacon Will" across the front, and after asking Mrs. Jeffrey to lead us in prayer, he started the meeting. While everyone talked, I took notes to myself, speaking up only when things started to wander. In fact, I thought the meeting had already dragged on too long—a few people had slipped out after an hour—when Will added a new item to the agenda.

"Before we adjourn," he announced, "I want us to try something out. This here's a church-based organization, and that means we devote a part of each meeting to reflection on ourselves, our relationships to each other, and our relationship to God. So I want everybody to take out just a minute to think about what brought them here tonight, some thoughts or feelings that you haven't talked about, and then I want you to share 'em with the group."

Will let the silence build for several minutes. "Anybody want to share their thoughts?" he repeated.

People looked down at the table uncomfortably.

"Okay," Will said. "I'll share something that's been on my mind for a while. Nothing big—just memories. You know, my folks weren't rich or nothing. We lived out in Altgeld. But when I think back on my own childhood, I remember some really good times. I remember going to Blackburn Forest with my folks to pick wild berries. I remember making skating carts with my cut buddies out of empty fruit crates and old roller skate wheels and racing around the parking lot. I remember going on field trips at school, and on the holidays meeting all the families in the park, everybody out and nobody scared, and then in the summers sleeping out in the yard together if it got too hot inside. A lot of good memories . . . seemed like I was smiling all the time, laughing—"

Will broke off suddenly and bowed his head. I thought he was preparing to sneeze, but when he raised his head back up, I saw tears rolling down his cheeks. He continued in a cracking voice, "And you know, I don't see kids smiling around here no more. You look at 'em listen to 'em . . . they seem worried all the time, mad about something. They got nothing they trust. Not their parents. Not God. Not themselves. And that's not right. That just ain't the way things supposed to be . . . kids not smiling."

He stopped again and pulled a handkerchief from his hip pocket to blow his nose. Then, as if the sight of this big man weeping had watered the dry surface of their hearts, the others in the room began speaking about their own memories in solemn, urgent tones. They talked about life in small Southern towns: the corner stores where men had gathered to learn the news of the day or lend a hand to women with their groceries, the way adults looked after each other's children ("Couldn't get away with nothing, 'cause your momma had eyes and ears up and down the whole block"), the sense of public decorum that such familiarity had helped sustain. In their voices was no little bit of nostalgia, elements of selective memory; but the whole of what they recalled rang vivid and true, the sound of shared loss. A feeling of witness, of frustration and hope, moved about the room from mouth to mouth, and when the last person had spoken, it hovered in the air, static and palpable. Then we all joined hands, Mr. Green's thick, callused hand in my left, Mrs. Turner's, slight and papery to the touch, in my right, and together we asked for the courage to turn things around.

I helped Will and Mary put back the chairs, rinse out the coffee pot, lock up, and turn off the lights. Outside, the night was cold and clear. I turned up my collar and quickly evaluated the meeting: Will needed to watch the time; we had to research the issue of city services before the next meeting and interview everyone who had come. At the end of my checklist, I put my arm around Will's shoulders.

"That reflection at the end was pretty powerful, Will."

He looked at Mary and they both smiled. "We noticed you didn't share anything with the group," Mary said.

"The organizer's supposed to keep a low profile."

"Who says?"

"It's in my organizer's handbook. Come on, Mary, I'll give you a ride home."

Will mounted his bike and waved good-bye, and Mary and I drove the four blocks to her house. I let her out in front of her door and watched her take a few steps before I stretched across the passenger seat and rolled down the window.

"Hey, Mary."

She came back and bent down to look at me.

"You know what you were asking before. About why I do this. It had something to do with the meeting tonight. I mean . . . I don't think our reasons are all that different."

She nodded, and walked up the path to her daughters.

A week later, I was back out in Altgeld, trying to stuff Angela, Mona, and Shirley into my subcompact car. Mona, who was sitting in the back, complained about the lack of room.

"What kinda car is this anyway?" she asked.

Shirley moved her seat up. "It's built for the skinny little girls Barack goes out with."

"Who are we meeting with again?"

I had scheduled three meetings, hoping to find a job strategy that would meet the needs of people in Altgeld. For now at least a new manufacturing boom appeared out of our reach: The big manufacturers had opted for well-scrubbed suburban corridors, and not even Gandhi could have gotten them to relocate near Altgeld anytime soon. On the other hand, there did remain a part of the economy that could be called local, I thought, a second-level consumer economy—of shops, restaurants, theaters, and services—that in other areas of the city continued to function as an incubator of civic life. Places where families might invest their savings and make a go of a business, and where entry-level jobs might be had; places where the economy remained on a human scale, transparent enough for people to understand.

The closest thing to a shopping district in the area was in Roseland, and so we followed the bus route up Michigan Avenue, with its wig shops and liquor stores, discount clothing stores and pizzerias, until we arrived in front of a two-story former warehouse. We entered the building through a heavy metal door and took a narrow set of stairs down into a basement filled with old furniture. In a small office sat a slight, wiry man with a goatee and a skullcap that accentuated a pair of prominent ears.

"Can I help you?"

I explained who we were and that we had spoken on the phone.

"That's right, that's right." He gestured to two large men standing on either side of his desk and they walked past us with a nod. "Listen, we're gonna have to make this quick 'cause something's come up. Rafiq al Shabazz."

"I know you," Shirley said as we shook hands with Rafiq. "You're Mrs. Thompson's boy, Wally. How's your momma doing?"

Rafiq forced a smile and offered us all a seat. He explained that he was the president of the Roseland Unity Coalition, an organization that engaged in a range of political activities to promote the black cause and claimed considerable credit for helping Mayor Washington get elected. When we asked him how our churches could encourage local economic development, he handed us a leaflet accusing Arab stores of selling bad meat.

"That's the real deal, right here," Rafiq said. "People from outside our community making money off us and showing our brothers and sisters disrespect. Basically what you got here is Koreans and Arabs running the stores, the Jews still owning most of the buildings. Now, in the short term, we're here to make sure that the interests of black people are looked after, you understand. When we hear one of them Koreans is mistreating a customer, we gonna be on the case. We gonna insist that they respect us and make a contribution back to the community—fund our programs, what have you.

"That's the short term. This"—Rafiq pointed to a map of Roseland that hung on the wall, with certain areas marked off in red ink—"is the long term. It's all about ownership. A comprehensive plan for the area. Black businesses, community centers—the whole nine yards. Some of

the properties, we've already started negotiating with the white own-
ers to sell them to us at a fair price. So if y'all are interested in jobs,
then you can help by spreading the message about this here plan. The
problem we got right now is not enough support from the folks in
Roseland. Instead of taking a stand, they'd rather follow white folks out
into the suburbs. But see, white folks ain't stupid. They just waiting for
us to move out of the city so they can come back, 'cause they know that
the value of the property we sitting on right now is worth a mint."

One of the burly men reentered Rafiq's office, and Rafiq stood up.
"I gotta get going," he said abruptly. "But hey, we'll talk again." He
shook all our hands before his assistant led us to the door.

"Sounds like you knew him, Shirley," I said once we were out of
the building.

"Yeah, before he got that fancy name of his, he was plain old Wally
Thompson. He can change his name but he can't hide them ears he's
got. He grew up in Altgeld—in fact, I think him and Will used to be
in school together. Wally was a big-time gang-banger before he
became a Muslim."

"Once a thug, always a thug," Angela said.

Our next stop was the local Chamber of Commerce, located on
the second floor of what looked like a pawnshop. Inside, we found a
plump black man who was busy packing boxes.

"We're looking for Mr. Foster," I said to the man.

"I'm Foster," he said, not looking up.

"We were told that you were the president of the Chamber—"

"Well, you right about that. I *was* the president. Just resigned last
week."

He offered us three chairs and talked as he worked. He explained
that he had owned the stationery store down the street for fifteen
years now, had been the president of the Chamber for the last five.
He had done his best to organize the local merchants, but lack of
support had finally left him discouraged.

"You won't hear me complaining about the Koreans," he said, stacking a few boxes by the door. "They're the only ones that pay their dues into the Chamber. They understand business, what it means to cooperate. They pool their money. Make each other loans. We don't do that, see. The black merchants around here, we're all like crabs in a bucket." He straightened up and wiped his brow with a handkerchief. "I don't know. Maybe you can't blame us for being the way we are. All those years without opportunity, you have to figure it took something out of us. And it's tougher now than it was for the Italian or the Jew thirty years ago. These days, a small store like mine has to compete against the big chains. It's a losing battle unless you do like these Koreans—work your family sixteen hours a day, seven days a week. As a people, we're not willing to do that anymore. I guess we worked so long for nothing, we feel like we shouldn't have to break our backs just to survive. That's what we tell our children anyway. I can't say I'm any different. I tell my sons I don't want them taking over the business. I want them to go work for some big company where they can be comfortable. . . ."

Before we left, Angela asked about the possibility of part-time work for the youth in Altgeld. Mr. Foster looked up at her like she was crazy.

"Every merchant around here turns down thirty applications a day," he said. "Adults. Senior citizens. Experienced workers willing to take whatever they can get. I'm sorry."

As we walked back to the car, we passed a small clothing store full of cheap dresses and brightly colored sweaters, two aging white mannequins now painted black in the window. The store was poorly lit, but toward the back I could make out the figure of a young Korean woman sewing by hand as a child slept beside her. The scene took me back to my childhood, back to the markets of Indonesia: the hawkers, the leather workers, the old women chewing betelnut and swatting flies off their fruit with whisk brooms.

I'd always taken such markets for granted, part of the natural order of things. Now, though, as I thought about Altgeld and Roseland, Rafiq and Mr. Foster, I saw those Djakarta markets for what they were: fragile, precious things. The people who sold their goods there might have been poor, poorer even than folks out in Altgeld. They hauled fifty pounds of firewood on their backs every day, they ate little, they died young. And yet for all that poverty, there remained in their lives a discernible order, a tapestry of trading routes and middlemen, bribes to pay and customs to observe, the habits of a generation played out every day beneath the bargaining and the noise and the swirling dust.

It was the absence of such coherence that made a place like Altgeld so desperate, I thought to myself; it was that loss of order that had made both Rafiq and Mr. Foster, in their own ways, so bitter. For how could we go about stitching a culture back together once it was torn? How long might it take in this land of dollars?

Longer than it took a culture to unravel, I suspected. I tried to imagine the Indonesian workers who were now making their way to the sorts of factories that had once sat along the banks of the Calumet River, joining the ranks of wage labor to assemble the radios and sneakers that sold on Michigan Avenue. I imagined those same Indonesian workers ten, twenty years from now, when their factories would have closed down, a consequence of new technology or lower wages in some other part of the globe. And then the bitter discovery that their markets have vanished; that they no longer remember how to weave their own baskets or carve their own furniture or grow their own food; that even if they remember such craft, the forests that gave them wood are now owned by timber interests, the baskets they once wove have been replaced by more durable plastics. The very existence of the factories, the timber interests, the plastics manufacturer, will have rendered their culture obsolete; the values of hard work and individual initiative turn out to have depended on a system of belief that's been scrambled by migration and urbanization and imported TV reruns. Some of them would prosper in this new order. Some would move to America. And the others, the millions left behind in Djakarta, or Lagos, or the West Bank, they would settle into their own Altgeld Gardens, into a deeper despair.

We drove in silence to our final meeting, with the administrator of a local branch of the Mayor's Office of Employment and Training, or MET, which helped refer the unemployed to training programs throughout the city. We had trouble finding the place—it turned out to be a forty-five-minute drive from Altgeld, on a back street in Vrdolyak's ward—and by the time we arrived the administrator was gone. Her assistant didn't know when she would be back but handed us a pile of glossy brochures.

"This ain't no help at all," Shirley said as she started for the door. "We might as well have stayed home."

Mona noticed I was lingering in the office. "What's he looking at?" she asked Angela.

I showed them the back of one of the brochures. It contained a list of all the MET programs in the city. None of them were south of Ninety-fifth.

"This is it," I said.

"What?"

"We just found ourselves an issue."

As soon as we got back to the Gardens, we drafted a letter to Ms. Cynthia Alvarez, the city-wide director of MET. Two weeks later, she agreed to meet with us out in the Gardens. Determined not to repeat my mistakes, I drove both myself and the leadership to exhaustion: preparing a script for the meeting, pushing hard for the other churches to send their people, developing a clear demand—a job intake and training center in the Far South Side—that we thought MET could deliver.

Two weeks of preparation and yet, the night of the meeting, my stomach was tied up in knots. At six forty-five only three people had shown up: a young woman with a baby who was drooling onto her tiny jumper, an older woman who carefully folded a stack of cookies into a napkin that she then stuffed into her purse, and a drunken man who immediately slouched into a light slumber in a back-row seat. As the minutes ticked away, I imagined once again the empty chairs, the official's change of mind at the last minute, the look of disappointment on the leadership's faces—the deathly smell of failure.

Then, at two minutes before seven, people began to trickle in. Will and Mary brought a group from West Pullman; then Shirley's children and grandchildren walked in, filling up an entire row of seats; then other Altgeld residents who owed Angela or Shirley or Mona a favor. There were close to a hundred people in the room by the time Ms. Alvarez showed up—a large imperious, Mexican-American woman with two young white men in suits trailing behind her.

"I didn't even know this was out here," I heard one of the aides whisper to the other as they walked through the door. I asked him if I could take his coat, and he shook his head nervously.

"No, no . . . I'll, uh . . . I'll just hang on to mine, thanks."

The leadership acquitted themselves well that night. Angela laid out the issue for the crowd and explained to Ms. Alvarez what we expected from her. When Ms. Alvarez avoided giving a definite response, Mona jumped in and pushed for a yes-or-no answer. And when Ms. Alvarez finally promised to have a MET intake center in the area within six months, the crowd broke into hearty applause. The only glitch came about halfway through the meeting, when the drunk in the back stood up and began shouting that he needed a job. Immediately, Shirley walked over to the man and whispered something in his ear that caused him to drop back into his seat.

"What did you tell him?" I asked Shirley later.

"You're too young to know."

The meeting was over in an hour—Ms. Alvarez and her aides sped off in a big blue car, and people went up to shake Mona's and Angela's hands. In the evaluation, the women were all smiles.

"You did a terrific job, Barack," Angela said, giving me a big hug.

"Hey, didn't I promise we were gonna make something happen?"

"He sure enough did," Mona said with a wink.

I told them that I'd leave them alone for at least a couple of days, and went out to my car feeling slightly light-headed. I can do this job, I said to myself. Have this whole damn town organized by the time we're through. I lit a cigarette and, in my self-congratulatory mood, imagined taking the leadership downtown to sit down with Harold and discuss the fate of the city. Then, under a streetlight a few feet away, I saw the drunk from the meeting spinning around in slow circles, looking down at his elongated shadow. I got out of my car and asked him if he needed some help getting home.

"I don't need no help!" he shouted, trying to steady himself "Not from nobody, you understand me! Punk-ass motherfucker . . . try to tell me shit . . ."

His voice trailed off. Before I could say anything more, he turned and began to wobble down the center of the road, disappearing into the darkness.

CHAPTER TEN

....

Winter came and the city turned monochrome—black trees against gray sky above white earth. Night now fell in midafternoon, especially when the snowstorms rolled in, boundless prairie storms that set the sky close to the ground, the city lights reflected against the clouds.

The work was tougher in such weather. Mounds of fine white powder blew through the cracks of my car, down my collar and into the openings in my coat. On rounds of interviews, I never spent enough time in one place to thaw properly, and parking spaces became scarce on the snow-narrowed streets—everyone, it seemed, had a cautionary tale about fights breaking out over parking spaces after a heavy snow, the resulting brawl or shooting. Attendance at evening meetings became more sporadic; people called at the last minute to say they had the flu or their car wouldn't start; those who did come looked damp and resentful. At times, driving home from such evenings, with the northern gusts off the lake shaking my car across the lane dividers, I would momentarily forget where I was, my thoughts a numbed reflection of the silence.

Marty suggested that I take more time off, build a life for myself away from the job. His concerns were professional, he explained:

Without some personal support outside the work, an organizer lost perspective and could quickly burn out. There was something to what he said, for it was true that the people I met on the job were generally much older than me, with a set of concerns and demands that created barriers to friendship. When I wasn't working, the weekends would usually find me alone in an empty apartment, making do with the company of books.

I didn't heed Marty's advice, though, perhaps because, as the bonds between myself and the leadership grew stronger, I found them offering more than simple friendship. After meetings, I might go with one of the men to a local tavern to watch the news or listen to oldies—the Temptations, the O'Jays—thump from a dinged-up corner jukebox. On Sunday, I'd visit the various church services and let the women tease me over my confusion with communion and prayer. At a Christmas party in the Gardens, I danced with Angela, Mona, and Shirley under a globe that sent sparkling beads across the room; I swapped sports stories over stale cheese puffs and meatballs with husbands who had been reluctantly dragged to the affair; I counseled sons or daughters on their college applications, and played with grandchildren who sat on my knee.

It was during such times, when familiarity or weariness dissolved the lines between organizer and leader, that I began to understand what Marty had meant when he insisted that I move toward the centers of people's lives. I remember, for instance, sitting in Mrs. Crenshaw's kitchen one afternoon, gulping down the burned cookies she liked to force on me every time I stopped by. It was getting late, the purpose of my visit had begun to blur in my head, and almost as an afterthought I decided to ask her why she still participated in the PTA so long after her own children had grown. Scooting her chair up closer to mine, she started to tell me about growing up in Tennessee, how she'd been forced to stop her own education because her family could afford to send only one child to college, a brother who would later die in World War II. Both she and her husband had spent years working in a factory, she said, just to see to it that their own son never had to stop his education—a son who had gone on to get a law degree from Yale.

A simple enough story to understand, I thought: the generational sacrifice, the vindication of a family's faith. Only, when I asked Mrs. Crenshaw what her son was doing these days, she went on to tell me that he had been diagnosed with schizophrenia a few years earlier and that he now spent his days reading newspapers in his room, afraid to leave the house. As she spoke, her voice never wavered; it was the voice of someone who has forced a larger meaning out of tragedy.

Or there was the time that I found myself sitting in the St. Helena's basement with Mrs. Stevens waiting for a meeting to start. I didn't know Mrs. Stevens well, knew only that she was interested in renovating the local hospital. By way of small talk I asked her why she was so concerned with improving health care in the area; her family seemed healthy enough. And she told me how, in her twenties, she had almost lost her sight from cataracts. She had been working as a secretary at the time, and although her condition grew so bad her doctor declared her legally blind, she had kept her ailment from her boss for fear of being fired. Day after day, she had snuck off to the bathroom to read her boss's memos with a magnifying glass, memorizing each line before she went back to type, staying at the office long after the others had left to finish the reports that needed to be ready the following morning. In this way she had maintained her secret for close to a year, until she finally saved enough money for an operation.

Or there was Mr. Marshall, a single man in his early thirties who worked as a bus driver for the Transit Authority. He was not typical of the leadership—he had no children, lived in an apartment—and so I wondered why he was so interested in doing something about drug use among teenagers. When I offered to give him a ride one day to pick up a car he had left in the shop, I asked him the question. And he told me about his father's dreams of wealth in a nowhere town in Arkansas; how the various business ventures had gone sour and how other men had cheated him; how his father had turned to gambling and drink, lost his home and family; how his father was finally pulled out of a ditch somewhere, suffocated in his own vomit.

That's what the leadership was teaching me, day by day: that the self-interest I was supposed to be looking for extended well beyond the immediacy of issues, that beneath the small talk and sketchy biographies and received opinions people carried within them some central explanation of themselves. Stories full of terror and wonder, studded with events that still haunted or inspired them. Sacred stories.

And it was this realization, I think, that finally allowed me to share more of myself with the people I was working with, to break out of the larger isolation that I had carried with me to Chicago. I was tentative at first, afraid that my prior life would be too foreign for South Side sensibilities; that I might somehow disturb people's expectations of me. Instead, as people listened to my stories of Toot or Lolo or my mother and father, of flying kites in Djakarta or going to school dances at Punahou, they would nod their heads or shrug or laugh, wondering how someone with my background had ended up, as Mona put it, so "country-fied," or, most puzzling to them, why anyone would willingly choose to spend a winter in Chicago when he could be sunning himself on Waikiki Beach. Then they'd offer a story to match or confound mine, a knot to bind our experiences together—a lost father, an adolescent brush with crime, a wandering heart, a moment of simple grace. As time passed, I found that these stories, taken together, had helped me bind my world together, that they gave me the sense of place and purpose I'd been looking for. Marty was right: There was always a community there if you dug deep enough. He was wrong, though, in characterizing the work. There was poetry as well—a luminous world always present beneath the surface, a world that people might offer up as a gift to me, if I only remembered to ask.

Not to say that everything I learned from the leaders cheered my heart. If they often revealed a strength of spirit that I hadn't imagined, they also forced me to acknowledge the unspoken forces that retarded our efforts, secrets that we kept from each other as well as from ourselves.

That's how it was with Ruby, for example. After our aborted meeting with the police commander, I had worried that she might back away from organizing. Instead, she had thrown herself headlong into the project, working hard to build a network of neighbors that could be regularly delivered to our events, coming up with ideas for registering voters or working with school parents. She was what every organizer dreamed about—someone with untapped talent, smart, steady, excited by the idea of a public life, eager to learn. And I liked her son, Kyle Jr. He had just turned fourteen, and in all of his awkwardness— one moment frisky and bumping into me while we shot baskets together in the neighborhood park, the next instant bored and sullen— I could see all the contours of my own youthful struggles. Sometimes Ruby would question me about him, exasperated with a mediocre report card or a cut on his chin, baffled by a young man's unruly mind.

"Last week he said he was going to be a rap artist," she would report. "Today he tells me he's going to the Air Force Academy to be a fighter pilot. When I ask him why, he just says 'So I can fly.' Like I was stupid. I swear, Barack, sometimes I don't know whether to hug him or beat his skinny behind."

"Try both," I would tell her.

One day just before Christmas, I asked Ruby to stop by my office so I could give her a present for Kyle. I was on the phone when she walked in, and out of the corner of my eye I thought I saw something different about her, but I couldn't quite put my finger on what it was. Only after I had hung up and she turned toward me did I realize that her eyes, normally a warm, dark brown that matched the color of her skin, had turned an opaque shade of blue, as if someone had glued plastic buttons over her irises. She asked me if something was wrong.

"What did you do to your eyes?"

"Oh, *these.*" Ruby shook her head and laughed. "They're just contacts, Barack. The company I work for makes cosmetic lenses, and I get them at a discount. You like them?"

"Your eyes looked just fine the way they were."

"It's just for fun," she said, looking down. "Something different, you know."

I stood there, not knowing what to say. Finally I remembered Kyle's gift and handed it to her. "For Kyle," I said. "A book on airplanes . . . I thought he might like it."

Ruby nodded and put the book inside her purse. "That's nice of you, Barack. I'm sure he will." Then, abruptly, she stood up and straightened her skirt. "Well, I better get going," she said, and hurried out the door.

For the rest of the day and into the next, I thought about Ruby's eyes. I had handled the moment badly, I told myself, made her feel ashamed for a small vanity in a life that could afford few vanities. I realized that a part of me expected her and the other leaders to possess some sort of immunity from the onslaught of images that feed every American's insecurities—the slender models in the fashion magazines, the square-jawed men in fast cars—images to which I myself was vulnerable and from which I had sought protection. When I mentioned the incident to a black woman friend of mine, she stated the issue more bluntly.

"What are you surprised about?" my friend said impatiently. "That black people still hate themselves?"

No, I told her, it wasn't exactly surprise that I was feeling. Since my first frightening discovery of bleaching creams in *Life* magazine, I'd become familiar with the lexicon of color consciousness within the black community—good hair, bad hair; thick lips or thin; if you're light, you're all right, if you're black, get back. In college, the politics of black fashion, and the questions of self-esteem that fashion signified, had been a frequent, if delicate, topic of conversation for black students, especially among the women, who would smile bitterly at the sight of the militant brother who always seemed to be dating light-skinned girls—and tongue-lash any black man who was foolish enough to make a remark about black women's hairstyles.

Mostly I had kept quiet when these subjects were broached, privately measuring my own degree of infection. But I noticed that such conversations rarely took place in large groups, and never in front of whites. Later, I would realize that the position of most black students in predominantly white colleges was already too tenuous, our identities too scrambled, to admit to ourselves that our black pride remained incomplete. And to admit our doubt and confusion to whites, to open up our psyches to general examination by those who had caused so much of the damage in the first place, seemed ludicrous, itself an expression of self-hatred—for there seemed no reason to expect that whites would look at our private struggles as a mirror into their own souls, rather than yet more evidence of black pathology.

It was in observing that division, I think, between what we talked about privately and what we addressed publicly, that I'd learned not to put too much stock in those who trumpeted black self-esteem as a cure for all our ills, whether substance abuse or teen pregnancy or black-on-black crime. By the time I reached Chicago, the phrase *self-esteem* seemed to be on everyone's lips: activists, talk show hosts, educators, and sociologists. It was a handy catchall to describe our hurt, a sanitized way of talking about the things we'd been keeping to ourselves. But whenever I tried to pin down this idea of self-esteem, the specific qualities we hoped to inculcate, the specific means by which

we might feel good about ourselves, the conversation always seemed
to follow a path of infinite regress. Did you dislike yourself because
of your color or because you couldn't read and couldn't get a job? Or
perhaps it was because you were unloved as a child—only, were you
unloved because you were too dark? Or too light? Or because your
mother shot heroin into her veins . . . and why did she do that anyway? Was the sense of emptiness you felt a consequence of kinky hair
or the fact that your apartment had no heat and no decent furniture?
Or was it because deep down you imagined a godless universe?

Maybe one couldn't avoid such questions on the road to personal
salvation. What I doubted was that all the talk about self-esteem could
serve as the centerpiece of an effective black politics. It demanded too
much honest self-reckoning from people; without such honesty, it easily degenerated into vague exhortation. Perhaps with more self-esteem
fewer blacks would be poor, I thought to myself, but I had no doubt
that poverty did nothing for our self-esteem. Better to concentrate on
the things we might all agree on. Give that black man some tangible
skills and a job. Teach that black child reading and arithmetic in a safe,
well-funded school. With the basics taken care of, each of us could
search for our own sense of self-worth.

Ruby shook up this predisposition of mine, the wall I had erected
between psychology and politics, the state of our pocketbooks and the
state of our souls. In fact, that particular episode was only the most
dramatic example of what I was hearing and seeing every day. It was
expressed when a black leader casually explained to me that he never
dealt with black contractors ("A black man'll just mess it up, and I'll
end up paying white folks to do it all over again"); or in another
leader's rationale for why she couldn't mobilize other people in her
church ("Black folks are just lazy, Barack—don't wanna do nothing").
Often the word *nigger* replaced *black* in such remarks, a word I'd once
liked to think was spoken in jest, with a knowing irony, the inside joke
that marked our resilience as a people. Until the first time I heard a

young mother use it on her child to tell him he wasn't worth shit, or watched teenage boys use it to draw blood in a quick round of verbal sparring. The transformation of the word's original meaning was never complete; like the other defenses we erected against possible hurt, this one, too, involved striking out at ourselves first.

If the language, the humor, the stories of ordinary people were the stuff out of which families, communities, economies would have to be built, then I couldn't separate that strength from the hurt and distortions that lingered inside us. And it was the implications of that fact, I realized, that had most disturbed me when I looked into Ruby's eyes. The stories that I had been hearing from the leadership, all the records of courage and sacrifice and overcoming of great odds, hadn't simply arisen from struggles with pestilence or drought, or even mere poverty. They had arisen out of a very particular experience with hate. That hate hadn't gone away; it formed a counternarrative buried deep within each person and at the center of which stood white people— some cruel, some ignorant, sometimes a single face, sometimes just a faceless image of a system claiming power over our lives. I had to ask myself whether the bonds of community could be restored without collectively exorcising that ghostly figure that haunted black dreams. Could Ruby love herself without hating blue eyes?

Rafiq al-Shabazz had settled such questions to his own satisfaction. I had begun to see him more regularly, for the morning after DCP met with the Mayor's Office of Employment and Training he had called me up and launched into a rapid-fire monologue about the job center we had asked for from the city.

"We gotta talk, Barack," he said. "What y'all are trying to do with job training needs to fit into the overall comprehensive development plan I've been working on. Can't think about this thing in isolation . . . got to look at the big picture. You don't understand the forces at work out here. Is big, man. All kinds of folks ready to stab you in the back."

"Who is this?"

"Rafiq. What's the matter, too early for you?"

It was. I put him on hold and got a cup of coffee, then asked him to start all over again, more slowly this time. I eventually gathered that Rafiq had an interest in having the new MET intake center we'd proposed to the city locate in a certain building near his office on Michigan Avenue. I didn't ask the particular nature of that interest: I doubted that I could get a straight answer out of him, and anyway, I figured that we might be able to use an ally in what was proving to be a series of sticky negotiations with Ms. Alvarez. If the storefront he had in mind met the necessary specifications, I said, then I was willing to propose it as one possible alternative.

So Rafiq and I formed an uneasy alliance, one that didn't go over too well with the DCP leaders. I understood their concerns: Whenever we sat down with Rafiq to discuss our joint strategy, he would interrupt the discussion with long lectures about secret machinations afoot, and all the black people willing to sell their people down the river. It was an effective negotiating ploy, for with his voice progressively rising, the veins in his neck straining, Angela and Will and the others would suddenly drop into a curious silence, watching Rafiq as if he were an epileptic in the midst of seizure. More than once, I'd have to jump in and start shouting back at him, not so much in anger as simply to slow him down, until finally a small smile would curl under his mustache and we could get back to work.

When the two of us were alone, though, Rafiq and I could sometimes have normal conversations. Over time I arrived at a grudging admiration for his tenacity and bravado, and, within his own terms, a certain sincerity. He confirmed that he had been a gang leader growing up in Altgeld; he had found religion, he said, under the stewardship of a local Muslim leader unaffiliated with Minister Louis Farrakhan's Nation of Islam. "If it hadn't been for Islam, man, I'd probably be dead," he told me one day. "Just had a negative attitude, you understand. Growing up in Altgeld, I'd soaked up all the poison the white man feeds us. See, the folks you're working with got the same problem, even though they don't realize it yet. They spend half they lives worrying about what white folks think. Start blaming themselves for the shit they see every day, thinking they can't do no better till the white man decides they all right. But deep down they know that ain't right. They know what this country has done to their momma, their daddy, their sister. So the truth is they hate white folks, but they can't admit it to themselves. Keep it all bottled up, fighting themselves. Waste a lot of energy that way.

"I tell you one thing I admire about white folks," he continued. "They know who they are. Look at the Italians. They didn't care about the American flag and all that when they got here. First thing they did is put together the Mafia to make sure their interests were met. The Irish—they took over the city hall and found their boys jobs. The Jews, same thing . . . you telling me they care more about some black kid in the South Side than they do 'bout they relatives in Israel? Shit. It's about blood, Barack, looking after your own. Period. Black people the only ones stupid enough to worry about their enemies."

That was the truth as Rafiq saw it, and he didn't waste energy picking that truth apart. His was a Hobbesian world where distrust was a given and loyalties extended from family to mosque to the black race—whereupon notions of loyalty ceased to apply. This narrowing vision, of blood and tribe, had provided him with a clarity of sorts, a means of focusing his attention. Black self-respect had delivered the mayor's seat, he could argue, just as black self-respect turned around the lives of drug addicts under the tutelage of the Muslims. Progress was within our grasp so long as we didn't betray ourselves.

But what exactly constituted betrayal? Ever since the first time I'd picked up Malcolm X's autobiography, I had tried to untangle the twin strands of black nationalism, arguing that nationalism's affirming message—of solidarity and self-reliance, discipline and communal responsibility—need not depend on hatred of whites any more than it depended on white munificence. We could tell this country where it was wrong, I would tell myself and any black friends who would listen, without ceasing to believe in its capacity for change.

In talking to self-professed nationalists like Rafiq, though, I came to see how the blanket indictment of everything white served a central function in their message of uplift; how, psychologically, at least, one depended on the other. For when the nationalist spoke of a reawakening of values as the only solution to black poverty, he was expressing an implicit, if not explicit, criticism to black listeners: that we did not have to live as we did. And while there were those who could take such an unadorned message and use it to hew out a new life for themselves—those with the stolid dispositions that Booker T. Washington had once demanded from his followers—in the ears of many blacks such talk smacked of the explanations that whites had always offered for black poverty: that we continued to suffer from, if not genetic inferiority, then cultural weakness. It was a message that ignored causality or fault, a message outside history, without a script or plot that might insist on progression. For a people already stripped of their history, a people often ill equipped to retrieve that history in any form other than what fluttered across the television screen, the testimony of what we saw every day seemed only to confirm our worst suspicions about ourselves.

Nationalism provided that history, an unambiguous morality tale that was easily communicated and easily grasped. A steady attack on the white race, the constant recitation of black people's brutal experience in this country, served as the ballast that could prevent the ideas of personal and communal responsibility from tipping into an ocean of despair. Yes, the nationalist would say, whites are responsible for your sorry state, not any inherent flaws in you. In fact, whites are so heartless and devious that we can no longer expect anything from them. The self-loathing you feel, what keeps you drinking or thieving, is planted by them. Rid them from your mind and find your true power liberated. *Rise up, ye mighty race!*

This process of displacement, this means of engaging in self-criticism while removing ourselves from the object of criticism, helped explain the much-admired success of the Nation of Islam in turning around the lives of drug addicts and criminals. But if it was especially well suited to those at the bottom rungs of American life, it also spoke to all the continuing doubts of the lawyer who had run hard for the gold ring yet still experienced the awkward silence when walking into the clubhouse; those young college students who warily measured the distance between them and life on Chicago's mean streets, with the danger that distance implied; all the black people who, it turned out, shared with me a voice that whispered inside them—"You don't really belong here."

In a sense, then, Rafiq was right when he insisted that, deep down, all blacks were potential nationalists. The anger was there, bottled up and often turned inward. And as I thought about Ruby and her blue eyes, the teenagers calling each other "nigger" and worse, I wondered whether, for now at least, Rafiq wasn't also right in preferring that that anger be redirected; whether a black politics that suppressed rage toward whites generally, or one that failed to elevate race loyalty above all else, was a politics inadequate to the task.

It was a painful thought to consider, as painful now as it had been years ago. It contradicted the morality my mother had taught me, a morality of subtle distinctions—between individuals of goodwill and those who wished me ill, between active malice and ignorance or indifference. I had a personal stake in that moral framework; I'd discovered that I couldn't escape it if I tried. And yet perhaps it was a framework that blacks in this country could no longer afford; perhaps it weakened black resolve, encouraged confusion within the ranks. Desperate times called for desperate measures, and for many blacks, times were chronically desperate. If nationalism could create a strong and effective insularity, deliver on its promise of self-respect, then the hurt it might cause well-meaning whites, or the inner turmoil it caused people like me, would be of little consequence.

If nationalism could deliver. As it turned out, questions of effectiveness, and not sentiment, caused most of my quarrels with Rafiq. Once, after a particularly thorny meeting with MET, I asked him whether he could turn out his followers if a public showdown with the city became necessary.

"I don't got time to run around passing out flyers trying to explain everything to the public," he said. "Most of the folks out here don't care one way or another. The ones that do are gonna be double-crossing Negroes trying to mess things up. Important thing is to get our plan tight and get the city signed on. That's how stuff gets done—not with a big crowd and noise and all that. Once we got a done deal, then y'all announce it any way you like."

I disagreed with Rafiq's approach; for all his professed love of black people, he seemed to distrust them an awful lot. But I also knew his approach was dictated by a lack of capacity: Neither his organization nor his mosque, I had discovered, could claim a membership of more than fifty persons. His influence arose not from any strong organizational support but from his willingness to show up at every meeting that remotely affected Roseland and shout his opponents into submission.

What held true for Rafiq was true throughout the city; without the concentrating effect of Harold's campaign, nationalism dissipated into an attitude rather than any concrete program, a collection of grievances and not an organized force, images and sounds that crowded the airwaves and conversation but without any corporeal existence. Among the handful of groups to hoist the nationalist banner, only the Nation of Islam had any significant following: Minister Farrakhan's sharply cadenced sermons generally drew a packed house, and still more listened to his radio broadcasts. But the Nation's active membership in Chicago was considerably smaller—several thousand, perhaps, roughly the size of one of Chicago's biggest black congregations—a base that was rarely, if ever, mobilized around political races or in support of broad-based programs. In fact, the physical presence of the Nation in the neighborhoods was nominal, restricted mainly to the clean-cut men in suits and bow ties who stood at the intersections of major thoroughfares selling the Nation's newspaper, *The Final Call.*

I would occasionally pick up the paper from these unfailingly polite men, in part out of sympathy to their heavy suits in the summer, their thin coats in winter; or sometimes because my attention was caught by the sensational, tabloid-style headlines (CAUCASIAN WOMAN ADMITS: WHITES ARE THE DEVIL). Inside the front cover, one found reprints of the minister's speeches, as well as stories that could have been picked straight off the AP news wire were it not for certain editorial embellishments ("*Jewish* Senator Metzenbaum announced today . . ."). The paper also carried a health section, complete with Minister Farrakhan's pork-free recipes; advertisements for Minister Farrakhan's speeches on videocassette (VISA or MasterCard accepted); and promotions for a line of toiletries—toothpaste and the like—that the Nation had launched under the brand name POWER, part of a strategy to encourage blacks to keep their money within their own community.

After a time, the ads for POWER products grew less prominent in *The Final Call*; it seems that many who enjoyed Minister Farrakhan's speeches continued to brush their teeth with Crest. That the POWER campaign sputtered said something about the difficulty that faced any black business—the barriers to entry, the lack of finance, the leg up that your competitors possessed after having kept you out of the game for over three hundred years.

But I suspected that it also reflected the inevitable tension that arose when Minister Farrakhan's message was reduced to the mundane realities of buying toothpaste. I tried to imagine POWER's product manager looking over his sales projections. He might briefly wonder whether it made sense to distribute the brand in national supermarket chains where blacks preferred to shop. If he rejected that idea, he might consider whether any black-owned supermarket trying to compete against the national chains could afford to give shelf space to a product guaranteed to alienate potential white customers. Would black consumers buy toothpaste through the mail? And what of the likelihood that the cheapest supplier of whatever it was that went into making toothpaste was a white man?

Questions of competition, decisions forced by a market economy and majoritarian rule; issues of power. It was this unyielding reality—that whites were not simply phantoms to be expunged from our dreams but were an active and varied fact of our everyday lives—that finally explained how nationalism could thrive as an emotion and flounder as a program. So long as nationalism remained a cathartic curse on the white race, it could win the applause of the jobless teenager listening on the radio or the businessman watching late-night TV. But the descent from such unifying fervor to the practical choices blacks confronted every day was steep. Compromises were everywhere. The black accountant asked: How am I going to open an account at the black-owned bank if it charges me extra for checking and won't even give me a business loan because it says it can't afford the risk? The black nurse said: White folks I work with ain't so bad, and even if they were, I can't be quitting my job—who's gonna pay my rent tomorrow, or feed my children today?

Rafiq had no ready answers to such questions; he was less interested in changing the rules of power than in the color of those who had it and who therefore enjoyed its spoils. There was never much room at the top of the pyramid, though; in a contest framed in such terms, the wait for black deliverance would be long indeed. During that wait, funny things happened. What in the hands of Malcolm had once seemed a call to arms, a declaration that we would no longer tolerate the intolerable, came to be the very thing Malcolm had sought to root out: one more feeder of fantasy, one more mask for hypocrisy, one more excuse for inaction. Black politicians less gifted than Harold discovered what white politicians had known for a very long time: that race-baiting could make up for a host of limitations. Younger leaders, eager to make a name for themselves, upped the ante, peddling conspiracy theories all over town—the Koreans were funding the Klan, Jewish doctors were injecting black babies with the AIDS virus. It was a shortcut to fame, if not always fortune; like sex or violence on TV, black rage always found a ready market.

Nobody I spoke with in the neighborhood seemed to take such talk very seriously. As it was, many had already given up the hope that politics could actually improve their lives, much less make demands on them; to them, a ballot, if cast at all, was simply a ticket to a good show. Blacks had no real power to act on the occasional slips into anti-Semitism or Asian-bashing, people would tell me; and anyway, black folks needed a chance to let off a little steam every once in a while— man, what do you think those folks say about us behind our backs?

Just talk. Yet what concerned me wasn't just the damage loose talk caused efforts at coalition building, or the emotional pain it caused others. It was the distance between our talk and our action, the effect it was having on us as individuals and as a people. That gap corrupted both language and thought; it made us forgetful and encouraged fabrication; it eventually eroded our ability to hold either ourselves or each other accountable. And while none of this was unique to black politicians or to black nationalists—Ronald Reagan was doing quite well with his brand of verbal legerdemain, and white America seemed ever willing to spend vast sums of money on suburban parcels and private security forces to deny the indissoluble link between black and white—it was blacks who could least afford such make-believe. Black survival in this country had always been premised on a minimum of delusions; it was such an absence of delusions that continued to operate in the daily lives of most black people I met. Instead of adopting such unwavering honesty in our public business, we seemed to be loosening our grip, letting our collective psyche go where it pleased, even as we sank into further despair.

The continuing struggle to align word and action, our heartfelt desires with a workable plan—didn't self-esteem finally depend on just this? It was that belief which had led me into organizing, and it was that belief which would lead me to conclude, perhaps for the final time, that notions of purity—of race or of culture—could no more serve as the basis for the typical black American's self-esteem than it could for mine. Our sense of wholeness would have to arise from something more fine than the bloodlines we'd inherited. It would have to find root in Mrs. Crenshaw's story and Mr. Marshall's story, in Ruby's story and Rafiq's; in all the messy, contradictory details of our experience.

I went away for two weeks to visit my family. When I returned, I called Ruby and told her I needed her to come to a meeting that Saturday night.

A long pause. "What about?"

"You'll see. Be ready by six . . . we'll grab a bite to eat first."

Our destination was a full hour away from Ruby's apartment, in one of the north-side neighborhoods where jazz and blues had migrated in search of a paying audience. We found a Vietnamese restaurant, and over a plate of noodles and shrimp we talked about her boss at work, the problems she was having with her back. The conversation seemed forced, though, without pause or reflection; as we spoke, we kept skirting each other's gaze.

By the time we'd paid the restaurant bill and walked next door, the theater was already full. An usher showed us to our seats, which turned out to be in front of a group of black teenage girls out on a field trip. Some of the girls diligently thumbed through their programs, taking their cue from the older woman—a teacher, I assumed—who sat beside them. Most of the girls, though, were too excited to sit still; they whispered and giggled about the play's lengthy title and wondered how to pronounce the playwright's name, Ntozake Shange.

The room was suddenly blanketed in darkness, and the girls fell quiet. Then the lights rose, a dim blue now, and seven black women appeared on the stage dressed in flowing skirts and scarves, their bodies frozen in awkward contortions. One of them, a big woman dressed in brown, began to cry out:

> *. . . half-notes scattered*
> *without rhythm / no tune*
> *distraught laughter fallin'*
> *over a black girl's shoulder*
> *it's funny / it's hysterical*
> *the melody-less-ness of her dance*
> *don't tell a soul*
> *she's dancing on beer cans and shingles . . .*

As she spoke, the other women slowly came to life, a chorus of many shades and shapes, mahogany and cream, round and slender, young and not so young, stretching their limbs across the stage.

> *somebody / anybody*
> *sing a black girl's song*
> *bring her out*
> *to know herself*
> *to know you*
> *but sing her rhythms*

carin' / struggle / hard times
sing her song of life . . .

For the next hour, the women took turns telling their stories, singing their songs. They sang about lost time and discarded fantasies and what might have been. They sang of the men who loved them, betrayed them, raped them, embraced them; they sang of the hurt inside these men, hurt that was understood and sometimes forgiven. They showed each other their stretch marks and the calluses on their feet; they revealed their beauty in the lilt of their voice, the flutter of a hand, beauty waning, ascendant, elusive. They wept over the aborted children, the murdered children, the children they once were. And through all of their songs, violent, angry, sweet, unflinching, the women danced, each of them, double-dutch and rhumba and bump and solitary waltz; sweat-breaking, heart-breaking dances. They danced until they all seemed one spirit. At the end of the play, that spirit began to sing a single, simple verse:

I found god in myself
and I loved her / I loved her fiercely

Lights came up; bows were taken; the girls behind us cheered wildly. I helped Ruby with her coat and we walked out to the parking lot. The temperature had dropped; the stars glinted like ice against the black sky. As we waited for the car to warm up, Ruby leaned over and kissed me on the cheek.

"Thanks."

Her eyes, deep brown, were shimmering. I grabbed her gloved hand and gave it a quick squeeze before starting to drive. Nothing more was said; for the entire ride back to the South Side, until I left her at her door and wished her good-night, we never broke that precious silence.

CHAPTER ELEVEN

．．．

I PULLED INTO THE AIRPORT parking lot at a quarter past three and ran to the terminal as fast as I could. Panting for breath, I spun around several times, my eyes scanning the crowds of Indians, Germans, Poles, Thais, and Czechs gathering their luggage.

Damn! I knew I should have left earlier. Maybe she had gotten worried and tried to call. Had I given her my office number? What if she'd missed her flight? What if she had walked right past me and I hadn't even known it?

I looked down at the photograph in my hand, the one she had sent me two months earlier, smudged now from too much handling. Then I looked up, and the picture came to life: an African woman emerging from behind the customs gate, moving with easy, graceful steps, her bright, searching eyes now fixed on my own, her dark, round, sculpted face blossoming like a wood rose as she smiled.

"Barack?"

"Auma?"

"Oh my. . ."

I lifted my sister off the ground as we embraced, and we laughed and laughed as we looked at each other. I picked up her bag and we began to walk to the parking garage, and she slipped her arm through mine. And I knew at that moment, somehow, that I loved her, so naturally, so easily and fiercely, that later, after she was gone, I would find myself mistrusting that love, trying to explain it to myself. Even now I can't explain it; I only know that the love was true, and still is, and I'm grateful for it.

"So, brother," Auma said as we drove into the city, "you have to tell me everything."

"About what?"

"Your life, of course."

"From the beginning?"

"Start anywhere."

I told her about Chicago and New York, my work as an organizer, my mother and grandparents and Maya—she had heard so much about them from our father, she said, she felt as if she already knew them. She described Heidelberg, where she was trying to finish a master's degree in linguistics, and the trials and tribulations of living in Germany.

"I have no right to complain, I suppose," she said. "I have a scholarship, a flat. I don't know what I would be doing if I was still in Kenya. Still, I don't care for Germany so much. You know, the Germans like to think of themselves as very liberal when it comes to Africans, but if you scratch the surface you see they still have the attitudes of their childhood. In German fairy tales, black people are always the goblins. Such things one doesn't forget so easily. Sometimes I try to imagine what it must have been like for the Old Man, leaving home for the first time. Whether he felt that same loneliness . . ."

The Old Man. That's what Auma called our father. It sounded right to me, somehow, at once familiar and distant, an elemental force that isn't fully understood. In my apartment, Auma held up the picture of him that sat on my bookshelf, a studio portrait that my mother had saved.

"He looks so innocent, doesn't he? So young." She held the picture next to my face. "You have the same mouth."

I told her she should lie down and get some rest while I went to my office for a few hours of work.

She shook her head. "I'm not tired. Let me go with you."

"You'll feel better if you take a nap."

She said, "Agh, Barack! I see you're bossy like the Old Man as well. And you only met him once? It must be in the blood."

I laughed, but she didn't; instead, her eyes wandered over my face as if it were a puzzle to solve, another piece to a problem that, beneath the exuberant chatter, nagged at her heart.

I gave her a tour of the South Side that afternoon, the same drive I had taken in my first days in Chicago, only with some of my own memories now. When we stopped by my office, Angela, Mona, and Shirley happened to be there. They asked Auma all about Kenya and how she braided her hair and how come she talked so pretty, like the queen of England, and the four of them enjoyed themselves thoroughly talking about me and all my strange habits.

"They seem very fond of you," Auma said afterward. "They remind me of our aunties back home." She rolled down the window and stuck her face into the wind, watching Michigan Avenue pass by: the gutted remains of the old Roseland Theatre, a garage full of rusted cars. "Are you doing this for them, Barack?" she asked, turning back to me. "This organizing business, I mean?"

I shrugged. "For them. For me."

That same expression of puzzlement, and fear, returned to Auma's face. "I don't like politics much," she said.

"Why's that?"

"I don't know. People always end up disappointed."

There was a letter waiting for her in my mailbox when we got home; it was from a German law student she said she'd been seeing.

The letter was voluminous, at least seven pages long, and as I prepared dinner, she sat at the kitchen table and laughed and sighed and clicked her tongue, her face suddenly soft and wistful.

"I thought you didn't like Germans," I said.

She rubbed her eyes and laughed. "Yah—Otto is different. He's so sweet! And sometimes I treat him so badly! I don't know, Barack. Sometimes I think it's just impossible for me to trust anybody completely. I think of what the Old Man made of his life, and the idea of marriage gives me, how do you say . . . the shivers. Also, with Otto and his career, we would have to live in Germany, you see. I start imagining what it would be like for me, living my entire life as a foreigner, and I don't think I could take it."

She folded her letter and put it back in the envelope. "What about you, Barack?" she asked. "Do you have these problems, or is it just your sister who's so confused?"

"I think I know what you're feeling."

"Tell me."

I went to the refrigerator and pulled out two green peppers, setting them on the cutting board. "Well . . . there was a woman in New York that I loved. She was white. She had dark hair, and specks of green in her eyes. Her voice sounded like a wind chime. We saw each other for almost a year. On the weekends, mostly. Sometimes in her apartment, sometimes in mine. You know how you can fall into your own private world? Just two people, hidden and warm. Your own language. Your own customs. That's how it was.

"Anyway, one weekend she invited me to her family's country house. The parents were there, and they were very nice, very gracious. It was autumn, beautiful, with woods all around us, and we paddled a canoe across this round, icy lake full of small gold leaves that collected along the shore. The family knew every inch of the land. They knew how the hills had formed, how the glacial drifts had created the lake, the names of the earliest white settlers—their ancestors—and before that, the names of the Indians who'd once hunted the land. The house was very old, her grandfather's house. He had inherited it from his grandfather. The library was filled with old books and pictures of the grandfather with famous people he had known—presidents, diplomats, industrialists. There was this tremendous gravity to the room. Standing in that room, I realized that our two worlds, my friend's and mine, were as distant from each other as Kenya is from Germany. And I knew that if we stayed together I'd eventually live in hers. After all, I'd been doing it most of my life. Between the two of us, I was the one who knew how to live as an outsider."

"So what happened."

I shrugged. "I pushed her away. We started to fight. We started thinking about the future, and it pressed in on our warm little world. One night I took her to see a new play by a black playwright. It was a very angry play, but very funny. Typical black American humor. The audience was mostly black, and everybody was laughing and clapping and hollering like they were in church. After the play was over, my friend started talking about why black people were so angry all the time. I said it was a matter of remembering—nobody asks why Jews remember the Holocaust, I think I said—and she said that's different, and I said it wasn't, and she said that anger was just a dead end. We had a big fight, right in front of the theater. When we got back to the car she started crying. She couldn't be black, she said. She would if she could, but she couldn't. She could only be herself, and wasn't that enough."

"That's a sad story, Barack."

"I suppose. Maybe even if she'd been black it still wouldn't have worked out. I mean, there are several black ladies out there who've broken my heart just as good." I smiled and scraped the cut-up peppers into the pot, and then turned back to Auma. "The thing is," I said, no longer smiling, "whenever I think back to what my friend said to me, that night outside the theater, it somehow makes me ashamed."

"Do you ever hear from her?"

"I got a postcard at Christmas. She's happy now; she's met some-one. And I have my work."

"Is that enough?"

"Sometimes."

I took the next day off, and we spent the day together, visiting the Art Institute (I wanted to go see the shrunken heads at the Field Museum, but Auma refused), digging old photos out of my closet, visiting the supermarket, where Auma decided that Americans were friendly and overweight. She was stubborn sometimes, sometimes impish, some-times burdened with the weight of the world, and always asserting a self-reliance that I recognized as a learned response—my own re-sponse to uncertainty.

We didn't speak much about our father, though; it was as if our conversation stopped whenever we threatened to skirt his memory. It was only that night, after dinner and a long walk along the lake's crumbling break wall, that we both sensed we couldn't go any further until we opened up the subject. I made us some tea and Auma began to tell me about the Old Man, at least what she could remember.

"I can't say I really knew him, Barack," she began. "Maybe nobody did . . . not really. His life was so scattered. People only knew scraps and pieces, even his own children.

"I was scared of him. You know, he was already away when I was born. In Hawaii with your mum, and then at Harvard. When he came back to Kenya, our oldest brother, Roy, and I were small chil-dren. We had lived with our mum in the country, in Alego, up until then. I was too young to remember much about him coming. I was four, but Roy was six, so maybe he can tell you more about what hap-pened. I just remember that he came back with an American woman named Ruth, and that he took us from our mother to go live with them in Nairobi. I remember that this woman, Ruth, was the first white person I'd ever been near, and that suddenly she was supposed to be my new mother."

"Why didn't you stay with your own mother?"

Auma shook her head. "I don't know exactly. In Kenya, men get to keep children in a divorce—if they want them, that is. I asked my mum about this, but it's difficult for her to talk about. She only says that the Old Man's new wife refused to live with another wife, and that she—my mum—thought us children would be better off living with the Old Man because he was rich.

"In those first years, the Old Man was doing really well, you see. He was working for an American oil company—Shell, I think. It was only a few years after independence, and the Old Man was well connected with all the top government people. He had gone to school with many of them. The vice-president, ministers, they would all come to the house sometimes and drink with him and talk about politics. He had a big house and a big car, and everybody was impressed with him because he was so young but he already had so much education from abroad. And he had an American wife, which was still rare—although later, when he was still married to Ruth, he would go out sometimes with my real mum. As if he had to show people, you see. That he could also have this beautiful African woman whenever he chose. Our four other brothers were born at this time. Mark and David, they were Ruth's children, born in our big house in Westlands. Abo and Bernard, they were my mum's children, and lived with her and her family upcountry. Roy and I didn't know Abo and Bernard then. They never came to the house to see us, and when the Old Man visited them, he would always go alone, without telling Ruth.

"I didn't think about this much until later, the way our lives were divided in two, because I was so young. I think it was harder on Roy, because he was old enough to remember what it had been like in Alego, living in the village with our mum and our people. For me, things were okay. Ruth, our new mother, was nice enough to us then. She treated us almost like her own children. Her parents were rich, I think, and they would send us beautiful presents from the States. I'd get really excited whenever a package came from them. But I remember sometimes Roy would refuse to take their gifts, even when they sent us sweets. I remember once he refused some chocolates they had sent, but later in the night, when he thought I was asleep, I saw him taking some of the chocolates that I had left on our dresser. But I didn't say anything, because I think I knew that he was unhappy.

"Then things began to change. When Ruth gave birth to Mark and David, her attention shifted to them. The Old Man, he left the American company to work in the government, for the Ministry of Tourism. He may have had political ambitions, and at first he was doing well in the government. But by 1966 or 1967, the divisions in Kenya had become more serious. President Kenyatta was from the largest tribe, the Kikuyus. The Luos, the second largest tribe, began to complain that Kikuyus were getting all the best jobs. The government was full of intrigue. The vice-president, Odinga, was a Luo, and he said the government was becoming corrupt. That, instead of serving those who had fought for independence, Kenyan politicians had taken the place of the white colonials, buying up businesses and land that should be redistributed to the people. Odinga tried to start his own party, but was placed under house arrest as a Communist. Another popular Luo minister, Tom M'boya, was killed by a Kikuyu gunman. Luos began to protest in the streets, and the government police cracked down. People were killed. All this created more suspicion between the tribes.

"Most of the Old Man's friends just kept quiet and learned to live with the situation. But the Old Man began to speak up. He would tell people that tribalism was going to ruin the country and that unqualified men were taking the best jobs. His friends tried to warn him about saying such things in public, but he didn't care. He always thought he knew what was best, you see. When he was passed up for a promotion, he complained loudly. 'How can you be my senior,' he would say to one of the ministers, 'and yet I am teaching you how to do your job properly?' Word got back to Kenyatta that the Old Man was a troublemaker, and he was called in to see the president. According to the stories, Kenyatta said to the Old Man that, because he could not keep his mouth shut, he would not work again until he had no shoes on his feet.

"I don't know how much of these details are true. But I know that with the president as an enemy things became very bad for the Old Man. He was banished from the government—blacklisted. None of the ministries would give him work. When he went to foreign companies to look for a post, the companies were warned not to hire him. He began looking abroad and was hired to work for the African Development Bank in Addis Ababa, but before he could join them, the government revoked his passport, and he couldn't even leave Kenya.

"Finally, he had to accept a small job with the Water Department. Even this was possible only because one of his friends pitied him. The job kept food on the table, but it was a big fall for him. The Old Man began to drink heavily, and many of the people he knew stopped coming to visit because now it was dangerous to be seen with him. They told him that maybe if he apologized, changed his attitude, he would be all right. But he refused and continued to say whatever was on his mind.

"I understood most of this only when I was older. At the time, I just saw that life at home became very difficult. The Old Man never spoke to Roy or myself except to scold us. He would come home very late, drunk, and I could hear him shouting at Ruth, telling her to cook him food. Ruth became very bitter at how the Old Man had changed. Sometimes, when he wasn't home, she would tell Roy and myself that our father was crazy and that she pitied us for having such a father. I didn't blame her for this—I probably agreed. But I noticed that, even more than before, she treated us differently from her own two sons. She would say that we were not her children and there was only so much she could do to help us. Roy and I began to feel like we had no one. And when Ruth left the Old Man, that feeling was not so far from the truth.

"She left when I was twelve or thirteen, after the Old Man had had a serious car accident. He had been drinking, I think, and the driver of the other car, a white farmer, was killed. For a long time the Old Man was in the hospital, almost a year, and Roy and I lived basically on our own. When the Old Man finally got out of the hospital, that's when he went to visit you and your mum in Hawaii. He told us that the two of you would be coming back with him and that then we would have a proper family. But you weren't with him when he returned, and Roy and I were left to deal with him by ourselves.

"Because of the accident, the Old Man had now lost his job at the Water Department, and we had no place to live. For a while, we bounced around from relative to relative, but eventually they would put us out because they had their own troubles. Then we found a run-down house in a rough section of town, and we stayed there for several years. That was a terrible time. The Old Man had so little money, he would have to borrow from relatives just for food. This made him more ashamed, I think, and his temper got worse. Despite all our troubles, he would never admit to Roy or myself that anything was wrong. I think that's what hurt the most—the way he still put on airs about how we were the children of Dr. Obama. We would have empty cupboards, and he would make donations to charities just to keep up appearances! I would argue with him sometimes, but he would just say that I was a foolish young girl and didn't understand.

"It was worse between him and Roy. They would have terrific fights. Finally Roy just left. He just stopped coming home and started living with different people. So I was left alone with the Old Man. Sometimes I would stay up half the night, waiting to hear him come through the door, worrying that something terrible had happened. Then he would stagger in drunk and come into my room and wake me because he wanted company or something to eat. He would talk about how unhappy he was and how he had been betrayed. I would be so sleepy, I wouldn't understand anything he was saying. Secretly, I began to wish that he would just stay out one night and never come back.

"The only thing that saved me was Kenya High School. It was a girls' school that had once been reserved for the British. Very strict, and still very racist—it was only when I was there, after most of the white students had left, that they allowed African teachers to lecture. But despite these things, I became active there. It was a boarding school, so during the school term I would stay there instead of with the Old Man. The school gave me some sense of order, you see. Something to hold on to.

"One year, the Old Man couldn't even pay my school fees, and I was sent home. I was so ashamed, I cried all night. I didn't know what I would do. But I was lucky. One of the headmistresses heard about my situation and gave me a scholarship that let me stay on. It's sad to say, but as much as I cared for the Old Man, and worried about him, I was glad not to have to live with him. I just left him to himself and never looked back.

"In my last two years in high school, the Old Man's situation improved. Kenyatta died, and somehow the Old Man was able to work again in government. He got a job with the Ministry of Finance and started to have money again, and influence. But I think he never got over the bitterness of what had happened to him, seeing his other age-mates who had been more politically astute rise ahead of him. And it was too late to pick up the pieces of his family. For a long time he lived alone in a hotel room, even when he could afford again to buy a house. He would have different women for short spells—Europeans, Africans—but nothing ever lasted. I almost never saw him, and when I did, he didn't know how to behave with me. We were like strangers, but you know, he still wanted to pretend that he was a model father and could tell me how to behave. I remember when I got my scholarship to study in Germany, I was afraid to tell him. I thought he might say I was too young to go and interfere with my student visa, which had to be approved by the government. So I just left without saying good-bye.

"It was only in Germany that I began to let go of some of the anger I felt towards him. With distance, I could see what he had gone through, how even he had never really understood himself. Only at the end, after making such a mess of his life, do I think he was maybe beginning to change. The last time I saw him, he was on a business trip, representing Kenya at an international conference in Europe. I was apprehensive, because we hadn't spoken for so long. But when he arrived in Germany he seemed really relaxed, almost peaceful. We had a really good time. You know, even when he was being completely unreasonable he could be so charming! He took me with him to London, and we stayed in a fancy hotel, and he introduced me to all his friends at a British club. He was pulling out chairs for me and making a great fuss, telling all his friends how proud he was of me. On the flight back from London, I noticed a little glass tumbler his whiskey was being served in, and I said I was going to filch it, and he said, 'There's no need for such things.' He called the stewardess and asked her to bring me a whole set of the glasses, as if he owned the plane. When the stewardess handed them to me, I felt like a little girl again. Like his princess.

"On the last day of his visit, he took me to lunch, and we talked about the future. He asked me if I needed money and insisted that I take something. He told me that once I returned to Kenya, he would find me a proper husband. It was touching, you know, what he was trying to do . . . as if he could make up for all the lost time. By then, he had just fathered another son, George, with a young woman he was living with. So I told him, 'Roy and myself, we're already adults. We have our own ways, our own memories, and what has happened between all of us is hard to undo. But with George, the baby, he is a clean slate. You have a chance to really do right by him.' And he just nodded, as if . . . as if . . ."

For some time, Auma had been staring at our father's photograph, soft-focused in the dim light. Now she stood up and went to the window, her back turned to me. She was clutching herself, her hands inching over her hunched shoulders. She began to shake violently, and I came up behind her and put my arms around her as she wept, the sorrow washing through her in slow, deep waves. "Do you see, Barack?" she said between sobs. "I was just starting to know him. It was just getting to the point where . . . where he might have explained himself. Sometimes I think he might have really turned the corner, found some inner peace. When he died, I felt so . . . so cheated. As cheated as you must have felt."

Outside, a car screeched around a corner; a solitary man crossed under the yellow circle of a streetlight. As if by force of will, Auma's body suddenly straightened, her breath steadied, and she wiped her eyes with her shirtsleeve. "Ah, look at what you've made your sister do," she said, and let out a fragile laugh. She turned to me. "You know, the Old Man used to talk about you so much! He would show off your picture to everybody and tell us how well you were doing in school. I guess your mum and him used to exchange letters. I think those letters really comforted him. During the really bad times, when everybody seemed to have turned against him, he would bring her letters into my room and start reading them out loud. He would wake me up and make me listen, and when he was finished, he would shake the letter in his hand and say how kind your mum had been. 'You see!' he would say. 'At least there are people who truly care for me.' He'd say this to himself over and over again. . . ."

While Auma brushed her teeth, I prepared the convertible sofa for her. Soon she was curled up under a blanket, sound asleep. But I remained awake, propped up in a chair with the desk light on, looking

at the stillness of her face, listening to the rhythm of her breathing, trying to make some sense out of all that she'd said. I felt as if my world
had been turned on its head; as if I had woken up to find a blue sun in
the yellow sky, or heard animals speaking like men. All my life, I had
carried a single image of my father, one that I had sometimes rebelled
against but had never questioned, one that I had later tried to take as
my own. The brilliant scholar, the generous friend, the upstanding
leader—my father had been all those things. All those things and more,
because except for that one brief visit in Hawaii, he had never been
present to foil the image, because I hadn't seen what perhaps most men
see at some point in their lives: their father's body shrinking, their
father's best hopes dashed, their father's face lined with grief and
regret.

Yes, I'd seen weakness in other men—Gramps and his disappointments, Lolo and his compromise. But these men had become object
lessons for me, men I might love but never emulate, white men and
brown men whose fates didn't speak to my own. It was into my
father's image, the black man, son of Africa, that I'd packed all the
attributes I sought in myself, the attributes of Martin and Malcolm,
DuBois and Mandela. And if later I saw that the black men I knew—
Frank or Ray or Will or Rafiq—fell short of such lofty standards; if I
had learned to respect these men for the struggles they went through,
recognizing them as my own—my father's voice had nevertheless
remained untainted, inspiring, rebuking, granting or withholding
approval. You do not work hard enough, Barry. You must help in
your people's struggle. Wake up, black man!

Now, as I sat in the glow of a single light bulb, rocking slightly on
a hard-backed chair, that image had suddenly vanished. Replaced
by . . . what? A bitter drunk? An abusive husband? A defeated, lonely
bureaucrat? To think that all my life I had been wrestling with nothing more than a ghost! For a moment I felt giddy; if Auma hadn't
been in the room, I would have probably laughed out loud. The king

is overthrown, I thought. The emerald curtain is pulled aside. The rabble of my head is free to run riot; I can do what I damn well please. For what man, if not my own father, has the power to tell me otherwise? Whatever I do, it seems, I won't do much worse than he did.

The night wore on; I tried to regain my balance, sensing that there was little satisfaction to be had from my newfound liberation. What stood in the way of my succumbing to the same defeat that had brought down the Old Man? Who might protect me from doubt or warn me against all the traps that seem laid in a black man's soul? The fantasy of my father had at least kept me from despair. Now he was dead, truly. He could no longer tell me how to live.

All he could tell me, perhaps, was what had happened to him. It occurred to me that for all the new information, I still didn't know the man my father had been. What had happened to all his vigor, his promise? What had shaped his ambitions? I imagined once again the first and only time we'd met, the man I now knew must have been as apprehensive as I was, the man who had returned to Hawaii to sift through his past and perhaps try and reclaim that best part of him, the part that had been misplaced. He hadn't been able to tell me his true feelings then, any more than I had been able to express my ten-year-old desires. We had been frozen by the sight of the other, unable to escape the suspicion that under examination our true selves would be found wanting. Now, fifteen years later, I looked into Auma's sleeping face and saw the price we had paid for that silence.

Ten days later, Auma and I sat in the hard plastic seats of an airport terminal, looking out at the planes through the high wall of glass. I asked her what she was thinking about, and she smiled softly.

"I was thinking about Alego," she said. "Home Square—our grandfather's land, where Granny still lives. It's the most beautiful place, Barack. When I'm in Germany, and it's cold outside, and I'm feeling lonely, sometimes I close my eyes and imagine I'm there. Sitting in the compound, surrounded by big trees that our grandfather planted. Granny is talking, telling me something funny, and I can hear the cow swishing its tall behind us, and the chickens pecking at the edges of the field, and the smell of the fire from the cooking hut. And under the mango tree, near the cornfields, is the place where the Old Man is buried. . . ."

Her flight was starting to board. We remained seated, and Auma closed her eyes, squeezing my hand.

"We need to go home," she said. "We need to go home, Barack, and see him there."

CHAPTER TWELVE

RAFIQ HAD DONE HIS best to spruce the place up. There was a new sign above the entrance, and the door had been propped open to let in the spring light. The floors were freshly scrubbed, the furniture rearranged. Rafiq wore a black suit and a black leather tie; his leather *kufu* was polished to a high gloss. For several minutes, he fussed over a long folding table set up on one side of the room, instructing a couple of his men on how to arrange the cookies and punch, fidgeting with the picture of Harold that hung from the wall.

"That look straight to you?" he asked me.

"It's straight, Rafiq."

The mayor was coming to cut the ribbon for the new MET intake center opening in Roseland. It was considered a great coup, and for weeks Rafiq had begged to have the activities start at his building. He wasn't the only one. The alderman had said he'd be happy to host a briefing with the mayor at his office. The state senator, an old ward heeler who'd made the mistake of backing one of the white candidates in the last mayoral election, had promised to help us get money for any project we wanted if we just got him on the program. Even Reverend Smalls had called, suggesting that we'd be helping ourselves by letting him introduce his "good friend Harold." Whenever I walked into the DCP office, my secretary would hand me the latest batch of messages.

"You've sure become popular, Barack," she would say before the phone started ringing again.

I looked now at the crowd that had gathered inside Rafiq's warehouse, mostly politicians and hangers-on, all of them taking peeks out the door every few minutes while plainclothes policemen spoke into their walkie-talkies and surveyed the scene. Wading my way across the room, I found Will and Angela and pulled them aside.

"You guys ready?"

They nodded.

"Remember," I said, "try to get Harold to commit to come to our rally in the fall. Do it while his scheduler is around. Tell him about all the work we're doing out here, and why—"

At that moment, a murmur ran through the crowd, then a sudden stillness. A large motorcade pulled up, a limousine door opened, and from behind a phalanx of policemen I saw the Man himself. He wore a plain blue suit and a rumpled trench coat; his gray hair looked a little frazzled, and he was shorter than I had expected. Still, his presence was undeniable, his smile that of a man at the height of his powers. Immediately, the crowd began chanting—"Ha-rold! Ha-rold!"—and the mayor made a small pirouette, his hand held up in acknowledgment. With Ms. Alvarez and the plainclothes cops leading the way, he began making his way through the throng. Past the senator and the alderman. Past Rafiq and me. Past Reverend Smalls's outstretched hand. Until he finally came to a stop directly in front of Angela.

"Ms. Rider." He took her hand, and made a slight bow. "It's a pleasure. I've heard excellent things about your work."

Angela looked like she was going to pass out. The mayor asked if she would introduce him to her associates, and she began to laugh and flutter about before gathering enough composure to take him down the row of leaders. They all stood at attention like a line of scouts, each one wearing the same helpless grin. When the review was over, the mayor offered Angela his arm, and together they walked toward the door, the crowd pressing behind them.

"Honey, can you believe this?" Shirley whispered to Mona.

The ceremony lasted about fifteen minutes. Police had closed off two blocks of Michigan Avenue, and a small stage had been set up in front of the storefront where the MET center would soon open. Angela introduced all the church members who'd worked on the project, as well as the politicians in attendance; Will gave a brief speech about DCP. The mayor congratulated us on our civic involvement, while the senator, Reverend Smalls, and the alderman jockeyed for position behind him, smiling widely for the photographers they'd hired. The ribbon was cut, and that was it. As the limousine sped away to the next event, the crowd dispersed almost instantly, leaving just a few of us standing in the litter-blown road.

I walked over to Angela, who was busy talking to Shirley and Mona. "When I heard him say 'Ms. Rider,'" she was saying, "I swear I just about died."

Shirley shook her head. "Girl, don't I know it."

"We got the pictures to prove it," Mona said, holding up her Instamatic camera.

I tried to break in. "Did we get a date for the rally?"

"So then he tells me that I look too young to have a fourteen-year-old daughter. Can you imagine?"

"Did he agree to come to our rally?" I repeated.

The three of them looked at me impatiently. "What rally?"

I threw up my hands and started stomping down the street. As I reached my car, I heard Will coming up from behind.

"Where you off to in such a hurry?" he said.

"I don't know. Somewhere." I tried to light a cigarette, but the wind kept blowing out the match. I cursed, tossing the matches to the ground, and turned to Will. "You wanna know something, Will?"

"What."

"We're trifling. That's what we are. Trifling. Here we are, with a chance to show the mayor that we're real players in the city, a group he needs to take seriously. So what do we do? We act like a bunch of starstruck children, that's what. Standing around, cheesing and grinning, worrying about whether we got a picture taken with him—"

"You mean you didn't get yourself a picture?" Will smiled cheerfully and held up a Polaroid shot, then put a hand on my shoulder. "You mind if I tell you something, Barack? You need to lighten up a little bit. What you call trifling was the most fun Angela and them have had all year. Ten years from now, they'll still be bragging about it. It made 'em feel important. And you made it happen. So what if they forgot to invite Harold to a rally? We can always call him back."

I climbed into my car and rolled down the window. "Forget it, Will. I'm just frustrated."

"Yeah, I can see that. But you should be asking yourself *why* you so frustrated."

"Why do you think?"

Will shrugged. "I think you're just trying to do a good job. But I also think you ain't never satisfied. You want everything to happen fast. Like you got something to prove out here."

"I'm not trying to prove anything, Will." I started the car and began to pull away, but not fast enough to avoid hearing Will's parting words.

"You don't have to prove nothing to us, Barack. We love you, man. Jesus loves you!"

Almost a year had passed since my arrival in Chicago, and our labor had finally begun to bear fruit. Will's and Mary's street corner group had grown to fifty strong; they organized neighborhood cleanups, sponsored career days for area youth, won agreements from the alderman to improve sanitation services. Farther north, Mrs. Crenshaw and Mrs. Stevens had pressed the Park District into overhauling run-down parks and playlots; work there had already begun. Streets had been repaired, sewers rooted, crime-watch programs instituted. And now the new job intake center, where once only an empty storefront had been.

As the organization's stock had grown, so had my own. I began receiving invitations to sit on panels and conduct workshops; local politicians knew my name, even if they still couldn't pronounce it. As far as our leadership was concerned, I could do little wrong. "You should have seen him when he first got here," I'd overhear Shirley tell a new leader one day. "He was just a boy. I swear, you look at him now, you'd think he was a different person." She spoke like a proud parent: I'd become a sort of surrogate prodigal son.

The appreciation of those you worked with, concrete improvements in the neighborhood, things you could hang a price tag on. It should have been enough. And yet what Will had said was true. I wasn't satisfied.

Maybe it was connected to Auma's visit and the news she had brought of the Old Man. Where once I'd felt the need to live up to his expectations, I now felt as if I had to make up for all his mistakes. Only the nature of those mistakes still wasn't clear in my mind; I still couldn't read the signposts that might warn me away from the wrong turns he'd taken. Because of that confusion, because my image of him remained so contradictory—sometimes one thing, sometimes another, but never the two things at once—I would find myself, at random moments in the day, feeling as if I was living out a preordained script, as if I were following him into error, a captive to his tragedy.

Then there were my problems with Marty. We had officially separated our respective efforts that spring; since then he'd been spending most of his time with the suburban churches, where it turned out that parishioners, black and white, were less concerned about jobs than they were about the same pattern of white flight and dropping property values that had swept through the South Side a decade before.

These were difficult issues, rife with the racialism and delicacy that Marty found so distasteful. So he had decided to move on. He had hired another organizer to do most of the day-to-day work in the suburbs and was now busy starting a new organization in Gary, a city where the economy had long ago collapsed—where things were so bad, Marty said, that no one would care about the color of an organizer. One day, he asked me to come with him.

"This is a bad training situation for you," he explained. "The South Side's too big. Too many distractions. It's not your fault. I should have known better."

"I can't just leave, Marty. I just got here."

He looked at me with infinite patience. "Listen, Barack, your loyalty is admirable. But right now you need to worry about your own development. Stay here and you're bound to fail. You'll give up organizing before you gave it a real shot."

He had it all worked out in his head: how much time it would take to hire and train a replacement for me, the need to leave a respectable budget in place. As I listened to him lay out his plans, it occurred to me that he'd made no particular attachments to people or place during his three years in the area, that whatever human warmth or connection he might require came from elsewhere: from his gracious wife, from his handsome young son. In his work, it was only the idea that drove him, the idea that a closed plant symbolized but that was larger than the plant, larger than Angela or Will or the lonely priests who had agreed to work with him. That idea might take spark anywhere; for Marty, it was simply a matter of finding the right combination of circumstances, the right mix of compounds.

"Marty."

"What?"

"I'm not going anywhere."

We had eventually come to an agreement: He would provide me the consultation I still desperately needed; the fee he received would help subsidize his work elsewhere. In our weekly meetings, though, he would remind me of the choice I'd made, that there was no risk in my modest accomplishments, that the men in fancy suits downtown were still calling all the shots. "Life is short, Barack," he would say. "If you're not trying to really change things out here, you might as well forget it."

Ah, yes. *Real* change. It had seemed like such an attainable goal back in college, an extension of my personal will and my mother's faith, like boosting my grade point average or giving up liquor: a matter of taking and assigning responsibility. Only now, after a year of organizing, nothing seemed simple. Who was responsible for a place like Altgeld? I found myself asking. There were no cigar-chomping crackers like Bull Connor out there, no club-wielding Pinkerton thugs. Just a small band of older black men and women, a group characterized less by malice or calculation than by fear and small greeds. People like Mr. Anderson, the Altgeld project manager, a balding, older man one year short of retirement. Or Mrs. Reece, a plump woman with a pincushion face who was president of the official tenant council and spent most of her time protecting the small prerogatives that came with her office: a stipend and a seat at the yearly banquet; the ability to see that her daughter got a choice apartment, her nephew a job in the CHA bureaucracy. Or Reverend Johnson, Mrs. Reece's pastor and head of the only large church in Altgeld, who, the first and only time that we met, had stopped me the minute I mentioned the word *organizing*.

"CHA ain't the problem," the good reverend had said. "Problem is these young girls out here, engaging in all manner of fornication."

Some tenants in Altgeld would tell me that Mr. Anderson didn't repair the apartments of anybody who opposed Mrs. Reece and her slate of candidates during LAC elections, that Mrs. Reece was in turn controlled by Reverend Johnson, that Reverend Johnson owned a security guard service under contract with CHA. I couldn't say that any of this was true, nor in the end did it seem to matter much. The three of them only reflected the attitudes of most of the people who worked in Altgeld: teachers, drug counselors, policemen. Some were there only for the paycheck; others sincerely wanted to help. But whatever their motives, they would all at some point confess a common weariness, a weariness that was bone-deep. They had lost whatever confidence they might have once had in their ability to reverse the deterioration they saw all around them. With that loss of confidence came a loss in the capacity for outrage. The idea of responsibility—their own, that of others—slowly eroded, replaced with gallows humor and low expectations.

In a sense, then, Will was right: I did feel that there was something to prove—to the people of Altgeld, to Marty, to my father, to myself. That what I did counted for something. That I wasn't a fool chasing pipe dreams. Later, when I tried to explain some of this to Will, he would laugh and shake his head, preferring to attribute my grumpy attitude that day at the ribbon cutting to a case of youthful jealousy. "See, you like the young rooster, Barack," he told me, "and Harold's like the old rooster. Old rooster came in, and the hens gave him all the attention. Made the young rooster realize he's got a thing or two to learn."

Will seemed to enjoy the comparison, and I had laughed along with him. But secretly I knew he had misunderstood my ambitions. More than anything, I wanted Harold to succeed; like my real father, the mayor and his achievements seemed to mark out what was possible; his gifts, his power, measured my own hopes. And in listening to him speak to us that day, full of grace and good humor, all I had been able to think about was the constraints on that power. At the margins, Harold could make city services more equitable. Black professionals now got a bigger share of city business. We had a black school superintendent, a black police chief, a black CHA director.

Harold's presence consoled, as Will's Jesus consoled, as Rafiq's nationalism consoled. But beneath the radiance of Harold's victory, in Altgeld and elsewhere, nothing seemed to change.

I wondered whether, away from the spotlight, Harold thought about those constraints. Whether, like Mr. Anderson or Mrs. Reece or any number of other black officials who now administered over inner city life, he felt as trapped as those he served, an inheritor of sad history, part of a closed system with few moving parts, a system that was losing heat every day, dropping into low-level stasis.

I wondered whether he, too, felt a prisoner of fate.

It was Dr. Martha Collier who eventually lifted me out my funk. She was the principal of Carver Elementary, one of the two elementary schools out in Altgeld. The first time I called her for an appointment, she didn't ask too many questions.

"I can use any help I can get," she said. "See you at eight-thirty."

The school, three large brick structures that formed a horseshoe around a broad, pitted dirt lot, was at the southern border of Altgeld. Inside, a security guard showed me to the main office, where a sturdily built, middle-aged black woman in a blue suit was talking to a taut and disheveled younger woman.

"You go home now and get some rest," Dr. Collier said, throwing her arm over the woman's shoulder. "I'm gonna make some calls and see if we can't get this thing sorted out." She led the woman to the door, then turned to me. "You must be Obama. Come on in. You want some coffee?"

Before I had a chance to reply, she had turned to her secretary. "Get Mr. Obama here a cup of coffee. Did those painters arrive yet?"

The secretary shook her head, and Dr. Collier frowned. "Hold all calls," she said as I followed her into her office, "except for that good-for-nothing building engineer. I want to tell him just what I think of his sorry ass."

Her office was sparsely furnished, the walls bare except for a few community service awards and a poster of a young black boy that read "God Don't Make No Junk." Dr. Collier pulled up a chair and said, "That girl just leaving my office, she's the mother of one of our kids. A junkie. Her boyfriend was arrested last night and can't make bail. So tell me—what can your organization do for someone like her?"

The secretary came in with my coffee. "I was hoping you'd have some suggestions," I said.

"Short of tearing this whole place down and giving people a chance to start over, I'm not sure."

She had been a teacher for two decades, a principal for ten years. She was accustomed to skirmishes with superiors—once all-white, now mostly black—over supplies and curriculum and hiring policies. Since coming to Carver, she'd set up a child-parent center that brought teenage parents into the classroom to learn with their children. "Most of the parents here want what's best for their child," Dr. Collier explained. "They just don't know how to provide it. So we counsel them on nutrition, health care, how to handle stress. We teach the ones who need it how to read so they can read to their child at home. Where we can, we help them get their high school equivalency, or hire them as teaching assistants."

Dr. Collier took a sip of her coffee. "What we can't do is change the environment these girls and their babies go back to every day. Sooner or later, the child leaves us, and the parents stop coming—"

Her phone buzzed; the painter was here.

"I tell you what, Obama," Dr. Collier said, rising to her feet. "You come in and talk to our parent group next week. Find out what's on their mind. I'm not encouraging you, now. But if the parents decide they want to raise some hell with you, I can't stop them, can I?"

She laughed cheerfully and walked me into the hallway, where a wobbly line of five- and six-year-olds was preparing to enter a class-

room. A few of them waved and smiled at us; a pair of boys toward
the rear spun around and around, their arms tight against their sides;
a tiny little girl struggled to yank a sweater over her head and got tangled up in the sleeves. As the teacher tried to direct them up the
stairs, I thought how happy and trusting they all seemed, that despite
the rocky arrivals many of them had gone through—delivered prematurely, perhaps, or delivered into addiction, most of them already
smudged with the ragged air of poverty—the joy they seemed to find
in simple locomotion, the curiosity they displayed toward every new
face, seemed the equal of children anywhere. They made me think
back to those words of Regina's, spoken years ago, in a different time
and place: *It's not about you.*

"Beautiful, aren't they?" Dr. Collier said.

"They really are."

"The change comes later. In about five years, although it seems
like it's coming sooner all the time."

"What change is that?"

"When their eyes stop laughing. Their throats can still make the
sound, but if you look at their eyes, you can see they've shut off
something inside."

I began spending several hours a week with those children and their
parents. The mothers were all in their late teens or early twenties;
most had spent their lives in Altgeld, raised by teenage mothers
themselves. They spoke without self-consciousness about pregnancy
at fourteen or fifteen, the dropping out of school, the tenuous links
to the fathers who slipped in and out of their lives. They told me
about working the system, which involved mostly waiting: waiting to
see the social worker, waiting at the currency exchange to cash their
welfare checks, waiting for the bus that would take them to the nearest supermarket, five miles away, just to buy diapers on sale.

They had mastered the tools of survival in their tightly bound world and made no apologies for it. They weren't cynical, though; that surprised me. They still had ambitions. There were girls like Linda and Bernadette Lowry, two sisters Dr. Collier had helped get high school equivalencies. Bernadette was now taking classes at the community college; Linda, pregnant again, stayed at home to look after Bernadette's son, Tyrone, and her own daughter, Jewel—but she said she'd be going to college, too, once her new baby was born. After that they would both find jobs, they said—in food management, maybe, or as secretaries. Then they would move out of Altgeld. In Linda's apartment one day, they showed me an album they kept full of clippings from *Better Homes and Gardens*. They pointed to the bright white kitchens and hardwood floors, and told me they would have such a home one day. Tyrone would take swimming lessons, they said; Jewel would dance ballet.

Sometimes, listening to such innocent dreams, I would find myself fighting off the urge to gather up these girls and their babies in my arms, to hold them all tight and never let go. The girls would sense that impulse, I think, and Linda, with her dark, striking beauty, would smile at Bernadette and ask me why I wasn't already married.

"Haven't found the right woman, I guess," I would say.

And Bernadette would slap Linda on the arm, saying, "Stop it! You making Mr. Obama blush." And they would both start to laugh, and I would realize that in my own way, I must have seemed as innocent to them as they both seemed to me.

My plan for the parents was simple. We didn't yet have the power to change state welfare policy, or create local jobs, or bring substantially more money into the schools. But what we could do was begin to improve basic services in Altgeld—get the toilets fixed, the heaters working, the windows repaired. A few victories there, and I imagined the parents forming the nucleus of a genuinely independent tenants' organization. With that strategy in mind, I passed out a set of com-

plaint forms at the next full parents' meeting, asking everyone to canvass the block where they lived. They agreed to the plan, but when
the meeting was over, one of the parents, a woman named Sadie
Evans, approached me holding a small newspaper clipping.

"I saw this in the paper yesterday, Mr. Obama," Sadie said. "I don't
know if it means anything, but I wanted to see what you thought."

It was a legal notice, in small print, run in the classified section. It
said that the CHA was soliciting bids from qualified contractors to
remove asbestos from Altgeld's management office. I asked the parents if any of them had been notified about potential asbestos exposure. They shook their heads.

"You think it's in our apartments?" Linda asked.

"I don't know. But we can find out. Who wants to call Mr. Anderson over at the management office?"

I glanced around the room, but no hands went up. "Come on,
somebody. I can't make the call. I don't live here."

Finally Sadie raised her hand. "I'll do it," she said.

Sadie wouldn't have been my first choice. She was a small, slight
woman with a squeaky voice that made her seem painfully shy. She
wore knee-length dresses and carried a leather-bound Bible wherever
she went. Unlike the other parents, she was married, to a young man
who worked as a store clerk by day but was training to be a minister;
they didn't associate with people outside their church.

All this made her something of a misfit in the group, and I wasn't
sure she'd be tough enough to deal with the CHA. But when I got
back to the office that day, my secretary passed on the message that
Sadie had already set up the appointment with Mr. Anderson and had
called all the other parents to let them know. The following morning, I found Sadie standing out in front of the Altgeld management
office, looking like an orphan, alone in the clammy mist.

"Don't look like anybody else is showing up, does it, Mr. Obama?"
she said, looking at her watch.

"Call me Barack," I said. "Listen, do you still want to go through with this? If you're not comfortable, we can reschedule the meeting until we have some other parents."

"I don't know. Do you think I can get in trouble?"

"I think you've got the right to information that could affect your health. But that doesn't mean Mr. Anderson is gonna think so. I'll stand behind you, and so will the other parents, but you need to do what makes sense for you."

Sadie pulled her overcoat tightly around herself and looked again at her watch. "We shouldn't keep Mr. Anderson waiting," she said, and plunged through the door.

From the expression on Mr. Anderson's face when we walked into his office, it was clear that I hadn't been expected. He offered us a seat and asked us if we wanted some coffee.

"No thank you," Sadie said. "I really appreciate you seeing us on such short notice." With her coat still on, she pulled out the legal notice and set it carefully on Mr. Anderson's desk. "Some of the parents at the school saw this in the paper, and we were worried . . . well, we wondered if this asbestos maybe was in our apartments."

Mr. Anderson glanced at the notice, then set it aside. "This is nothing to worry about, Mrs. Evans," he said. "We're just doing renovation on this building, and after the contractors tore up one of the walls, they found asbestos on the pipes. It's just being removed as a precautionary measure."

"Well . . . shouldn't the same thing, the same precautionary measures, I mean, be taken in our apartments? I mean, isn't there asbestos there, too?"

The trap was laid, and Mr. Anderson's eyes met mine. A cover-up would generate as much publicity as the asbestos, I had told myself. Publicity would make my job easier. And yet, as I watched Mr. Anderson shift around in his seat, trying to take measure of the situation, there was a part of me that wanted to warn him off. I had the unsettling feeling that his soul was familiar to me, that of an older man who feels betrayed by life—a look I had seen so often in my grandfather's eyes. I wanted to somehow let Mr. Anderson know that I understood his dilemma, wanted to tell him that if he would just explain that the problems in Altgeld preceded him and admit that he, too, needed help, then some measure of salvation might alight in the room.

Instead, I said nothing, and Mr. Anderson turned away. "No, Mrs. Evans," he said to Sadie. "There's no asbestos in the residential units. We've tested them thoroughly."

"Well, that's a relief," Sadie said. "Thank you. Thank you very much." She rose, shook Mr. Anderson's hand, and started for the door. I was just about to say something when she turned back toward the project manager.

"Oh, I'm sorry," she said. "I forgot to ask you something. The other parents . . . well, they'd like to see a copy of these tests you took. The results, I mean. You know, just so we can make everybody feel their kids are safe."

"I . . . the records are all at the downtown office," Mr. Anderson stammered. "Filed away, you understand."

"Do you think you can get us a copy by next week?"

"Yes, well . . . of course. I'll see what I can do. Next week."

When we got outside, I told Sadie she had done well.

"Do you think he's telling the truth?"

"I don't know. We'll find out soon enough."

A week passed. Sadie called Mr. Anderson's office: She was told that the results would take another week to produce. Two weeks passed, and Sadie's calls went unreturned. We tried to reach Mrs. Reece, then the CHA district manager, then sent a letter to the executive director of the CHA with a copy to the mayor's office. No response.

"What do we do now?" Bernadette asked.

"We go downtown. If they won't come to us, we'll go to them."

The next day we planned our action. Another letter to the CHA executive director was drafted, informing him that we would appear at his office in two days to demand an answer to the asbestos question. A short press release was issued. The children of Carver were sent home with a flyer pinned to their jackets urging their parents to join us. Sadie, Linda, and Bernadette spent most of the evening calling their neighbors.

But when the day of reckoning arrived, I counted only eight heads in the yellow bus parked in front of the school. Bernadette and I stood in the parking lot trying to recruit other parents as they came to pick up their children. They said they had doctors' appointments or couldn't find baby-sitters. Some didn't bother with excuses, walking past us as if we were panhandlers. When Angela, Mona, and Shirley arrived to see how things were shaping up, I insisted they ride with us to lend moral support. Everyone looked depressed, everyone except Tyrone and Jewel, who were busy making faces at Mr. Lucas, the only father in the group. Dr. Collier came up beside me.

"I guess this is it," I said.

"Better than I expected," she said. "Obama's Army."

"Right."

"Good luck," she said, and clapped me on the back.

The bus rolled past the old incinerator and the Ryerson Steel plant, through Jackson Park, and then onto Lake Shore Drive. As we approached downtown, I passed out a script for the action and asked everyone to read it over carefully. Waiting for them to finish, I noticed that Mr. Lucas had a deep frown carved into his forehead. He was a short, gentle man with a bit of a stutter; he did odd jobs around Altgeld and helped out the mother of his children whenever he could. I came up beside him and asked if something was wrong.

"I don't read so good," he said quietly.

We both looked down at the page of crowded type.

"That's okay." I walked to the front of the bus. "Listen up, everybody! We're going to go over the script together to make sure we've got it straight. What do we want?"

"A meeting with the director!"

"Where?"

"In Altgeld!"

"What if they say they'll give us an answer later?"

"We want an answer now!"

"What if they do something we don't expect?"

"We caucus!"

"Crackers!" Tyrone shouted.

The CHA office was in a stout gray building in the center of the Loop. We filed off the bus, entered the lobby, and mashed onto the elevator. On the fourth floor, we entered a brightly lit lobby where a receptionist sat behind an imposing desk.

"Can I help you?" she said, scarcely glancing up from her magazine.

"We'd like to see the director, please," Sadie said.

"Do you have an appointment?"

"He . . ." Sadie turned to me.

"He knows we're coming," I said.

"Well, he's not in the office right now."

Sadie said, "Could you please check with his deputy?"

The receptionist looked up with an icy stare, but we stood our ground. "Have a seat," she said finally.

The parents sat down, and everyone fell into silence. Shirley started to light a cigarette, but Angela elbowed her in the ribs.

"We're supposed to be concerned about health, remember?"

"It's too late for me, girl," Shirley muttered, but the pack went back into her purse. A group of men in suits and ties came out of the door behind the receptionist's desk and gave our contingent the once-over as they walked to the elevator. Linda whispered something to Bernadette; Bernadette whispered back.

"What's everybody whispering for?" I asked loudly.

The children giggled. Bernadette said, "I feel like I'm waiting to see the principal or something."

"You hear that, everybody," I said. "They build these big offices to make you feel intimidated. Just remember that this is a *public* author-ity. Folks who work here are responsible to you."

"Excuse me," the receptionist said to us, her voice rising to match mine. "I've been told that the director will not be able to see you today. You should report any problems you have to Mr. Anderson out in Altgeld."

"Look, we've already seen Mr. Anderson," Bernadette said. "If the director's not here, we'd like to see his deputy."

"I'm sorry but that's not possible. If you don't leave right now, I'll have to call Security."

At that moment, the elevator doors opened and several TV film crews came in, along with various reporters. "Is this the protest about asbestos?" one of the reporters asked me.

I pointed to Sadie. "She's the spokesperson."

The TV crews began to set up, and the reporters took out their notebooks. Sadie excused herself and dragged me aside.

"I don't wanna talk in front of no cameras."

"Why's that?"

"I don't know. I never been on TV before."

"You'll be fine."

In a few minutes the cameras were rolling, and Sadie, her voice quavering slightly, held her first press conference. As she started to field questions, a woman in a red suit and heavy mascara rushed into the reception area. She smiled tightly at Sadie, introducing herself as the director's assistant, Ms. Broadnax. "I'm so sorry that the director isn't here," Ms. Broadnax said. "If you'll just come this way, I'm sure we can clear up this whole matter."

"Is there asbestos in all CHA units?" a reporter shouted.

"Will the director meet with the parents?"

"We're interested in the best possible outcome for the residents," Ms. Broadnax shouted over her shoulder. We followed her into a large room where several gloomy officials were already seated around a conference table. Ms. Broadnax remarked on how cute the children were and offered everyone coffee and doughnuts.

"We don't need doughnuts," Linda said. "We need answers."

And that was it. Without a word from me, the parents found out that no tests had been done and obtained a promise that testing would start by the end of the day. They negotiated a meeting with the director, collected a handful of business cards, and thanked Ms. Broadnax for her time. The date of the meeting was announced to the press before we crammed back into the elevator to meet our bus. Out on the street, Linda insisted that I treat everybody, including the bus driver, to caramel popcorn. As the bus pulled away, I tried to conduct an evaluation, pointing out the importance of preparation, how everyone had worked as a team.

"Did you see that woman's face when she saw the cameras?"

"What about her acting all nice to the kids? Just trying to cozy up to us so we wouldn't ask no questions."

"Wasn't Sadie terrific? You did us proud, Sadie."

"I got to call my cousin to make sure she gets her VCR set up. We gonna be on TV."

I tried to stop everybody from talking at once, but Mona tugged on my shirt. "Give it up, Barack. Here." She handed me a bag of popcorn. "Eat."

I took a seat beside her. Mr. Lucas hoisted the children up onto his lap for the view of Buckingham Fountain. As I chewed on the gooey popcorn, looking out at the lake, calm and turquoise now, I tried to recall a more contented moment.

I changed as a result of that bus trip, in a fundamental way. It was the sort of change that's important not because it alters your concrete circumstances in some way (wealth, security, fame) but because it hints at what might be possible and therefore spurs you on, beyond the immediate exhilaration, beyond any subsequent disappointments, to retrieve that thing that you once, ever so briefly, held in your hand. That bus ride kept me going, I think. Maybe it still does.

The publicity was nice, of course. The evening after we got back from the CHA office, Sadie's face was all over the television. The press, smelling blood, discovered that another South Side project contained pipes lined with rotting asbestos. Aldermen began calling for immediate hearings. Lawyers called about a class-action suit.

But it was away from all that, as we prepared for our meeting with the CHA director, that I began to see something wonderful happening. The parents began talking about ideas for future campaigns. New parents got involved. The block-by-block canvass we'd planned earlier was put into effect, with Linda and her swollen belly waddling door-to-door to collect complaint forms; Mr. Lucas, unable to read the forms himself, explaining to neighbors how to fill them out properly. Even those who'd opposed our efforts began to come around: Mrs. Reece agreed to cosponsor the event, and Reverend Johnson allowed some of his members to make an announcement at Sunday service. It was as though Sadie's small, honest step had broken into a reservoir of hope, allowing people in Altgeld to reclaim a power they had had all along.

The meeting was to be held in Our Lady's gymnasium, the only building in Altgeld that could accommodate the three hundred people we hoped would turn up. The leaders arrived an hour early, and we went over our demands one last time—that a panel of residents work with CHA to assure containment of asbestos, and that CHA establish a firm timetable for making repairs. As we discussed a few last-minute details, Henry, the maintenance man, waved me over to the public address system.

"What's the matter?"

"System's dead. A short or something."

"So we don't have a microphone?"

"Not outta here. Gonna have to make do with this thing here." He pointed to a solitary amplifier, the size of a small suitcase, with a loose microphone that hung by a single, frayed cord. Sadie and Linda came up beside me and stared down at the primitive box.

"You're joking," Linda said.

I tapped on the mike. "It'll be okay. You guys will just have to speak up." Then, looking down at the amp again, I said, "Try not to let the director hog the microphone, though. He'll end up talking for hours. Just hold it up to him after you've asked the questions. You know, like Oprah."

"If nobody comes," Sadie said, looking at her watch, "we won't need no mike."

People came. From all across the Gardens, people came—senior citizens, teenagers, tots. By seven o'clock five hundred people had arrived; by seven-fifteen, seven hundred. TV crews began setting up cameras, and the local politicians on hand asked us for a chance to warm up the crowd. Marty, who had come to watch the event, could barely contain himself.

"You've really got something here, Barack. These people are ready to move."

There was just one problem: The director still hadn't arrived. Ms. Broadnax said he was caught in traffic, so we decided to go ahead with the first part of the agenda. By the time the preliminaries were over, it was almost eight. I could hear people starting to grumble, fanning themselves in the hot, airless gym. Near the door, I saw Marty trying to lead the crowd in a chant. I pulled him aside.

"What are you doing?"

"You're losing people. You have to do something to keep them fired up."

"*Sit down*, will you please."

I was about to cut our losses and go ahead with Ms. Broadnax when a murmur rose from the back of the gym and the director walked through the door surrounded by a number of aides. He was a dapper black man of medium build, in his early forties. Straightening his tie, he grimly made his way to the front of the room.

"Welcome," Sadie said into the mike. "We've got a whole bunch of people who want to talk to you."

The crowd applauded; we heard a few catcalls. The TV lights switched on.

"We're here tonight," Sadie said, "to talk about a problem that threatens the health of our children. But before we talk about asbestos, we need to deal with problems we live with every day. Linda?"

Sadie handed the microphone to Linda, who turned to the director and pointed to the stack of complaint forms.

"Mr. Director. All of us in Altgeld don't expect miracles. But we do expect basic services. That's all, just the basics. Now these people here have gone out of their way to fill out, real neat-like, all the things they keep asking the CHA to fix but don't never get fixed. So our question is, will you agree here tonight, in front of all these residents, to work with us to make these repairs?"

The next moments are blurry in my memory. As I remember it, Linda leaned over to get the director's response, but when he reached for the microphone, Linda pulled it back.

"A yes-or-no answer, please," Linda said. The director said something about responding in his own fashion and again reached for the mike. Again, Linda pulled it back, only this time there was the slightest hint of mockery in the gesture, the movement of a child who's goading a sibling with an ice-cream cone. I tried to wave at Linda to forget what I'd said before and give up the microphone, but I was standing too far in the rear for her to see me. Meanwhile, the director had gotten his hand on the cord, and for a moment a struggle ensued between the distinguished official and the pregnant young woman in stretch pants and blouse. Behind them, Sadie stood motionless, her face shining, her eyes wide. The crowd, not clear on what was happening, began shouting, some at the director, others at Linda.

Then . . . pandemonium. The director released his grip and headed for the exit. Like some single-celled creature, people near the door lurched after him, and he broke into a near trot. I ran myself, and by the time I had fought my way outside, the director had secured himself in his limousine while a swell of people surrounded the car, some pressing their faces against the tinted glass, others laughing, still others cursing, most just standing about in confusion. Slowly the limo lurched forward, an inch at a time, until a path onto the road opened up and the car sped away, lumping over the cratered street, running over a curb, vanishing from sight.

I walked back toward the gymnasium in a daze, against the current of people now going home. Near the door, a small circle was gathered around a young man in a brown leather jacket whom I recognized as an aide to the alderman.

"The whole thing was put together by Vrdolyak, see," he was telling the group. "You saw that white man egging the folks on. They just trying to make Harold look bad."

A few feet away, I spotted Mrs. Reece and several of her lieutenants. "See what you done!" she snapped at me. "This is what happens when you try and get these young folks involved. Embarrassed the whole Gardens, on TV and everything. White folks seeing us act like a bunch of niggers! Just like they expect."

Inside, only a few of the parents remained. Linda stood alone in one corner, sobbing. I came up and put my arm around her shoulder.

"You okay?"

"I'm so embarrassed," she said, gulping down a sob. "I don't know what happened, Barack. With all the people . . . seems like I just always mess things up."

"You didn't mess up," I said. "If anybody messed up, it was me." I called the others together into a circle and tried to offer encouragement. The turnout was great, I said, which meant people were willing to get involved. Most of the residents would still support our effort. We would learn from our mistakes.

"And the director sure knows who we are now," Shirley said.

This last line drew some weak laughter. Sadie said she had to get home; I told the group that I could take care of cleaning up. As I watched Bernadette pick up Tyrone in one arm and carry his slumbering weight across the gymnasium floor, I felt my stomach constrict. Dr. Collier tapped me on the shoulder.

"So who's gonna cheer you up?" she asked.

I shook my head.

"You take some chances, things are gonna blow once in a while."

"But the looks on their faces . . ."

"Don't worry," Dr. Collier said. "They're tough. Not as tough as they sound—none of us are, including you. But they'll get over it. Something like this is just part of growing up. And sometimes growing up hurts."

The fallout from the meeting could have been worse. Because we had run so late, only one TV station replayed the tug-of-war between Linda and the director. The morning paper noted the frustration residents felt with CHA's slow response to the asbestos problem, as well as the director's tardiness that evening. In fact, we could claim the meeting as a victory of sorts, for the following week men dressed in moon-suits and masks were seen all over the Gardens, sealing any asbestos that posed an immediate threat. CHA also announced that it had asked the U.S. Department of Housing and Urban Development for several million dollars in emergency cleanup funds.

Such concessions helped to lift the spirits of some of the parents, and after a few weeks of licking our wounds, we started meeting again to make sure that CHA followed up on its commitments. Still, in Altgeld at least, I couldn't shake the feeling that the window of possibility that had been pried open so briefly had slammed shut once again. Linda, Bernadette, Mr. Lucas—they would all continue to work with DCP, but only reluctantly, out of loyalty to me rather than to each other. Other residents who had joined us during the weeks leading up to the meeting dropped away. Mrs. Reece refused to speak to us anymore, and while few people paid attention to her attacks on our methods and motives, the squabbling only served to reinforce the suspicion among residents that no amount of activism would alter their condition, except maybe to bring trouble that they didn't need.

A month or so after the initial cleanup, we met with HUD to lobby for CHA's budget request. In addition to the emergency cleanup funds, CHA had asked the feds for over a billion dollars to make basic repairs on projects all over the city. A tall, dour white man from HUD went over the line items.

"Let me be blunt," he told us. "CHA has no chance of getting even half the appropriation it's requested. You can have the asbestos removed. Or you can have new plumbing and roofing where it's needed. But you can't have both."

"So you're telling us that after all this, we gonna be worse off than we was," Bernadette said.

"Well, not exactly. But these are the budget priorities coming out of Washington these days. I'm sorry."

Bernadette hoisted Tyrone up on her lap. "Tell that to him."

Sadie didn't join us for that meeting. She had called me to say that she had decided to stop working with DCP.

"My husband doesn't think it's a good idea, me spending all this time instead of looking after my own family. He says that the publicity went to my head . . . that I became prideful."

I suggested that as long as her family lived in the Gardens, she'd have to stay involved.

"Ain't nothing gonna change, Mr. Obama," she said. "We just gonna concentrate on saving our money so we can move outta here as fast as we can."

CHAPTER THIRTEEN

....

"I'M TELLING YOU, MAN, the world is a *place*."

"Say, the world is a place, huh."

"That's just what I'm saying."

We were walking back to the car after dinner in Hyde Park, and Johnnie was in an expansive mood. He often got like this, especially after a good meal and wine. The first time I met him, when he was still working with a downtown civic group, he had started explaining the relationship between jazz and Eastern religion, then swerved into an analysis of black women's behinds, before coming to a stop on the subject of Federal Reserve Bank policy. In such moments his eyes would grow wide; his voice would speed up; his round, bearded face would glow with a childlike wonder. That was part of the reason I'd hired Johnnie, I suppose, that curiosity of his, his appreciation of the absurd. He was a philosopher of the blues.

"I'll give you an example," Johnnie was saying to me now. "The other day, I'm headed for a meeting up in the State of Illinois Building. You know how it's open in the middle, right . . . big atrium and all that. Well, the guy I'm supposed to be meeting with is late, so I'm just standing there looking down at the lobby from the twelfth floor, checking out the architecture, when all of a sudden this body flies past me. A suicide."

"You didn't tell me about that—"

"Yeah, well, shook me up pretty good. High up as I was, I could hear the body land like it was right there next to me. Terrible sound. Soon as it happened, these office workers rushed up to the guardrail to see what was going on. We're all looking down, and sure enough the body's lying there, all twisted and limp. People started screaming, covering their eyes. But the strange thing was, after people got through screaming, they'd go back to the railing to get a second look. Then they'd scream and cover their eyes all over again. Now why would they do that? Like, what do they expect the second time around? But see, folks are funny like that. We can't help ourselves with that morbid shit. . . .

"Anyway, the cops come, they rope things off and take the body away. Then the building crew starts cleaning up. Nothing special, you know—just a broom and a mop. Sweeping up a life. Whole thing's cleaned up in maybe five minutes. Makes sense, I guess. . . . I mean, it's not like you need special equipment or suits or something. But it starts me thinking, How's that gonna feel to be one of those janitors, mopping up somebody's remains? Somebody's got to do it, right? But how you gonna feel that night eating dinner?"

"Who was it that jumped?"

"That's the other thing, Barack!" Johnnie took a drag from his cigarette and let the smoke roll from his mouth. "It was a young white girl, man, sixteen maybe, seventeen. One of these punk rock types, with blue hair and a ring through her nose. Afterward, I'm wondering what she was thinking about while she was riding up the elevator. I mean, folks musta been standing right next to her on the way up. Maybe they looked her over, decided she was a freak, and went back to thinking about their own business. You know, their promotion, or the Bulls game, or whatever. And the whole time this girl's just standing there next to them with all that pain inside her. Got to be a lot of pain, doc, 'cause right before she jumps, you figure she looks down and knows that shit is gonna hurt."

Johnnie stamped out his cigarette. "So that's what I'm saying, Barack. Whole panorama of life out there. Crazy shit going on. You got to ask yourself, is this kinda stuff happening elsewhere? Is there any precedent for all this shit? You ever ask yourself that?"

"The world's a place," I repeated.

"See there! It's serious, man."

We'd almost reached Johnnie's car when we heard a small pop, compact and brief, like a balloon bursting. We looked in the direction of the sound, and watched a young man appear from around the corner diagonal to us. I don't clearly recall his features or what he wore, although he couldn't have been older than fifteen. I just remember that he ran at a desperate pace, his sneakered feet silent against the sidewalk, his lanky limbs pumping wildly, his chest jutting out as if straining for an imaginary tape.

Johnnie dropped flat onto a small plot of grass in front of one of the apartments, and I quickly followed suit. A few seconds later, two more boys came around the same corner, also running at full speed. One of them, short, fattish, with pants that bunched around his ankles, was waving a small pistol. Without stopping to aim, he let out three quick shots in the direction of the first boy. Then, realizing that his target was out of range, he slowed to a walk, stuffing the weapon under his shirt. His companion, skinny and big-eared, came alongside.

"Stupid motherfucker," the skinny boy said. He spat with satisfaction, and the two of them laughed to each other before continuing down the street, children again, their figures casting squat shadows on the asphalt.

Another fall, another winter. I had recovered from the disappointments of the asbestos campaign, developed other issues and found other leaders. Johnnie's presence had helped relieve my workload, and our budget was stable; what I'd lost in youthful enthusiasm I made up for in experience. And in fact, it may have been that growing familiarity with the landscape, the counsel of time, that gave me the sense that something different was going on with the children of the South Side that spring of 1987; that an invisible line had been crossed, a blind and ugly corner turned.

There was nothing definite I could point to, no hard statistics. The drive-by shootings, the ambulance sirens, the night sounds of neighborhoods abandoned to drugs and gang war and phantom automobiles, where police or press rarely ventured until after the body was found on the pavement, blood spreading in a glistening, uneven pool—none of this was new. In places like Altgeld, prison records had been passed down from father to son for more than a generation; during my very first days in Chicago I had seen the knots of young men, fifteen or sixteen, hanging out on the corners of Michigan or Halsted, their hoods up, their sneakers unlaced, stomping the ground in a desultory rhythm during the colder months, stripped down to T-shirts in the summer, answering their beepers on the corner pay phones: a knot that unraveled, soon to reform, whenever the police cars passed by in their barracuda silence.

No, it was more a change of atmosphere, like the electricity of an approaching storm. I felt it when, driving home one evening, I saw four tall boys walking down a tree-lined block idly snapping a row of young saplings that an older couple had just finished planting in front of their house. I felt it whenever I looked into the eyes of the young men in wheelchairs that had started appearing on the streets that spring, boys crippled before their prime, their eyes without a trace of self-pity, eyes so composed, already so hardened, that they served to frighten rather than to inspire.

That's what was new: the arrival of a new equilibrium between hope and fear; the sense, shared by adults and youth alike, that some, if not most, of our boys were slipping beyond rescue. Even lifelong South Siders like Johnnie noticed the change. "I ain't never seen it like this, Barack," he would tell me one day as we sat in his apartment sipping beer. "I mean, things were tough when I was coming up, but there were limits. We'd get high, get into fights. But out in public, at home, if an adult saw you getting loud or wild, they would say something. And most of us would listen, you know what I'm saying?

"Now, with the drugs, the guns—all that's disappeared. Don't take a whole lot of kids carrying a gun. Just one or two. Somebody says something to one of 'em, and—pow!—kid wastes him. Folks hear stories like that, they just stop trying to talk to these young cats out here. We start generalizing about 'em just like the white folks do. We see 'em hanging out, we head the other way. After a while, even the good kid starts realizing ain't nobody out here gonna look out for him. So he figures he's gonna have to look after himself. Bottom line, you got twelve-year-olds making their own damn rules."

Johnnie took a sip of his beer, the foam collecting on his mustache. "I don't know, Barack. Sometimes *I'm* afraid of 'em. You got to be afraid of somebody who just doesn't care. Don't matter how young they are."

After I was back in my own apartment, I thought about what Johnnie had said. Was I afraid? I didn't think so . . . at least not in the way Johnnie had meant it. Wandering through Altgeld or other tough neighborhoods, my fears were always internal: the old fears of not belonging. The idea of physical assault just never occurred to me. Same thing with the distinction Johnnie made between good kids and bad kids—the distinction didn't compute in my head. It seemed based on a premise that defied my experience, an assumption that children could somehow set the terms of their own development. I thought about Bernadette's five-year-old son, scampering about the broken roads of Altgeld, between a sewage plant and a dump. Where did he sit along the spectrum of goodness? If he ended up in a gang or in jail, would that prove his essence somehow, a wayward gene . . . or just the consequences of a malnourished world?

And what about Kyle: How did one explain what he was going through? I leaned back in my chair, thinking about Ruby's son. He had just turned sixteen; the two years since my arrival had given him several inches, added bulk, and the shadow above his upper lip, first efforts at a mustache. He was still polite to me, still willing to talk about the Bulls—this'd be the year Jordan took 'em to the finals, he said. But he was usually gone whenever I stopped by, or on his way out with his friends. Some nights, Ruby would call me at home just to talk about him, how she never knew where he was anymore, how his grades had continued to drop in school, how he hid things from her, the door to his room always closed.

Don't worry, I would tell her; I was a lot worse at Kyle's age. I don't think she believed that particular truth, but hearing the words seemed to make her feel better. One day I volunteered to sound Kyle out, inviting him to join me for a pick-up basketball game at the University of Chicago gym. He was quiet most of the ride up to Hyde Park, fending off questions with a grunt or a shrug. I asked him if he was still thinking about the air force, and he shook his head; he'd stay in Chicago, he said, find a job and get his own place. I asked him what had changed his mind. He said that the air force would never let a black man fly a plane.

I looked at him crossly. "Who told you that mess?"

Kyle shrugged. "Don't need somebody to tell me that. Just is, that's all."

"Man, that's the wrong attitude. You can do whatever you want if you're willing to work for it."

Kyle smirked and turned his head toward the window, his breath misting the glass. "Yeah, well . . . how many black pilots do you know?"

The gym wasn't crowded when we arrived, and we had to wait only one game before we got onto the court. It had been at least six months since I'd even seen a basketball, and the cigarettes had taken their toll. On the first play of the game, the man guarding me stripped the ball clean out of my hands and I called a foul, causing the players on the sidelines to hoot with derision. By the second game I was walking across the half-court line, feeling slightly dizzy.

To spare myself further embarrassment, I decided to sit out the third game and watch Kyle play. His game wasn't bad, but he was guarding a brother a few years older than me, an orderly at the hospital—short but aggressive, and very quick. After a few plays, it became clear that the man had Kyle's number. He scored three baskets in a row, then started talking the usual talk.

"You can't do no better than that, boy? How you gonna let an old man like me make you look so bad?"

Kyle didn't answer, but the play between them became rough. The next time down the floor, as the man made his move for the basket, Kyle bumped him hard. The man threw the ball at Kyle's chest, then turned to one of his partners. "You see that? This punk can't guard me—"

Suddenly, without any warning, Kyle swung. His fist landed square on the man's jaw, dropping him to the floor. I ran onto the court as the other players pulled Kyle away. His eyes were wide, his voice trembling as he watched the orderly struggle to his feet and spit out a wad of blood.

"I ain't no punk," Kyle muttered. And then again, "I ain't no punk."

We were lucky; somebody had called the security guard downstairs, but the orderly was too embarrassed to admit to the incident. On the drive back, I gave Kyle a long lecture about keeping his cool, about violence, about responsibility. My words sounded trite, and Kyle sat without answering, his eyes fixed on the road. When I was finished he turned to me and said, "Just don't tell my momma, all right?"

I thought that was a good sign. I said I wouldn't tell Ruby what had happened so long as he did, and he grudgingly agreed.

Kyle was a good kid; he still cared about something. Would that be enough to save him?

The week after Johnnie's and my adventure in Hyde Park, I decided it was time to take on the public schools.

It seemed like a natural issue for us. Segregation wasn't much of an issue anymore; whites had all but abandoned the system. Neither was overcrowding, at least in black neighborhood high schools; only half the incoming students bothered to stick around for graduation. Otherwise, Chicago's schools remained in a state of perpetual crisis—annual budget shortfalls in the hundreds of millions; shortages of textbooks and toilet paper; a teachers' union that went out on strike at least once every two years; a bloated bureaucracy and an indifferent state legislature. The more I learned about the system, the more convinced I became that school reform was the only possible solution for the plight of the young men I saw on the street; that without stable families, with no prospects for blue-collar work that could support a family of their own, education was their last best hope. And so in April, in between working on other issues, I developed an action plan for the organization and started peddling it to my leadership.

The response was underwhelming.

Some of it was a problem of self-interest, constituencies misaligned. Older church members told me they had already raised their children; younger parents, like Angela and Mary, sent their children to Catholic schools. The biggest source of resistance was rarely talked about, though—namely, the uncomfortable fact that every one of our churches was filled with teachers, principals, and district superintendents. Few of these educators sent their own children to public schools; they knew too much for that. But they would defend the status quo with the same skill and vigor as their white counterparts of two decades before. There wasn't enough money to do the job right, they told me (which was certainly true). Efforts at reform—decentralization, say, or cutbacks in the bureaucracy—were part of a white effort to wrest back control (not so true). As for the students, well, they were impossible. Lazy. Unruly. Slow. Not the children's fault, maybe, but certainly not the schools'. There may not be any bad kids, Barack, but there sure are a lot of bad parents.

In my mind, these conversations came to serve as a symbol of the unspoken settlement we had made since the 1960s, a settlement that allowed half of our children to advance even as the other half fell further behind. More than that, the conversations made me angry; and so despite lukewarm support from our board, Johnnie and I decided to go ahead and visit some of the area schools, hoping to drum up a constituency beyond the young parents of Altgeld.

We started with Kyle's high school, the one in the area with the best reputation. It was a single building, relatively new but with a careless, impersonal feel: bare concrete pillars, long stark corridors, windows that couldn't be opened and had already clouded, like the windows in a greenhouse. The principal, an attentive, personable man named Dr. Lonnie King, said he was eager to work with community groups like ours. Then he mentioned that one of his school counselors, a Mr. Asante Moran, was trying to start a mentorship program for young men at the school and suggested that we might want to meet him.

We followed Dr. King's directions to a small office toward the rear of the building. It was decorated with African themes: a map of the continent, posters of ancient Africa's kings and queens, a collection of drums and gourds and a kente-cloth wall hanging. Behind the desk sat a tall and imposing man with a handlebar mustache and a prominent jaw. He was dressed in an African print, an elephant-hair bracelet around one thick wrist. He seemed a bit put off at first—he had a stack of SAT practice exams on his desk, and I sensed that Dr. King's call had been an unwelcome interruption. Nevertheless, he offered us seats, told us to call him Asante, and as our interest became more apparent, began to explain some of his ideas.

"The first thing you have to realize," he said, looking at Johnnie and me in turn, "is that the public school system is not about educating black children. Never has been. Inner-city schools are about social control. Period. They're operated as holding pens—miniature jails, really. It's only when black children start breaking out of their pens and bothering white people that society even pays any attention to the issue of whether these children are being educated.

"Just think about what a real education for these children would involve. It would start by giving a child an understanding of *him*self, *his* world, *his* culture, *his* community. That's the starting point of any educational process. That's what makes a child hungry to learn—the promise of being part of something, of mastering his environment. But for the black child, everything's turned upside down. From day one, what's he learning about? Someone else's history. Someone else's culture. Not only that, this culture he's supposed to learn is the same culture that's systematically rejected him, denied his humanity."

Asante leaned back in his chair, his hands folded across his belly. "Is it any wonder that the black child loses interest in learning? Of course not. It's worst for the boys. At least the girls have older women to talk to, the example of motherhood. But the boys have nothing. Half of them don't even know their own fathers. There's nobody to guide them through the process of becoming a man . . . to explain to them the meaning of manhood. And that's a recipe for disaster. Because in every society, young men are going to have violent tendencies. Either those tendencies are directed and disciplined in creative pursuits or those tendencies destroy the young men, or the society, or both.

"So that's what we're dealing with here. Where I can, I try to fill the void. I expose students to African history, geography, artistic traditions. I try to give them a different values orientation—something to counteract the materialism and individualism and instant gratification that's fed to them the other fifteen hours of their day. I teach them that Africans are a communal people. That Africans respect their elders. Some of my European colleagues feel threatened by this, but I tell them it's not about denigrating other cultures. It's about giving these young people a base for themselves. Unless they're rooted in their own traditions, they won't ever be able to appreciate what other cultures have to offer—"

There was a knock on the door, and a gangly young man peeked into the office. Asante apologized; he had another appointment but would be happy to meet with us again to discuss possible youth programs for the area. Walking Johnnie and me to the door, Asante asked me about my name, and I told him about my background.

"I thought so!" Asante smiled. "You know, that's where I went for my first trip to the continent. Kenya. Fifteen years ago, but I remember that trip like it was yesterday. Changed my life forever. The people were so welcoming. And the land—I'd never seen anything so beautiful. It really felt like I had come home." His face glowed with the memory. "When was the last time you were back?"

I hesitated. "Actually, I've never been there."

Asante looked momentarily confused. "Well . . ." he said after a pause, "I'm sure that when you do make the trip, it'll change your life, too." With that, he shook our hands, waved in the young man waiting in the hall, and shut the door behind him.

Johnnie and I were quiet for most of the ride back to our office. We hit a patch of traffic, and Johnnie turned and said, "Can I ask you something, Barack?"

"Sure."

"Why haven't you ever gone to Kenya?"

"I don't know. Maybe I'm scared of what I'll find out."

"Huh." Johnnie lit a cigarette and rolled down the window to let out the smoke. "It's funny," he said, "how listening to Asante back there made me think about my old man. I mean, it's not like my old man is real educated or nothing. He doesn't know anything about Africa. After my mother died, he had to raise me and my brothers on his own. Drove a delivery truck for Spiegel's for twenty years. They laid him off before his pension vested, so he's still working—for another company, but doing the same thing every day. Lifting other people's furniture.

"Never seemed like he really enjoyed life, you know what I mean? On weekends, he'd just hang around the house, and some of my uncles would come over and they'd drink and listen to music. They'd complain about what their bosses had done to 'em this week. The Man did this. The Man did that. But if one of 'em actually started talking about doing something different, or had a new idea, the rest of 'em would just tear the guy up. 'How's some no-'count nigger like you gonna start himself a business?' one of 'em'd say. And somebody else'd say, 'Take that glass away from Jimmy—that wine done gone to his head.' They'd all be laughing, but I could tell they weren't laughing inside. Sometimes, if I was around, my uncles'd start talking about me. 'Hey, boy, that sure is a knobby head you got.' 'Hey, boy, you starting to sound just like a white man, with all them big words.'"

Johnnie blew a stream of smoke into the hazy air. "When I was in high school, I got to feeling ashamed of him. My old man, I mean. Working like a dog. Sitting there, getting drunk with his brothers. I swore I'd never end up like that. But you know, when I thought about it later, I realized my old man never laughed when I talked about wanting to go to college. I mean, he never said anything one way or the other, but he always made sure me and my brother got up for school, that we didn't have to work, that we had a little walking-around money. The day I graduated, I remember he showed up in a jacket and tie, and he just shook my hand. That's all . . . just shook my hand, then went back to work. . . ."

Johnnie stopped talking; the traffic cleared. I started thinking about those posters back in Asante's office—posters of Nefertiti, regal and dark-hued in her golden throne; and Shaka Zulu, fierce and proud in his leopard-skin tunic—and then further back to that day years ago, before my father came for his visit to Hawaii, when I had gone to the library in search of my own magic kingdom, my own glorious birthright. I wondered how much difference those posters would make to the boy we had just left in Asante's office. Probably not as much as Asante himself, I thought. A man willing to listen. A hand placed on a young man's shoulders.

"He was there," I said to Johnnie.

"Who?"

"Your father. He was there for you."

Johnnie scratched his arm. "Yeah, Barack. I guess he was."

"You ever tell him that?"

"Naw. We're not real good at talking." Johnnie looked out the window, then turned to me. "Maybe I should though, huh."

"Yeah, John," I said, nodding. "Maybe you should."

Over the next two months, Asante and Dr. Collier helped us develop a proposal for a youth counseling network, something to provide at-risk teenagers with mentoring and tutorial services and to involve parents in a long-term planning process for reform. It was an exciting project, but my mind was elsewhere. When the proposal was finished, I told Johnnie that I'd be gone for a few days but that he should go ahead with some of the meetings we'd scheduled, to start lining up broader support.

"Where're you going?" he asked me.

"To see my brother."

"I didn't know you had a brother."

"I haven't had one that long."

The next morning, I flew down to Washington, D.C., where my brother Roy now lived. We had first spoken to each other during Auma's visit to Chicago; she had told me then that Roy had married an American Peace Corps worker and had moved to the States. One day we had called him up just to say hello. He had seemed happy to hear from us, his voice deep and unruffled, as if we had talked only yesterday. His job, his wife, his new life in America—everything was "lovely," he said. The word rolled out of him slowly, the syllables drawn out. "Looove-leee." A visit from me would be "fan-taaas-tic." Staying with him and his wife would be "nooo prooob-lem." After we got off the phone, I had told Auma that he sounded well. She looked at me doubtfully.

"Yah, you never know with Roy," she had said. "He doesn't always show his true feelings. He's like the Old Man in that way. In fact, although they didn't get along, he really reminds me of the Old Man in many ways. At least that's how he was in Nairobi. I haven't seen him since David's funeral, though, so maybe marriage has settled him down."

She didn't say much more than that; I should get to know him for myself, she said. And so Roy and I had arranged a visit; I would fly to D.C. for the long weekend, we would see the sights, it would be a wonderful time. Only now, as I searched the emptying gate at National, Roy was nowhere to be found. I called his house and he answered, sounding apologetic.

"Listen, brother—you think maybe you can stay in a hotel tonight?"

"Why? Is something wrong?"

"Nothing serious. It's just, well, me and the wife, we had a little argument. So having you here tonight might not be so good, you understand?"

"Sure. I—"

"You call me when you find a hotel, okay? We'll meet tonight and have dinner. I'll pick you up at eight."

I checked into the cheapest room I could find and waited. At nine, I heard a knock. When I opened the door, I found a big man standing there with his hands in his pockets, an even-toothed grin breaking across his ebony face.

"Hey, brother," he said. "How's life?"

In the pictures I had of Roy, he was slender, dressed in African print, with an Afro, a goatee, a mustache. The man who embraced me now was much heavier, over two hundred pounds, I guessed, the flesh on his cheeks pressing out beneath a thick pair of glasses. The goatee was gone; the African shirt had been replaced by a gray sports coat, white shirt, and tie. Auma had been right, though; his resemblance to the Old Man was unnerving. Looking at my brother, I felt as if I were ten years old again.

"You've gained some weight," I said as we walked to his car.

Roy looked down at his generous belly and gave it a pat. "Eh, it's this fast food, man. It's everywhere. McDonald's. Burger King. You don't even have to get out of the car to have these things. Two all–beef patties, special sauce, lettuce, cheese. The Double Whopper with cheese." He shook his head. "They tell me I can have it right away. *My way! Fantastic!*"

He threw back his head to laugh, a magical, inward sound that made his whole body shake, as if he couldn't get over the wonders this new life had to offer. It was infectious, his laughter—although I wasn't laughing as we made our way to dinner. His Toyota was too small for his bulk—he looked like a kid in a carnival bumper car—and it didn't seem as if he'd yet mastered a stick shift or the rules of the road, including the speed limit. Twice we almost collided with oncoming cars; once, at a turn, we careened over a high curb.

"You always drive this way?" I shouted over the music blasting out of his tape deck.

Roy smiled, shifting into fifth. "I'm not so good, eh? Mary, my wife, she's always complaining, too. Especially since the accident . . ."

"What accident?"

"Ah, it was nothing. You see I'm still here. Alive and breathing!" And again he laughed and shook his head, as if the car worked independently of him, as if our safe arrival would be yet one more example of God's ample blessings.

The restaurant was Mexican, beside a marina, and we chose a table with a view out over the water. I ordered a beer, Roy a margarita, and for a while we made small talk about my work and his accounting job at a large mortgage finance company. He ate with gusto, drank a second margarita; he laughed and joked about his adventures in America. But as the meal wore on, the effort he was making began to show. Eventually, I came around to asking him why his wife hadn't joined us. His smile evaporated.

"Ah, I think we're getting divorced," he said.

"I'm sorry."

"She says she's tired of me staying out late. She says I drink too much. She says I'm becoming just like the Old Man."

"What do you think?"

"What do I think?" He lowered his head, then looked at me somberly, the flame of the tea candles dancing like tiny bonfires across the lenses of his glasses. "The truth is," he said, leaning his weight forward, "I don't think I really like myself. And I blame the Old Man for this."

For the next hour, he recounted all the hard times that Auma had spoken of—of being yanked away from his mother and everything familiar; the Old Man's sudden descent into poverty; the arguments and breakdown and eventual flight. He told me about his life after leaving our father's house; how, bouncing from relative to relative, he had gained admission to the University of Nairobi, then secured a job with a local accounting firm after graduation; how he had taught himself the discipline of work, always arriving at his job early and completing his tasks no matter how late he was out the night before. Listening to him, I felt the same admiration that I'd felt when listening to Auma talk about her life, the resilience they had both displayed, the same stubborn strength that had lifted them out of bad circumstances. Except in Auma I had also sensed a willingness to put the past behind her, a capacity to somehow forgive, if not necessarily forget. Roy's memories of the Old Man seemed more immediate, more taunting; for him the past remained an open sore.

"Nothing was ever good enough for him," he told me as the busboy took our plates away. "He was smart, and he couldn't ever let you forget. If you came home with the second best grades in the class, he would ask why you weren't first. 'You are an Obama,' he would say. 'You should be the best.' He would really believe this. And then I would see him drunk, with no money, living like a beggar. I would ask myself, How can someone so smart fall so badly? It made no sense to me. No sense.

"Even after I was living on my own, even after his death, I would try to figure out this puzzle. It was as if I couldn't escape him. I remember we had to take his body to Alego for the funeral, and as the eldest son, I was responsible for making the arrangements. The government wanted a Christian burial. The family wanted a Muslim burial. People came to Home Square from everywhere, and we had to mourn him according to Luo tradition, burning a log for three days, listening to people cry and moan. Half these people, I didn't even know who they were. They wanted food. They wanted beer. Some people whispered that the Old Man had been poisoned, that I must take revenge. Some people stole things from the house. Then our relatives began to fight about the Old Man's inheritance. The Old Man's last girlfriend, the mother of our baby brother, George—

she wanted everything. Some people, like our Aunt Sarah, sided with her. Others lined up with my mum's side of the family. I'm telling you, it was crazy! Everything seemed to be going wrong.

"After the funeral was over, I didn't want to be with anyone. The only person I trusted was David, our younger brother. That guy, let me tell you, he was okay. He looked like you a little bit, only younger . . . fifteen, sixteen. His mother, Ruth, had tried to raise him like an American. But David, he rebelled. He loved everybody, you see. He ran away from home and came to live with me. I told him he should go home, but he refused. He didn't want to be an American, he said. He was an African. He was an Obama.

"When David died, that was it for me. I was sure our whole family was cursed. I started drinking, fighting—I didn't care. I figured if the Old Man could die, if David could die, that I would have to die, too. Sometimes I wonder what would have happened if I had stayed in Kenya. As it was, there was Nancy, this American girl I had been seeing. She'd returned to the States, so one day I just called her and said I wanted to come. When she said yes, I bought a ticket and caught the next plane out. I didn't pack, or tell my office, or say good-bye to anyone, or anything.

"I thought I could start over, you see. But now I know you can never start over. Not really. You think you have control, but you are like a fly in somebody else's web. Sometimes I think that's why I like accounting. All day, you are only dealing with numbers. You add them, multiply them, and if you are careful, you will always have a solution. There's a sequence there. An order. With numbers, you can have control. . . ."

Roy took another sip from his drink, and suddenly his speech slowed, as if he'd dropped deep into another place, as if our father had taken possession of him. "I am the oldest, you see. In Luo tradition, I am now head of the household. I am responsible for you, and for Auma, and for all the younger boys. It's my responsibility to set things right. To pay the boys' school fees. To see that Auma is properly married. To build a proper house and bring the family together."

I reached across the table and touched his hand. "You don't have to do it alone, brother," I said. "We can share the load."

But it was as if he hadn't heard me. He just stared out the window, and then, as if snapping out of a trance, he waved the waitress over.

"You want another drink?"

"Why don't we just get the check?"

Roy looked at me and smiled. "I can tell you worry too much, Barack. That's my problem, as well. I think we need to learn to go with the flow. Isn't that what you say in America? *Just go with the flow. . . .*" Roy laughed again, loud enough for the people at the next table to turn around. Only the magic was gone out of it now; it sounded hollow, as if it were traveling across a vast, empty distance.

I caught a flight out the next day—Roy needed to spend some time with his wife, and I didn't have the money for another night at the hotel. We had breakfast together, and in the morning light he seemed in better spirits. At the airport gate, we shook hands and hugged, and he promised to come visit me once things had settled down. The entire flight back to Chicago, though, and through the rest of the weekend, I couldn't rid myself of the sense that Roy was in danger somehow, that old demons were driving him toward an abyss, and that if only I was a better brother, my intervention would prevent his fall.

Roy was still on my mind when Johnnie walked into my office late Monday afternoon.

"You're back early," Johnnie said. "How was your trip?"

"It was good. Good to see my brother." I nodded, tapping on the edge of my desk. "So what happened while I was gone?"

Johnnie dropped into a chair. "Well," he said, "we met with the state senator. He committed to introducing a bill to get funding for a pilot program. Maybe not the whole half million, but enough."

"That's terrific. How about the high school principals?"

"Just got back from a meeting with Dr. King, the principal at Asante's school. The rest of 'em haven't returned my calls."

"That's all right. What did Dr. King have to say?"

"Oh, he was all smiles," Johnnie said. "Said he really liked the proposal. He got real excited when he heard we might get funding. Said he'd encourage the other principals to work with us and that we'd have his full support. 'Nothing's more important than saving our youth,' he said."

"Sounds good."

"Right. *Sounds* good. So then, I'm about to walk out of his office when suddenly he gives me *this*." Johnnie reached into his briefcase, pulled out a piece of paper, and handed it to me. I read over a few lines before handing it back.

"A résumé?"

"Not just any résumé, Barack. His *wife's* résumé. Seems she's kinda bored around the house, see, and Dr. King thinks she'd make an 'excellent' director for our program. No pressure, you understand. Just once the money is allocated, some consideration, you know what I mean."

"He gave you his wife's résumé—"

"Not just his wife's résumé." Johnnie reached into his briefcase and pulled out another piece of paper, waving it in the air. "Got his daughter's, too! Tells me *she'd* make an 'excellent' counselor—"

"Naw—"

"I'm telling you, Barack, he had the whole thing figured out. And you know what? The whole time we're talking, he's not batting an eye. Acting like what he's doing is the most natural thing in the world. It was unbelievable." Johnnie shook his head, then suddenly shouted out like a preacher. "Yessuh! Doctah Lonnie King! Now there's a brother with some nerve! An enterprising brother! Program hasn't even started yet, he's already thinking ahead."

I started to laugh.

"He don't just want *one* job! He gotta have *two*! Go in to talk about some kids, he gonna hand you his whole goddamn *family's* résumé. . . ."

I shouted out, catching the spirit. "Doctah Lonnie King!"

"Yessuh! Doctah Lonnie King!" Johnnie started to giggle, which made me laugh even harder, until soon we were doubled over in loud guffaws, catching our breath only long enough to repeat that name again—"Doctah Lonnie King!"—as if it now contained the most obvious truth, the most basic element in an elemental world. We laughed until our faces were hot and our sides hurt, until tears came to our eyes, until we felt emptied out and couldn't laugh anymore, and decided to take the rest of the afternoon off and go find ourselves a beer.

That night, well past midnight, a car pulls up in front of my apartment building carrying a troop of teenage boys and a set of stereo speakers so loud that the floor of my apartment begins to shake. I've learned to ignore such disturbances—where else do they have to go? I say to myself. But on this particular evening I have someone staying over; I know that my neighbors next door have just brought home their newborn child; and so I pull on some shorts and head downstairs for a chat with our nighttime visitors. As I approach the car, the voices stop, the heads within all turn my way.

"Listen, people are trying to sleep around here. Why don't y'all take it someplace else."

The four boys inside say nothing, don't even move. The wind wipes away my drowsiness, and I feel suddenly exposed, standing in a pair of shorts on the sidewalk in the middle of the night. I can't see the faces inside the car; it's too dark to know how old they are, whether they're sober or drunk, good boys or bad. One of them could be Kyle. One of them could be Roy. One of them could be Johnnie.

One of them could be me. Standing there, I try to remember the days when I would have been sitting in a car like that, full of inarticulate resentments and desperate to prove my place in the world. The feelings of righteous anger as I shout at Gramps for some forgotten reason. The blood rush of a high school brawl. The swagger that carries me into a classroom drunk or high, knowing that my teachers will smell beer or reefer on my breath, just daring them to say something. I start picturing myself through the eyes of these boys, a figure of random authority, and know the calculations they might now be making, that if one of them can't take me out, the four of them certainly can.

That knotted, howling assertion of self—as I try to pierce the darkness and read the shadowed faces inside the car, I'm thinking that while these boys may be weaker or stronger than I was at their age, the only difference that matters is this: The world in which I spent those difficult times was far more forgiving. These boys have no margin for error; if they carry guns, those guns will offer them no protection from that truth. And it is that truth, a truth that they surely sense but can't admit and, in fact, must refuse if they are to wake up tomorrow, that has forced them, or others like them, eventually to shut off access to any empathy they may once have felt. Their unruly maleness will not be contained, as mine finally was, by a sense of sadness at an older man's injured pride. Their anger won't be checked by the intimation of danger that would come upon me whenever I split another boy's lip or raced down a highway with gin clouding my head. As I stand there, I find myself thinking that somewhere down the line both guilt and empathy speak to our own buried sense that an order of some sort is required, not the social order that exists, necessarily, but something more fundamental and more demanding; a sense, further, that one has a stake in this order, a wish that, no matter how fluid this order sometimes appears, it will not drain out of the universe. I suspect that these boys will have to search long and hard for that order—indeed, any order that includes them as more than objects of fear or derision. And that suspicion terrifies me, for I now have a place in the world, a job, a schedule to follow. As much as I might tell myself otherwise, we are breaking apart, these boys and me, into different tribes, speaking a different tongue, living by a different code.

The engine starts, and the car screeches away. I turn back toward my apartment knowing that I've been both stupid and lucky, knowing that I am afraid after all.

CHAPTER FOURTEEN

....

I T WAS AN OLD BUILDING, in one of the South Side's older neighborhoods, still sound but badly in need of tuck-pointing and perhaps a new roof. The sanctuary was dark, with several pews that had cracked and splintered; the reddish carpet gave off a musty, damp odor; and at various points the floorboards beneath bucked and dipped like welts in a meadow. Reverend Philips's office had this same chipped, worn quality, lit only by an antique desk lamp that cast the room in a dull, amber glow. And Reverend Philips himself—he was old. With the window shades drawn, surrounded by stacks of dusty old books, he seemed now to be receding into the wall, as still as a portrait, only his snow-white hair clearly visible, his voice sonorous and disembodied, like the voice of a dream.

We had been talking for close to an hour, mostly about the church. Not his church so much as *the* church, the historically black church, the church as an institution, the church as an idea. He was an erudite man and began our conversation with a history of slave religion, telling me about the Africans who, newly landed on hostile shores, had sat circled around a fire mixing newfound myths with ancient rhythms, their songs becoming a vessel for those most radical of ideas—survival, and freedom, and hope. The reverend went on to recall the Southern church of his own youth, a small, whitewashed wooden place, he said, built with sweat and pennies saved from sharecropping, where on bright, hot Sunday mornings all the quiet terror and open wounds of the week drained away in tears and shouts of gratitude; the clapping, waving, fanning hands reddening the embers of those same stubborn ideas—survival, and freedom, and hope. He discussed Martin Luther King's visit to Chicago and the jealousy he had witnessed among some of King's fellow ministers, their fear of being usurped; and the emergence of the Muslims, whose anger Reverend Philips understood: It was his own anger, he said, an anger that he didn't expect he would ever entirely escape but that through prayer he had learned to control—and that he had tried not to pass down to his children.

Now he was explaining the history of churches in Chicago. There were thousands of them, and it seemed as if he knew them all: the tiny storefronts and the large stone edifices; the high-yella congregations that sat stiff as cadets as they sang from their stern hymnals, and the charismatics who shook as their bodies expelled God's unintelligible tongue. Most of the larger churches in Chicago had been a blend of these two forms, Reverend Philips explained, an example of segregation's hidden blessings, the way it forced the lawyer and the doctor to live and worship right next to the maid and the laborer. Like a great pumping heart, the church had circulated goods, information, values, and ideas back and forth and back again, between rich and poor, learned and unlearned, sinner and saved.

He wasn't sure, he said, how much longer his church would continue to serve that function. Most of his better-off members had moved away to tidier neighborhoods, suburban life. They still drove back every Sunday, out of loyalty or habit. But the nature of their involvement had changed. They hesitated to volunteer for anything—a tutoring program, a home visitation—that might keep them in the city after dark. They wanted more security around the church, a fenced-in parking lot to protect their cars. Reverend Philips expected that once he passed on, many of those members would stop coming back. They would start new churches, tidy like their new streets. He feared that the link to the past would be finally broken, that the children would no longer retain the memory of that first circle, around a fire. . . .

His voice began to trail off; I felt he was getting tired. I asked him for introductions to other pastors who might be interested in organizing, and he mentioned a few names—there was a dynamic young pastor, he said, a Reverend Jeremiah Wright, Jr., pastor of Trinity United Church of Christ, who might be worth talking to; his message seemed to appeal to young people like me. Reverend Philips gave me his number, and as I got up to leave, I said, "If we could bring just fifty churches together, we might be able to reverse some of the trends you've been talking about."

Reverend Philips nodded and said, "You may be right, Mr. Obama. You have some interesting ideas. But you see, the churches around here are used to doing things their own way. Sometimes, the congregations even more than the pastors." He opened the door for me, then paused. "By the way, what church do you belong to?"

"I . . . I attend different services."

"But you're not a member anywhere?"

"Still searching, I guess."

"Well, I can understand that. It might help your mission if you had a church home, though. It doesn't matter where, really. What you're asking from pastors requires us to set aside some of our more priestly concerns in favor of prophecy. That requires a good deal of faith on our part. It makes us want to know just where you're getting yours from. Faith, that is."

Outside, I put on my sunglasses and walked past a group of older men who had set out their lawn chairs on the sidewalk for a game of bid whist. It was a gorgeous day, seventy-five in late September.

Instead of driving straight to my next appointment, I decided to linger, letting my legs hang out the open car door, watching the old men play their game. They didn't talk much, these men. They reminded me of the men Gramps used to play bridge with—the same thick, stiff hands; the same thin, natty socks and improbably slender shoes; the same beads of sweat along the folds of their necks, just beneath their flat caps. I tried to remember the names of those men back in Hawaii, what they had done for a living, wondering what residue of themselves they'd left in me. They had been mysteries to me then, those old black men; that mystery was part of what had brought me to Chicago. And now, now that I was leaving Chicago, I wondered if I understood them any better than before.

I hadn't told anyone except Johnnie about my decision. I figured there would be time for an announcement later; I wouldn't even hear back from the law schools until January. Our new youth program would be up and running by then; I would have raised next year's budget, hopefully brought in a few more churches. I had told Johnnie only because I needed to know whether he'd be willing to stay on and take my place as lead organizer—and maybe, too, because he was my friend and I needed to explain myself. Except Johnnie hadn't seen the need for explanations. The minute I told him the schools to which I'd applied—Harvard, Yale, Stanford—he had grinned and slapped me on the back.

"I *knew* it!" he shouted.

"Knew what?"

"That it was just a matter of time, Barack. Before you were outta here."

"Why'd you think that?"

Johnnie shook his head and laughed. "Damn, Barack . . . 'cause you got *options*, that's why. 'Cause you *can* leave. I mean, I know you're a conscientious brother and all that, but when somebody's got a choice between Harvard and Roseland, it's only so long somebody's gonna keep choosing Roseland." Again he shook his head. "Harvard! Goddamn. I just hope you remember your friends when you up in that fancy office downtown."

For some reason, Johnnie's laughter had made me defensive. I insisted that I would be coming back to the neighborhood. I told him that I didn't plan on being dazzled by the wealth and power that Harvard represented, and that he shouldn't be either. Johnnie put his hands up in mock surrender.

"Hey, you don't need to be telling *me* all this. I ain't the one going nowhere."

I grew quiet, embarrassed by my outburst. "Yeah, well . . . I'm just saying that I'll be back, that's all. I don't want you or the leaders to get the wrong idea."

Johnnie smiled gently. "Ain't nobody gonna get the wrong idea, Barack. Man, we're just proud to see you succeed."

The sun was now slipping behind a cloud; a couple of the old card-players pulled on the windbreakers they had hung on the backs of their chairs. I lit a cigarette and tried to decipher that conversation with Johnnie. Had he doubted my intentions? Or was it just me that mistrusted myself? It seemed like I had gone over my decision at least a hundred times. I needed a break, that was for sure. I wanted to go to Kenya: Auma was already back in Nairobi, teaching at the university for a year; it would be an ideal time for an extended visit.

And I had things to learn in law school, things that would help me bring about real change. I would learn about interest rates, corporate mergers, the legislative process; about the way businesses and banks were put together; how real estate ventures succeeded or failed. I would learn power's currency in all its intricacy and detail, knowledge that would have compromised me before coming to Chicago but that I could now bring back to where it was needed, back to Roseland, back to Altgeld; bring it back like Promethean fire.

That's the story I had been telling myself, the same story I imagined my father telling himself twenty-eight years before, as he had boarded the plane to America, the land of dreams. He, too, had probably believed he was acting out some grand design, that he wasn't simply fleeing from possible inconsequence. And, in fact, he had returned to Kenya, hadn't he? But only as a divided man, his plans, his dreams, soon turned to dust. . . .

Would the same thing happen to me? Maybe Johnnie was right; maybe once you stripped away the rationalizations, it always came down to a simple matter of escape. An escape from poverty or boredom or crime or the shackles of your skin. Maybe, by going to law school, I'd be repeating a pattern that had been set in motion centuries before, the moment white men, themselves spurred on by their own fears of inconsequence, had landed on Africa's shores, bringing with them their guns and blind hunger, to drag away the conquered in chains. That first encounter had redrawn the map of black life, recentered its universe, created the very idea of escape—an idea that lived on in Frank and those other old black men who had found refuge in Hawaii; in green-eyed Joyce back at Occidental, just wanting to be an individual; in Auma, torn between Germany and Kenya; in Roy, finding out that he couldn't start over. And here, in the South Side, among members of Reverend Philips's church, some of whom had probably marched alongside Dr. King, believing then that they marched for a higher purpose, for rights and for principles and for all God's children, but who at some point had realized that power was unyielding and principles unstable, and that even after laws were passed and lynchings ceased, the closest thing to freedom would still involve escape, emotional if not physical, away from ourselves, away from what we knew, flight into the outer reaches of the white man's empire—or closer into its bosom.

The analogies weren't exactly right. The relationship between black and white, the meaning of escape, would never be quite the same for me as it had been for Frank, or for the Old Man, or even for

Roy. And as segregated as Chicago was, as strained as race relations were, the success of the civil rights movement had at least created some overlap between communities, more room to maneuver for people like me. I could work in the black community as an organizer or a lawyer and still live in a high rise downtown. Or the other way around: I could work in a blue-chip law firm but live in the South Side and buy a big house, drive a nice car, make my donations to the NAACP and Harold's campaign, speak at local high schools. A role model, they'd call me, an example of black male success.

Was there anything wrong with that? Johnnie obviously didn't think so. He had smiled, I realized now, not because he judged me but precisely because he didn't; because he, like my leaders, didn't see anything wrong with such success. That was one of the lessons I'd learned these past two and a half years, wasn't it?—that most black folks weren't like the father of my dreams, the man in my mother's stories, full of high-blown ideals and quick to pass judgment. They were more like my stepfather, Lolo, practical people who knew life was too hard to judge each other's choices, too messy to live according to abstract ideals. No one expected self-sacrifice from me—not Rafiq, who of late had been pestering me about helping him raise money from white foundations for his latest scheme; not Reverend Smalls, who had decided to run for the state senator's seat and was anxious for our support. As far as they were concerned, my color had always been a sufficient criterion for community membership, enough of a cross to bear.

Was that all that had brought me to Chicago, I wondered—the desire for such simple acceptance? That had been part of it, certainly, one meaning to community. But there had been another meaning, too, a more demanding impulse. Sure, you could be black and still not give a damn about what happened in Altgeld or Roseland. You didn't have to care about boys like Kyle, young mothers like Bernadette or Sadie. But to be right with yourself, to do right by others, to lend meaning to a community's suffering and take part in its healing—that required something more. It required the kind of commitment that Dr. Collier made every day out in Altgeld. It required the kind of sacrifices a man like Asante had been willing to make with his students.

It required faith. I glanced up now at the small, second-story window of the church, imagining the old pastor inside, drafting his sermon for the week. Where did your faith come from? he had asked. It suddenly occurred to me that I didn't have an answer. Perhaps, still, I had faith in myself. But faith in one's self was never enough.

I stamped out my cigarette and started the car. I looked into my rearview mirror and, driving off, watched the old, silent cardplayers recede from my sight.

With Johnnie handling the organization's day-to-day activities, I met with more black ministers in the area, hoping to convince them to join the organization. It was a slow process, for unlike their Catholic counterparts, most black pastors were fiercely independent, secure in their congregations and with little obvious need for outside assistance. Whenever I first reached them on the phone, they would often be suspicious or evasive, uncertain as to why this Muslim—or worse yet, this Irishman, O'Bama—wanted a few minutes of their time. And a handful I met with conformed to the prototypes found in Richard Wright novels or Malcolm X speeches: sanctimonious graybeards preaching pie-in-the-sky, or slick Holy Rollers with flashy cars and a constant eye on the collection plate.

For the most part, though, once I'd had a chance to meet these men face-to-face, I would come away impressed. As a group, they turned out to be thoughtful, hardworking men, with a confidence, a certainty of purpose, that made them by far the best organizers in the neighborhood. They were generous with their time, interested in the issues, surprisingly willing to open themselves to my scrutiny. One minister talked about a former gambling addiction. Another told me about his years as a successful executive and a secret drunk. They all mentioned periods of religious doubt; the corruption of the world and their own hearts; the striking bottom and shattering of pride; and then finally the resurrection of self, a self alloyed to something larger. That was the source of their confidence, they insisted: their personal fall, their subsequent redemption. It was what gave them the authority to preach the Good News.

Had I heard the Good News? some of them would ask me.

Do you know where it is that *your* faith is coming from?

When I asked for other pastors to talk to, several gave me the name of Reverend Wright, the same minister Reverend Philips had mentioned that day at his church. Younger ministers seemed to regard Reverend Wright as a mentor of sorts, his church a model for what they themselves hoped to accomplish. Older pastors were more cautious with their praise, impressed with the rapid growth of Trinity's congregation but somewhat scornful of its popularity among young black professionals. ("A buppie church," one pastor would tell me.)

Toward the end of October I finally got a chance to pay Reverend Wright a visit and see the church for myself. It sat flush on Ninety-fifth Street in a mostly residential neighborhood a few blocks down from the Louden Home projects. I had expected something imposing, but it turned out to be a low, modest structure of red brick and angular windows, landscaped with evergreens and sculpted shrubs and a small sign spiked into the grass—FREE SOUTH AFRICA in simple block letters. Inside, the church was cool and murmured with activity. A group of small children waited to be picked up from day care. A crew of teenage girls passed by, dressed for what looked like an African dance class. Four elderly women emerged from the sanctuary, and one of them shouted "God is good!" causing the others to respond giddily "All the time!"

Eventually a pretty woman with a brisk, cheerful manner came up and introduced herself as Tracy, one of Reverend Wright's assistants.

She said that the reverend was running a few minutes late and asked if I wanted some coffee. As I followed her back into a kitchen toward the rear of the church, we began to chat, about the church mostly, but also a little about her. It had been a difficult year, she said: Her husband had recently died, and in just a few weeks she'd be moving out to the suburbs. She had wrestled long and hard with the decision, for she had lived most of her life in the city. But she had decided the move would be best for her teenage son. She began to explain how there were a lot more black families in the suburbs these days; how her son would be free to walk down the street without getting harassed; how the school he'd be attending had music courses, a full band, free instruments and uniforms.

"He's always wanted to be in a band," she said softly.

As we were talking, I noticed a man in his late forties walking toward us. He had silver hair, a silver mustache and goatee; he was dressed in a gray three-piece suit. He moved slowly, methodically, as if conserving energy, sorting through his mail as he walked, humming a simple tune to himself.

"Barack," he said as if we were old friends, "let's see if Tracy here will let me have a minute of your time."

"Don't pay him no mind, Barack," Tracy said, standing up and straightening out her skirt. "I should have warned you that Rev likes to act silly sometimes."

Reverend Wright smiled and led me into a small, cluttered office. "Sorry for being late," he said, closing the door behind him. "We're trying to build a new sanctuary, and I had to meet with the bankers. I'm telling you, doc, they always want something else from you. Latest thing is another life insurance policy on me. In case I drop dead tomorrow. They figure the whole church'll collapse without me."

"Is it true?"

Reverend Wright shook his head. "I'm not the church, Barack. If I die tomorrow, I hope the congregation will give me a decent burial.

I like to think a few tears will be shed. But as soon as I'm six feet under, they'll be right back on the case, figuring out how to make this church live up to its mission."

He had grown up in Philadelphia, the son of a Baptist minister. He had resisted his father's vocation at first, joining the Marines out of college, dabbling with liquor, Islam, and black nationalism in the sixties. But the call of his faith had apparently remained, a steady tug on his heart, and eventually he'd entered Howard, then the University of Chicago, where he spent six years studying for a Ph.D. in the history of religion. He learned Hebrew and Greek, read the literature of Tillich and Niebuhr and the black liberation theologians. The anger and humor of the streets, the book learning and occasional twenty-five-cent word, all this he had brought with him to Trinity almost two decades ago. And although it was only later that I would learn much of this biography, it became clear in that very first meeting that, despite the reverend's frequent disclaimers, it was this capacious talent of his—this ability to hold together, if not reconcile, the conflicting strains of black experience—upon which Trinity's success had ultimately been built.

"We got a lot of different personalities here," he told me. "Got the Africanist over here. The traditionalist over here. Once in a while, I have to stick my hand in the pot—smooth things over before stuff gets ugly. But that's rare. Usually, if somebody's got an idea for a new ministry, I just tell 'em to run with it and get outta their way."

His approach had obviously worked: the church had grown from two hundred to four thousand members during his tenure; there were organizations for every taste, from yoga classes to Caribbean clubs. He was especially pleased with the church's progress in getting more men involved, although he admitted that they still had a way to go.

"Nothing's harder than reaching young brothers like yourself," he said. "They worry about looking soft. They worry about what their buddies are gonna say about 'em. They tell themselves church is a woman's thing—that it's a sign of weakness for a man to admit that he's got spiritual needs."

The reverend looked up at me then, a look that made me nervous. I decided to shift the conversation to more familiar ground, telling him about DCP and the issues we were working on, explaining the need for involvement from larger churches like his. He sat patiently and listened to my pitch, and when I was finished he gave a small nod.

"I'll try to help you if I can," he said. "But you should know that having us involved in your effort isn't necessarily a feather in your cap."

"Why's that?"

Reverend Wright shrugged. "Some of my fellow clergy don't appreciate what we're about. They feel like we're too radical. Others, we ain't radical enough. Too emotional. Not emotional enough. Our emphasis on African history, on scholarship—"

"Some people say," I interrupted, "that the church is too upwardly mobile."

The reverend's smile faded. "That's a lot of bull," he said sharply. "People who talk that mess reflect their own confusion. They've bought into the whole business of class that keeps us from working together. Half of 'em think that the former gang-banger or the former Muslim got no business in a Christian church. Other half think any black man with an education or a job, or any church that respects scholarship, is somehow suspect.

"We don't buy into these false divisions here. It's not about income, Barack. Cops don't check my bank account when they pull me over and make me spread-eagle against the car. These miseducated brothers, like that sociologist at the University of Chicago, talking about 'the declining significance of race.' Now, what country is he living in?"

But wasn't there a reality to the class divisions, I wondered? I mentioned the conversation I'd had with his assistant, the tendency of those with means to move out of the line of fire. He took off his glasses and rubbed what I now saw to be a pair of tired eyes.

"I've given Tracy my opinion about moving out of the city," he said quietly. "That boy of hers is gonna get out there and won't have a clue about where, or who, he is."

"It's tough to take chances with your child's safety."

"Life's not safe for a black man in this country, Barack. Never has been. Probably never will be."

A secretary buzzed, reminding Reverend Wright of his next appointment. We shook hands, and he agreed to have Tracy prepare a list of members for me to meet. Afterward, in the parking lot, I sat in my car and thumbed through a silver brochure that I'd picked up in the reception area. It contained a set of guiding principles—a "Black Value System"—that the congregation had adopted in 1979. At the top of the list was a commitment to God, "who will give us the strength to give up prayerful passivism and become Black Christian activists, soldiers for Black freedom and the dignity of all humankind." Then a commitment to the black community and black family, education, the work ethic, discipline, and self-respect.

A sensible, heartfelt list—not so different, I suspected, from the values old Reverend Philips might have learned in his whitewashed country church two generations before. There was one particular passage in Trinity's brochure that stood out, though, a commandment more self-conscious in its tone, requiring greater elaboration. "A Disavowal of the Pursuit of Middleclassness," the heading read. "While it is permissible to chase 'middleincomeness' with all our might," the text stated, those blessed with the talent or good fortune to achieve success in the American mainstream must avoid the "psychological entrapment of Black 'middleclassness' that hypnotizes the successful brother or sister into believing they are better than the rest and teaches them to think in terms of 'we' and 'they' instead of 'US'!"

My thoughts would often return to that declaration in the weeks that followed as I met with various members of Trinity. I decided that Reverend Wright was at least partly justified in dismissing the church's critics, for the bulk of its membership was solidly working class, the same teachers and secretaries and government workers one found in other big black churches throughout the city. Residents from the nearby housing project had been actively recruited, and programs designed to meet the needs of the poor—legal aid, tutorials, drug programs—took up a substantial amount of the church's resources.

Still, there was no denying that the church had a disproportionate number of black professionals in its ranks: engineers, doctors, accountants, and corporate managers. Some of them had been raised in Trinity; others had transferred in from other denominations. Many confessed to a long absence from any religious practice—a conscious choice for some, part of a political or intellectual awakening, but more often because church had seemed irrelevant to them as they'd pursued their careers in largely white institutions.

At some point, though, they all told me of having reached a spiritual dead end; a feeling, at once inchoate and oppressive, that they'd been cut off from themselves. Intermittently, then more regularly, they had returned to the church, finding in Trinity some of the same things every religion hopes to offer its converts: a spiritual harbor and the chance to see one's gifts appreciated and acknowledged in a way that a paycheck never can; an assurance, as bones stiffened and hair began to gray, that they belonged to something that would outlast their own lives—and that, when their time finally came, a community would be there to remember.

But not all of what these people sought was strictly religious, I thought; it wasn't just Jesus they were coming home to. It occurred to me that Trinity, with its African themes, its emphasis on black history, continued the role that Reverend Philips had described earlier as a redistributor of values and circulator of ideas. Only now the redistribution didn't run in just a single direction from the schoolteacher or the physician who saw it as a Christian duty to help the sharecropper or the young man fresh from the South adapt to big-city life. The flow of culture now ran in reverse as well; the former gang-banger, the teenage mother, had their own forms of valida-tion—claims of greater deprivation, and hence authenticity, their presence in the church providing the lawyer or doctor with an edu-cation from the streets. By widening its doors to allow all who would enter, a church like Trinity assured its members that their fates remained inseparably bound, that an intelligible "us" still remained.

It was a powerful program, this cultural community, one more pli-ant than simple nationalism, more sustaining than my own brand of organizing. Still, I couldn't help wondering whether it would be enough to keep more people from leaving the city or young men out of jail. Would the Christian fellowship between a black school administrator, say, and a black school parent change the way the schools were run? Would the interest in maintaining such unity allow Reverend Wright to take a forceful stand on the latest proposals to reform public housing? And if men like Reverend Wright failed to take a stand, if churches like Trinity refused to engage with real power and risk genuine conflict, then what chance would there be of holding the larger community intact?

Sometimes I would put such questions to the people I met with. They would respond with the same bemused look Reverend Philips and Reverend Wright had given me. For them, the principles in Trinity's brochure were articles of faith no less than belief in the Res-urrection. You have some good ideas, they would tell me. Maybe if you joined the church you could help us start a community program. Why don't you come by on Sunday?

And I would shrug and play the question off, unable to confess that I could no longer distinguish between faith and mere folly, between faith and simple endurance; that while I believed in the sincerity I heard in their voices, I remained a reluctant skeptic, doubtful of my own motives, wary of expedient conversion, having too many quarrels with God to accept a salvation too easily won.

The day before Thanksgiving, Harold Washington died.

It occurred without warning. Only a few months earlier, Harold had won reelection, handily beating Vrdolyak and Byrne, breaking the deadlock that had prevailed in the city for the previous four years. He had run a cautious campaign this time out, professionally managed, without any of the fervor of 1983; a campaign of consolidation, of balanced budgets and public works. He reached out to some of the old-time Machine politicians, the Irish and the Poles, ready to make peace. The business community sent him their checks, resigned to his presence. So secure was his power that rumblings of discontent had finally surfaced within his own base, among black nationalists upset with his willingness to cut whites and Hispanics into the action, among activists disappointed with his failure to tackle poverty head-on, and among people who preferred the dream to the reality, impotence to compromise.

Harold didn't pay such critics much attention. He saw no reason to take any big risks, no reason to hurry. He said he'd be mayor for the next twenty years.

And then death: sudden, simple, final, almost ridiculous in its ordinariness, the heart of an overweight man giving way.

It rained that weekend, cold and steady. In the neighborhood, the streets were silent. Indoors and outside, people cried. The black radio stations replayed Harold's speeches, hour after hour, trying to summon the dead. At City Hall, the lines wound around several blocks as mourners visited the body, lying in state. Everywhere black people appeared dazed, stricken, uncertain of direction, frightened of the future.

By the time of the funeral, Washington loyalists had worked

through the initial shock. They began to meet, regroup, trying to decide on a strategy for maintaining control, trying to select Harold's rightful heir. But it was too late for that. There was no political organization in place, no clearly defined principles to follow. The entire of black politics had centered on one man who radiated like a sun. Now that he was gone, no one could agree on what that presence had meant.

The loyalists squabbled. Factions emerged. Rumors flew. By Monday, the day the city council was to select a new mayor to serve until the special election, the coalition that had first put Harold in office was all but extinguished. I went down to City Hall that evening to watch this second death. People, mostly black, had been gathering outside the city council's chambers since late afternoon—old people, curiosity seekers, men and women with banners and signs. They shouted at the black aldermen who had cut deals with the white bloc. They waved dollar bills at the soft-spoken black alderman—a holdover from Machine days—behind whom the white aldermen had thrown their support. They called this man a sellout and an Uncle Tom. They chanted and stomped and swore never to leave.

But power was patient and knew what it wanted; power could outwait slogans and prayers and candlelight vigils. Around midnight, just before the council got around to taking a vote, the door to the chambers opened briefly and I saw two of the aldermen off in a huddle. One, black, had been Harold's man; the other, white, Vrdolyak's. They were whispering now, smiling briefly, then looking out at the still-chanting crowd and quickly suppressing their smiles, large, fleshy men in double-breasted suits with the same look of hunger in their eyes—men who knew the score.

I left after that. I pushed through the crowds that overflowed into the street and began walking across Daley Plaza toward my car. The wind whipped up cold and sharp as a blade, and I watched a handmade sign tumble past me. HIS SPIRIT LIVES ON, the sign read in heavy block letters. And beneath the words that picture I had seen so many times while waiting for a chair in Smitty's Barbershop: the handsome, grizzled face; the indulgent smile; the twinkling eyes; now blowing across the empty space, as easily as an autumn leaf.

The months passed at a breathless pace, with constant reminders of all the things left undone. We worked with a citywide coalition in support of school reform. We held a series of joint meetings with Mexicans in the Southeast Side to craft a common environmental strategy for the region. I drove Johnnie nuts trying to cram him with the things it had taken me three years to learn.

"So who did you meet with this week?" I would ask.

"Well, there's this woman, Mrs. Banks, over at True Vine Holiness Church. Seems like she's got potential . . . hold on, yeah, here it is. Teacher, interested in education. I think she'll definitely work with us."

"What does her husband do?"

"You know, I forgot to ask her—"

"What does she think of the teachers' union?"

"Damn, Barack, I only had half an hour. . . ."

In February, I received my acceptance from Harvard. The letter came with a thick packet of information. It reminded me of the packet I'd received from Punahou that summer fourteen years earlier. I remembered how Gramps had stayed up the whole night reading from the catalog about music lessons and advanced placement courses, glee clubs and baccalaureates; how he had waved that catalog and told me it would be my meal ticket, that the contacts I made at a school like Punahou would last me a lifetime, that I would move in charmed circles and have all the opportunities that he'd never had. I remembered how, at the end of the evening, he had smiled and tousled my hair, his breath smelling of whiskey, his eyes shining as if he were about to cry. And I had smiled back at him, pretending to understand but actually wishing I was still in Indonesia running bare-foot along a paddy field, with my feet sinking into the cool, wet mud, part of a chain of other brown boys chasing after a tattered kite.

I felt something like that now.

I had scheduled a luncheon that week at our office for the twenty or so ministers whose churches had agreed to join the organization. Most of the ministers we'd invited showed up, as did most of our key leadership. Together we discussed strategies for the coming year, the lessons learned from Harold's death. We set dates for a training retreat, agreed on a schedule of dues, talked about the continued need to recruit more churches. When we were finished, I announced that I would be leaving in May and that Johnnie would be taking over as director.

No one was surprised. They all came up to me afterward and offered their congratulations. Reverend Philips assured me I had made a wise choice. Angela and Mona said they always knew I'd amount to something someday. Shirley asked me if I'd be willing to advise a nephew of hers who had fallen down a manhole and wanted to sue.

Only Mary seemed upset. After most of the ministers had left, she helped Will, Johnnie, and me clean up. When I asked her if she needed a ride, she started shaking her head.

"What is it with you men?" she said, looking at Will and myself. Her voice trembled slightly as she pulled on her coat. "Why is it you're always in a hurry? Why is it that what you have isn't ever good enough?"

I started to say something, then thought about Mary's two daughters at home, the father that they would never know. Instead, I walked her to the door and gave her a hug. When she was gone, I returned to the meeting room, where Will was working on a plate of leftover chicken wings.

"Want some?" he asked in between bites.

I shook my head, taking a seat across the table from him. He watched me for a while, chewing silently, sucking hot sauce off his fingers.

"Place kinda grows on you, don't it?" he said finally.

I nodded. "Yeah, Will. It does."

He took a sip from his soda and let out a small burp. "Three years ain't that long to be gone," he said.

"How do you know I'm gonna be back?"

"I don't know *how* I know," he said, pushing away his plate. "I just *know*, that's all." Without another word he went to wash his hands, before mounting his bike and riding off down the street.

I woke up at six A.M. that Sunday. It was still dark outside. I shaved, brushed the lint from my only suit, and arrived at the church by seven-thirty. Most of the pews were already filled. A white-gloved usher led me past elderly matrons in wide plumaged hats, tall unsmiling men in suits and ties and mud-cloth *kufis*, children in their Sunday best. A parent from Dr. Collier's school waved at me; an official from the CHA with whom I'd had several run-ins nodded curtly. I shunted through to the center of a row and stuffed myself between a plump older woman who failed to scoot over and a young family of four, the father already sweating in his coarse woolen jacket, the mother telling the two young boys beside her to stop kicking each other.

"Where's God?" I overheard the toddler ask his brother.

"Shut up," the older boy replied.

"Both of you settle down right now," the mother said.

Trinity's associate pastor, a middle-aged woman with graying hair and a no-nonsense demeanor, read the bulletin and led sleepy voices through a few traditional hymns. Then the choir filed down the aisle dressed in white robes and kente-cloth shawls, clapping and singing as they fanned out behind the altar, an organ following the quickening drums:

I'm so glad, Jesus lifted me!
I'm so glad, Jesus lifted me!
I'm so glad, Jesus lifted me!
Singing Glory, Ha-le-lu-yah!
Jesus lifted me!

As the congregation joined in, the deacons, then Reverend Wright, appeared beneath the large cross that hung from the rafters. The reverend remained silent while devotions were read, scanning the faces in front of him, watching the collection basket pass from hand to hand. When the collection was over, he stepped up to the pulpit and read the names of those who had passed away that week, those who were ailing, each name causing a flutter somewhere in the crowd, the murmur of recognition.

"Let us join hands," the reverend said, "as we kneel and pray at the foot of an old rugged cross—"

"Yes . . ."

"Lord, we come first to thank you for what you've already done for us. . . . We come to thank you most of all for Jesus. Lord, we come from different walks of life. Some considered high, and some low . . . but all on equal ground at the foot of this cross. Lord, thank you! For Jesus, Lord . . . our burden bearer and heavy load sharer, we thank you. . . ."

The title of Reverend Wright's sermon that morning was "The Audacity of Hope." He began with a passage from the Book of Samuel—the story of Hannah, who, barren and taunted by her rivals, had wept and shaken in prayer before her God. The story reminded him, he said, of a sermon a fellow pastor had preached at a conference some years before, in which the pastor described going to a museum and being confronted by a painting titled *Hope*.

"The painting depicts a harpist," Reverend Wright explained, "a woman who at first glance appears to be sitting atop a great mountain. Until you take a closer look and see that the woman is bruised and bloodied, dressed in tattered rags, the harp reduced to a single frayed string. Your eye is then drawn down to the scene below, down to the valley below, where everywhere are the ravages of famine, the drumbeat of war, a world groaning under strife and deprivation.

"It is this world, a world where cruise ships throw away more food in a day than most residents of Port-au-Prince see in a year, where white folks' greed runs a world in need, apartheid in one hemisphere, apathy in another hemisphere . . . That's the world! On which hope sits!"

And so it went, a meditation on a fallen world. While the boys next to me doodled on their church bulletin, Reverend Wright spoke of Sharpsville and Hiroshima, the callousness of policy makers in the White House and in the State House. As the sermon unfolded, though, the stories of strife became more prosaic, the pain more immediate. The reverend spoke of the hardship that the congregation would face tomorrow, the pain of those far from the mountaintop, worrying about paying the light bill. But also the pain of those closer to the metaphorical summit: the middle-class woman who seems to have all her worldly needs taken care of but whose husband is treating her like "the maid, the household service, the jitney service, and the escort service all rolled into one"; the child whose wealthy parents worry more about "the texture of hair on the outside of the head than the quality of education inside the head."

"Isn't that . . . the world that each of us stands on?"

"Yessuh!"

"Like Hannah, we have known bitter times! Daily, we face rejection and despair!"

"Say it!"

"And yet consider once again the painting before us. Hope! Like Hannah, that harpist is looking upwards, a few faint notes floating upwards towards the heavens. She dares to hope. . . . She has the audacity . . . to make music . . . and praise God . . . on the one string . . . she has left!"

People began to shout, to rise from their seats and clap and cry out, a forceful wind carrying the reverend's voice up into the rafters. As I watched and listened from my seat, I began to hear all the notes from the past three years swirl about me. The courage and fear of Ruby and Will. The race pride and anger of men like Rafiq. The desire to let go, the desire to escape, the desire to give oneself up to a God that could somehow put a floor on despair.

And in that single note—hope!—I heard something else; at the foot of that cross, inside the thousands of churches across the city, I imagined the stories of ordinary black people merging with the stories of David and Goliath, Moses and Pharaoh, the Christians in the lion's den, Ezekiel's field of dry bones. Those stories—of survival, and freedom, and hope—became our story, my story; the blood that had spilled was our blood, the tears our tears; until this black church, on this bright day, seemed once more a vessel carrying the story of a people into future generations and into a larger world. Our trials and triumphs became at once unique and universal, black and more than black; in chronicling our journey, the stories and songs gave us a means to reclaim memories that we didn't need to feel shamed about, memories more accessible than those of ancient Egypt, memories that all people might study and cherish—and with which we could start to rebuild. And if a part of me continued to feel that this Sunday communion sometimes simplified our condition, that it could sometimes disguise or suppress the very real conflicts among us and would fulfill its promise only through action, I also felt for the first time how that spirit carried within it, nascent, incomplete, the possibility of moving beyond our narrow dreams.

"The audacity of hope! I still remember my grandmother, singing in the house, 'There's a bright side somewhere . . . don't rest till you find it. . . .'"

"That's right!"

"The audacity of hope! Times when we couldn't pay the bills.

Times when it looked like I wasn't ever going to amount to anything . . . at the age of fifteen, busted for grand larceny auto theft . . .
and yet and still my momma and daddy would break into a song . . .

> *Thank you, Jesus.* Thank you, Jesus.
> *Thank you, Jesus.* Thank you, Jesus.
> *Thank you, Je-sus,*
> *Thank you, Lo-ord.*
> *You brought me fro-om*
> *A mighty long way,* mighty long way.

"And it made no sense to me, this singing! Why were they thanking
Him for all of their troubles? I'd ask myself. But see, I was only looking at the horizontal dimension of their lives!"

"Tell it now!"

"I didn't understand that they were talking about the vertical
dimension! About their relationship to God! I didn't understand that
they were thanking Him in advance for all that they dared to hope
for in me! Oh, I thank you, Jesus, for not letting go of me when I let
go of you! Oh yes, Jesus, I thank you. . . ."

As the choir lifted back up into song, as the congregation began to
applaud those who were walking to the altar to accept Reverend
Wright's call, I felt a light touch on the top of my hand. I looked
down to see the older of the two boys sitting beside me, his face
slightly apprehensive as he handed me a pocket tissue. Beside him,
his mother glanced at me with a faint smile before turning back
toward the altar. It was only as I thanked the boy that I felt the tears
running down my cheeks.

"Oh, Jesus," I heard the older woman beside me whisper softly.
"Thank you for carrying us this far."

PART THREE

Kenya

CHAPTER FIFTEEN

．．．

I FLEW OUT OF HEATHROW Airport under stormy skies. A group of young British men dressed in ill-fitting blazers filled the back of the plane, and one of them—a pale, gangly youth, still troubled with acne—took the seat beside me. He read over the emergency instructions twice with great concentration, and once we were airborne, he turned to ask where I was headed. I told him I was traveling to Nairobi to visit my family.

"Nairobi's a beautiful place, I hear. Wouldn't mind stopping off there one of these days. Going to Johannesburg, I am." He explained that as part of a degree program in geology, the British government had arranged for him and his classmates to work with South African mining companies for a year. "Seems like they have a shortage of trained people there, so if we're lucky they'll take us on for a permanent spot. Best chance we have for a decent wage, I reckon—unless you're willing to freeze out on some bleeding North Sea oil rig. Not for me, thank you."

I mentioned that if given the chance, a lot of black South Africans might be interested in getting such training.

"Well, I'd imagine you're right about that," he said. "Don't much agree with the race policy there. A shame, that." He thought for a

299

moment. "But then the rest of Africa's falling apart now, isn't it? Least from what I can tell. The blacks in South Africa aren't starving to death like they do in some of these Godforsaken countries. Don't envy them, mind you, but compared to some poor bugger in Ethiopia—"

A stewardess came down the aisle with headphones for rent, and the young man pulled out his wallet. "'Course, I try and stay out of politics, you know. Figure it's none of my business. Same thing back home—everybody on the dole, the old men in Parliament talking the same old rubbish. Best thing to do is mind your own little corner of the world, that's what I say." He found the outlet for the headphones and slipped them over his ears.

"Wake me up when they bring the food, will you," he said before reclining his seat for a nap.

I pulled out a book from my carry-on bag and tried to read. It was a portrait of several African countries written by a Western journalist who'd spent a decade in Africa; an old Africa hand, he would be called, someone who apparently prided himself on the balanced assessment. The book's first few chapters discussed the history of colonialism at some length: the manipulation of tribal hatreds and the caprice of colonial boundaries, the displacements, the detentions, the indignities large and small. The early heroism of independence figures like Kenyatta and Nkrumah was duly noted, their later drift toward despotism attributed at least in part to various Cold War machinations.

But by the book's third chapter, images from the present had begun to outstrip the past. Famine, disease, the coups and counter-coups led by illiterate young men wielding AK-47s like shepherd sticks—if Africa had a history, the writer seemed to say, the scale of current suffering had rendered such history meaningless.

Poor buggers. Godforsaken countries.

I set the book down, feeling a familiar anger flush through me, an anger all the more maddening for its lack of a clear target. Beside me the young Brit was snoring softly now, his glasses askew on his fin-shaped nose. Was I angry at him? I wondered. Was it his fault that, for all my education, all the theories in my possession, I had had no ready answers to the questions he'd posed? How much could I blame him for wanting to better his lot? Maybe I was just angry because of his easy familiarity with me, his assumption that I, as an American, even a black American, might naturally share in his dim view of Africa; an assumption that in his world at least marked a progress of sorts, but that for me only underscored my own uneasy status: a Westerner not entirely at home in the West, an African on his way to a land full of strangers.

I'd been feeling this way all through my stay in Europe—edgy, defensive, hesitant with strangers. I hadn't planned it that way. I had thought of the layover there as nothing more than a whimsical detour, an opportunity to visit places I had never been before. For three weeks I had traveled alone, down one side of the continent and up the other, by bus and by train mostly, a guidebook in hand. I took tea by the Thames and watched children chase each other through the chestnut groves of Luxembourg Garden. I crossed the Plaza Major at high noon, with its De Chirico shadows and sparrows swirling across cobalt skies; and watched night fall over the Palatine, waiting for the first stars to appear, listening to the wind and its whispers of mortality.

And by the end of the first week or so, I realized that I'd made a mistake. It wasn't that Europe wasn't beautiful; everything was just as I'd imagined it. It just wasn't mine. I felt as if I were living out someone else's romance; the incompleteness of my own history stood between me and the sites I saw like a hard pane of glass. I began to suspect that my European stop was just one more means of delay, one more attempt to avoid coming to terms with the Old Man. Stripped of language, stripped of work and routine—stripped even of the racial obsessions to which I'd become so accustomed and which I had taken (perversely) as a sign of my own maturation—I had been forced to look inside myself and had found only a great emptiness there.

Would this trip to Kenya finally fill that emptiness? The folks back in Chicago thought so. It'll be just like *Roots*, Will had said at my going-away party. A pilgrimage, Asante had called it. For them, as for me, Africa had become an idea more than an actual place, a new promised land, full of ancient traditions and sweeping vistas, noble struggles and talking drums. With the benefit of distance, we engaged Africa in a selective embrace—the same sort of embrace I'd once offered the Old Man. What would happen once I relinquished that distance? It was nice to believe that the truth would somehow set me free. But what if that was wrong? What if the truth only disappointed, and my father's death meant nothing, and his leaving me behind meant nothing, and the only tie that bound me to him, or to Africa, was a name, a blood type, or white people's scorn?

I switched off the overhead light and closed my eyes, letting my mind drift back to an African I'd met while traveling through Spain, another man on the run. I had been waiting for a night bus in a roadside tavern about halfway between Madrid and Barcelona. A few old men sat at tables and drank wine from short, cloudy glasses. There was a pool table off to one side, and for some reason I had racked up the balls and started to play, remembering those late evenings with Gramps in the bars on Hotel Street, with their streetwalkers and pimps and Gramps the only white man in the joint.

As I was finishing up the table, a man in a thin wool sweater had appeared out of nowhere and asked if he could buy me some coffee. He spoke no English, and his Spanish wasn't much better than mine, but he had a winning smile and the urgency of someone in need of company. Standing at the bar, he told me he was from Senegal, and was crisscrossing Spain for seasonal work. He showed me a battered photograph he kept in his wallet of a young girl with round, smooth cheeks. His wife, he said; he had had to leave her behind. They would be reunited as soon as he saved the money. He would write and send for her.

We ended up riding to Barcelona together, neither of us talking much, him turning to me every so often to try to explain the jokes on the Spanish program being shown on a TV-video contraption hooked up above the driver's seat. Shortly before dawn, we were deposited in front of an old bus depot, and my friend gestured me over to a short, thick palm that grew beside the road. From his knapsack he pulled out a toothbrush, a comb, and a bottle of water that he handed to me with great ceremony. And together we washed ourselves under the morning mist, before hoisting our bags over our shoulders and heading toward town.

What was his name? I couldn't remember now; just another hungry man far away from home, one of the many children of former colonies—Algerians, West Indians, Pakistanis—now breaching the barricades of their former masters, mounting their own ragged, haphazard invasion. And yet, as we walked toward the Ramblas, I had felt as if I knew him as well as any man; that, coming from opposite ends of the earth, we were somehow making the same journey. When we finally parted company, I had remained in the street for a long, long time, watching his slender, bandy-legged image shrink into the distance, one part of me wishing then that I could go with him into a life of open roads and other blue mornings; another part realizing that such a wish was also a romance, an idea, as partial as my image of the Old Man or my image of Africa. Until I settled on the fact that this man from Senegal had bought me coffee and offered me water, and that was real, and maybe that was all any of us had a right to expect: the chance encounter, a shared story, the act of small kindness. . . .

The airplane shook with some turbulence; the flight crew came to serve us dinner. I woke up the young Brit, who ate with impressive precision, describing, between bites, what it had been like to grow up in Manchester. Eventually I dozed off into a fitful sleep. When I

awoke, the stewardess was passing out customs forms in preparation
for landing. Outside it was still dark, but, pressing my face against the
glass, I began to see scattered lights, soft and hazy like fireflies, gradually swarming into the shape of a city below. A few minutes later, a
slope of rounded hills appeared, black against a long strand of light
on the eastern horizon. As we touched down on an African dawn I
saw high thin clouds streak the sky, their underbellies glowing with a
reddish hue.

Kenyatta International Airport was almost empty. Officials sipped at
their morning tea as they checked over passports; in the baggage
area, a creaky conveyor belt slowly disgorged luggage. Auma was
nowhere in sight, so I took a seat on my carry-on bag and lit a cigarette. After a few minutes, a security guard with a wooden club
started to walk toward me. I looked around for an ashtray, thinking I
must be in a no-smoking area, but instead of scolding me, the guard
smiled and asked if I had another cigarette to spare.

"This is your first trip to Kenya, yes?" he asked as I gave him a light.

"That's right."

"I see." He squatted down beside me. "You are from America. You
know my brother's son, perhaps. Samson Otieno. He is studying
engineering in Texas."

I told him that I'd never been to Texas and so hadn't had the
opportunity to meet his nephew. This seemed to disappoint him, and
he took several puffs from his cigarette in quick succession. By this
time, the last of the other passengers on my flight had left the terminal. I asked the guard if any more bags were coming. He shook his
head doubtfully.

"I don't think so," he said, "but if you will just wait here, I will find
someone who can help you."

He disappeared around a narrow corridor, and I stood up to
stretch my back. The rush of anticipation had drained away, and I

smiled with the memory of the homecoming I had once imagined for myself, clouds lifting, old demons fleeing, the earth trembling as ancestors rose up in celebration. Instead I felt tired and abandoned. I was about to search for a telephone when the security guard reappeared with a strikingly beautiful woman, dark, slender, close to six feet tall, dressed in a British Airways uniform. She introduced herself as Miss Omoro and explained that my bag had probably been sent on to Johannesburg by mistake.

"I'm awfully sorry about the inconvenience," she said. "If you will just fill out this form, we can call Johannesburg and have it delivered to you as soon as the next flight comes in."

I completed the form and Miss Omoro gave it the once-over before looking back at me. "You wouldn't be related to Dr. Obama, by any chance?" she asked.

"Well, yes—he was my father."

Miss Omoro smiled sympathetically. "I'm very sorry about his passing. Your father was a close friend of my family's. He would often come to our house when I was a child."

We began to talk about my visit, and she told me of her studies in London, as well as her interest in traveling to the States. I found myself trying to prolong the conversation, encouraged less by Miss Omoro's beauty—she had mentioned a fiancé—than by the fact that she'd recognized my name. That had never happened before, I realized; not in Hawaii, not in Indonesia, not in L.A. or New York or Chicago. For the first time in my life, I felt the comfort, the firmness of identity that a name might provide, how it could carry an entire history in other people's memories, so that they might nod and say knowingly, "Oh, you are so and so's son." No one here in Kenya would ask how to spell my name, or mangle it with an unfamiliar tongue. My name belonged and so I belonged, drawn into a web of relationships, alliances, and grudges that I did not yet understand.

"Barack!" I turned to see Auma jumping up and down behind

another guard, who wasn't letting her pass into the baggage area. I excused myself and rushed over to her, and we laughed and hugged, as silly as the first time we'd met. A tall, brown-skinned woman was smiling beside us, and Auma turned and said, "Barack, this is our Auntie Zeituni. Our father's sister."

"Welcome home," Zeituni said, kissing me on both cheeks.

I told them about my bag and said that there was someone here who had known the Old Man. But when I looked back to where I'd been standing, Miss Omoro was nowhere in sight. I asked the security guard where she had gone. He shrugged and said that she must have left for the day.

Auma drove an old, baby-blue Volkswagen Beetle. The car was something of a business venture for her: Since Kenyan nationals living abroad could ship a car back to Kenya free of a hefty import tax, she had figured that she could use it during the year that she'd be teaching at the University of Nairobi and then sell it for the cost of shipping and perhaps a small profit. Unfortunately, the engine had come down with a tubercular knock, and the muffler had fallen off on the way to the airport. As we sputtered out onto the four-lane highway, Auma clutching the steering wheel with both hands, I couldn't keep from laughing.

"Should I get out and push?"

Zeituni frowned. "Eh, Barry, don't say anything about this car. This is a beautiful car. It just needs some new paint. In fact, Auma has already promised that I will have this car after she leaves."

Auma shook her head. "Your aunt is trying to cheat me now, Barack. I promised we would talk about it, that's all."

"What's there to talk about?" Zeituni said, winking at me. "I tell you, Auma, I will give you the best price."

The two of them began to talk at the same time, asking how my trip had been, telling me all the plans they had made, listing all the people

I had to see. Wide plains stretched out on either side of the road, savannah grass mostly, an occasional thorn tree against the horizon, a landscape that seemed at once ancient and raw. Gradually the traffic thickened, and crowds began to pour out of the countryside on their way to work, the men still buttoning their flimsy shirts; the women straight-backed, their heads wrapped in bright-colored scarves. Cars meandered across lanes and roundabouts, dodging potholes, bicycles, and pedestrians, while rickety jitneys—called *matatus*, I was told—stopped without any warning to cram on more passengers. It all seemed strangely familiar, as if I had been down the same road before. And then I remembered other mornings in Indonesia, with my mother and Lolo talking in the front seat, the same smell of burning wood and diesel, the same stillness that lingered at the center of the morning rush, the same look on people's faces as they made their way into a new day, with few expectations other than making it through, and perhaps a mild hope that their luck would change, or at least hold out.

We went to drop off Zeituni at Kenya Breweries, a large, drab complex where she worked as a computer programmer. Stepping out of the car, she leaned over again to kiss me on the cheek, then wagged her finger at Auma. "You take good care of Barry now," she said. "Make sure he doesn't get lost again."

Once we were back on the highway, I asked Auma what Zeituni had meant about my getting lost. Auma shrugged.

"It's a common expression here," she said. "Usually, it means the person hasn't seen you in a while. 'You've been lost,' they'll say. Or 'Don't get lost.' Sometimes it has a more serious meaning. Let's say a son or husband moves to the city, or to the West, like our Uncle Omar, in Boston. They promise to return after completing school. They say they'll send for the family once they get settled. At first they write once a week. Then it's just once a month. Then they stop writing completely. No one sees them again. They've been lost, you see. Even if people know where they are."

The Volkswagen struggled up an ascending road shaded by thick groves of eucalyptus and liana vines. Elegant old homes receded behind the hedges and flower beds, homes that had once been exclusively British, Auma said, but that now mostly served government officials and foreign embassy staffs. At the top of the rise we made a sharp right and parked at the end of a gravel driveway next to a yellow two-story apartment building that the university rented out to its faculty. A huge lawn sloped down from the apartments to meet patches of banana trees and high forest and, farther down, a narrow, murky stream that ran through a wide gully pitted with stones.

Auma's apartment, a small but comfortable space with French doors that let sunlight wash through the rooms, was on the first floor. There were stacks of books everywhere, and a collage of photographs hanging on one wall, studio portraits and Polaroid shots, a patchwork of family that Auma had stitched together for herself. Above Auma's bed, I noticed a large poster of a black woman, her face tilted upward toward an unfolding blossom, the words "I Have a Dream" printed below.

"So what's your dream, Auma?" I said, setting down my bags.

Auma laughed. "That's my biggest problem, Barack. Too many dreams. A woman with dreams always has problems."

My exhaustion from the trip must have showed, because Auma suggested that I take a nap while she went to the university to teach her class. I dropped onto the cot she'd prepared and fell asleep to the buzz of insects outside the window. When I awoke it was dusk and Auma was still gone. From the kitchen, I noticed a troop of black-faced monkeys gathered beneath a banyan tree. The older ones sat warily at the tree's base watching with knotted brows as pups scampered about through the long, winding roots. Rinsing my face in the sink, I put water on for tea, then opened the door that led into the yard. The monkeys all froze in their tracks; their eyes turned toward me in unison. A few feet away, the air filled with the beat of huge green wings, and I watched the dreamy ascent of a long-necked bird as it sent out a series of deep-throated cries and drifted toward distant canopies.

We decided to stay in that night, cooking stew and catching up on each other's news. The next morning we walked into town and wandered without any particular destination in mind, just taking in the sights. The city center was smaller than I'd expected, with much of the colonial architecture still intact: row after row of worn, whitewashed stucco from the days when Nairobi was little more than an outpost to service British railway construction. Alongside these buildings, another city emerged, a city of high-rise offices and elegant shops, hotels with lobbies that seemed barely distinguishable from their counterparts in Singapore or Atlanta. It was an intoxicating, elusive mixture, a contrast that seemed to repeat itself wherever we went: in front of the Mercedes-Benz dealership, where a train of Masai women passed by on the way to market, their heads shaven clean, their slender bodies wrapped in red *shukas*, their earlobes elongated and ringed with bright beads; or at the entrance to an open-air mosque, where we watched a group of bank officers carefully remove their wing-tipped shoes and bathe their feet before joining farmers and ditchdiggers in afternoon prayer. It was as if Nairobi's history refused to settle in orderly layers, as if what was then and what was now fell in constant, noisy collision.

We wandered into the old marketplace, a cavernous building that smelled of ripe fruit and a nearby butchery. A passage to the rear of the building led into a maze of open-air stalls where merchants hawked fabrics, baskets, brass jewelry, and other curios. I stopped in front of one of them, where a set of small wooden carvings was set out for display. I recognized the figures as my father's long-ago gift to me: elephants, lions, drummers in tribal headdress. They are only small things, the Old Man had said. . . .

"Come, mister," the young man who was minding the stall said to me. "A beautiful necklace for your wife."

"This is my sister."

"She is a very beautiful sister. Come, this is nice for her."

"How much?"

"Only five hundred shillings. Beautiful."

Auma frowned and said something to the man in Swahili. "He's giving you the *wazungu* price," she explained. "The white man's price."

The young man smiled. "I'm very sorry, sister," he said. "For a Kenyan, the price is three hundred only."

Inside the stall, an old woman who was stringing glass beads together pointed at me and said something that made Auma smile.

"What'd she say?"

"She says that you look like an American to her."

"Tell her I'm Luo," I said, beating my chest.

The old woman laughed and asked Auma my name. The answer made the old woman laugh even harder, and she called for me to stand beside her, taking my hand. "She says you don't look much like a Luo," Auma said, "but you have a kind face. She says she has a daughter you should meet and that, if you buy her a soda, you can have two carvings and the necklace she's making for five hundred shillings."

The young man went to buy sodas for all of us, and we sat on wooden stools that the old woman pulled out from behind a large chest. She told us about her business, the rent she had to pay the government for the use of her stall, how her other son joined the army because there was no land left to work in their village. Across from us, another woman wove colored straw into baskets; beside her, a man cut a hide into long strips to be used for some purse straps.

I watched these nimble hands stitch and cut and weave, and listened to the old woman's voice roll over the sounds of work and barter, and for a moment the world seemed entirely transparent. I began to imagine an unchanging rhythm of days, lived on firm soil where you could wake up each morning and know that all was how it had been yesterday, where you saw how the things that you used had been made and could recite the lives of those who had made them and could believe that it would all hang together without computer terminals or fax machines. And all of this while a steady procession of black faces passed before your eyes, the round faces of babies and the chipped, worn faces of the old; beautiful faces that made me understand the transformation that Asante and other black Americans claimed to have undergone after their first visit to Africa. For a span of weeks or months, you could experience the freedom that comes from not feeling watched, the freedom of believing that your hair grows as it's supposed to grow and that your rump sways the way a rump is supposed to sway. You could see a man talking to himself as just plain crazy, or read about the criminal on the front page of the daily paper and ponder the corruption of the human heart, without having to think about whether the criminal or lunatic said something about your own fate. Here the world was black, and so you were just you; you could discover all those things that were unique to your life without living a lie or committing betrayal.

How tempting, I thought, to fly away with this moment intact. To have this feeling of ease wrapped up as neatly as the young man was now wrapping Auma's necklace, and take it back with me to America to slip on whenever my spirits flagged.

But of course that wasn't possible. We finished our sodas. Money changed hands. We left the marketplace. The moment slipped away.

We turned onto Kimathi Street, named after one of the leaders of the Mau-Mau rebellion. I had read a book about Kimathi before leaving Chicago and remembered a photograph of him: one in a group of dreadlocked men who lived in the forest and spread secret oaths among the native population—the prototype guerrilla fighter. It was a clever costume he had chosen for himself (Kimathi and the other Mau-Mau leaders had served in British regiments in their previous lives), an image that played on all the fears of the colonial West, the same sort of fear that Nat Turner had once evoked in the antebellum

South and coke-crazed muggers now evoked in the minds of whites in Chicago.

Of course, the Mau-Mau lay in Kenya's past. Kimathi had been captured and executed. Kenyatta had been released from prison and inaugurated Kenya's first president. He had immediately assured whites who were busy packing their bags that businesses would not be nationalized, that landholdings would be kept intact, so long as the black man controlled the apparatus of government. Kenya became the West's most stalwart pupil in Africa, a model of stability, a useful contrast to the chaos of Uganda, the failed socialism of Tanzania. Former freedom fighters returned to their villages or joined the civil service or ran for a seat in Parliament. Kimathi became a name on a street sign, thoroughly tamed for the tourists.

I took the opportunity to study these tourists as Auma and I sat down for lunch in the outdoor café of the New Stanley Hotel. They were everywhere—Germans, Japanese, British, Americans—taking pictures, hailing taxis, fending off street peddlers, many of them dressed in safari suits like extras on a movie set. In Hawaii, when we were still kids, my friends and I had laughed at tourists like these, with their sunburns and their pale, skinny legs, basking in the glow of our obvious superiority. Here in Africa, though, the tourists didn't seem so funny. I felt them as an encroachment, somehow; I found their innocence vaguely insulting. It occurred to me that in their utter lack of self-consciousness, they were expressing a freedom that neither Auma nor I could ever experience, a bedrock confidence in their own parochialism, a confidence reserved for those born into imperial cultures.

Just then I noticed an American family sit down a few tables away from us. Two of the African waiters immediately sprang into action, both of them smiling from one ear to the other. Since Auma and I hadn't yet been served, I began to wave at the two waiters who remained standing by the kitchen, thinking they must have somehow failed to see us. For some time they managed to avoid my glance, but eventually an older man with sleepy eyes relented and brought us over two menus. His manner was resentful, though, and after several more minutes he showed no signs of ever coming back. Auma's face began to pinch with anger, and again I waved to our waiter, who continued in his silence as he wrote down our orders. At this point, the Americans had already received their food and we still had no place settings. I overheard a young girl with a blond ponytail complain that there wasn't any ketchup. Auma stood up.

"Let's go."

She started heading for the exit, then suddenly turned and walked back to the waiter, who was watching us with an impassive stare.

"You should be ashamed of yourself," Auma said to him, her voice shaking. "You should be ashamed."

The waiter replied brusquely in Swahili.

"I don't care how many mouths you have to feed, you cannot treat your own people like dogs. Here . . ." Auma snapped open her purse and took out a crumpled hundred-shilling note. "You see!" she shouted. "I can pay for my own damn food."

She threw the note to the ground, then marched out onto the street. For several minutes we wandered without apparent direction, until I finally suggested we sit down on a bench beside the central post office.

"You okay?" I asked her.

She nodded. "That was stupid, throwing away money like that." She set down her purse beside her and we watched the traffic pass. "You know, I can't go to a club in any of these hotels if I'm with another African woman," she said eventually. "The *askaris* will turn us away, thinking we are prostitutes. The same in any of these big office buildings. If you don't work there, and you are African, they will stop you until you tell them your business. But if you're with a German friend, then they're all smiles. 'Good evening, miss,' they'll say. 'How are you tonight?'" Auma shook her head. "That's why Kenya, no matter what its GNP, no matter how many things you can buy here, the rest of Africa laughs. It's the whore of Africa, Barack. It opens its legs to anyone who can pay."

I told Auma she was being too hard on the Kenyan, that the same sort of thing happened in Djakarta or Mexico City—just an unfortunate matter of economics. But as we started back toward the apartment, I knew my words had done nothing to soothe her bitterness. I suspected that she was right: not all the tourists in Nairobi had come for the wildlife. Some came because Kenya, without shame, offered to re-create an age when the lives of whites in foreign lands rested comfortably on the backs of the darker races; an age of innocence before Kimathi and other angry young men in Soweto or Detroit or the Mekong Delta started to lash out in street crime and revolution. In Kenya, a white man could still walk through Isak Dinesen's home and imagine romance with a mysterious young baroness, or sip gin under the ceiling fans of the Lord Delamare Hotel and admire portraits of Hemingway smiling after a successful hunt, surrounded by grim-faced coolies. He could be served by a black man without fear or guilt, marvel at the exchange rate, and leave a generous tip; and if he felt a touch of indigestion at the sight of leprous beggars outside the hotel, he could always administer a ready tonic. Black rule has come, after all. This is their country. We're only visitors.

Did our waiter know that black rule had come? Did it mean anything to him? Maybe once, I thought to myself. He would be old enough to remember independence, the shouts of "*Uhuru!*" and the raising of new flags. But such memories may seem almost fantastic to him now, distant and naive. He's learned that the same people who controlled the land before independence still control the same land, that he still cannot eat in the restaurants or stay in the hotels that the white man has built. He sees the money of the city swirling above his head, and the technology that spits out goods from its robot mouth.

If he's ambitious he will do his best to learn the white man's language and use the white man's machines, trying to make ends meet the same way the computer repairman in Newark or the bus driver back in Chicago does, with alternating spurts of enthusiasm or frustration but mostly with resignation. And if you say to him that he's serving the interests of neocolonialism or some other such thing, he will reply that yes, he will serve if that is what's required. It is the lucky ones who serve; the unlucky ones drift into the murky tide of hustles and odd jobs; many will drown.

Then again, maybe that's not all that the waiter is feeling. Maybe a part of him still clings to the stories of Mau-Mau, the same part of him that remembers the hush of a village night or the sound of his mother grinding corn under a stone pallet. Something in him still says that the white man's ways are not his ways, that the objects he may use every day are not of his making. He remembers a time, a way of imagining himself, that he leaves only at his peril. He can't escape the grip of his memories. And so he straddles two worlds, uncertain in each, always off balance, playing whichever game staves off the bottomless poverty, careful to let his anger vent itself only on those in the same condition.

A voice says to him yes, changes have come, the old ways lie broken, and you must find a way as fast as you can to feed your belly and stop the white man from laughing at you.

A voice says no, you will sooner burn the earth to the ground.

That evening, we drove east to Kariako, a sprawling apartment complex surrounded by dirt lots. The moon had dropped behind thick clouds, and light drizzle had begun to fall. As we climbed the dark stairwell, a young man bounded past us onto the broken pavement and into the night. At the top of three flights, Auma pushed against a door that was slightly ajar.

"Barry! You've finally come!"

A short, stocky woman with a cheerful brown face gave me a tight squeeze around the waist. Behind her were fifteen or so people, all of them smiling and waving like a crowd at a parade. The short woman looked up at me and frowned.

"You don't remember me, do you?"

"I . . ."

"I'm your Aunt Jane. It is me that called you when your father died." She smiled and took me by the hand. "Come. You must meet everybody here. Zeituni you have already met. This . . ." she said, leading me to a handsome older woman in a green patterned dress, "this is my sister, Kezia. She is mother to Auma and to Roy Obama."

Kezia took my hand and said my name together with a few words of Swahili.

"She says her other son has finally come home," Jane said.

"My son," Kezia repeated in English, nodding and pulling me into a hug. "My son has come home."

We continued around the room, shaking hands with aunts, cousins, nephews, and nieces. Everyone greeted me with cheerful curiosity but very little awkwardness, as if meeting a relative for the first time was an everyday occurrence. I had brought a bag of chocolates for the children, and they gathered around me with polite stares as the adults tried to explain who I was. I noticed a young man, sixteen or seventeen, standing against the wall with a watchful expression.

"That's one of your brothers," Auma said to me. "Bernard."

I went over to the young man and we shook hands, studying each other's faces. I found myself at a loss for words but managed to ask him how he had been.

"Fine, I guess," he answered softly, which brought a round of laughter from everyone.

After the introductions were over, Jane pushed me toward a small table set with bowls of goat curry, fried fish, collards, and rice. As we ate, people asked me about everyone back in Hawaii, and I tried to describe my life in Chicago and my work as an organizer. They nodded politely but seemed a bit puzzled, so I mentioned that I'd be studying law at Harvard in the fall.

"Ah, this is good, Barry," Jane said as she sucked on a bone from the curry. "Your father studied at this school, Harvard. You will make us all proud, just like him. You see, Bernard, you must study hard like your brother."

"Bernard thinks he's going to be a football star," Zeituni said.

I turned to Bernard. "Is that right, Bernard?"

"No," he said, uncomfortable that he'd attracted attention. "I used to play, that's all."

"Well . . . maybe we can play sometime."

He shook his head. "I like to play basketball now," he said earnestly. "Like Magic Johnson."

The meal smothered some of the initial excitement, and the children turned to a large black-and-white TV that was showing the munificence of the president: the president opens a school; the president denounces foreign journalists and various Communist elements; the president encourages the nation to follow the path of *nyayo*—"footsteps toward progress." I went with Auma to see the rest of the apartment, which consisted of two bedrooms, both jammed from one end to the other with old mattresses.

"How many people live here?" I asked.

"I'm not sure right now," Auma said. "It always changes. Jane doesn't know how to say no to anybody, so any relative who moves to the city or loses a job ends up here. Sometimes they stay a long time. Or they leave their children here. The Old Man and my mum left Bernard here a lot. Jane practically raised him."

"Can she afford it?"

"Not really. She has a job as a telephone operator, which doesn't pay so much. She doesn't complain, though. She can't have her own children, so she looks after others'."

We returned to the living room, and I sank down into an old sofa. In the kitchen, Zeituni directed the younger women in cleaning the dishes; a few of the children were now arguing about the chocolate I'd brought. I let my eyes wander over the scene—the well-worn furniture, the two-year-old calendar, the fading photographs, the blue ceramic cherubs that sat on linen doilies. It was just like the apartments in Altgeld, I realized. The same chain of mothers and daughters and children. The same noise of gossip and TV. The perpetual motion of cooking and cleaning and nursing hurts large and small. The same absence of men.

We said our good-byes around ten, promising to visit each and every relative in turn. As we walked to the door, Jane pulled us aside and lowered her voice. "You need to take Barry to see your Aunt Sarah," she whispered to Auma. And then to me: "Sarah is your father's older sister. The firstborn. She wants to see you very badly."

"Of course," I said. "But why wasn't she here tonight? Does she live far away?"

Jane looked at Auma, and some unspoken thought passed between them. "Come on, Barack," Auma said finally. "I'll explain it to you in the car."

The roads were empty and slick with rain. "Jane is right, Barack," Auma told me as we passed the university. "You should go see Sarah. But I won't go with you."

"Why not?"

"It's this business with the Old Man's estate. Sarah is one of the people who has disputed the will. She's been telling people that Roy, Bernard, myself—that none of us are the Old Man's children." Auma sighed. "I don't know. A part of me sympathizes with her. She's had a hard life. She never had the chances the Old Man had, you see, to study or go abroad. It made her very bitter. She thinks that somehow my mum, myself, that we are to blame for her situation."

"But how much could the Old Man's estate be worth?"

"Not much. Maybe a small government pension. A piece of worthless land. I try to stay out of it. Whatever is there has probably been spent on lawyers by now. But you see, everyone expected so much from the Old Man. He made them think that he had everything, even when he had nothing. So now, instead of getting on with their lives, they just wait and argue among themselves, thinking that the Old Man somehow is going to rescue them from his grave. Bernard's learned this same waiting attitude. You know, he's really smart, Barack, but he just sits around all day doing nothing. He dropped out of school and doesn't have much prospect for finding work. I've told him that I would help him get into some sort of trade school, whatever he wants, just so he's doing something, you know. He'll say okay, but when I ask if he's gotten any applications or talked to the schoolmasters, nothing's been done. Sometimes I feel like, unless I take every step with him, nothing will happen."

"Maybe I can help."

"Yes. Maybe you can talk to him. But now that you're here, coming from America, you're part of the inheritance, you see. That's why Sarah wants to see you so much. She thinks I'm hiding you from her because you're the one with everything."

The rain had started up again as we parked the car. A single light bulb jutting from the side of the building sent webbed, liquid shadows across Auma's face. "The whole thing gets me so tired, Barack," she said softly. "You wouldn't believe how much I missed Kenya when I was in Germany. All I could do was think about getting back home. I thought how I never feel lonely here, and family is everywhere, nobody sends their parents to an old people's home or leaves their children with strangers. Then I'm here and everyone is asking me for help, and I feel like they are all just grabbing at me and that I'm going to sink. I feel guilty because I was luckier than them. I went to a university. I can get a job. But what can I do, Barack? I'm only one person."

I took Auma's hand and we remained in the car for several minutes, listening to the rain as it slackened. "You asked me what my dream was," she said finally. "Sometimes I have this dream that I will build a beautiful house on our grandfather's land. A big house where we can all stay and bring our families, you see. We could plant fruit trees like our grandfather, and our children would really know the land and speak Luo and learn our ways from the old people. It would belong to them."

"We can do all that, Auma."

She shook her head. "Let me tell you what I start thinking then. I think of who will take care of the house if I'm not here? I think, who can I count on to make sure that a leak gets fixed or that the fence gets mended? It's terrible, selfish, I know. All I can do when I think this way is to get mad at the Old Man because he didn't build this house for us. We are the children, Barack. Why do we have to take care of everyone? Everything is upside down, crazy. I had to take care of myself, just like Bernard. Now I'm used to living my own life, just like a German. Everything is organized. If something is broken, I fix it. If something goes wrong, it's my own fault. If I have it, I send money to the family, and they can do with it what they want, and I won't depend on them, and they won't depend on me."

"It sounds lonely."

"Oh, I know, Barack. That's why I keep coming home. That's why I'm still dreaming."

After two days, I still hadn't recovered my bag. The airline office downtown told us to call the airport, but whenever we tried the lines were always busy. Auma finally suggested that we drive out there ourselves. At the British Airways desk we found two young women discussing a nightclub that had just opened. I interrupted their conversation to ask about my bag, and one of them thumbed listlessly through a stack of papers.

"We have no record of you here," she said.

"Please check again."

The woman shrugged. "If you wish, you can come back tonight at midnight. A flight from Johannesburg comes in at that time."

"I was told my bag would be delivered to me."

"I'm sorry, but I have no record of your bag here. If you like, you can fill out another form."

"Is Miss Omoro here? She—"

"Omoro is on vacation."

Auma bumped me aside. "Who else can we talk to here, since you don't seem to know anything."

"Go downtown if you want to talk to someone else," the woman said curtly before returning to her conversation.

Auma was still muttering under her breath when we stepped into the British Airways downtown office. It was in a high-rise building whose elevators announced each floor electronically in crisp Victorian tones; a receptionist sat beneath photographs of lion cubs and dancing children. She repeated that we should check the airport.

"Let me talk to the manager," I said, trying not to shout.

"I'm sorry, but Mr. Maduri is in a meeting."

"Look, miss, we have just come from the airport. They told us to come here. Two days ago I was told my bag would be delivered. Now I'm told that no one even knows it's missing. I—" I stopped in midsentence. The receptionist had withdrawn behind a stony mask, a place where neither pleading nor bluster could reach. Auma apparently saw the same thing, for the air seemed to go out of her as well. Together we slumped into a pair of lounge chairs, not knowing what to do next, when a hand suddenly appeared on Auma's shoulder. Auma turned to find the hand attached to a dark, wiry man dressed in a blue blazer.

"Eh, Uncle! What are you doing here?"

Auma introduced me to the man, who was related to us in a sequence that I couldn't quite follow. He asked us if we were planning a trip, and Auma told him what had happened.

"Listen, don't worry," our uncle said. "Maduri, he is a good friend of mine. In fact, just now I am about to have lunch with him." Our uncle turned crossly to the receptionist, who had been watching our conversation with considerable interest.

"Mr. Maduri already knows you are here," she said, smiling.

Mr. Maduri turned out to be a heavyset man with a bulbous nose and a raspy voice. After we had repeated our story, he immediately picked up the phone. "Hello? Yes, this is Maduri. Who is this? Listen, I have Mr. Obama here who is looking for his luggage. Yes, Obama. He has been expecting his bag for some time now. What? Yes, look now, please." A few minutes later the phone rang. "Yes . . . okay, send it to . . ." He relayed Auma's office address, then hung up the phone and told us that the bag would be delivered there that same afternoon.

"Call me if you have any more problems," he said.

We thanked both men profusely and immediately excused ourselves, worried that our luck might change at any moment. Downstairs, I stopped in front of a large photograph of Kenyatta that was hanging in an office window. His eyes dazzled with confidence and cunning; his powerful, bejeweled hand clutched the carved staff of a Kikuyu chieftain. Auma came and stood beside me.

"That's where it all starts," she said. "The Big Man. Then his assistant, or his family, or his friend, or his tribe. It's the same whether you want a phone, or a visa, or a job. Who are your relatives? Who do you know? If you don't know somebody, you can forget it. That's what the Old Man never understood, you see. He came back here thinking that because he was so educated and spoke his proper English and understood his charts and graphs everyone would somehow put him in charge. He forgot what holds everything together here."

"He was lost," I said quietly.

Walking back to the car, I remembered a story Auma had told me about the Old Man after his fall from grace. One evening, he had told Auma to go to the store and fetch him some cigarettes. She reminded him that they had no money, but the Old Man had shaken his head impatiently.

"Don't be silly," he told her. "Just tell the storekeeper that you are Dr. Obama's daughter and that I will pay him later."

Auma went to the store and repeated what the Old Man had said. The storekeeper laughed and sent her away. Afraid to go home, Auma called on a cousin the Old Man had once helped get a job, who lent her the few shillings she needed. When she got home, the Old Man took the cigarettes, scolding her for taking so long.

"You see," he said to her as he opened the pack. "I told you that you would have no problems. Everyone here knows Obama."

I feel my father's presence as Auma and I walk through the busy street. I see him in the schoolboys who run past us, their lean, black legs moving like piston rods between blue shorts and oversized shoes. I hear him in the laughter of the pair of university students who sip sweet, creamed tea and eat samosas in a dimly lit teahouse. I smell him in the cigarette smoke of the businessman who covers one ear and shouts into a pay phone; in the sweat of the day laborer who loads gravel into a wheelbarrow, his face and bare chest covered with dust. The Old Man's here, I think, although he doesn't say anything to me. He's here, asking me to understand.

CHAPTER SIXTEEN

· ·

B ERNARD RANG THE DOORBELL at ten o'clock sharp. He wore faded blue shorts and a T-shirt several sizes too small; in his hands was a bald orange basketball, held out like an offering.

"Ready?" he asked.

"Almost. Give me a second to put on my shoes."

He followed me into the apartment and stepped over to the desk where I had been working. "You've been reading again, Barry," he said, shaking his head. "Your woman will get bored with you, always spending time with books."

I sat down to tie my sneakers. "I've been told."

He tossed the ball into the air. "Me, I'm not so interested in books. I'm a man of action. Like Rambo."

I smiled. "Okay, Rambo," I said, standing up and opening the door. "Let's see how you do running down to the courts."

Bernard looked at me doubtfully. "The courts are far away. Where's the car?"

"Auma took it to work." I went out onto the veranda and started stretching. "Anyway, she told me it's just a mile. Good for warming up those young legs of yours."

He followed me halfheartedly through a few stretching exercises before we started up the graveled driveway onto the main road. It was a perfect day, the sun cut with a steady breeze, the road empty except for a distant woman, walking with a basket of kindling on top of her head. After less than a quarter of a mile, Bernard stopped dead in his tracks, beads of sweat forming on his high, smooth forehead.

"I'm warmed up, Barry," he said, gulping for air. "I think now we should walk."

The University of Nairobi campus took up a couple of acres near the center of town. The courts were above the athletic field on a slight rise, their pebbled asphalt cracked with weeds. I watched Bernard as we took turns shooting, and thought about what a generous and easy companion he'd been these last few days, taking it upon himself to guide me through the city while Auma was busy grading exams. He would clutch my hand protectively as we made our way through the crowded streets, infinitely patient whenever I stopped to look at a building or read a sign that he passed by every day, amused by my odd ways but with none of the elaborate gestures of boredom or resistance that I would have shown at his age.

That sweetness, the lack of guile, made him seem much younger than his seventeen years. But he was seventeen, I reminded myself, an age where a little more independence, a sharper edge to his character, wouldn't be such a bad thing. I realized that he had time for me partly because he had nothing better to do. He was patient because he had no particular place he wanted to go. I needed to talk to him about that, as I'd promised Auma I would—a man-to-man talk. . . .

"You have seen Magic Johnson play?" Bernard asked me now, gathering himself for a shot. The ball went through the netless rim, and I passed the ball back out to him.

"Just on TV."

Bernard nodded. "Everybody has a car in America. And a telephone." They were more statements than questions.

"Most people. Not everybody."

He shot again and the ball clanged noisily off the rim. "I think it is better there," he said. "Maybe I will come to America. I can help you with your business."

"I don't have a business right now. Maybe after I finish law school—"

"It must be easy to find work."

"Not for everybody. Actually, lots of people have a tough time in the States. Black people especially."

He held the ball. "Not as bad as here."

We looked at each other, and I tried to picture the basketball courts back in the States. The sound of gunshots nearby, a guy peddling nickel hits in the stairwell—that was one picture. The laughter of boys playing in their suburban backyard, their mother calling them in for lunch. That was true, too. The two pictures collided, leaving me tongue-tied. Satisfied with my silence, Bernard returned to his dribbling.

When the sun became too strong, we walked to an ice-cream parlor a few blocks from the university. Bernard ordered a chocolate sundae and began eating methodically, measuring out the ice cream half a teaspoon at a time. I lit a cigarette and leaned back in my chair.

"Auma tells me that you're thinking about trade school," I said.

He nodded, his expression noncommittal.

"What kind of courses are you interested in?"

"I don't know." He dipped his spoon in his sundae and thought for a moment. "Maybe auto mechanics. Yes . . . I think auto mechanics is good."

"Have you tried to get into some sort of program?"

"No. Not really." He stopped to take another bite. "You must pay fees."

"How old are you now, Bernard?"

"Seventeen," he said cautiously.

"Seventeen." I nodded, blowing smoke at the ceiling. "You know what that means, don't you? It means you're almost a man. Somebody with responsibilities. To your family. To yourself. What I'm trying to say is, it's time you decided on something that interested you. Could be auto mechanics. Could be something else. But whatever it is, you're gonna have to set some goals and follow through. Auma and I can help you with school fees, but we can't live your life for you. You've got to put in some effort. You understand?"

Bernard nodded. "I understand."

We both sat in silence for a while, watching Bernard's spoon twirl through the now-liquid mess. I began to imagine how hollow my words must be sounding to this brother of mine, whose only fault was having been born on the wrong side of our father's cloven world. He didn't resent me for this, it seemed. Not yet. Only he must have been wondering why I was pretending that my rules somehow applied to him. All he wanted was a few tokens of our relationship—Bob Marley cassettes, maybe my basketball shoes once I was gone. So little to ask for, and yet anything else that I offered—advice, scoldings, my ambitions for him—would seem even less.

I stamped out my cigarette and suggested we get going. As we stepped into the street, Bernard draped his arm over my shoulder.

"It's good to have a big brother around," he said before waving good-bye and vanishing into the crowd.

What is a family? Is it just a genetic chain, parents and offspring, people like me? Or is it a social construct, an economic unit, optimal for child rearing and divisions of labor? Or is it something else entirely: a store of shared memories, say? An ambit of love? A reach across the void?

I could list various possibilities. But I'd never arrived at a definite answer, aware early on that, given my circumstances, such an effort was bound to fail. Instead, I drew a series of circles around myself, with borders that shifted as time passed and faces changed but that nevertheless offered the illusion of control. An inner circle, where love was constant and claims unquestioned. Then a second circle, a realm of negotiated love, commitments freely chosen. And then a circle for colleagues, acquaintances; the cheerful gray-haired lady who rang up my groceries back in Chicago. Until the circle finally widened to embrace a nation or a race, or a particular moral course, and the commitments were no longer tied to a face or a name but were actually commitments I'd made to myself.

In Africa, this astronomy of mine almost immediately collapsed. For family seemed to be everywhere: in stores, at the post office, on streets and in the parks, all of them fussing and fretting over Obama's long-lost son. If I mentioned in passing that I needed a notebook or shaving cream, I could count on one of my aunts to insist that she take me to some far-off corner of Nairobi to find the best bargains, no matter how long the trip took or how much it might inconvenience her.

"Ah, Barry . . . what is more important than helping my brother's son?"

If a cousin discovered, much to his distress, that Auma had left me to fend for myself, he might walk the two miles to Auma's apartment on the off chance that I was there and needed company.

"Ah, Barry, why didn't you call on me? Come, I will take you to meet some of my friends."

And in the evenings, well, Auma and I simply surrendered ourselves to the endless invitations that came our way from uncles, nephews, second cousins or cousins once removed, all of whom demanded, at the risk of insult, that we sit down for a meal, no matter what time it happened to be or how many meals we had already eaten.

"Ah, Barry . . . we may not have much in Kenya—but so long as you are here, you will always have something to eat!"

At first I reacted to all this attention like a child to its mother's bosom, full of simple, unquestioning gratitude. It conformed to my idea of Africa and Africans, an obvious contrast to the growing isolation of American life, a contrast I understood, not in racial, but in cultural terms. A measure of what we sacrificed for technology and mobility, but that here—as in the kampongs outside Djakarta or in the country villages of Ireland or Greece—remained essentially intact: the insistent pleasure of other people's company, the joy of human warmth.

As the days wore on, though, my joy became tempered with tension and doubt. Some of it had to do with what Auma had talked about that night in the car—an acute awareness of my relative good fortune, and the troublesome questions such good fortune implied. Not that our relatives were suffering, exactly. Both Jane and Zeituni had steady jobs; Kezia made do selling cloth in the markets. If cash got too short, the children could be sent upcountry for a time; that's where another brother, Abo, was staying, I was told, with an uncle in Kendu Bay, where there were always chores to perform, food on the table and a roof over one's head.

Still, the situation in Nairobi was tough and getting tougher. Clothes were mostly secondhand, a doctor's visit reserved for the direst emergency. Almost all the family's younger members were unemployed, including the two or three who had managed, against stiff competition, to graduate from one of Kenya's universities. If Jane or Zeituni ever fell ill, if their companies ever closed or laid them off, there was no government safety net. There was only family, next of kin; people burdened by similar hardship.

Now I was family, I reminded myself; now I had responsibilities. But what did that mean exactly? Back in the States, I'd been able to translate such feelings into politics, organizing, a certain self-denial. In Kenya, these strategies seemed hopelessly abstract, even self-indulgent. A commitment to black empowerment couldn't help find Bernard a job. A faith in participatory democracy couldn't buy Jane a new set of sheets. For the first time in my life, I found myself thinking deeply about money: my own lack of it, the pursuit of it, the crude but undeniable peace it could buy. A part of me wished I could live up to the image that my new relatives imagined for me: a corporate lawyer, an American businessman, my hand poised on the spigot, ready to rain down like manna the largesse of the Western world.

But of course I wasn't either of those things. Even in the States, wealth involved trade-offs for those who weren't born to it, the same sorts of trade-offs that I could see Auma now making as she tried, in her own way, to fulfill the family's expectations. She was working two jobs that summer, teaching German classes to Kenyan businessmen along with her job at the university. With the money she saved, she wanted not only to fix up Granny's house in Alego but also to buy a bit of land around Nairobi, something that would appreciate in value, a base from which to build. She had plans, schedules, budgets, and deadlines—all the things she'd learned were required to negotiate a modern world. The problem was that her schedules also meant begging off from family affairs; her budgets meant saying no to the constant requests for money that came her way. And when this happened— when she insisted on going home before Jane served dinner because things had started two hours late, or when she refused to let eight people pile into her VW because it was designed for four and they would tear up the seats—the looks of unspoken hurt, barely distinguishable from resentment, would flash across the room. Her restlessness, her independence, her constant willingness to project into the future—all of this struck the family as unnatural somehow. Unnatural . . . and un-African.

It was the same dilemma that old Frank had posed to me the year I left Hawaii, the same tensions that certain children in Altgeld might suffer if they took too much pleasure in doing their schoolwork, the same perverse survivor's guilt that I could expect to experience if I ever did try to make money and had to pass the throngs of young black men on the corner as I made my way to a downtown office. Without power for the group, a group larger, even, than an extended family, our success always threatened to leave others behind. And perhaps it was that fact that left me so unsettled—the fact that even here, in Africa, the same maddening patterns still held sway; that no one here could tell me what my blood ties demanded or how those demands could be reconciled with some larger idea of human association. It was as if we—Auma, Roy, Bernard, and I—were all making it up as we went along. As if the map that might have once measured the direction and force of our love, the code that would unlock our blessings, had been lost long ago, buried with the ancestors beneath a silent earth.

Toward the end of my first week in Nairobi, Zeituni took me to visit our other aunt, Sarah. Auma had remained unwilling to go, but because it turned out that her mechanic lived near Sarah, she offered to give us a ride to her garage; from there, she said, we could travel by foot. On Saturday morning, Auma and I picked up Zeituni and headed east, past cinder-block apartments and dry, garbage-strewn lots, until we finally came to the rim of a wide valley known as Mathare. Auma pulled off to the shoulder and I looked out the window to see the shantytown below, miles and miles of corrugated rooftops shimmering under the sun like wet lily pads, buckling and dipping in an unbroken sequence across the valley floor.

"How many people live there?" I asked.

Auma shrugged and turned to our aunt. "What would you say, Auntie? Half a million, maybe?"

Zeituni shook her head. "That was last week. This week, it must be one million."

Auma started the car back up. "Nobody knows for sure, Barack. The place is growing all the time. People come in from the countryside looking for work and end up staying permanently. For a while, the city council tried to tear the settlement down. They said it was a health hazard—an affront to Kenya's image, you see. Bulldozers came, and people lost what little they had. But of course, they had nowhere else to go. As soon as the bulldozers left, people rebuilt just like before."

We came to a stop in front of a slanting tin shed where a mechanic and several apprentices emerged to look Auma's car over. Promising to be back in an hour, Zeituni and I left Auma at the garage and began our walk down a wide, unpaved road. It was already hot, the road bereft of shade; on either side were rows of small hovels, their walls a patchwork of wattle, mud, pieces of cardboard, and scavenged plywood. They were neat, though, the packed earth in front of each home cleanly swept, and everywhere we could see tailors and shoe repairers and furniture makers plying their trades out of roadside stalls, and women and children selling vegetables from wobbly wood tables.

Eventually we came to one edge of Mathare, where a series of concrete buildings stood along a paved road. The buildings were eight, maybe twelve stories tall, and yet curiously unfinished, the wood beams and rough cement exposed to the elements, like they'd suffered an aerial bombardment. We entered one of them, climbed a narrow flight of stairs, and emerged at the end of a long unlit hallway, at the other end of which we saw a teenage girl hanging out clothes to dry on a small cement patio. Zeituni went to talk to the girl, who led us wordlessly to a low, scuffed door. We knocked, and a dark, middle-aged woman appeared, short but sturdily built, with hard, glassy eyes set in a wide, rawboned face. She took my hand and said something in Luo.

"She says she is ashamed to have her brother's son see her in such a miserable place," Zeituni translated.

We were shown into a small room, ten feet by twelve, large enough to fit a bed, a dresser, two chairs, and a sewing machine. Zeituni and I each took one of the chairs, and the young woman who had shown us Sarah's room returned with two warm sodas. Sarah sat on the bed and leaned forward to study my face. Auma had said that Sarah knew some English, but she spoke mostly in Luo now. Even without the benefit of Zeituni's translation, I guessed that she wasn't happy.

"She wants to know why you have taken so long to visit her," Zeituni explained. "She says that she is the eldest child of your grandfather, Hussein Onyango, and that you should have come to see her first."

"Tell her I meant no disrespect," I said, looking at Sarah but not sure what she understood. "Everything's been so busy since my arrival—it was hard to come sooner."

Sarah's tone became sharp. "She says that the people you stay with must be telling you lies."

"Tell her that I've heard nothing said against her. Tell her that the dispute about the Old Man's estate has just made Auma uncomfortable about coming here."

Sarah snorted after the translation and started up again, her voice rumbling against the close walls. When she finally stopped, Zeituni remained quiet.

"What'd she say, Zeituni?"

Zeituni's eyes stayed on Sarah as she answered my question. "She says the trial is not her fault. She says that it's Kezia's doing—Auma's mum. She says that the children who claim to be Obama's are not Obama's. She says they have taken everything of his and left his true people living like beggars."

Sarah nodded, and her eyes began to smolder. "Yes, Barry," she said suddenly in English. "It is me who looks after your father when he is a small boy. My mother, Akumu, is also your father's mother. Akumu is your true grandmother, not this one you call Granny. Akumu, the woman who gives your father life—you should be helping her. And me, your brother's sister. Look how I live. Why don't you help us, instead of these others?"

Before I could answer, Zeituni and Sarah began to argue with each other in Luo. Eventually, Zeituni stood up and straightened her skirt. "We should go now, Barry."

I began to rise out of my chair, but Sarah took my hand in both of hers, her voice softening.

"Will you give me something? For your grandmother?"

I reached for my wallet and felt the eyes of both aunts as I counted out the money I had on me—perhaps thirty dollars' worth of shillings. I pressed them into Sarah's dry, chapped hands, and she quickly slipped the money down the front of her blouse before clutching my hand again.

"Stay here, Barry," Sarah said. "You must meet—"

"You can come back later, Barry," Zeituni said. "Let's go."

Outside, a hazy yellow light bathed the road; my clothes hung limp against my body in the windless heat. Zeituni was quiet now, visibly upset. She was a proud woman, this aunt; the scene with Sarah must have embarrassed her. And then, that thirty dollars—Lord knows, she could have used it herself. . . .

We had walked for ten minutes before I asked Zeituni what she and Sarah had been arguing about.

"Ah, it's nothing, Barry. This is what happens to old women who have no husbands." Zeituni tried to smile, but the tension creased the corners of her mouth.

"Come on, Auntie. Tell me the truth."

Zeituni shook her head. "I don't *know* the truth. At least not all of it. I know that even growing up, Sarah was always closer to her real mum, Akumu. Barack, he cared only for my mum, Granny, the one who raised them after Akumu left."

"Why did Akumu leave?"

"I'm not sure. You will have to ask Granny about that."

Zeituni signaled for us to cross the street, then resumed talking. "You know, your father and Sarah were actually very similar, even though they did not always get along. She was smart like him. And independent. She used to tell me, when we were children, that she wanted to get an education so that she would not have to depend on

any man. That's why she ended up married to four different husbands. None of them lasted. The first one died, but the others she
left, because they were lazy, or tried to abuse her. I admire her for
this. Most women in Kenya put up with anything. I did, for a long
time. But Sarah also paid a price for her independence."

Zeituni wiped the sweat on her forehead with the back of her hand.
"Anyway, after Sarah's first husband died, she decided that your father
should support her and her child, since he had received all the education. That's why she disliked Kezia and her children. She thought
Kezia was just a pretty girl who wanted to take everything. You must
understand, Barry—in Luo custom, the male child inherits everything. Sarah feared that once your grandfather died, everything would
belong to Barack and his wives, and she would be left with nothing."

I shook my head. "That's no excuse for lying about who the Old
Man's children are."

"You're right. But. . ."

"But what?"

Zeituni stopped walking and turned to me. She said, "After your
father went off to live with his American wife, Ruth . . . well, he
would go to Kezia sometimes. You must understand that traditionally
she was still his wife. It was during such a visit that Kezia became
pregnant with Abo, the brother you haven't met. The thing was,
Kezia also lived with another man briefly during this time. So when
she became pregnant again, with Bernard, no one was sure who—"
Zeituni stopped, letting the thought finish itself.

"Does Bernard know about this?"

"Yes, he knows by now. You understand, such things made no difference to your father. He would say that they were all his children.
He drove this other man away, and would give Kezia money for the
children whenever he could. But once he died, there was nothing to
prove that he'd accepted them in this way."

We turned a corner onto a busier road. In front of us, a pregnant goat bleated as it scuttered out of the path of an oncoming *matatu*. Across the way, two little girls in dusty red school uniforms, their round heads shaven almost clean, held hands and sang as they skipped across a gutter. An old woman with her head under a faded shawl motioned to us to look at her wares: two margarine tins of dried beans, a neat stack of tomatoes, dried fish hanging from a wire like a chain of silver coins. I looked into the old woman's face, drawn beneath the shadows. Who was this woman? I wondered. My grandmother? A stranger? And what about Bernard—should my feelings for him somehow be different now? I looked over at a bus stop, where a crowd of young men were streaming out into the road, all of them tall and black and slender, their bones pressing against their shirts. I suddenly imagined Bernard's face on all of them, multiplied across the landscape, across continents. Hungry, striving, desperate men, all of them my brothers. . . .

"Now you see what your father suffered."

"What?" I rubbed my eyes and looked up to find my aunt staring at me.

"Yes, Barry, your father suffered," she repeated. "I am telling you, his problem was that his heart was too big. When he lived, he would just give to everybody who asked him. And they all asked. You know, he was one of the first in the whole district to study abroad. The people back home, they didn't even know anyone else who had ridden in an airplane before. So they expected everything from him. 'Ah, Barack, you are a big shot now. You should give me something. You should help me.' Always these pressures from family. And he couldn't say no, he was so generous. You know, even me he had to take care of when I became pregnant, he was very disappointed in me. He had wanted me to go to college. But I would not listen to him, and went off with my husband. And despite this thing, when my husband became abusive and I had to leave, no money, no job, who do you think took me in? Yes—it was him. That's why, no matter what others sometimes say, I will always be grateful to him."

We were approaching the garage shop; up ahead, we could see Auma talking to her mechanic and hear the engine of the old VW whine. Beside us, a naked boy, maybe three years old, wandered out from behind a row of oil drums, his feet caked with what looked like tar. Again Zeituni stopped, this time as if suddenly ill, and spat into the dust.

"When your father's luck changed," she said, "these same people he had helped, they forgot him. They laughed at him. Even family refused to have him stay in their houses. Yes, Barry! Refused! They would tell Barack it was too dangerous. I knew this hurt him, but he wouldn't pass blame. Your father never held a grudge. In fact, when he was rehabilitated and doing well again, I would find out that he was giving help to these same people who had betrayed him. Ah, I could not understand this thing. I would tell him, 'Barack, you should only look after yourself and your children! These others, they have treated you badly. They are just too lazy to work for themselves.' And you know what he would say to me? He would say, 'How do you know that man does not need this small thing more than me?'"

My aunt turned away and, forcing a smile, waved to Auma. And as we began to walk forward, she added, "I tell you this so you will know the pressure your father was under in this place. So you don't judge him too harshly. And you must learn from his life. If you have something, then everyone will want a piece of it. So you have to draw the line somewhere. If everyone is family, no one is family. Your father, he never understood this, I think."

I remember a conversation I had once in Chicago when I was still organizing. It was with a woman who'd grown up in a big family in rural Georgia. Five brothers and three sisters, she had told me, all crowded under a single roof. She told me about her father's ultimately futile efforts to farm his small plot of land, her mother's vegetable garden, the two pigs they kept penned out in the yard, and the trips with her siblings to fish the murky waters of a river nearby. Listening to her speak, I began to realize that two of the three sisters she'd mentioned had actually died at birth, but that in this woman's mind they had remained with her always, spirits with names and ages and characters, two sisters who accompanied her while she walked to school or did chores, who soothed her cries and calmed her fears. For this woman, family had never been a vessel just for the living. The dead, too, had their claims, their voices shaping the course of her dreams.

So now it was for me. I remember how, a few days after my visit to Sarah's, Auma and I happened to run into an acquaintance of the Old Man's outside Barclay's Bank. I could tell that Auma didn't remember his name, so I held out my hand and introduced myself. The man smiled and said, "My, my—you have grown so tall. How's your mother? And your brother Mark—has he graduated from university yet?"

At first I was confused. Did I know this person? And then Auma explained in a low voice that no, I was a different brother, Barack, who grew up in America, the child of a different mother. David had passed away. And then the awkwardness on all sides—the man nodding his head ("I'm sorry, I didn't know") but taking another look at me, as if to make sure what he'd heard was true; Auma trying to appear as if the situation, while sad, was somehow the normal stuff of tragedy; me standing to the side, wondering how to feel after having been mistaken for a ghost.

Later, back in her apartment, I asked Auma when she had last seen Mark and Ruth. She leaned her head against my shoulder and looked up at the ceiling.

"David's funeral," she said. "Although by then they had stopped speaking to us for a long time."

"Why?"

"I told you that Ruth's divorce from the Old Man was very bitter. After they separated, she married a Tanzanian and had Mark and David take his name. She sent them to an international school, and they were raised like foreigners. She told them that they should have nothing to do with our side of the family."

Auma sighed. "I don't know. Maybe because he was older, Mark came to share Ruth's attitudes and had no contact with us after that. But for some reason, once David was a teenager, he began to rebel against Ruth. He told her he was an African, and started calling himself Obama. Sometimes he would sneak off from school to visit the Old Man and the rest of the family, which is how we got to know him. He became everybody's favorite. He was so sweet, you know, and funny, even if he was sometimes too wild.

"Ruth tried to enroll him in a boarding school, hoping it would settle him down. But David ended up running away instead. Nobody saw him for months. Then Roy happened to bump into him outside a rugby match. He was dirty, thin, begging money from strangers. He laughed when he saw Roy, and bragged about his life on the streets, hustling *bhang* with his friends. Roy told him to go home, but he refused, so Roy took David to his own apartment, sending word to Ruth that her son was safe and staying with him. When Ruth heard this, she was relieved but also furious. She begged David to come back, but when he again refused, she tacitly accepted the arrangement with Roy, hoping that eventually David would change his mind."

Auma sipped on her tea. "That's when David died. While he was living with Roy. His death broke everybody's heart—Roy's especially. The two of them were really close, you see. But Ruth never understood that. She thought we had corrupted David. Stolen her baby away. And I don't think she's ever forgiven us for it."

I decided to stop talking about David after that; I could tell that

Auma found the memories too painful. But only a few days later, Auma and I came home to find a car waiting for us outside the apartment. The driver, a brown-skinned man with a prominent Adam's apple, handed Auma a note.

"What is it?" I asked.

"It's an invitation from Ruth," she said. "Mark's back from America for the summer. She wants to have us over for lunch."

"Do you want to go?"

Auma shook her head, a look of disgust on her face. "Ruth knows I've been here almost six months now. She doesn't care about me. The only reason she's invited us is because she's curious about you. She wants to compare you to Mark."

"I think maybe I should go," I said quietly.

Auma looked at the note again, then handed it back to the driver and said something to him in Swahili. "We'll both go," she said, and walked into the apartment.

Ruth lived in Westlands, an enclave of expensive homes set off by wide lawns and well-tended hedges, each one with a sentry post manned by brown-uniformed guards. It was raining as we drove toward her house, sending a soft, gentle spray through the big, leafy trees. The coolness reminded me of the streets around Punahou, Manoa, Tantalus, the streets where some of my wealthier classmates had lived back in Hawaii. Staring out Auma's car window, I thought back to the envy I'd felt toward those classmates whenever they invited me over to play in their big backyards or swim in their swimming pools. And along with that envy, a different impression—the sense of quiet desperation those big, pretty houses seemed to contain. The sound of someone's sister crying softly behind the door. The sight of a mother sneaking a tumbler of gin in midafternoon. The expression on a father's face as he sat alone in his den, his features clenched as he flicked between college football games on TV. An impression of loneliness that perhaps wasn't true, perhaps was just a projection of my own heart, but that, either way, had made me want to run, just as, an ocean away, David had run, back into the marketplace and noisy streets, back into disorder and the laughter disorder produced, back into the sort of pain a boy could understand.

We came to one of the more modest houses on the block and parked along the curve of a looping driveway. A white woman with a long jaw and graying hair came out of the house to meet us. Behind her was a black man of my height and complexion with a bushy Afro and horn-rimmed glasses.

"Come in, come in," Ruth said. The four of us shook hands stiffly and entered a large living room, where a balding, older black man in a safari jacket was bouncing a young boy on his lap. "This is my husband," Ruth said, "and this is Mark's little brother, Joey."

"Hey, Joey," I said, bending down to shake his hand. He was a beautiful boy, with honey-colored skin and two front teeth missing. Ruth tousled the boy's big curls, then looked at her husband and said, "Weren't you two on your way to the club?"

"Yes, yes," the man said, standing up. "Come on, Joey . . . it was nice to meet you both." The boy stood fast, staring up at Auma and me with a bright, curious smile until his father finally picked him up and carried him out the door.

"Well, here we are," Ruth said, leading us to the couch and pouring lemonade. "I must say it was quite a surprise to find out you were here, Barry. I told Mark that we just had to see how this other son of Obama's turned out. Your name is Obama, isn't it? But your mother remarried. I wonder why she had you keep your name?"

I smiled as if I hadn't understood the question. "So, Mark," I said, turning to my brother, "I hear you're at Berkeley."

"Stanford," he corrected. His voice was deep, his accent perfectly American. "I'm in my last year of the physics program there."

"It must be tough," Auma offered.

Mark shrugged. "Not really."

"Don't be so modest, dear," Ruth said. "The things Mark studies are so complicated only a handful of people really understand it all." She patted Mark on the hand, then turned to me. "And Barry, I understand you'll be going to Harvard. Just like Obama. You must have gotten some of his brains. Hopefully not the rest of him, though. You know Obama was quite crazy, don't you? The drinking made it worse. Did you ever meet him? Obama, I mean?"

"Only once. When I was ten."

"Well, you were lucky then. It probably explains why you're doing so well."

That's how the next hour passed, with Ruth alternating between stories of my father's failure and stories of Mark's accomplishments. Any questions were directed exclusively to me, leaving Auma to fiddle silently with Ruth's lasagna. I wanted to leave as soon as the meal was over, but Ruth suggested that Mark show us the family album while she brought out the dessert.

"I'm sure they're not interested, Mother," Mark said.

"Of course they're interested," Ruth said. Then, her voice oddly distant: "There are pictures of Obama. From when he was young. . . ."

We followed Mark to the bookcase, and he pulled down a large photo album. Together we sat on the couch, slowly thumbing through laminate pages. Auma and Roy, dark and skinny and tall, all legs and big eyes, holding the two smaller children protectively in their arms. The Old Man and Ruth mugging it up at a beach some-where. The entire family dressed up for a night out on the town. They were happy scenes, all of them, and all strangely familiar, as if I were glimpsing some alternative universe that had played itself out behind my back. They were reflections, I realized, of my own long-held fantasies, fantasies that I'd kept secret even from myself. The fantasy of the Old Man's having taken my mother and me back with him to Kenya. The wish that my mother and father, sisters and brothers, were all under one roof. Here it was, I thought, what might have been. And the recognition of how wrong it had all turned out, the harsh evidence of life as it had really been lived, made me so sad that after only a few minutes I had to look away.

On the drive back, I apologized to Auma for having put her through the ordeal. She waved it off.

"It could have been worse," she said. "I feel sorry for Mark, though. He seems so alone. You know, it's not easy being a mixed child in Kenya."

I looked out the window, thinking about my mother, Toot, and Gramps, and how grateful I was to them—for who they were, and for the stories they'd told. I turned back to Auma, and said, "She still hasn't gotten over him, has she?"

"Who?"

"Ruth. She hasn't gotten over the Old Man."

Auma thought for a moment. "No, Barack. I guess she hasn't. Just like the rest of us."

The following week, I called Mark and suggested that we go out to lunch. He seemed a bit hesitant, but eventually agreed to meet me at an Indian restaurant downtown. He was more relaxed than he had been during our first meeting, making a few self-deprecatory jokes, offering his observations about California and academic infighting. As the meal wore on, I asked him how it felt being back for the summer.

"Fine," he said. "It's nice to see my mom and dad, of course. And Joey—he's really a great kid." Mark cut off a bite of his samosa and put it into his mouth. "As for the rest of Kenya, I don't feel much of an attachment. Just another poor African country."

"You don't ever think about settling here?"

Mark took a sip from his Coke. "No," he said. "I mean, there's not much work for a physicist, is there, in a country where the average person doesn't have a telephone."

I should have stopped then, but something—the certainty in this brother's voice, maybe, or our rough resemblance, like looking into a foggy mirror—made me want to push harder. I asked, "Don't you ever feel like you might be losing something?"

Mark put down his knife and fork, and for the first time that afternoon his eyes looked straight into mine.

"I understand what you're getting at," he said flatly. "You think that somehow I'm cut off from my roots, that sort of thing." He wiped his mouth and dropped the napkin onto his plate. "Well, you're right. At a certain point, I made a decision not to think about who my real father was. He was dead to me even when he was still alive. I knew that he was a drunk and showed no concern for his wife or children. That was enough."

"It made you mad."

"Not mad. Just numb."

"And that doesn't bother you? Being numb, I mean?"

"Towards him, no. Other things move me. Beethoven's symphonies. Shakespeare's sonnets. I know—it's not what an African is supposed to care about. But who's to tell me what I should and shouldn't care about? Understand, I'm not ashamed of being half Kenyan. I just don't ask myself a lot of questions about what it all means. About who I *really* am." He shrugged. "I don't know. Maybe I should. I can acknowledge the possibility that if I looked more carefully at myself, I would . . ."

For the briefest moment I sensed Mark hesitate, like a rock climber losing his footing. Then, almost immediately, he regained his composure and waved for the check.

"Who knows?" he said. "What's certain is that I don't need the stress. Life's hard enough without all that excess baggage."

We stood up to leave, and I insisted on paying the bill. Outside we exchanged addresses and promised to write, with a dishonesty that made my heart ache. When I got home, I told Auma how the meeting had gone. She looked away for a moment, then broke out with a short, bitter laugh.

"What's so funny?"

"I was just thinking about how life is so strange. You know, as soon as the Old Man died, the lawyers contacted all those who might have a claim to the inheritance. Unlike my mum, Ruth has all the documents needed to prove who Mark's father was. So of all of the Old Man's kids, Mark's claim is the only one that's uncontested."

Again Auma laughed, and I looked up at the picture hanging on her wall, the same picture pasted inside Ruth's album, of three brothers and a sister, smiling sweetly for the camera.

CHAPTER SEVENTEEN

· ·

TOWARD THE END OF my second week in Kenya, Auma and I went on a safari.

Auma wasn't thrilled with the idea. When I first showed her the brochure, she grimaced and shook her head. Like most Kenyans, she could draw a straight line between the game parks and colonialism. "How many Kenyans do you think can afford to go on a safari?" she asked me. "Why should all that land be set aside for tourists when it could be used for farming? These *wazungu* care more about one dead elephant than they do for a hundred black children."

For several days we parried. I told her she was letting other people's attitudes prevent her from seeing her own country. She said she didn't want to waste the money. Eventually she relented, not because of my persuasive powers but because she took pity on me.

"If some animal ate you out there," she said, "I'd never forgive myself."

And so, at seven o'clock on a Tuesday morning, we watched a sturdily built Kikuyu driver named Francis load our bags onto the roof of a white minivan. With us were a spindly cook named Rafael, a dark-haired Italian named Mauro, and a British couple in their early forties, the Wilkersons.

We drove out of Nairobi at a modest pace, passing soon into countryside, green hills and red dirt paths and small *shambas* surrounded by plots of wilting, widely spaced corn. Nobody spoke, a discomfiting silence that reminded me of similar moments back in the States, the pause that would sometimes accompany my personal integration of a bar or hotel. It made me think about Auma and Mark, my grandparents back in Hawaii, my mother still in Indonesia, and the things Zeituni had told me.

If everyone is family, then no one is family.

Was Zeituni right? I'd come to Kenya thinking that I could somehow force my many worlds into a single, harmonious whole. Instead, the divisions seemed only to have become more multiplied, popping up in the midst of even the simplest chores. I thought back to the previous morning, when Auma and I had gone to book our tickets. The travel agency was owned by Asians; most small businesses in Nairobi were owned by Asians. Right away, Auma had tensed up.

"You see how arrogant they are?" she had whispered as we watched a young Indian woman order her black clerks to and fro. "They call themselves Kenyans, but they want nothing to do with us. As soon as they make their money, they send it off to London or Bombay."

Her attitude had touched a nerve. "How can you blame Asians for sending their money out of the country," I had asked her, "after what happened in Uganda?" I had gone on to tell her about the close Indian and Pakistani friends I had back in the States, friends who had supported black causes, friends who had lent me money when I was tight and taken me into their homes when I'd had no place to stay. Auma had been unmoved.

"Ah, Barack," she had said. "Sometimes you're so naive."

I looked at Auma now, her face turned toward the window. What had I expected my little lecture to accomplish? My simple formulas for Third World solidarity had little application in Kenya. Here, persons of Indian extraction were like the Chinese in Indonesia, the

Koreans in the South Side of Chicago, outsiders who knew how to trade and kept to themselves, working the margins of a racial caste system, more visible and so more vulnerable to resentment. It was nobody's fault necessarily. It was just a matter of history, an unfortunate fact of life.

Anyway, the divisions in Kenya didn't stop there; there were always finer lines to draw. Between the country's forty black tribes, for example. They, too, were a fact of life. You didn't notice the tribalism so much among Auma's friends, younger university-educated Kenyans who'd been schooled in the idea of nation and race; tribe was an issue with them only when they were considering a mate, or when they got older and saw it help or hinder careers. But they were the exceptions. Most Kenyans still worked with older maps of identity, more ancient loyalties. Even Jane or Zeituni could say things that surprised me. "The Luo are intelligent but lazy," they would say. Or "The Kikuyu are money-grubbing but industrious." Or "The Kalenjins—well, you can see what's happened to the country since they took over."

Hearing my aunts traffic in such stereotypes, I would try to explain to them the error of their ways. "It's thinking like that that holds us back," I would say. "We're all part of one tribe. The black tribe. The human tribe. Look what tribalism has done to places like Nigeria or Liberia."

And Jane would say, "Ah, those West Africans are all crazy anyway. You know they used to be cannibals, don't you?"

And Zeituni would say, "You sound just like your father, Barry. He also had such ideas about people."

Meaning he, too, was naive; he, too, liked to argue with history. Look what happened to him. . . .

The van suddenly came to a stop, shaking me out of my reverie. We were in front of a small *shamba*, and our driver, Francis, asked us all to stay put. A few minutes later, he emerged from the house with a young African girl, maybe twelve or thirteen, who was dressed in jeans and a neatly pressed blouse and carried a small duffel bag. Francis helped her into the back and pointed to the seat next to Auma.

"Is this your daughter?" Auma asked, scooting over to make room for the girl.

"No," Francis said. "My sister's. She likes to see the animals and is always nagging me to take her along. Nobody minds, I hope."

Everyone shook their heads and smiled at the girl, who suffered bravely under the attention.

"What is your name?" the British woman, Mrs. Wilkerson, asked.

"Elizabeth," the girl whispered.

"Well, Elizabeth, you can share my tent if you like," Auma said. "My brother, I think he snores."

I made a face. "Don't listen to her," I said, and held out a package of biscuits. Elizabeth took one and nibbled neatly around its edges. Auma reached for the bag and turned to Mauro.

"Want some?" she asked.

The Italian smiled and took one, before Auma passed them around to the others.

We followed the road into cooler hills, where women walked barefoot carrying firewood and water and small boys switched at donkeys from their rickety carts. Gradually the *shambas* became less frequent, replaced by tangled bush and forest, until the trees on our left dropped away without warning and all we could see was the wide-open sky.

"The Great Rift Valley," Francis announced.

We piled out of the van and stood at the edge of the escarpment looking out toward the western horizon. Hundreds of feet below, stone and savannah grass stretched out in a flat and endless plain, before it met the sky and carried the eye back through a series of high white clouds. To the right, a solitary mountain rose like an island in a silent sea; beyond that, a row of worn and shadowed ridges. Only two signs of man's presence were visible—a slender road leading west, and a satellite station, its massive white dish cupped upward toward the sky.

A few miles north, we turned off the main highway onto a road of pulverized tarmac. It was slow going: at certain points the potholes yawned across the road's entire width, and every so often trucks would approach from the opposite direction, forcing Francis to drive onto embankments. Eventually, we arrived at the road we'd seen from above and began to make our way across the valley floor. The landscape was dry, mostly bush grass and scruffy thorn trees, gravel and patches of hard dark stone. We began to pass small herds of gazelle; a solitary wildebeest feeding at the base of a tree; zebra and a giraffe, barely visible in the distance. For almost an hour we saw no other person, until a solitary Masai herdsman appeared in the distance, his figure as lean and straight as the staff that he carried, leading a herd of long-horned cattle across an empty flat.

I hadn't met many Masai in Nairobi, although I'd read quite a bit about them. I knew that their pastoral ways and fierceness in war had earned them a grudging respect from the British, so that even as treaties had been broken and the Masai had been restricted to reservations, the tribe had become mythologized in its defeat, like the Cherokee or Apache, the noble savage of picture postcards and coffee table books. I also knew that this Western infatuation with the Masai infuriated other Kenyans, who thought their ways something of an embarrassment, and who hankered after Masai land. The government had tried to impose compulsory education on Masai children, and a system of land title among the adults. The black man's burden, officials explained: to civilize our less fortunate brethren.

I wondered, as we drove deeper into their country, how long the Masai could hold out. In Narok, a small trading town where we stopped for gas and lunch, a group of children dressed in khaki shorts and old T-shirts surrounded our van with the aggressive enthusiasm of their Nairobi counterparts, peddling cheap jewelry and snacks.

Two hours later, when we arrived at the adobe gate leading into the preserve, a tall Masai man in a Yankees cap and smelling of beer leaned through the window of our van and suggested we take a tour of a traditional Masai *boma*.

"Only forty shillings," the man said with a smile. "Pictures extra."

While Francis attended to some business in the game warden's office, the rest of us got out and followed the Masai man into a large circular compound walled in by thornbrush. Along the perimeter were small mud-and-dung huts; in the center of the compound, several cattle and a few naked toddlers stood side by side in the dirt. A group of women waved us over to look at their bead-covered gourds, and one of them, a lovely young mother with a baby slung on her back, showed me a U.S. quarter that someone had foisted on her. I agreed to exchange it for Kenya shillings, and in return she invited me into her hut. It was a cramped, pitch-black space with a five-foot-high ceiling. The woman told me her family cooked, slept, and kept newborn calves in it. The smoke was blinding, and after a minute I had to leave, fighting the urge to brush away the flies that formed two solid rings around the baby's puffed eyes.

Francis was waiting for us when we returned to the van. We drove through the gate, following the road up a small, barren rise. And there, on the other side of the rise, I saw as beautiful a land as I'd ever seen. It swept out forever, flat plains undulating into gentle hills, dun-colored and as supple as a lion's back, creased by long gallery forests and dotted with thorn trees. To our left, a huge herd of zebra, ridiculously symmetrical in their stripes, harvested the wheat-colored grass; to our right, a troop of gazelle leaped into bush. And in the center, thousands of wildebeest, with mournful heads and humped shoulders that seemed too much for their slender legs to carry. Francis began to inch the van through the herd, and the animals parted before us, then merged in our wake like a school of fish, their hoofs beating against the earth like a wave against the shore.

I looked over at Auma. She had her arm around Elizabeth, and the two of them were wearing the same wordless smile.

We set up camp above the banks of a winding brown stream, beneath a big fig tree filled with noisy blue starlings. It was getting late, but after setting up our tents and gathering firewood, we had time for a short drive to a nearby watering hole where topi and gazelle had gathered to drink. A fire was going when we got back, and as we sat down to feed on Rafael's stew, Francis began telling us a little bit about himself. He had a wife and six children, he said, living on his homestead in Kikuyuland. They tended an acre of coffee and corn; on his days off, he did the heavier work of hoeing and planting. He said he enjoyed his work with the travel agency but disliked being away from his family. "If I could, I might prefer farming full-time," he said, "but the KCU makes it impossible."

"What's the KCU?" I asked.

"The Kenyan Coffee Union. They are thieves. They regulate what we can plant and when we can plant it. I can only sell my coffee to them, and they sell it overseas. They say to us that prices are dropping, but I know they still get one hundred times what they pay to me. The rest goes where?" Francis shook his head with disgust. "It's a terrible thing when the government steals from its own people."

"You speak very freely," Auma said.

Francis shrugged. "If more people spoke up, perhaps things might change. Look at the road that we traveled this morning coming into the valley. You know, that road was supposed to have been repaired only last year. But they used only loose gravel, so it washed out in the first rains. The money that was saved probably went into building some big man's house."

Francis looked into the fire, combing his mustache with his fingers. "I suppose it is not only the government's fault," he said after a while. "Even when things are done properly, we Kenyans don't like to pay taxes. We don't trust the idea of giving our money to someone. The poor man, he has good reason for this suspicion. But the big men who own the trucks that use the roads, they also refuse to pay their share. They would rather have their equipment break down all the time than give up some of their profits. This is how we like to think, you see. Somebody else's problem."

I tossed a stick into the fire. "Attitudes aren't so different in America," I told Francis.

"You are probably right," he said. "But you see, a rich country like America can perhaps afford to be stupid."

At that moment, two Masai approached the fire. Francis welcomed them, and as they sat down on one of the benches, he explained that they would provide security during the night. They were quiet, handsome men, their high cheekbones accentuated by the fire, their lean limbs jutting out of their blood-red *shukas*, their spears stuck into the ground before them, casting long shadows toward the trees. One of them, who said his name was Wilson, spoke Swahili, and he told us that he lived in a *boma* a few miles to the east. His silent companion began to pan the darkness with the beam of his flashlight, and Auma asked if the camp had ever been attacked by animals. Wilson grinned.

"Nothing serious," he said. "But if you have to go to the bathroom at night, you should call one of us to go with you."

Francis began to question the men about the movement of various animals, and I drifted away from the fire to glance up at the stars. It had been years since I'd seen them like this; away from the lights of the city, they were thick and round and bright as jewels. I noticed a patch of haze in the otherwise clear sky and stepped farther away from the fire, thinking perhaps it was the smoke, then deciding that it must be a cloud. I was wondering why the cloud hadn't moved when I heard the sound of footsteps behind me.

"I believe that's the Milky Way," Mr. Wilkerson said, looking up at the sky.

"No kidding."

He held up his hand and traced out the constellations for me, the points of the Southern Cross. He was a slight, soft-spoken man with round glasses and pasty blond hair. Initially I had guessed he spent his life indoors, an accountant or professor. I noticed, though, as the day had passed, that he possessed all sorts of practical knowledge, the kinds of things I had never got around to knowing but wished that I had. He could talk at length with Francis about Land Rover engines, had his tent up before I drove in my first stake, and seemed to know the name of every bird and every tree that we saw.

I wasn't surprised, then, when he told me that he had spent his childhood in Kenya, on a tea plantation in the White Highlands. He seemed reluctant to talk about the past; he said only that his family had sold the land after independence and had moved back to England, to settle in a quiet suburb of London. He had gone to medical school, then practiced with the National Health Service in Liverpool, where he had met his wife, a psychiatrist. After a few years, he had convinced her to return with him to Africa. They had decided against living in Kenya, where there was a surplus of doctors relative to the rest of the continent, and instead settled on Malawi, where they both had worked under government contract for the past five years.

"I oversee eight doctors for a region with a population of half a million," he told me now. "We never have enough supplies—at least half of what the government purchases ends up on the black market. So we can only focus on the basic, which in Africa is really what's needed anyway. People die from all sorts of preventable disease. Dysentery. Chicken pox. And now AIDS—the infection rate in some villages has reached fifty percent. It can be quite maddening."

The stories were grim, but as he continued to tell me the tasks of his life—digging wells, training outreach workers to inoculate children, distributing condoms—he seemed neither cynical nor sentimental. I asked him why he thought he had come back to Africa and he answered without a pause, as if he'd heard the question many times.

"It's my home, I suppose. The people, the land . . ." He took off his glasses and wiped them with a handkerchief. "It's funny, you know. Once you've lived here for a time, the life in England seems terribly cramped. The British have so much more, but seem to enjoy things less. I felt a foreigner there."

He put his glasses back on and shrugged. "Of course, I know that in the long run I need to be replaced. That's part of my job—making myself unnecessary. The Malawian doctors I work with are excellent, really. Competent. Dedicated. If we could just build a training hospital, some decent facilities, we could triple their number in no time. And then . . ."

"And then?"

He turned toward the campfire, and I thought his voice began to waver. "Perhaps I can never call this place home," he said. "Sins of the father, you know. I've learned to accept that." He paused for a moment, then looked at me.

"I do love this place, though," he said before walking back to his tent.

Dawn. To the east, the sky lightens above a black grove of trees, deep blue, then orange, then creamy yellow. The clouds lose their purple tint slowly, then dissipate, leaving behind a single star. As we pull out of camp, we see a caravan of giraffe, their long necks at a common slant, seemingly black before the rising red sun, strange markings against an ancient sky.

It was like that for the rest of the day, as if I were seeing as a child once again, the world a pop-up book, a fable, a painting by Rousseau. A pride of lions, yawning in the broken grass. Buffalo in the marshes, their horns like cheap wigs, tick birds scavenging off their mud-crusted backs. Hippos in the shallow riverbeds, pink eyes and nostrils like marbles bobbing on the water's surface. Elephants fanning their vegetable ears.

And most of all the stillness, a silence to match the elements. At twilight, not far from our camp, we came upon a tribe of hyenas feeding on the carcass of a wildebeest. In the dying orange light they looked like demon dogs, their eyes like clumps of black coal, their chins dripping with blood. Beside them, a row of vultures waited with stern, patient gazes, hopping away like hunchbacks whenever one of the hyenas got too close. It was a savage scene, and we stayed there for a long time, watching life feed on itself, the silence interrupted only by the crack of bone or the rush of wind, or the hard thump of a vulture's wings as it strained to lift itself into the current, until it finally found the higher air and those long and graceful wings became motionless and still like the rest. And I thought to myself: This is what Creation looked like. The same stillness, the same crunching of bone. There in the dusk, over that hill, I imagined the first man stepping forward, naked and rough-skinned, grasping a chunk of flint in his clumsy hand, no words yet for the fear, the anticipation, the awe he feels at the sky, the glimmering knowledge of his own death. If only we could remember that first common step, that first common word—that time before Babel.

At night, after dinner, we spoke further with our Masai guardsmen. Wilson told us that both he and his friend had recently been *moran*, members of the bachelor class of young warriors who were at the center of the Masai legend. They had each killed a lion to prove their manhood, had participated in numerous cattle raids. But now there were no wars, and even cattle raids had become complicated—only last year, another friend had been shot by a Kikuyu rancher. Wilson had finally decided that being a *moran* was a waste of time. He had gone to Nairobi in search of work, but he had little schooling and had ended up as a security guard at a bank. The boredom drove him crazy, and eventually he had returned to the valley to marry and tend to his cattle. Recently one of the cattle had been killed by a lion, and although it was illegal now, he and four others had hunted the lion into the preserve.

"How do you kill a lion?" I asked.

"Five men surround it and throw their spears," Wilson said. "The lion will choose one man to pounce. That man, he curls under his shield while the other four finish the job."

"It sounds dangerous," I said stupidly.

Wilson shrugged. "Usually there are only scratches. But sometimes only four will come back."

The man didn't sound like he was boasting—more like a mechanic trying to explain a difficult repair. Perhaps it was that nonchalance that caused Auma to ask him where the Masai thought a man went after he died. At first, Wilson didn't seem to understand the question, but eventually he smiled and began shaking his head.

"This is not a Masai belief," he said, almost laughing, "this life after you die. After you die, you are nothing. You return to the soil. That is all."

"What do you say, Francis?" Mauro asked.

For some time Francis had been reading a small, red-bound Bible. He looked up now and smiled. "These Masai are brave men," he said.

"Were you raised a Christian?" Auma asked Francis.

Francis nodded. "My parents converted before I was born."

Mauro spoke, staring into the fire. "Me, I leave the Church. Too many rules. Don't you think, Francis, that sometimes Christianity not so good? For Africa, the missionary changes everything, yes? He brings . . . how do you say?"

"Colonialism," I offered.

"Yes—colonialism. White religion, no?"

Francis placed the Bible in his lap. "Such things troubled me when I was young. The missionaries were men, and they erred as men. Now that I am older, I understand that I also can fail. That is not

God's failure. I also remember that some missionaries fed people during drought. Some taught children to read. In this, I believe they were doing God's work. All we can do is aspire to live like God, though we will always fall short."

Mauro went to his tent and Francis returned to his Bible. Beside him, Auma began to read a story with Elizabeth. Dr. Wilkerson sat with his knees together, mending his pants while his wife stared at the fire beside him. I looked at the Masai, their faces silent and watchful, and wondered what they made of the rest of us. They might be amused, I decided. I knew that their courage, their hardness, made me question my own noisy spirit. And yet, as I looked around the fire, I thought I saw a courage no less admirable in Francis, and in Auma, and in the Wilkersons as well. Maybe it was that courage, I thought, that Africa most desperately needed. Honest, decent men and women with attainable ambitions, and the determination to see those ambitions through.

The fire began to die, and one by one the others made their way to bed, until only Francis and I and the Masai remained. As I stood up, Francis began to sing a deep-voiced hymn in Kikuyu, with a melody that I vaguely recognized. I listened a while, lost in my own thoughts. Walking back to my tent, I felt I understood Francis's plaintive song, imagining it transmitting upward, through the clear black night, directly to God.

The day we got back from Mara, Auma and I received word that Roy had arrived, a week earlier than expected. He had suddenly appeared in Kariakor with a suitcase in hand, saying that he'd felt restless waiting around in D.C. and had managed to talk his way onto an earlier flight. The family was thrilled by his arrival and had held off on a big feast only until Auma and I returned. Bernard, who brought us the news, said that we were expected soon; he fidgeted as he spoke, as if every minute away from our eldest brother were a dereliction of duty.

But Auma, still stiff from sleeping in tents for the past two days, insisted on taking the time for a bath.

"Don't worry," she said to Bernard. "Roy just likes to make everything seem so dramatic."

Jane's apartment was in a hubbub when we arrived. In the kitchen, the women were cleaning collards and yams, chopping chicken and stirring *ugali*. In the living room, younger children set the table or served sodas to the adults. And at the center of this rush sat Roy, his legs spread out in front of him, his arms flung along the back of the sofa, nodding with approval. He waved us over and offered us each a hug. Auma, who hadn't seen Roy since he'd moved to the States, stepped back to get a better look.

"You've become so fat!" she said.

"Fat, eh?" Roy laughed. "A man needs a man-sized appetite." He turned toward the kitchen. "Which reminds me . . . where's that other beer?"

No sooner had the words fallen from his mouth than Kezia came up with a beer in hand, smiling happily. "Barry," she said in English, "this is the eldest son. Head of the family."

Another woman whom I had never seen before, plump and heavy-breasted, with bright red lipstick, sidled up beside Roy and put her arm around him. Kezia's smile subsided, and she drifted back into the kitchen.

"Baby," the woman said to Roy, "do you have the cigarettes?"

"Yeah, hold on. . . ." Roy patted his shirt pockets carefully. "Have you met my brother, Barack? Barack, this is Amy. And you remember Auma." Roy found the cigarettes and lit one for Amy. Amy took a long drag and leaned forward toward Auma, exhaling round puffs of smoke as she spoke.

"*Of course* I remember Auma. How are you? Let me tell you, you look wonderful! And I like what you've done to your hair. Really, it's so . . . natural!"

Amy reached for Roy's bottle, and Roy went to the dinner table. He grabbed himself a plate and bent down to smell the steaming pots. *"Chapos!"* he exclaimed, dropping three chapatis onto his plate. *"Sukuma-wiki!"* he shouted at the collard greens before spooning a heap onto his plate. *"Ugali!"* he hollered, cutting off two big wedges of cornmeal cake. Bernard and the children followed his every step, repeating Roy's words at a more tentative volume. Around the table, our aunts and Kezia beamed with satisfaction. It was the happiest I had seen any of them since my arrival.

After dinner, while Amy helped the aunts wash up, Roy sat between Auma and me and announced that he had come back with big plans. He was going to start an import-export company, he said, selling Kenyan curios in the States. *"Chondos.* Fabrics. Wood carvings. These things are *big* over there! You sell them at festivals, art shows, specialty stores. I already bought some samples to take back with me."

"That's a great idea," Auma said. "Show me what you've got."

Roy told Bernard to fetch several pink plastic bags from one of the bedrooms. Inside the bags were several wood carvings, the sort of slick, mass-produced pieces that were sold at quick turnover to the tourists downtown. Auma turned them around in her hands with a doubtful expression on her face.

"How much did you pay for these?"

"Only four hundred shillings each."

"So much! Brother, I think you've been cheated. Bernard, why did you let him pay so much?"

Bernard shrugged. Roy looked a bit wounded.

"I told you, these are Just samples," he said as he folded the carvings back in their wrapping. "An investment, so I will know what the market wants. You can't make money unless you spend money, eh, Barack?"

"That's what they say."

Roy's enthusiasm quickly returned. "You see? Once I know the market, then I will send orders back to Zeituni. We'll build the business up slowly, you see. *Slow-ly.* Then, when we have a regular system, Bernard and Abo can go to work for the company. Eh, Bernard? You can work for me."

Bernard nodded vaguely. Auma studied her younger brother, then turned back to Roy. "So what's the other big plan?"

Roy smiled. "Amy," he said.

"Amy?"

"Amy. I'm going to marry her."

"*What?* How long has it been since you last saw her?"

"Two years. Three. What does it matter?"

"You haven't had much time to think about it."

"She's an African woman. I know *that*! She *understands* me. Not like these European women, always arguing with their men." Roy nodded emphatically, and then, as if he were being yanked by an invisible string, he jumped out of his seat and headed toward the kitchen. Taking Amy in one arm, he lifted his bottle of beer toward the ceiling.

"Listen, everybody! Now that we are all here, we must have a toast! To those who are not with us! And to a happy ending!" With solemn deliberation, he started to pour his beer onto the floor. At least half of the beer splashed on Auma's shoes.

"Aggh!" Auma shouted, jumping back. "What are you doing?"

"The ancestors must drink," Roy said cheerfully. "It is the African way."

Auma grabbed a napkin to wipe the beer off her legs. "That's outdoors, Roy! Not in somebody's house! I swear, sometimes you're so careless! Who will clean this up now? You?"

Roy was about to answer when Jane rushed up with a rag in her hand. "Don't worry, don't worry!" she said, wiping up the floor. "We are just happy to have this one home."

It had been decided that after dinner we would all go out dancing at a nearby club. As Auma and I headed down the stairs ahead of the others, I heard her muttering to herself in the darkness.

"You Obama men!" she said to me. "You get away with anything! Have you noticed how they treat him? As far as they are concerned, he can do no wrong. Like this thing with Amy. This is just an idea that has popped into his head because he's lonely. I have nothing against Amy, but she's as irresponsible as he is. When they're together, they make each other worse. My mum, Jane, Zeituni—they all know this. But will they say anything to him? No. Because they're so afraid to offend him, even if it's for his own good."

Auma opened the car door and looked back at the rest of the family. They had just emerged from the shadows of the apartment building, Roy's figure towering over the others like a tree, his arms spread out like branches over the shoulders of his aunts. The sight of him softened Auma's face just a bit.

"Yah, it's not really his fault, I suppose," she said, starting up the car. "You see how he is with them. He's always been more of a family person than me. They don't feel judged with him."

The club, Garden Square, turned out to be a low-roofed, dimly lit place. It was already packed when we arrived, the air thick with cigarette smoke. The clientele was almost all African, an older, after work crowd of clerks, secretaries, government workers, all gathered around wobbly Formica tables. We pushed together two empty tables away from the small stage, and the waiter took our orders. Auma sat down next to Amy.

"So, Amy. Roy tells me you two are thinking about getting married."

"Yes, isn't it wonderful! He's so much fun! When he settles down, he says I can come to stay with him in America."

"You don't worry about being apart? I mean . . ."

"Other women?" Amy laughed and winked at Roy. "I tell you honestly, I don't care about that." She swung her fleshy arm over Roy's shoulder. "As long as he treats me well, he can do what he likes. Right, baby?"

Roy maintained a poker face, as if the conversation didn't concern him. Both he and Amy had the sheen of too many beers, and I saw Jane sneak an anxious look at Kezia. I decided to change the subject, and asked Zeituni if she'd been to Garden Square before.

"Me?" Zeituni raised her eyebrows at my impertinence. "Let me tell you, Barry—if there is dancing somewhere, then I have been to that place. These people here will tell you that I am the champion dancer. What do you say, Auma?"

"Zeituni's the best."

Zeituni tilted her head proudly. "You see? Really, Barry, your auntie can dance! And you want to know who was always my best partner? Your father! That guy, he really loved to dance. We entered many contests together when we were young. In fact, I'll tell you this story about his dancing. It was when he had come home to Alego one time to visit with your grandfather. He had promised that evening to do some chore for the old man—I don't remember what it was—but instead of doing his work, he went out to meet Kezia and take her dancing. You remember, Kezia? This is before they were married. I wanted to go with them, but Barack said I was too young.

"Anyway, they came home late that night, and Barack had had a few too many beers. He tried to sneak Kezia into his hut, but the old man was still awake and heard their footsteps in the compound. Even as an old man, your grandfather's hearing was very keen. So right away he shouts for Barack to come. When Barack comes in, the old man doesn't say a word. He just looks at Barack and snorts like an angry bull. Hmmmph! Hmmmph! And this whole time, I am peeking through the window of the old man's house, because I'm sure that the old man will cane Barack and I'm still angry at Barack, for not letting me go to the dance hall.

"What happened next, I couldn't believe. Instead of apologizing for coming home late, Barack walked over to the old man's phonograph and started to play a record! Then he turned and shouted to Kezia, who was hiding outside. 'Woman!' Barack shouted. 'Come here!' Right away Kezia came into the house, too frightened to refuse, and Barack took her in his arms and began to dance with her, around and around in the old man's house, as if he were dancing in a palace ballroom."

Zeituni shook her head and laughed. "Well now . . . no one treated your grandfather this way, not even Barack. I was sure now that for this thing Barack must be beaten severely. For a long time, your grandfather said nothing. He just sat there, watching his son. Then, like an elephant, he shouted out even louder than Barack. 'Woman! Come here!' And right away my mum, the one you call Granny, rushed in from her own hut, where she had been mending clothes. She asked why everyone was shouting, and your grandfather stood up and held out his hand. My mum shook her head and accused your grandfather of trying to make a fool of her, but the old man was so determined that soon all four of them were dancing in the hut, the two men looking very serious, the women looking at each other as if now they were sure that their husbands were crazy."

We all laughed at the story, and Roy ordered another round for everyone. I started to ask Zeituni more about our grandfather, but just then the band took up their positions on stage. The group looked a bit ragged at first, but the moment they struck their first note, the place was transformed. Immediately, people began pouring out onto the dance floor, stepping to the *soukous* beat. Zeituni grabbed my hand, and Roy took Auma's, and Amy took Bernard's, and soon we were all dancing into a sweat, arms and hips and rumps swaying softly; tall, ink-black Luos and short, brown Kikuyus, Kamba and Meru and Kalenjin, everyone smiling and shouting and having a ball. Roy threw his arms over his head to do a slow, funky turn around

Auma, who was laughing at her brother's silliness, and right then I saw in my brother's face the same look I had seen years ago in Toot and Gramps's apartment back in Hawaii, when the Old Man had first taught me how to dance—that same look of unquestioned freedom.

After three or four numbers, Roy and I both relinquished our partners and carried our beers into the open courtyard out back. The cool air tickled my nose, and I felt a bit tipsy.

"It's good to be here," I said.

"You know it. Like a poet." Roy laughed, sipping his beer.

"No, really, I mean it. It's just good to be here, with you and Auma and everyone. It's as if we—"

Before I could finish, we heard a bottle crash to the floor behind us. I spun around to see two men at the far side of the courtyard pushing another, smaller, man down onto the ground. With one hand, the man on the ground appeared to be covering a cut on his head; with his free arm he was trying to shield himself from the swings of a billy club. I took a step forward, but Roy pulled me back.

"Mind your own business, brother," he whispered.

"But—"

"They may be police. I tell you, Barack, you don't know what it's like to spend a night in a Nairobi jail."

By now, the man on the ground had curled up into a tight ball, trying to protect himself from the haphazard blows. Then, like a trapped animal who senses an opening, the man suddenly jumped to his feet and climbed onto one of the tables to scramble over the wooden fence. His assailants looked as if they were going to give chase but apparently decided that it wasn't worth it. One of them noticed Roy and me but said nothing, and together the two of them sauntered back inside. I suddenly felt very sober.

"That was terrible," I said.

"Yah, well . . . you don't know what the other guy did first."

I rubbed the back of my neck. "When were you in jail anyway?"

Roy took another swig of beer and fell into one of the metal chairs. "The night David died."

I sat down beside him and he told me the story. They had gone out to drink, he said, in search of a party. They had taken Roy's motorcycle to a nearby club, and there Roy had met a woman. He had taken a fancy to her, and they started talking. He had bought her a beer, but before long another man had come up and started getting in Roy's face. The man said he was the woman's husband and grabbed her by the arm. The woman struggled and fell, and Roy told the man to leave her alone. A fight broke out. The police came, and Roy didn't have his identification papers, so they took him down to the station. He was thrown in a cell and left there for several hours, until David finally managed to get in to see him.

Give me the keys to the motorcycle, David had said, *and I can get you the papers you need.*

No. Just go home.

You can't stay here all night, brother. Give me the keys. . . .

Roy stopped talking. We sat and stared at the shadows, oversized and faint off the lattice fence.

"It was an accident, Roy," I said finally. "It wasn't your fault. You need to let it go."

Before I could say anything else, I heard Amy hollering behind us, her voice slurring slightly over the music.

"Hey, you two! We've been looking all over for you!"

I started to wave her off, but Roy jerked out of his chair, tipping it to the ground.

"Come on, woman," he said, taking Amy by the waist. "Let's go dance."

CHAPTER EIGHTEEN

A T FIVE-THIRTY IN the evening, our train rumbled out of the old Nairobi train station heading west for Kisumu. Jane had decided to stay behind, but the rest of the family was on board—Kezia, Zeituni, and Auma in one compartment; Roy, Bernard, and myself in the next. While everyone busied themselves with storing their luggage, I jiggled open a window and looked out at the curve of the tracks behind us, a line of track that had helped usher in Kenya's colonial history.

The railway had been the single largest engineering effort in the history of the British Empire at the time it was built—six hundred miles long, from Mombasa on the Indian Ocean to the eastern shores of Lake Victoria. The project took five years to complete, as well as the lives of several hundred imported Indian workers. When it was finished, the British realized there were no passengers to help defray the costs of their conceit. And so the push for white settlers; the consolidation of lands that could be used to help lure newcomers; the cultivation of cash crops like coffee and tea; the necessity of an administrative apparatus that could extend as far as the tracks, into the heart of an unknown continent. And missions and churches to vanquish the fear that an unknown land produced.

It seemed like ancient history. And yet I knew that 1895, the year that the first beams were laid, had also been the year of my grandfather's birth. It was the lands of that same man, Hussein Onyango, to which we were now traveling. The thought made the history of the train come alive for me, and I tried to imagine the sensations some nameless British officer might have felt on the train's maiden voyage, as he sat in his gas-lit compartment and looked out over miles of receding bush. Would he have felt a sense of triumph, a confidence that the guiding light of Western civilization had finally penetrated the African darkness? Or did he feel a sense of foreboding, a sudden realization that the entire enterprise was an act of folly, that this land and its people would outlast imperial dreams? I tried to imagine the African on the other side of the glass window, watching this snake of steel and black smoke passing his village for the first time. Would he have looked at the train with envy, imagining himself one day sitting in the car where the Englishman sat, the load of his days somehow eased? Or would he have shuddered with visions of ruin and war?

My imagination failed me, and I returned to the present landscape, no longer bush but the rooftops of Mathare stretching into the foothills beyond. Passing one of the slum's open-air markets, I saw a row of small boys wave to the train. I waved back, and heard Kezia's voice, speaking in Luo, behind me. Bernard yanked on my shirt.

"She says you should keep your head inside. Those boys will throw stones at you."

One of the train's crew came in to take our bedding order and tell us that food service had started, and so we all went into the dining car and found ourselves a table. The car was a picture of faded elegance—the original wood paneling still intact but dull, the silver real but not perfectly matched. The food was just fine, though, and the beer served cold, and by the end of the meal I was feeling content.

"How long will it take to get to Home Square?" I asked, wiping the last bit of sauce off my plate.

"All night to Kisumu," Auma said. "We'll take a bus or *matatu* from there—another five hours, maybe."

"By the way," Roy said to me, lighting a cigarette, "it's not Home *Square*. It's Home *Squared*."

"What does that mean?"

"It's something the kids in Nairobi used to say," Auma explained. "There's your ordinary house in Nairobi. And then there's your house in the country, where your people come from. Your ancestral home. Even the biggest minister or businessman thinks this way. He may have a mansion in Nairobi and build only a small hut on his land in the country. He may go there only once or twice a year. But if you ask him where he is from, he will tell you that that hut is his true home. So, when we were at school and wanted to tell somebody we were going to Alego, it was home twice over, you see. Home Squared."

Roy took a sip of his beer. "For you, Barack, we can call it Home Cubed."

Auma smiled and leaned back in her seat, listening to the rhythm of the train on the tracks. "This train brings back so many memories. You remember, Roy, how much we used to look forward to going home? It is so beautiful, Barack! Not at all like Nairobi. And Granny—she's so much fun! Oh, you will like her, Barack. She has such a good sense of humor."

"She had to have a good sense of humor," Roy said, "living with the Terror for so long."

"Who's the Terror?"

Auma said, "That's what we used to call our grandfather. Because he was so mean."

Roy shook his head and laughed. "Wow, that guy was *mean*! He would make you sit at the table for dinner, and served the food on china, like an Englishman. If you said one wrong thing, or used the wrong fork—pow! He would hit you with his stick. Sometimes when he hit you, you wouldn't even know why until the next day."

Zeituni waved them off, unimpressed. "Ah, you children knew him only when he was old and weak. When he was younger, aay! I was his favorite, you know. His pet. But still, if I did something wrong, I would hide from him all day, I would be so scared! You know, he was strict even with his guests. If they came to his house, he would kill many chickens in their honor. But if they broke custom, like washing their hands before someone who was older, he would have no hesitation in hitting them, even the adults."

"Doesn't sound like he was real popular," I said.

Zeituni shook her head. "Actually, he was well respected because he was such a good farmer. His compound in Alego was one of the biggest in the area. He had such a green thumb, he could make anything grow. He had studied these techniques from the British, you see. When he worked for them as a cook."

"I didn't know he was a cook."

"He had his lands, but for a long time he was a cook for *wazungu* in Nairobi. He worked for some very important people. During the World War he served a captain in the British army."

Roy ordered another beer. "Maybe that's what made him so mean."

"I don't know," Zeituni said. "I think my father was always that way. Very strict. But fair. I will tell you one story I remember, from when I was only a young girl. One day a man came to the edge of our compound with a goat on a leash. He wanted to pass through our land, because he lived on the other side, and he didn't want to walk around. So your grandfather told this man, 'When you are alone, you are always free to pass through my land. But today you cannot pass, because your goat will eat my plants.' Well, this man would not listen. He argued for a long time with your grandfather, saying that he would be careful and that the goat would do no harm. This man talked so much your grandfather finally called me over and said, 'Go bring me Alego.' That's what he called his *panga*, you see—"

"His machete."

"Yes, his machete. He had two that he kept very, very sharp. He would rub them on a stone all day. One *panga* he called Alego. The other he called Kogelo. So I ran back to his hut and brought him the one he called Alego. And now your grandfather tells this man, 'See here. I have already told you that you should not pass, but you are too stubborn to listen. So now I will make a bargain with you. You can pass with your goat. But if even one leaf is harmed—if even *one half* of one leaf of my plants is harmed—then I will cut down your goat also.'

"Well, even though I was very young at the time, I knew that this man must be so stupid, because he accepted my father's offer. We began to walk, the man and his goat in front, me and the old man following closely behind. We had walked maybe twenty steps when the goat stuck out its neck and started nibbling at a leaf. Then— Whoosh! My dad cut one side of the goat's head clean through. The goat owner was shocked, and started to cry out. 'Aalieey! Aaiieey! What have you done now, Hussein Onyango.' And your grandfather just wiped off his *panga* and said, 'If I say I will do something, I must do it. Otherwise how will people know that my word is true?' Later, the owner of the goat tried to sue your grandfather before the council of elders. The elders all felt pity for the man, for the death of a goat was not such a small thing. But when they heard his story, they had to send him away. They knew that your grandfather was right, because the man had been warned."

Auma shook her head. "Can you imagine, Barack?" she said, looking at me. "I swear, sometimes I think that the problems in this family all started with him. He is the only person whose opinion I think the Old Man really worried about. The only person he feared."

By this time, the dining car had emptied and the waiter was pacing back and forth impatiently, so we all decided to turn in. The bunks were narrow, but the sheets were cool and inviting, and I stayed up late listening to the trembling rhythm of the train and the even breath of my brothers, and thinking about the stories of our grandfather. It had all started with him, Auma had said. That sounded right somehow. If I could just piece together his story, I thought, then perhaps everything else might fall into place.

I finally fell asleep, and dreamed I was walking along a village road. Children, dressed only in strings of beads, played in front of the round huts, and several old men waved to me as I passed. But as I went farther along, I began to notice that people were looking behind me fearfully, rushing into their huts as I passed. I heard the growl of a leopard and started to run into the forest, tripping over roots and stumps and vines, until at last I couldn't run any longer and fell to my knees in the middle of a bright clearing. Panting for breath, I turned around to see the day turned night, and a giant figure loom- ing as tall as the trees, wearing only a loincloth and a ghostly mask. The lifeless eyes bored into me, and I heard a thunderous voice say- ing only that it was time, and my entire body began to shake violently with the sound, as if I were breaking apart. . . .

I jerked up in a sweat, hitting my head against the wall lamp that stuck out above the bunk. In the darkness, my heart slowly evened itself, but I couldn't get back to sleep again.

We arrived in Kisumu at daybreak and walked the half mile to the bus depot. It was crowded with buses and *matatus* honking and jockeying for space in the dusty open-air lot, their fenders painted with names like "Love Bandit" and "Bush Baby." We found a sad-looking vehicle with balding, cracked tires that was heading our way. Auma boarded first, then stepped back out, looking morose.

"There are no seats," she said.

"Don't worry," Roy said as our bags were hoisted up by a series of hands to the roof of the bus. "This is Africa, Auma . . . not Europe." He turned and smiled down at the young man who was collecting fares. "You can find us some seats, eh, brother?"

The man nodded. "No problem. This bus is first-class."

An hour later Auma was sitting on my lap, along with a basket of yams and somebody else's baby girl.

"I wonder what third-class looks like," I said, wiping a strand of spittle off my hand.

Auma pushed a strange elbow out of her face. "You won't be joking after we hit the first pothole."

Fortunately, the highway was well paved, the landscape mostly dry bush and low hills, the occasional cinder-block house soon replaced by mud huts with thatched, conical roofs. We got off in Ndori and spent the next two hours sipping on warm sodas and watching stray dogs snap at each other in the dust, until a *matatu* finally appeared to take us over the dirt road heading north. As we drove up the rocky incline a few shoeless children waved but did not smile, and a herd of goats ran before us, to drink at a narrow stream. Then the road widened and we finally stopped at a clearing. Two young men were sitting there, under the shade of a tree, and their faces broke into smiles as they saw us. Roy jumped out of the *matatu* to gather the two men into his arms.

"Barack," Roy said happily, "these are our uncles. This is Yusuf," he said, pointing to the slightly built man with a mustache. "And this," he said, pointing to the larger, clean-shaven man, "this is our father's youngest brother, Sayid."

"Ah, we have heard many great things about this one," Sayid said, smiling at me. "Welcome, Barry. Welcome. Come, let me have your bags."

We followed Yusuf and Sayid down a path running perpendicular to the main road, until we crossed a wall of tall hedges and entered a large compound. In the middle of the compound was a low, rectangular house with a corrugated-iron roof and concrete walls that had crumbled on one side, leaving their brown mud base exposed. Bougainvillea, red and pink and yellow with flowers, spread along one side in the direction of a large concrete water tank, and across the packed earth was a small round hut lined with earthenware pots where a few chickens pecked in an alternating rhythm. I could see two more huts in the wide grass yard that stretched out behind the house. Beneath a tall mango tree, a pair of bony red cows looked up at us before returning to feed.

Home Squared.

"Eh, Obama!" A big woman with a scarf on her head strode out of the main house drying her hands on the sides of her flowered skirt. She had a face like Sayid's, smooth and big-boned, with sparkling, laughing eyes. She hugged Auma and Roy as if she were going to wrestle them to the ground, then turned to me and grabbed my hand in a hearty handshake.

"Halo!" she said, attempting English.

"*Musawa!*" I said in Luo.

She laughed, saying something to Auma.

"She says she has dreamed about this day, when she would finally meet this son of her son. She says you've brought her a great happiness. She says that now you have finally come home."

Granny nodded and pulled me into a hug before leading us into the house. Small windows let in little of the afternoon light, and the house was sparsely furnished—a few wooden chairs, a coffee table, a worn couch. On the walls were various family artifacts: the Old Man's Harvard diploma; photographs of him and of Omar, the uncle who had left for America twenty-five years ago and had never come back. Beside these were two older, yellowing photographs, the first of a tall young woman with smoldering eyes, a plump infant in her lap, a young girl standing beside her; the second of an older man in a high-backed chair. The man was dressed in a starched shirt and a *kanga*; his legs were crossed like an Englishman's, but across his lap was what appeared to be some sort of club, its heavy head wrapped in an animal skin. His high cheekbones and narrow eyes gave his face an almost Oriental cast. Auma came up beside me.

"That's him. Our grandfather. The woman in the picture is our other grandmother, Akumu. The girl is Sarah. And the baby . . . that's the Old Man."

I studied the pictures for some time, until I noticed one last picture on the wall. It was a vintage print, the kind that grace old Coca-Cola ads, of a white woman with thick dark hair and slightly dreamy eyes. I asked what the print was doing there, and Auma turned to Granny, who answered in Luo.

"She says that that is a picture of one of our grandfather's wives. He told people that he had married her in Burma when he was in the war."

Roy laughed. "She doesn't look very Burmese, eh, Barack?"

I shook my head. She looked like my mother.

We sat down in the living room and Granny made us some tea. She explained that things were well, although she had given away some of the land to relatives, since she and Yusuf could not work it all by themselves. She made up the lost income by selling lunches to the children at the nearby school and bringing goods from Kisumu to the local market whenever she had some spare cash. Her only real problems were with the roof of the house—she pointed to a few threads of sunlight that ran from the ceiling to the floor—and the fact that she hadn't heard anything from her son Omar in over a year. She asked if I had seen him, and I had to say no. She grunted something in Luo, then started to gather up our cups.

"She says when you see him, you should tell him she wants nothing from him," Auma whispered. "Only that he should come visit his mother."

I looked at Granny, and for the first time since our arrival, her age showed on her face.

After we unpacked our bags, Roy gestured for me to follow him out into the backyard. At the edge of a neighboring cornfield, at the foot of a mango tree, I saw two long rectangles of cement jutting out of the earth like a pair of exhumed coffins. There was a plaque on one of the graves: HUSSEIN ONYANGO OBAMA, B. 1895. D. 1979. The other was covered with yellow bathroom tiles, with a bare space on the headstone where the plaque should have been. Roy bent down and brushed away a train of ants that marched along the length of the grave.

"Six years," Roy said. "Six years, and there's still nothing to say who is buried here. I tell you now, Barack—when I die, you make sure that my name is on the grave." He shook his head slowly before heading back toward the house.

How to explain the emotions of that day? I can summon each moment in my mind almost frame by frame. I remember Auma and myself joining Granny at the afternoon market, the same clearing where the *matatu* had first dropped us off, only now full of women who sat on straw mats, their smooth brown legs sticking straight out in front of them from under wide skirts; the sound of their laughter as they watched me help Granny pick stems off collard greens that she'd brought from Kisumu, and the nutty-sweet taste of a sugarcane stalk that one of the women put into my hand. I remember the rustle of corn leaves, the concentration on my uncles' faces, the smell of our sweat as we mended a hole in the fence bounding the western line of the property. I remember how, in the afternoon, a young boy named Godfrey appeared in the compound, a boy who Auma explained was staying with Granny because his family lived in a village where there was no school; I remember Godfrey's frantic steps as he chased a big black rooster through the banana and papaya trees, the knot in his young brow as the bird kept flapping out of his reach, the look in his eyes when finally Granny grabbed the rooster from behind with one hand and unceremoniously drew her knife across the bird's neck—a look that I remembered as my own.

It wasn't simply joy that I felt in each of these moments. Rather, it was a sense that everything I was doing, every touch and breath and word, carried the full weight of my life; that a circle was beginning to close, so that I might finally recognize myself as I was, here, now, in one place. Only once that afternoon would I feel that mood broken, when, on our way back from the market, Auma ran ahead to get her camera, leaving Granny and me alone in the middle of the road. After a long pause, Granny looked at me and smiled. "Halo!" she said. *"Musawa!"* I said. Our mutual vocabulary exhausted, we stared ruefully down at the dirt until Auma finally returned. And Granny then turned to Auma and said, in a tone I could understand, that it pained her not to be able to speak to the son of her son.

"Tell her I'd like to learn Luo, but it's hard to find time in the States," I said. "Tell her how busy I am."

"She understands that," Auma said. "But she also says that a man can never be too busy to know his own people."

I looked at Granny, and she nodded at me, and I knew then that at some point the joy I was feeling would pass and that that, too, was part of the circle: the fact that my life was neither tidy nor static, and that even after this trip hard choices would always remain.

Night fell quickly, the wind making swift tracks through the darkness. Bernard, Roy, and I went to the water tank and bathed ourselves in the open air, our soapy bodies glowing from the light of an almost full moon. When we returned to the house, the food was waiting for us, and we ate purposefully, without words. After dinner, Roy left, muttering that he had some people he wanted to visit. Yusuf went to his hut and brought back an old transistor radio that he said had once belonged to our grandfather. Fiddling with the knob, he caught a scratchy BBC newscast, fading in and out of range, the voices like hallucinatory fragments from another world. A moment later we heard a strange, low-pitched moan off in the distance.

"The night runners must be out tonight," Auma said.

"What are night runners?"

"They're like warlocks," Auma said. "Spirit men. When we were children, these people here"—she pointed at Granny and Zeituni—would tell us stories about them to make us behave. They told us that in daylight the night runners are like ordinary men. You might pass them in the market, or even have them to your house for a meal, and never know their true natures. But at night they take on the shape of leopards and speak to all the animals. The most powerful night runners can leave their bodies and fly to faraway places. Or hex you with only a glance. If you ask our neighbors, they will tell you that there are still many night runners around here."

"Auma! You act as if it is not true!"

In the flickering light of the kerosene lamp, I couldn't tell if Zeituni was joking. "Let me tell you, Barry," she said, "When I was young the night runners caused people many problems. They would steal our goats. Sometimes they took even our cattle. Only your grandfather was not afraid of them. I remember one time he heard his goats bleating in their pen, and when he went to check on them, he saw what looked like a huge leopard standing on its hind legs, like a man. It had a baby goat in its jaws, and when it saw your grandfather, it cried out in Luo before running into the forest. Your grandfather chased it deep into the hills, but just as he was about to strike it with his *panga*, the night runner flew up into the trees. Luckily, it dropped the goat when it jumped, and the goat suffered only a broken leg. Your grandfather brought the goat back to the compound and showed me how to make a splint. I cared for that goat myself until it was back to health."

We became quiet again; lamplight grew low and people began drifting off to bed. Granny brought out blankets and a twin-sized cot for Bernard and me, and we arranged ourselves on the narrow bed before blowing out the lamp. My body ached from exhaustion; inside Granny's bedroom, I could hear the murmur of her and Auma talking. I wondered where Roy had gone to, and thought about the yellow tiles on the Old Man's grave.

"Barry," Bernard whispered. "Are you awake?"

"Yeah."

"Did you believe what Zeituni told you? About night runners?"

"I don't know."

"Myself, I think there is no such thing as a night runner. They are probably just thieves who use these stories to make people afraid."

"You may be right."

There was a long pause.

"Barry?"

"What?"

"What made you finally come home?"

"I'm not sure, Bernard. Something told me it was time."

Bernard rolled over onto his side without answering. A moment later, I heard his soft snores beside me, and I opened my eyes to the darkness, waiting for Roy to return.

In the morning, Sayid and Yusuf suggested that Auma and I take a tour of the lands. As we followed them across the backyard and down a dirt path, through fields of corn and millet, Yusuf turned to me and said, "It must seem very primitive to you, compared to farms in America."

I told him that I didn't know much about farming but that, as far as I could tell, the land seemed quite fertile.

"Yes, yes," Yusuf said, nodding. "The land is good. The problem is that people here are uneducated. They don't understand much about development. Proper agricultural techniques and so forth. I try to explain to them about capital improvements and irrigation, but they refuse to listen. The Luo are very stubborn in this way."

I noticed Sayid frowning at his brother, but he said nothing. After a few minutes we came to a small, brown stream. Sayid shouted out a warning, and two young women emerged on the opposite bank, wrapped in their *kangas*, their hair still gleaming from their morning baths. They smiled shyly and stepped behind an island of rushes, and Sayid pointed to the hedges running alongside the water.

"This is where the land ends," he said. "Before, when my father lived, the fields were much bigger. But as my mother said, much of the land has now been given away."

Yusuf decided to go back at this point, but Sayid led Auma and me along the stream for a while, then across more fields, past the occasional compound. In front of some huts, we saw women sorting through millet spread across square strips of cloth, and we stopped to talk to one of them, a middle-aged woman in a faded red dress and red, laceless sneakers. She set aside her work to shake our hands and told us that she remembered our father—they had herded goats together as children, she said. When Auma asked how life had been treating her, she shook her head slowly.

"Things have changed," she said in a flat voice. "The young men leave for the city. Only the old men, women, and children remain. All the wealth has left us." As she spoke, an old man with a rickety bicycle came up beside us, then a spindly man whose breath smelled of liquor. They immediately picked up the woman's refrain about the hardness of life in Alego, and the children who had left them behind. They asked if we might give them something to tide them over, and Auma dropped a few shillings into each of their hands before we excused ourselves and started back toward the house.

"What's happened here, Sayid?" Auma said after we were out of earshot. "There never used to be such begging."

Sayid leaned down and cleared away a few fallen branches from between the rows of corn. "You are right," he said. "I believe they have learned this thing from those in the city. People come back from Nairobi or Kisumu and tell them, 'You are poor.' So now we have this idea of poverty. We didn't have this idea before. You look at my mother. She will never ask for anything. She has always something that she is doing. None of it brings her much money, but it is something, you see. It gives her pride. Anyone could do the same, but many people here, they prefer to give up."

"What about Yusuf?" Auma asked. "Couldn't he do more?"

Sayid shook his head. "My brother, he talks like a book, but I'm afraid he does not like to lead by example."

Auma turned to me. "You know, Yusuf was doing really well for a time. He did well in school, didn't he, Sayid? He received several good job offers. Then, I don't know what happened. He just dropped out. Now he just stays here with Granny, doing small chores for her. It's as if he's afraid to try to succeed."

Sayid nodded. "I think perhaps education doesn't do us much good unless it is mixed with sweat."

I thought about what Sayid had said as we continued to walk. Perhaps he was right; perhaps the idea of poverty had been imported to this place, a new standard of need and want that was carried like measles, by me, by Auma, by Yusuf's archaic radio. To say that poverty was just an idea wasn't to say that it wasn't real; the people we'd just met couldn't ignore the fact that some people had indoor toilets or ate meat every day, any more than the children of Altgeld could ignore the fast cars and lavish homes that flashed across their television sets.

But perhaps they could fight off the notion of their own helplessness. Sayid was telling us about his own life now: his disappointment at having never gone to the university, like his older brothers, for lack of funds; his work in the National Youth Corps, assigned to development projects around the country, a three-year stint that was now coming to an end. He had spent his last two holidays knocking on the doors of various businesses in Nairobi, so far without any success. Still, he seemed undaunted by his circumstances, certain that persistence would eventually pay off.

"To get a job these days, even as a clerk, requires that you know somebody," Sayid said as we approached Granny's compound. "Or you must grease the palm of some person very heavily. That's why I would like to start my own business. Something small only. But mine. That was your father's error, I think. For all his brilliance, he never had something of his own." He thought for a moment. "Of course, there's no point wasting time worrying about the mistakes of the past, am I correct? Like this dispute over your father's inheritance. From the beginning, I have told my sisters to forget this thing. We must get on with our lives. They do not listen to me, though. And in the meantime, the money they fight over goes where? To the lawyers. The lawyers are eating very well off this case, I believe. How does the saying go? When two locusts fight, it is always the crow who feasts."

"Is that a Luo expression?" I asked. Sayid's face broke into a bashful smile.

"We have similar expressions in Luo," he said, "but actually I must admit that I read this particular expression in a book by Chinua Achebe. The Nigerian writer. I like his books very much. He speaks the truth about Africa's predicament. The Nigerian, the Kenyan—it is the same. We share more than divides us."

Granny and Roy were sitting outside the house and talking to a man in a heavy suit when we returned. The man turned out to be the principal of the nearby school, and he had stopped to share news from town and enjoy the chicken stew left over from the night before. I noticed that Roy had his bag packed, and asked him where he was going.

"To Kendu Bay," he said. "The principal here is going that way, so myself, Bernard, and my mum, we're going to go catch a ride with him and bring Abo back here. You should come, too, and pay your respects to the family there."

Auma decided to stay back with Granny, but Sayid and I went to gather a change of clothes and piled into the principal's old jalopy.

The drive to Kendu turned out to be several hours long by the main highway; to the west, Lake Victoria appeared intermittently, its still, silver waters tapering off into flat green marsh. By late afternoon we were pulling down Kendu Bay's main street, a wide, dusty road lined with sand-colored shops. After thanking the principal, we caught a *matatu* down a maze of side streets, until all signs of town had disappeared and the landscape was once again open pasture and cornfields. At a fork in the road, Kezia signaled for us to get off, and we began walking along a deep, chalk-colored gully at the bottom of which flowed a wide, chocolate-brown river. Along the riverbank, we could see women slapping wet clothes against exposed rock; on a terrace above, a herd of goats chewed on the patches of yellow grass, their black, white, and roan markings like lichen against the earth. We turned down a narrower footpath and came to the entrance of a hedged-in compound. Kezia stopped and pointed to what looked like a random pile of rocks and sticks, saying something to Roy in Luo.

"That's Obama's grave," Roy explained. "Our great-grandfather. All the land around here is called *K'Obama*—'Land of the Obama.' We are *Jok'Obama*—'the people of Obama.' Our great-great-grandfather was raised in Alego, but he moved here when he was still a young man. This is where Obama settled, and where all his children were born."

"So why did our grandfather go back to Alego?"

Roy turned to Kezia, who shook her head. "You have to ask Granny that question," Roy said. "My mum thinks maybe he didn't get along with his brothers. In fact, one of his brothers is still living here. He's old now, but perhaps we can see him."

We came to a small wooden house where a tall, handsome woman was sweeping the yard. Behind her, a young shirtless man sat on the porch. The woman shaded her eyes with her forearm and began to wave, and the young man slowly turned our way. Roy went up to shake hands with the woman, whose name was Salina, and the young man stood up to greet us.

"Eh, you people finally came for me," Abo said, hugging each of us in turn. He reached for his shirt. "I had heard you were coming with Barry so long ago!"

"Yah, you know how it is," Roy said. "It took us a while to get organized."

"I'm just glad you came. I'm telling you, I need to get back to Nairobi."

"You don't like it here, eh?"

"It's so boring, man, you would not believe it. No TV. No clubs. These people in the country, I think they are slow. If Billy hadn't shown up, I would have gone crazy for sure."

"Billy's here?"

"Yah, he's around somewhere. . . ." Abo waved his hand vaguely, then turned to me and smiled. "So, Barry. What have you brought me from America?"

I reached into my bag and pulled out one of the portable cassette players that I had bought for him and Bernard. He turned it over in his hands with a thinly disguised look of disappointment.

"This brand is not a Sony, is it?" he said. Then, looking up, he quickly recovered himself and slapped me on the back. "That's okay, Barry. Thank you! Thank you."

I nodded at him, trying not to get angry. He was standing beside Bernard and their resemblance was striking: the same height, the same slender frame, the same smooth, even features. Just shave off Abo's mustache, I thought to myself, and they could almost Pass as twins. Except for . . . what? The look in Abo's eyes. That was it. Not just the telltale redness of some sort of high but something deeper, something that reminded me of young men back in Chicago. An element of guardedness, perhaps, and calculation. The look of someone who realizes early in life that he has been wronged.

We followed Salina inside the house, and she brought in a tray of sodas and biscuits. As she set down the tray, a strapping, mustached young man, as good-looking as Salina and as tall as Roy, walked through the door and let out a yell.

"Roy! What are you doing here?"

Roy stood up and they embraced. "You know me. Just looking for a meal. I should ask you the same thing."

"Me, I am only visiting my mother. If I don't come so often, she begins to complain." He kissed Salina on the cheek and took my hand in a crushing handshake. "So I see you've brought my American cousin! I've heard so much about you, Barry, I cannot believe you are now here." He turned to Salina. "Have you given Barry food?"

"Soon, Billy. Soon." Salina took Kezia's hand and turned to Roy. "You see what mothers must put up with? How is your granny, anyway?"

"Same."

She nodded thoughtfully. "That is not so bad," she said.

Together with Kezia, she went out of the room, and Billy fell onto the couch beside Roy.

"So, you still crazy, *bwana*? Look at you now! Well-fed, like a prize bull! You must be enjoying yourself in the States."

"It's okay," Roy said. "How's Mombasa? I hear you're working at the post office."

Billy shrugged. "The pay is all right. Not too much thinking, you know, but steady." He turned to me. "Let me tell you, Barry, this brother of yours, he was wild! Truthfully, we were all wild back then. We spent most of our time chasing the bush meat, eh Roy!" He slapped Roy on the thigh and laughed. "So tell me, how are these American women?"

Roy laughed, but he seemed relieved when Salina and Kezia brought in dinner. "You see, Barry," Billy said, setting down his plate on the low table in front of him, "your father and my father were age-mates. Very close. When Roy and I were growing up, we were also age-mates, so naturally we became very close. Let me tell you, your father, he was a very great man. I was closer to him than to my own father. If I was in trouble, it was my Uncle Barack that I went to first. And Roy, you would also go to my father, I believe."

"The men in our family were very good to other people's children," Roy said quietly. "With their own, they didn't want to look weak."

Billy nodded and licked his fingers. "You know, Roy, I think there's truth in what you say. Myself, I don't want to make the same mistakes. I don't want to mistreat my family." With his clean hand, Billy pulled his wallet out of his pocket and showed me a picture of his wife and their two young children. "I swear, *bwana*, marriage *takes* you! You should see me now, Roy. I've become so calm. A family man. Of course, there are limits to what a man should take. My wife, she knows not to cross me too often. What do you say, Sayid?"

I realized that Sayid hadn't spoken much since we arrived. He washed his hands now before turning to Billy.

"I am not yet married," he said, "so perhaps I should not speak. But I admit, I have been giving these matters some thought. I have concluded that the problem that is most serious for Africa is what?" He paused to look around the room. "This thing between men and women. Our men, we try to be strong, but our strength is often misplaced. Like this business with having more than one woman. Our fathers had many wives, so we also must have many women. But we do not stop and look at the consequences. What happens with all these women? They become jealous. The children, they are not close to their fathers. It is—"

Sayid caught himself suddenly and smiled. "Of course, I have not even one wife, so I shouldn't carry on so. Where there is no experience, I believe the wise man is silent."

"Achebe?" I asked.

Sayid laughed and clutched my hand. "No, Barry. That one was only me."

It was dark by the time we finished dinner, and, after thanking

Salina and Kezia for the food, we followed Billy outside onto a narrow footpath. Walking under a full moon, we soon came to a smaller house where the shadows of moths fluttered against a yellow window. Billy knocked on the door, and a short man with a scar along his forehead answered, his lips smiling but his eyes darting around like those of a man about to be struck. Behind him sat another man, tall, very thin, dressed in white and with a wispy goatee and mustache that made him look like an Indian *sadhu*. Together, the two men began shaking our hands feverishly, speaking to me in broken English.

"Your nephew!" the white-haired man said, pointing to himself.

The short one laughed and said, "His hair is white, but he calls you uncle! Ha-ha. You like this English? Come."

They led us to a wooden table set with an unlabeled bottle of clear liquid and three glasses. The white-haired man held up the bottle, then carefully poured what looked like a couple of shots into each glass. "This is better than whiskey, Barry," Billy said as he lifted his glass. "It makes a man very potent." He threw the drink down his throat, and Roy and I followed suit. I felt my chest explode, raining down shrapnel into my stomach. The glasses were refilled, but Sayid took a pass, so the short man held the extra drink in front of my eyes, his face distorted through the glass.

"More?"

"Not right now," I said, suppressing a cough. "Thanks."

"You may perhaps have something for me?" the white-haired man said. "T-shirt maybe? Shoes?"

"I'm sorry . . . I left everything back in Alego."

The short man kept smiling as if he hadn't understood and again offered me a drink. This time Billy pushed the man's hand away.

"Leave him be!" Billy shouted. "We can drink more later. First we should see our grandfather."

The two men led us into a small back room. There, in front of a kerosene lamp, sat what looked like the oldest man I had ever seen.

His hair was snow-white, his skin like parchment. He was motionless, his eyes closed, his fleshless arms propped on the armrests of his chair. I thought perhaps he was asleep, but when Billy stepped forward the old man's head tilted in our direction, and I saw a mirror image of the face I'd seen yesterday in Alego, in the faded photograph on Granny's wall.

Billy explained who was there, and the old man nodded and began to speak in a low, quaking voice that seemed to rise out of a chamber beneath the floor.

"He says that he is glad you have come," Roy translated. "He was your grandfather's brother. He wishes you well."

I said that I was happy to see him, and the old man nodded again.

"He says that many young men have been lost to . . . the white man's country. He says his own son is in America and has not come home for many years. Such men are like ghosts, he says. When they die, no one will be there to mourn them. No ancestors will be there to welcome them. So . . . he says it is good that you have returned."

The old man raised his hand and I shook it gently. As we got up to leave, the old man said something else, and Roy nodded his head before closing the door behind us.

"He says that if you hear of his son," Roy explained, "you should tell him that he should come home."

Perhaps it was the effects of the moonshine, or the fact that the people around me were speaking in a language I didn't understand. But when I try to remember the rest of that evening, it's as if I'm walking through a dream. The moon hangs low in the sky, while the figures of Roy and the others merge with the shadows of corn. We enter another small house and find more men, perhaps six, perhaps ten, the numbers constantly changing as the night wears on. In the center of a rough wooden table sit three more bottles, and the men begin pouring the moonshine into the glasses, ceremoniously at first,

then faster, more sloppily; the dull, labelless bottle passed from hand
to hand. I stop drinking after two more shots, but no one seems to
notice. Old faces and young faces all glow like jack-o'-lanterns in the
shifting lamplight, laughing and shouting, slumped in dark corners
or gesticulating wildly for cigarettes or another drink, anger or joy
pitching up to a crest, then just as quickly ebbing away, words of Luo
and Swahili and English running together in unrecognizable swirls,
the voices wheedling for money or shirts or the bottle, the voices
laughing and sobbing, the outstretched hands, the faltering angry
voices of my own sodden youth, of Harlem and the South Side; the
voices of my father.

I'm not sure how long we stayed. I know that at some point, Sayid
came up and shook my arm.

"Barry, we are going," he said. "Bernard is not feeling well."

I said I'd go with them, but as I stood up, Abo leaned over to me
and grabbed my shoulders.

"Barry! Where are you going?"

"To sleep, Abo."

"You must stay here with us! With me! And Roy!"

I looked up to see Roy slumped on the couch. Our eyes met, and I
nodded toward the door. It seemed then that the entire room became
silent, as if I were watching the scene on television and the sound had
gone off. I saw the white-haired man fill Roy's glass, and I thought
about pulling Roy out of the room. But Roy's eyes slid away from mine;
he laughed and poured the drink down his throat to much cheering
and applause, cheering that I still could hear even after Sayid, Bernard,
and I had started making our way back toward Salina's house.

"Those people were too drunk," Bernard said weakly as we walked
across the field.

Sayid nodded and turned to me. "I'm afraid Roy is too much like
my eldest brother. You know, your father was very popular in these

parts. Also in Alego. Whenever he came home, he would buy everyone drinks and stay out very late. The people here appreciated this.
They would tell him, 'You are a big man, but you have not forgotten
us.' Such words made him happy, I think. I remember once, he took
me to Kisumu town in his Mercedes. On the way, he saw a *matatu*
picking up passengers, and he said to me, 'Sayid, we will be *matatu*
drivers this evening!' At the next *matatu* stop, he picked up the
remaining people and told me to collect the regular fare from them.
I think we squeezed eight people into his car. He took them not only
to Kisumu but to their houses, or wherever they needed to go. And
when each of them got out, he gave them all their money back. The
people didn't understand why he did this thing, and I also didn't
understand at the time. After we were done, we went to the bar, and
he told the story of what we had done to all of his friends. He laughed
very well that night."

Sayid paused, choosing his words carefully.

"This is what made my brother such a good man, these things. But
I think also that once you are one thing, you cannot pretend that you
are something else. How could he be a *matatu* driver, or stay out all
night drinking, and also he is writing Kenya's economic plan? A man
does service for his people by doing what is right for him, isn't this
so? Not by doing what others think he should do. But my brother,
although he prided himself on his independence, I also think that he
was afraid of some things. Afraid of what people would say about him
if he left the bar too early. That perhaps he would no longer belong
with those he'd grown up with."

"I don't want to be that way," Bernard said.

Sayid looked at his nephew with something like regret. "I did not
mean to speak so freely, Bernard. You must respect your elders. They
clear the way for you so that your path is easier. But if you see them
falling into a pit, then you must learn to what?"

"Step around," Bernard said.

"You are right. Diverge from that path and make your own."

Sayid put his arm over the younger man's shoulders. As we approached Salina's house, I looked back behind me. I could still see the dim light of the old man's window, and sense his blind eyes staring out into the darkness.

CHAPTER NINETEEN

....

R OY AND ABO BOTH woke up with bad headaches, and along
with Kezia stayed in Kendu for another day. In slightly better
shape, I decided to make the trip back to Home Squared with Sayid
and Bernard by bus, a decision I soon regretted. We had to stand for
most of the way, our heads forced down by the bus's low roof. To make
matters worse, I'd come down with a case of the runs. My stomach
lurched with every bump. My head throbbed with each wayward turn.
And so it was in a cautious trot that I first appeared to Granny and
Auma upon our return, offering them a curt wave before racing across
the backyard, around an errant cow, and into the outhouse.

Twenty minutes later I emerged, blinking like a prisoner in the
light of the early afternoon. The women were gathered on straw mats
under the shade of a mango tree while Granny braided Auma's hair
and Zeituni braided the hair of a neighbor's girl.

"Did you have a nice time?" Auma said, trying not to smile.

"Wonderful." I sat down beside them and watched as a skinny old
woman came out of the house and took a spot next to Granny. The
old woman was in her early seventies, I guessed, but was dressed in a
bright pink sweater; she folded her legs to the side like a bashful
schoolgirl. She peered at me and spoke to Auma in Luo.

"She says you don't look so well."

The old woman smiled at me, revealing two missing bottom front teeth.

"This is our grandfather's sister, Dorsila," Auma continued. "The last child of our great-grandfather Obama. She lives in another village, but when she heard—Ow! I tell you, Barack, you are lucky you don't have braids to undo. What was I saying? Yah . . . Dorsila says that when she heard that we had come she walked all the way to see us. She brings greetings from all the people of her village."

Dorsila and I shook hands, and I mentioned that I'd met her older brother in Kendu Bay. She nodded and spoke again.

"She says her brother is very old," Auma translated. "When he was younger, he looked just like our grandfather. Sometimes even she couldn't tell them apart."

I agreed and took out my lighter. As I pulled at the flame, our great-aunt hooted and spoke rapidly to Auma.

"She wants to know where the fire comes from."

I handed Dorsila the lighter and showed her how it worked as she continued to speak. Auma explained, "She says that things are changing so fast it makes her head spin. She says that the first time she saw television, she assumed the people inside the box could also see her. She thought they were very rude, because when she spoke to them they never answered back."

Dorsila chuckled at herself good-humoredly, while Zeituni went into the cooking hut. A few minutes later, Zeituni came out with a mug in her hand. I asked her what had happened to Sayid and Bernard.

"They're asleep," she said, handing me the cup. "Here. Drink this."

I took a sniff of the steaming green liquid. It smelled like a swamp.

"What is it?"

"It's made from a plant that grows here. Trust me . . . it will firm up your stomach in a jiffy."

I took a tentative first sip. The brew tasted as bad as it looked, but

Zeituni stood over me until I had gulped down the last drop. "That is your grandfather's recipe," she said. "I told you he was a herbalist."

I took another puff from my cigarette and turned to Auma. "Ask Granny to tell me more about him," I said. "Our grandfather, I mean. Roy says that he actually grew up in Kendu, then moved to Alego on his own."

Granny nodded to Auma's translation. "Does she know why he left Kendu?"

Granny shrugged. "She says that originally his people came from this land," Auma said.

I asked Granny to start from the beginning. How did our great-grandfather Obama come to live in Kendu? Where did our grandfather work? Why did the Old Man's mother leave? As she started to answer, I felt the wind lift, then die. A row of high clouds crossed over the hills. And under the fanning shade of the mango tree, as hands wove black curls into even rows, I heard all our voices begin to run together, the sound of three generations tumbling over each other like the currents of a slow-moving stream, my questions like rocks roiling the water, the breaks in memory separating the currents, but always the voices returning to that single course, a single story. . . .

First there was Miwiru. It's not known who came before. Miwiru sired Sigoma, Sigoma sired Owiny, Owiny sired Kisodhi, Kisodhi sired Ogelo, Ogelo sired Otondi, Otondi sired Obongo, Obongo sired Okoth, and Okoth sired Opiyo. The women who bore them, their names are forgotten, for that was the way of our people.

Okoth lived in Alego. Before that, it is known only that families traveled a great distance, from the direction of what is now Uganda, and that we were like the Masai, migrating in search of water and grazing land for great herds of cattle. In Alego, the people settled and began to grow crops. Other

Luo settled by the lake and learned to fish. There were other tribes, who spoke Bantu, already living in Alego when the Luo came, and great wars were fought. Our ancestor Owiny was known as a great warrior and leader of his people. He helped to defeat the Bantu armies, but the Bantu were allowed to stay on and marry Luo, and taught us many things about farming and the new land.

Once people began to settle and farm, the land in Alego became crowded. Opiyo, son of Okoth, was a younger brother, so perhaps that is why he decided to move to Kendu Bay. When he moved there, he was landless, but in the custom of our people, a man could use any unused land. What a man did not use reverted to the tribe. So there was no shame in Opiyo's situation. He worked in the compounds of other men and cleared the land for his own farm. But before he could prosper, he died very young, leaving behind two wives and several children. One wife was taken in by Opiyo's brother, as was the custom then—she became the brother's wife, her children his children. But the other wife also died, and her oldest son, Obama, was orphaned when still a boy. He, too, lived with his uncle, but the resources of the family were strained, and so as Obama grew older, he began to work for other men as his father had done before him.

The family he worked for was wealthy, with many cattle. But they came to admire Obama, for he was enterprising and a very good farmer. When he sought to marry their oldest daughter, they agreed, and the uncles in this family provided the necessary dowry. And when this eldest daughter died, they agreed that Obama could marry the younger daughter, whose name was Nyaoke. Eventually Obama had four wives, who bore him many children. He cleared his own land and became prosperous, with a large compound and many cattle and goats. And because of his politeness and responsible ways, he became an elder in Kendu, and many came to seek his advice.

Your grandfather, Onyango, was Nyaoke's fifth son. Dorsila, who sits here, was the last child of Obama's last wife.

This is the time before the white man came. Each family had their own compound, but they all lived under the laws of the elders. Men had their own huts, and were responsible for clearing and cultivating their land, as well as protecting the cattle from wild animals and the raids of other tribes. Each wife had her own vegetable plot, which only she and her daughters would cultivate. She cooked the man's food, drew water, and maintained the huts. The elders regulated all plantings and the harvests. They organized families to rotate their work, so that each family helped the other, in doing these things. The elders distributed food to widows or those who had fallen on hard times, provided cattle as dowry for those men who had no cattle themselves, and settled all conflicts. The words of the elders were law and strictly followed—those who disobeyed would have to leave and start anew in another village.

The children did not go to school, but learned alongside their parents. The girls would accompany their mothers and learn how to grind the millet into porridge, how to grow vegetables and pack clay for the huts. The boys learned from their fathers how to herd and work *pangas* and throw spears. When a mother died, another would take the child in and suckle him as her own. At night, the daughters would eat with their mothers, while the sons would join their father in his hut, listening to stories and learning the ways of our people. Sometimes a harpist would come, and the entire village would come to listen to his songs. The harpists sang of great deeds of the past, the great warriors and wise elders. They would praise men who were good farmers, or women who were beautiful, and rebuke those who were lazy or cruel. All were recognized in these songs for their contributions to the village, good and bad, and in this way the traditions of the ancestors stayed alive in all who heard. When the children and women were gone, the men in the village would gather together and decide on the village affairs.

Even from the time that he was a boy, your grandfather Onyango was strange. It is said of him that he had ants up his anus, because he could not sit still. He would wander off on his own for many days, and when he returned he would not say where he had been. He was very serious always—he never laughed or played games with the other children, and never made jokes. He was always curious about other people's business, which is how he learned to be a herbalist. You should know that a herbalist is different from a shaman— what the white man calls a witch doctor. A shaman casts spells and speaks to the spirit world. The herbalist knows various plants that will cure certain illnesses or wounds, how to pack a special mud so that a cut will heal. As a boy, your grandfather sat in the hut of the herbalist in his village, watching and listening carefully while the other boys played, and in this way he gained knowledge.

When your grandfather was still a boy, we began to hear that the white man had come to Kisumu town. It was said that these white men had skin as soft as a child's, but that they rode on a ship that roared like thunder and had sticks that burst with fire. Before this time, no one in our village had seen white men—only Arab traders who sometimes came to sell us sugar and cloth. But even that was rare, for our people did not use much sugar, and we did not wear

cloth, only a goatskin that covered our genitals. When the
elders heard these stories, they discussed it among themselves and advised the men to stay away from Kisumu until
this white man was better understood.

Despite this warning, Onyango became curious and
decided that he must see these white men for himself. One
day he disappeared, and no one knew where he had gone.
Then, many months later, while Obama's other sons were
working the land, Onyango returned to the village. He was
wearing the trousers of a white man, and a shirt like a white
man, and shoes that covered his feet. The small children
were frightened, and his brothers didn't know what to make
of this change. They called Obama, who came out of his hut,
and the family gathered 'round to stare at Onyango's strange
appearance.

"What has happened to you?" Obama asked. "Why do
you wear these strange skins?" Onyango said nothing, and
Obama decided that Onyango must be wearing trousers to
hide the fact that he was circumcised, which was against Luo
custom. He thought that Onyango's shirt must be covering
a rash, or sores. Obama turned to his other sons and said,
"Don't go near this brother of yours. He is unclean." Then
he returned to his hut, and the others laughed and shunned
Onyango. Because of this, Onyango returned to Kisumu,
and would remain estranged from his father for the rest of
his life.

Nobody realized then that the white man intended to stay
in the land. We thought that they had come only to trade
their goods. Some of their customs we soon developed a
taste for, like the drinking of tea. With tea, we found that we
needed sugar, and teakettles, and cups. All these things we
bought with skins and meat and vegetables. Later we learned

to accept the white man's coin. But these things did not affect us deeply. Like the Arabs, the white men remained small in number, and we assumed they would eventually return to their own land. In Kisumu, some white men stayed on and built a mission. These men spoke of their god, who they said was all-powerful. But most people ignored them and thought their talk silly. Even when white men appeared with rifles, no one resisted because our lives were not yet touched by the death such weapons could bring. Many of us thought the guns were just fancy *ugali* stirrers.

Things began to change with the first of the white man's wars. More guns arrived, along with a white man who called himself district commissioner. We called this man *Bwana Ogalo*, which meant "the Oppressor." He imposed a hut tax that had to be paid in the white man's money. This forced many men to work for wages. He conscripted outright many of our men into his army to carry provisions and build a road that would allow automobiles to pass. He surrounded himself with Luos who wore clothes like the white man to serve as his agents and tax collectors. We learned that we now had chiefs, men who were not even in the council of elders. All these things were resisted, and many men began to fight. But those who did so were beaten or shot. Those who failed to pay taxes saw their huts burned to the ground. Some families fled farther into the countryside to start new villages. But most people stayed and learned to live with this new situation, although we now all realized that it had been foolish to ignore the white man's arrival.

During this time, your grandfather worked for the white man. Few people could speak English or Swahili in those days—men didn't like to send their sons to the white man's school, preferring that they work with them on the land. But

Onyango had learned to read and write, and understood the
white man's system of paper records and land titles. This
made him useful to the white man, and during the war he was
put in charge of road crews. Eventually he was sent to Tanganyika, where he stayed for several years. When he finally
returned, he cleared land for himself in Kendu, but it was
away from his father's compound and he rarely spoke to his
brothers. He didn't build a proper hut for himself, but instead
lived in a tent. People had never seen such a thing and they
thought he was crazy. After he had staked his claim, he traveled to Nairobi, where a white man had offered him a job.

In those days, few Africans could ride the train, so
Onyango walked all the way to Nairobi. The trip took him
more than two weeks. Later he would tell us of the adventures he had during this journey. Many times he chased away
leopards with his *panga*. Once he was chased into a tree by
an angry buffalo and had to sleep in the tree for two days.
Once he found a drum lying in the middle of the forest path
and when he opened it, a snake appeared and slid between
his feet into the bush. But no harm came to him, and he
eventually arrived in Nairobi to begin his work in the white
man's house.

He was not the only one who moved to town. After the
war, many Africans began working for wages, especially
those who had been conscripted or lived near the cities or
had joined the white missions. Many people had been dis-
placed during and immediately following the war. The war
had brought famine and disease in its wake, and it brought
large numbers of white settlers, who were allowed to confis-
cate the best land.

The Kikuyu felt these changes the most, for they lived in
the highlands around Nairobi, where white settlement was

heaviest. But the Luo also felt the white man's rule. All persons had to register with the colonial administration and hut taxes steadily increased. This pressured more and more men to work as laborers on the big white farms. In our village, more families now wore the white man's clothes, and more fathers agreed to send their children to mission school. Of course, even those who went to school could not do the things the white man did. Only whites were allowed to buy certain land or run certain businesses. Other enterprises were reserved by law for the Hindus and the Arabs.

Some men began to try to organize against these policies, to petition and hold demonstrations. But their numbers were few, and most people just struggled to live. Those Africans who did not work as laborers stayed in their villages, trying to maintain the old ways. But even in the villages, attitudes changed. The land was crowded, for with new systems of land ownership, there was no longer room for sons to start their own plots—everything was owned by someone. Respect for tradition weakened, for young people saw that the elders had no real power. Beer, which once had been made of honey and which men drank only sparingly, now came in bottles, and many men became drunks. Many of us began to taste the white man's life, and we decided that compared to him, our lives were poor.

By these standards, your grandfather prospered. In his job in Nairobi, he learned how to prepare the white man's food and organize the white man's house. Because of this, he was popular with employers and worked in the estates of some of the most important white men, even Lord Delamere. He saved his wages and bought land and cattle in Kendu. On these lands, he eventually built himself a hut. But the way he kept his hut was different from other people. His hut was so spotless, he would insist that people rinse their feet or take off their shoes before entering. Inside, he would eat all his meals at a table and chair, under mosquito netting, with a knife and a fork. He would not touch food that had not been washed properly and covered as soon as it had been cooked. He bathed constantly, and washed his clothes every night. To the end of his life he would be like this, very neat and hygienic, and he would become angry if you put something in the wrong place or cleaned something badly.

And he was very strict about his property. If you asked him, he would always give you something of his—his food, his money, his clothes even. But if you touched his things without asking, he would become very angry. Even later, when his children were born, he would tell them always that you do not touch other people's property.

The people of Kendu thought his manners strange. They would come to his house because he was generous with his food and always had something to eat. But among themselves, they would laugh because he had neither wives nor children. Perhaps Onyango heard this talk, for he soon decided that he needed a wife. His problem was, no woman could maintain his household the way he expected. He paid dowry on several girls, but whenever they were lazy or broke a dish, your grandfather would beat them severely. It was normal among the Luo for men to beat their wives if they misbehaved, but even among Luos Onyango's attitude was considered harsh, and eventually the women he took for himself would flee to their fathers' compounds. Your grandfather lost many cattle this way, for he would be too proud to ask for the return of his dowry.

Finally, he found a wife who could live with him. Her name was Helima. It isn't known how she felt toward your

grandfather, but she was quiet and polite—and most important, she could maintain your grandfather's high housekeeping standards. He built a hut for her in Kendu, where she
spent most of her time. Sometimes he would bring her to
Nairobi to stay in the house where he worked. After a few
years had passed, it was discovered that Helima could not
bear any children. Among the Luo, this was normally proper
grounds for divorce—a man could send a barren wife back
to his in-laws and ask that his dowry be returned. But your
grandfather chose to keep Helima, and in that sense, he
treated her well.

Still, it must have been lonely for Helima, for your grandfather worked all the time and had no time for friends or
entertainment. He did not drink with other men, and he did
not smoke tobacco. His only pleasure was going to the dance
halls in Nairobi once a month, for he liked to dance. But he
also was not such a good dancer—he was rough, and would
bump into people and step on their feet. Most people did
not say anything about this because they knew Onyango and
his temper. One night, though, a drunken man began to
complain about Onyango's clumsiness. The man became
rude, and told your grandfather, "Onyango, you are already
an older man. You have many cattle, and you have a wife,
and yet you have no children. Tell me, is something the matter between your legs?"

People who overheard the conversation began to laugh,
and Onyango beat this man severely. But the drunk man's
words must have stayed with your grandfather, for that month
he set out to find another wife. He returned to Kendu and
inquired about all the women in the village. Finally he made
up his mind on a young girl named Akumu, who was well
regarded for her beauty. She was already promised to another

man, who had paid her father six cattle in dowry, promising to deliver six more in the future. But Onyango knew the girl's father and he convinced him to send back these six cattle. In return, Onyango gave him fifteen cattle on the spot. The next day, your grandfather's friends captured Akumu while she was walking in the forest and dragged her back to Onyango's hut.

The young boy, Godfrey, appeared with the washbasin, and we all washed our hands for lunch. Auma. stood up to stretch her back, her hair still half undone, a troubled look on her face. She said something to Dorsila and Granny, and drew a lengthy response from both women.

"I was asking them if our grandfather took Akumu by force," Auma told me, spooning some meat onto her plate.

"What did they say?"

"They say that this thing about grabbing the woman was part of Luo custom. Traditionally, once the man pays the dowry, the woman must not seem too eager to be with him. She pretends to refuse him, and so the man's friends must capture her and take her back to his hut. Only after this ritual do they perform a proper marriage cere-mony." Auma took a small bite of her food. "I told them that in such a custom some women might not have been pretending."

Zeituni dipped her *ugali* into the stew. "Yah, Auma, it was not as bad as you say. If her husband behaved badly, the girl could always leave."

"But what good was that if her father would only end up choosing someone else for her? Tell me, what would happen if a woman refused her father's choice of a suitor?"

Zeituni shrugged. "She shamed herself and her family."

"You see?" Auma turned to ask Granny something, and whatever it was that Granny said in response made Auma hit Granny—only half playfully—on the arm.

"I asked her if the man would force the girl to sleep with him the night of her capture," Auma explained, "and she told me that no one knew what went on in a man's hut. But she also asked me how a man would know if he wanted the whole bowl of soup unless he first had a taste."

I asked Granny how old she had been when she married our grandfather. The question amused her so much that she repeated it to Dorsila, who giggled and slapped Granny on the leg.

"She told Dorsila that you wanted to know when Onyango seduced her," Auma said.

Granny winked at me, then told us she had been just sixteen when she married; our grandfather was a friend of her father's, she said. I asked if that had bothered her, and she shook her head.

"She says that it was common to marry an older man," Auma said. "She says in those days, marriage involved more than just two people. It brought together families and affected the whole village. You didn't complain, or worry about love. If you didn't learn to love your husband, you learned to obey him."

At this point, Auma and Granny began to speak at length, and Granny said something that again made the others laugh. Everyone except Auma, who stood up and began to stack the dishes.

"I give up," Auma said, exasperated.

"What did Granny say?"

"I asked her why our women put up with the arranged marriages. The way men make all the decisions. The wife-beating. You know what she said? She said that often the women needed to be beaten, because otherwise they would not do everything that was required of them. You see how we are? We complain, but still we encourage men to treat us like shit. Look at Godfrey over there. You think, when he hears these things Granny and Dorsila have said, that this won't affect his own attitudes?"

Granny couldn't understand the precise meaning of Auma's words, but she must have caught the tone, for her voice suddenly became serious.

"Much of what you say is true, Auma," she said in Luo. "Our women have carried a heavy load. If one is a fish, one does not try to fly—one swims with other fish. One only knows what one knows. Perhaps if I were young today, I would not have accepted these things. Perhaps I would only care about my feelings, and falling in love. But that's not the world I was raised in. I only know what I have seen. What I have not seen doesn't make my heart heavy."

I leaned back on the mat and thought about what Granny had said. There was a certain wisdom there, I supposed; she was speaking of a different time, another place. But I also understood Auma's frustration. I knew that, as I had been listening to the story of our grandfather's youth, I, too, had felt betrayed. My image of Onyango, faint as it was, had always been of an autocratic man—a cruel man, perhaps. But I had also imagined him an independent man, a man of his people, opposed to white rule. There was no real basis for this image, I now realized—only the letter he had written to Gramps saying that he didn't want his son marrying white. That, and his Muslim faith, which in my mind had become linked with the Nation of Islam back in the States. What Granny had told us scrambled that image completely, causing ugly words to flash across my mind. Uncle Tom. Collaborator. House nigger.

I tried to explain some of this to Granny, asking her if our grandfather had ever expressed his feelings about the white man. Just then, Sayid and Bernard emerged, groggy-eyed, from the house, and Zeituni directed them to the plates of food that had been set aside for them. It wasn't until they had settled down to eat, and Auma and the neighbor's girl resumed their positions in front of the older women, that Granny returned to her story.

I also did not always understand what your grandfather thought. It was difficult, because he did not like people to know him so well. Even when he spoke to you, he would look away for fear that you would know his thoughts. So it was with his attitude towards the white man. One day he would say one thing, and the next day it was as if he was saying something else. I know that he respected the white man for his power, for his machines and weapons and the way he organized his life. He would say that the white man was always improving himself, whereas the African was suspicious of anything new. "The African is thick," he would sometimes say to me. "For him to do anything, he needs to be beaten."

But despite these words, I don't think he ever believed that the white man was born superior to the African. In fact, he did not respect many of the white man's ways or their customs. He thought many things that they did were foolish or unjust. He himself, he would never allow himself to be beaten by a white man. This is how he lost many jobs. If the white man he worked for was abusive, he would tell the man to go to hell and leave to find other work. Once, an employer tried to cane him, and your grandfather grabbed the man's cane and thrashed him with it. For this he was arrested, but when he explained what had happened, the authorities let him off with a fine and a warning.

What your grandfather respected was strength. Discipline. This is why, even though he learned many of the white man's ways, he always remained strict about Luo traditions. Respect for elders. Respect for authority. Order and custom in all his affairs. This is also why he rejected the Christian religion, I think. For a brief time, he converted, and even changed his name to Johnson. But he could not understand such ideas as mercy towards your enemies, or that this man Jesus could wash away a man's sins. To your grandfather, this was foolish sentiment, something to comfort women. And so he converted to Islam—he thought its practices conformed more closely to his beliefs.

In fact, it was this hardness that caused so many problems between him and Akumu. By the time I came to live with him, she had already borne Onyango two children. The first was Sarah. Three years later came your father, Barack. I did not know Akumu well, for she and her children lived with Helima on your grandfather's compound in Kendu, while I stayed with him in Nairobi, to help him with his work there. But whenever I accompanied your grandfather to Kendu, I could see that Akumu was unhappy. Her spirit was rebellious, and she found Onyango too demanding. He would always complain that she kept a bad house. Even in child rearing, he was strict with her. He told her to keep the babies in cribs and dress them in fancy clothes that he brought from Nairobi. Whatever the babies touched had to be even cleaner than before. Helima tried to help Akumu, and cared for the children as if they were her own, but it didn't help. Akumu was only a few years older than me, and the pressure on her was great. And perhaps Auma is right . . . perhaps she still loved the man she was to have wed before Onyango took her away.

Whatever it was, more than once she tried to leave Onyango. Once after Sarah was born, and again after Barack. Despite his pride, Onyango followed her both times, for he believed that the children needed their mother. Both times, Akumu's family took his side, so she had no choice but to return. Eventually she learned to do what was expected of her. But she quietly clung to her bitterness.

Life became easier for her when the Second World War came. Your grandfather went overseas as the cook to the British captain, and I came to live with Akumu and Helima, helping both with the children and their crops. We did not see Onyango for some time. He traveled widely with the British regiments—to Burma and Ceylon, to Arabia, and also somewhere in Europe. When he returned three years later, he came with a gramophone and that picture of the woman he claimed to have married in Burma. The pictures you see on my wall—they are taken from this time.

Onyango was now almost fifty. More and more, he thought of quitting his work for the white man and returning to farm the land. He saw, though, that the land surrounding Kendu was crowded and overgrazed. So his mind went back to Alego, the land that his grandfather had abandoned. One day he came to his wives and told us that we should prepare ourselves to leave for Alego. I was young and adaptable, but the news came as a shock to Helima and Akumu. Both of their families lived in Kendu, and they had become accustomed to living there. Helima especially feared that she would be lonely in this new place, for she was almost as old as Onyango and had no children of her own. So she refused to go. Akumu also refused to go at first, but again her family convinced her that she must follow her husband and care for her children.

When we arrived in Alego, most of this land that you now see was bush, and life was hard for all of us. But your grandfather had studied modern farming techniques while in Nairobi and he put his ideas to work. He could make anything grow, and in less than a year he had grown enough crops to sell at market. He smoothed out the earth to make this wide lawn, and cleared the fields where his crops grew high and plentiful. He planted the mango and banana and pawpaw trees that you see today.

He even sold most of his cattle because he said that their grazing made the soil poor and caused it to wash away. With this money, he built large huts for Akumu and myself and a hut of his own. He had brought back a crystal set from

England that he displayed on a shelf, and on his gramophone he played strange music late into the night. When my first children, Omar and Zeituni, were born, he bought them cribs and gowns and separate mosquito nets, just as he had for Barack and Sarah. In the cooking hut, he built an oven in which he baked bread and cakes like you buy in a store.

His neighbors in Alego had never seen such things. At first they were suspicious of him and thought he was foolish—especially when he sold his cattle. But soon they came to respect his generosity, as well as what he taught them about farming and herbal medicines. They even came to appreciate his temper, for they discovered that he could protect them from witchcraft. In those days, shamans were consulted often and were widely feared. It was said that they could give you a love potion for the one you desired and other potions that would cause your enemies to fall dead. But your grandfather, because he had traveled widely and read books, didn't believe in such things. He thought they were tricksters who stole people's money.

Even now, many in Alego can tell you about the day that a shaman from another province came to kill one of our neighbors. This neighbor had courted a girl from nearby, and the families had agreed that they should be wed. However, another man hungered for this girl, and so the jealous suitor hired a shaman to kill his rival. When our neighbor heard of this plan, he became very afraid, and came to Onyango asking for advice. Your grandfather listened to the man's story, then picked up his *panga* and a hippo-hide whip, and went to wait for the shaman at the foot of the road.

Before long, Onyango saw the shaman approaching, carrying a small suitcase of potions in one hand. When the shaman was within shouting distance, your grandfather stood in the center of the road and said, "Go back to where you come from." The shaman didn't know who Onyango was, and made like he was going to pass, but Onyango blocked his way and said, "If you are as powerful as you claim, you must strike me now with lightning. If not, you should run, for unless you leave this village now, I will have to beat you." Again, the shaman made as if he was going to pass, but before he could take another step, Onyango had beaten him to the ground, taken his suitcase, and returned with it to his compound.

Well, this was a very serious matter, especially when your grandfather refused to return the shaman's potions. The next day, the council of elders gathered beneath a tree to resolve the dispute, and Onyango and the shaman were both told to appear and state their case. First the shaman stood and told the elders that if Onyango did not return the suitcase at once, a curse would be brought on the entire village. Then Onyango stood, and he repeated what he had said earlier. "If this man has strong magic, let him curse me now and strike me dead." The elders leaned away from Onyango, fearful that the spirits might miss their target. But they soon saw that no spirits came. So Onyango turned to the man who had hired the shaman and said, "Go and find yourself a new woman, and let this other woman be with the one to whom she is promised." And to the shaman Onyango said, "Go back to where you came from, because there will be no killings in this place."

To these things, all the elders agreed. But they insisted that Onyango must also return the shaman's suitcase, for they did not want to take any chances. Onyango also agreed, and when the meeting was finished, he brought the shaman to his hut. He told me to slaughter a chicken so the shaman could eat, and even gave the shaman money so that his trip to Alego would not have been wasted. But before your grandfather let the shaman leave, he made the man show him the contents of his suitcase and explain the properties of every potion, so that he would know all the tricks that the shaman performed.

Even if Onyango had used one of these potions on Akumu, I don't think he could have made her happy. No matter how much he beat her, she would argue with him. She was also proud and scornful of me, and often refused to help in the household chores. She had a third child—named Auma, like this one sitting here—and as she nursed this new baby, she secretly planned her escape. One night, when Sarah was twelve and Barack was nine, she made her move. She woke up Sarah and said that she was running away to Kendu. She told Sarah that it was too difficult a journey for children to make at night, but said that they should follow her as soon as they were older. Then she disappeared with her baby into the darkness.

When Onyango found out what had happened, he was furious. At first he thought he should finally let Akumu go, but when he saw that Barack and Sarah were still young, and that even I, with two children of my own, was little more than a girl, he again went to Akumu's family in Kendu and asked that she be returned. But this time the family refused. In fact, they had already accepted dowry for Akumu's remarriage to another man, and together Akumu and her new husband had left for Tanganyika. There was nothing Onyango could do, so he returned to Alego. He said to himself, "It does not matter," and he told me that I was now the mother of all his children.

Neither he nor I knew of Akumu's last visit to Sarah. But

Sarah had remembered her mother's instructions, and only a few weeks passed before she woke up Barack in the middle of the night, just as her mother had done to her. She told Barack to be quiet, helped him get dressed, and together they began to walk down the road to Kendu. I still wonder that they both survived. They were gone for almost two weeks, walking many miles each day, hiding from those who passed them on the road, sleeping in fields and begging for food. Not far from Kendu, they became lost, and a woman finally saw them and took pity on them, for they were filthy and almost starved. The woman took them in and fed them, and asked them their names; and when she realized who they were she sent for your grandfather. And when Onyango came to get them, and saw how badly they looked, this is the only time that anyone ever saw him cry.

The children never tried to run away again. But I don't think they ever forgot this journey they made. Sarah kept a careful distance from Onyango, and in her heart remained loyal to Akumu, for she was older, and perhaps had seen how the old man had treated her mother. I believe she also resented me for taking her mother's place. Barack reacted differently. He could not forgive his abandonment, and acted as if Akumu didn't exist. He told everyone that I was his mother, and although he would send Akumu money when he became a man, to the end of his life he would always act coldly towards her.

The strange thing was that in many ways Sarah was most like her father in personality. Strict, hardworking, easy to anger. Whereas Barack was wild and stubborn like Akumu. But of course such things one does not see in one's self.

As you might expect, Onyango was very strict with his children. He worked them hard, and would not allow them to play outside the compound, because he said other children were filthy and ill-mannered. Whenever Onyango went away, I would ignore these instructions, because children must play with other children, just as they must eat and sleep. But I would never tell your grandfather what I did, and I would have to scrub the children clean before your grandfather came home.

This was not easy, especially with Barack. That boy was so mischievous! In Onyango's presence, he appeared well-mannered and obedient, and never answered back when his father told him to do something. But behind the old man's back, Barack did as he pleased. When Onyango was away on business, Barack would take off his proper clothes and go off with other boys to wrestle or swim in the river, to steal the fruit from the neighbors' trees or ride their cows. The neighbors were afraid to go directly to Onyango, so they would come to me and complain about these things. But I could not get mad at Barack, and would always cover up his foolishness from Onyango, for I loved him as my own son.

Although he did not like to show it, your grandfather was also very fond of Barack, because the boy was so clever. When Barack was only a baby, Onyango would teach him the alphabet and numbers, and it was not long before the son could outdo the father in these things. This pleased Onyango, for to him knowledge was the source of all the white man's power, and he wanted to make sure that his son was as educated as any white man. He was less concerned with Sarah's education, although she was also quick like Barack. Most men thought educating their daughters was a waste of money. When Sarah was finished with primary school, she came to Onyango begging for school fees to go on to secondary school. He said to her, "Why should I spend school fees on you when you will come to live in another man's house? Go help your mother and learn how to be a proper wife."

This created more friction between Sarah and her younger brother, especially because she knew that Barack was not always serious about his studies. Everything came too easily to him. At first he went to the mission school nearby, but he came back after the first day and told his father that he could not study there because his class was taught by a woman and he knew everything she had to teach him. This attitude he had learned from his father, so Onyango could say nothing. The next closest school was six miles away, and I began to walk him to this school every morning. His teacher there was a man, but Barack discovered this didn't solve his problems. He always knew the answers, and sometimes would even correct the teacher's mistakes before the whole class. The teacher would scold Barack for his insolence, but Barack would refuse to back down. This caused Barack many canings at the hand of the headmaster. But it also might have taught him something, because the next year, when he switched to a class with a woman teacher, I noticed that he didn't complain.

Still, he was bored with school, and when he became older, he would stop going to school altogether for weeks at a time. A few days before exams, he would find a classmate and read through the lessons. He could sit down and teach himself everything in just a few days, and when the marks came in, he would always be first. The few times he did not come in first, he came to me in tears, for he was so used to being the best. But this happened only once or twice—usually he would come home laughing and boasting of his cleverness.

Barack did not mean his boasts cruelly—he was always good-natured towards his classmates, and would help them whenever they asked. His boasts were like those of a child who discovers that he can run fast or hunt well. So he did not understand that others might resent his ease. Even as a man, he did not understand such things. In a bar or a restaurant, he would see classmates of his who were now ministers or businessmen, and in front of everybody he would tell them their ideas were silly. He would say to them, "Oy, I remember that I had to teach you arithmetic, so how can you be such a big man now?" Then he would laugh and buy these men beers, for he was also fond of them. But these fellows would remember their school days, and know what Barack had said was true, and although they might not show it, his words made them angry.

By the time your father was a teenager, things were changing rapidly in Kenya. Many Africans had fought in the Second World War. They had carried arms and distinguished themselves as great warriors in Burma and Palestine. They had seen the white man fight his own people, and had died beside white men, and had killed many white men themselves. They had learned that an African could work the white man's machines and had met blacks from America who flew airplanes and performed surgery. When they returned to Kenya, they were eager to share this new knowledge and were no longer satisfied with the white man's rule.

People began to talk about independence. Meetings and demonstrations were held, and petitions were presented to the administration complaining about land confiscation and the power of chiefs to commission free labor for government projects. Even Africans who had been educated in mission schools now rebelled against their home churches and accused whites of distorting Christianity to demean everything African. As before, most of this activity centered in Kikuyuland, for that tribe bore the white man's yoke most heavily. But the Luo, too, were oppressed, a main source of forced labor. Men in our area began to join the Kikuyu in demonstrations. And later, when the British declared their Emergency, many men were detained, some never to be seen again.

Like other boys, your father would be influenced by the early talk of independence, and he would come home from school talking about the meetings he had seen. Your grandfather agreed with many of the demands of the early parties like KANU, but he remained skeptical that the independence movement would lead to anything, because he thought Africans could never win against the white man's army. "How can the African defeat the white man," he would tell Barack, "when he cannot even make his own bicycle?" And he would say that the African could never win against the white man because the black man only wanted to work with his own family or clan, while all white men worked to increase their power. "The white man alone is like an ant," Onyango would say. "He can be easily crushed. But like an ant, the white man works together. His nation, his business—these things are more important to him than himself. He will follow his leaders and not question orders. Black men are not like this. Even the most foolish black man thinks he knows better than the wise man. That is why the black man will always lose."

Despite his attitude, your grandfather would once find himself detained. An African who worked for the district commissioner was jealous of your grandfather's lands. This man had once been rebuked by your grandfather because he would collect excessive taxes and pocket the money for himself. During the Emergency, this man placed Onyango's name on a list of KANU supporters and told the white man that Onyango was a subversive. One day, the white man's *askaris* came to take Onyango away, and he was placed in a detention camp. Eventually he received a hearing, and he was found innocent. But he had been in the camp for over six months, and when he returned to Alego he was very thin and dirty. He had difficulty walking, and his head was full of lice. He was so ashamed, he refused to enter his house or tell us what had happened. Instead, he called me to boil him water and bring him one of his razors. He shaved off his hair, and I had to help him bathe for a very long time, just where you are now sitting. And from that day on, I saw that he was now an old man.

Barack was away at the time and only learned about this detention later. He had taken the district examination, and had been admitted to Maseno Mission School, some fifty miles south, near the equator. This should have been a great honor for Barack, because few Africans were allowed to get secondary education, and only the best students got into Maseno, but your father's rebellious nature caused the school much grief. He would sneak girls into his dormitory, for he could always talk very sweetly to girls and promise them all that they dreamed. He and his friends would raid nearby farms for chickens and yams, because they did not like the dormitory food. The teachers at the school over-looked many of these infractions, for they saw how smart he was. But eventually Barack went too far with his mischief and was finally expelled.

Onyango was so furious when he found out, he beat Barack with a stick until Barack's back was bleeding. But Barack refused to run or cry out, or even explain himself to his father. Finally, Onyango told Barack, "If you cannot behave properly in my compound, I have no use for you here!" The following week, Onyango told Barack that he had arranged for him to travel to the coast, where he would work as a clerk. "You will learn the value of education now," the old man said. "I will see how you enjoy yourself, earning your own meals."

Barack had no choice but to obey his father. He went to Mombasa and took the job, in the office of an Arab merchant. But after a short time, he had an argument with the Arab and left without collecting his pay. He found another clerk's job, but it paid much less. He was too proud to ask his father for help or admit that he had been wrong. Nevertheless, word got back to Onyango, and when Barack came home for a visit, his father shouted to him that he would amount to nothing. Barack tried to tell Onyango that the new job paid much better than the one Onyango had arranged. He said that he was earning one hundred and fifty shillings every month. So Onyango said, "Let me see your wage book, if you are such a wealthy man." And when Barack said nothing, Onyango knew that his son had lied. He went into his hut and told Barack to go away because he had brought shame on his father.

Barack moved to Nairobi and found a job working as a clerk for the railway. But he was bored, and he became distracted by the politics of the country. The Kikuyu had begun their warfare in the forests. Everywhere there were rallies calling for Kenyatta's release from prison. Barack began to attend political meetings after work and came to know some of the KANU leadership. At one of these meetings, the police came, and Barack was arrested for violating the meeting law. He was jailed, and sent word to his father that he needed money for bail. But Onyango refused to give Barack the money he'd asked for, and told me that his son needed to learn his lesson well.

Because he was not a leader in KANU, Barack was released after a few days. But there was no happiness in his release, for he had begun to think that perhaps what his father had said was true—that he would amount to nothing. He was a man of twenty and what did he have? He had been fired from his railway job. He was estranged from his father, without money or prospects. And he now had a wife and a child. He had met Kezia when he was only eighteen. She lived in Kendu with her family then. He was struck by her beauty, and after a brief courtship he decided that he would marry her. To do so, he knew that his father would have to help him with the dowry payment, and so he asked me to intercede on his behalf. At first Onyango resisted, and Sarah, who had moved back to Alego after her first husband died, also disapproved. She told your grandfather that Kezia only wanted to live off the family's wealth. But I told Onyango that it would be improper for Barack to have to beg from other relatives for a dowry when everyone knew he was the son of a well-off man. Onyango saw that I spoke the truth, and he relented. One year after Barack and Kezia were married, Roy was born. Two years later came Auma.

To support this family, Barack had to take any work he could find, and he finally convinced another Arab, named Suleiman, to take him on as an office boy. But Barack remained deeply depressed, almost desperate. Many of his age-mates from Maseno, the ones who were not as gifted as him, were already leaving for Makarere University in Uganda. Some had even gone to London to study. They could expect big jobs when they returned to a liberated Kenya. Barack saw that he might end up working as the clerk of these men for the rest of his life.

Then, good fortune struck, in the form of two American

women. They were teaching in Nairobi, connected to some religious organization, I think, and one day they came into the office where Barack was working. Your father struck up a conversation with them, and soon these women became his friends. They loaned him books to read and invited him to their house, and when they saw how smart he was, they told him that he should go to a university. He explained that he had no money and no secondary school certificate, but these women said they could arrange for him to take a correspondence course that would give him the certificate he needed. If he was successful, they said, they would try to help him get into a university in America.

Barack became very excited and immediately wrote away for this correspondence course. For the first time in his life he worked diligently. Every night, and during his lunch hours, he would study his books and do the lessons in his notebooks. A few months later, he sat for the exam at the American embassy. The exam took several months to score, and during this wait he was so nervous he could barely eat. He became so thin that we thought he would die. One day, the letter came. I was not there to see him open it. I know that when he told me the news, he was still shouting out with happiness. And I laughed along with him, for it was just as things had been so many years before, when he used to come home after school to boast about his marks.

He still had no money, though, and no university had yet accepted him. Onyango had softened towards his son when he saw that he was becoming more responsible, but even he could not raise the money to pay university fees and transport abroad. Some in the village were willing to help, but many were afraid that if Barack went off with their money they would never see him again. So Barack wrote to universities in America. He wrote and he wrote. Finally, a university in Hawaii wrote back and told him they would give him a scholarship. No one knew where this place was, but Barack didn't care. He gathered up his pregnant wife and son and dropped them off with me, and in less than a month he was gone.

What happened in America, I cannot say. I know that after less than two years we received a letter from Barack saying that he had met this American girl, Ann, and that he would like to marry her. Now, Barry, you have heard that your grandfather disapproved of this marriage. This is true, but it is not for the reasons you say. You see, Onyango did not believe your father was behaving responsibly. He wrote back to Barack, saying, "How can you marry this white woman when you have responsibilities at home? Will this woman return with you and live as a Luo woman? Will she accept that you already have a wife and children? I have not heard of white people understanding such things. Their women are jealous and used to being pampered. But if I am wrong in this matter, let the girl's father come to my hut and discuss the situation properly. For this is the affairs of elders, not children." He also wrote to your grandfather Stanley and said many of these same things.

As you know, your father went ahead with the marriage. He only told Onyango what had happened after you were born. We are all happy that this marriage took place, because without it we would not have you here with us now. But your grandfather was very angry at the time, and threatened to have Barack's visa revoked. And because he had lived with white people, perhaps Onyango did understand the white people's customs better than Barack did. For when Barack finally returned to Kenya, we discovered that you and your mother had stayed behind, just as Onyango had warned.

Soon after Barack came, a white woman arrived in Kisumu looking for him. At first we thought this must be your mother, Ann. Barack had to explain that this was a different woman, Ruth. He said that he had met her at Harvard and that she had followed him to Kenya without his knowledge. Your grandfather didn't believe this story and thought that again Barack had disobeyed him. But I wasn't so sure, for, in fact, Barack did seem reluctant to marry Ruth at first. I'm not sure what finally swayed him. Maybe he felt Ruth would be better suited to his new life. Or maybe he heard gossip that Kezia had enjoyed herself too much during his absence, even though I told him that this gossip was not true. Or maybe he just cared for Ruth more than he liked to admit.

Whatever the reason, I know that once Barack agreed to marry Ruth, she could not accept the idea of his having Kezia as a second wife. That is how the children went to live with their father and his new wife in Nairobi. When Barack brought Auma and Roy back to visit, Ruth would refuse to accompany him and would not let Barack bring David or Mark. Onyango did not discuss this directly with Barack. But he would say to his friends, in such a way that Barack could hear him, "My son is a big man, but when he comes home his mother must cook for him instead of his wife."

The others have told you what happened to your father in Nairobi. We saw him rarely, and he would usually stay only a short time. Whenever he came, he would bring us expensive gifts and money and impress all the people with his big car and fine clothes. But your grandfather continued to speak harshly to him, as if he were a boy. Onyango was now very old. He walked with a cane and was almost blind. He could not even bathe without my help, which I think caused him shame. But age did not soften his temper.

Later, when Barack fell from power, he would try to hide his problems from the old man. He continued to bring gifts that he could no longer afford, although we noticed that he arrived in a taxi instead of in his own car. Only to me would he confide his unhappiness and disappointments. I would tell him he was too stubborn in his dealings with the government. He would talk to me about principles, and I would tell him that his principles weighed heavily on his children. He would say I didn't understand, just as his father had said to me. So I stopped giving advice and just listened.

That is what Barack needed most, I think—someone to listen to him. Even after things had improved again for him, and he had built this house for us, he remained heavy-hearted. With his children, he behaved just as Onyango had behaved towards him. He saw that he was pushing them away, but there was nothing he could do. He still liked to boast and laugh and drink with the men. But his laughter was empty. I remember the last time he visited Onyango before the old man died. The two of them sat in their chairs, facing each other and eating their food, but no words passed between them. A few months later, when Onyango finally went to join his ancestors, Barack came home to make all the arrangements. He said very little, and it is only when he sorted through a few of the old man's belongings that I saw him begin to weep.

Granny stood up and brushed the grass off her skirt. The yard was hushed, the silence broken only by a bird's anxious trill. "It's going to rain," she said, and we all gathered up the mats and cups and carried them into the house.

Once inside, I asked Granny if she had anything left of the Old Man's or our grandfather's. She went into her bedroom, sorting through the contents of an old leather trunk. A few minutes later, she emerged with a rust-colored book the size of a passport, along with a few papers of different colors, stapled together and chewed at an angle along one side.

"I'm afraid this is all I could find," she said to Auma. "The rats got to the papers before I had a chance to put them away."

Auma and I sat down and set the book and papers on the low table in front of us. The binding on the red book had crumbled away, but the cover was still legible: *Domestic Servant's Pocket Register,* it read, and in smaller letters, *Issued under the Authority of the Registration of Domestic Servant's Ordinance, 1928, Colony and Protectorate of Kenya.* On the book's inside cover, we found a two-shilling stamp above Onyango's left and right thumbprints. The swirls were still clear, like an imprint of coral. The box was empty where the photograph once had been.

The preamble explained: *The object of this Ordinance is to provide every person employed in a domestic capacity with a record of such employment, and to safeguard his or her interests as well as to protect employers against the employment of persons who have rendered themselves unsuitable for such work.*

The term *servant* was defined: *cook, house servant, waiter, butler, nurse, valet, bar boy, footmen, or chauffeur, or washermen.* The rules governing the carrying of such passbooks: servants found to be working without such books, or in any way injuring such books, *are liable to a fine not exceeding one hundred shillings or to imprisonment not exceeding six months or to both.* And then, the particulars of said Registered Servant, filled out in the elegant, unhurried script of a nameless clerk:

Name: *Hussein II Onyango.*
Native Registration Ordinance No.: *Rwl A NBI 0976717.*

Race or Tribe: *Ja'Luo.*
Usual Place of Residence When Not Employed: *Kisumu.*
Sex: *M.*
Age: *35.*
Height and Build: *6'0"* Medium.
Complexion: *Dark.*
Nose: *Flat.*
Mouth: *Large.*
Hair: *Curly.*
Teeth: *Six Missing.*
Scars, Tribal Marks, or Other Peculiarities: *None.*

Toward the back of the book, we found the particulars of employment, *signed and* testified to by various employers. Capt. C. Harford of Nairobi's Government House said that Onyango *performed his duties as personal boy with admirable diligence.* Mr. A. G. Dickson found his cooking excellent—*he can read and write English and follows any recipes . . . apart from other things his pastries are excellent.* He no longer needed Onyango's services since *I am no longer on Safari.* Dr. H. H. Sherry suggested that Onyango *is a capable cook but the job is not big enough for him.* On the other hand, Mr. Arthur W. H. Cole of the East Africa Survey Group says that after a *week on* the job, Onyango was *found to be unsuitable and certainly not worth 60 shillings per month.*

We moved to the stack of letters. They were from our father, addressed to various universities in the States. There were more than thirty of them, to the presidents of Morgan State, Santa Barbara Junior College, San Francisco State.

Dear President Calhoun, one letter began. *I have heard of your college from Mrs. Helen Roberts of Palo Alto, California, who is now in Nairobi here. Mrs. Roberts, knowing how much desirous I am to further my studies in the United States of America, has asked me to apply to your esteemed college for admission. I shall therefore be very much pleased if you will kindly*

*forward me your application form and information regarding the possibil-
ity of such scholarships as you may be aware of.* Attached to several letters
were recommendations from Miss Elizabeth Mooney, a literacy spe-
cialist from Maryland. *It is not possible to obtain Mr. O'Bama's school
transcripts*, she wrote, *since he has been out of school for some years.* However, she expressed confidence in our father's talents, noting that she
had *observed him making use of algebra and geometry.* She added that
there was a great need in Kenya for capable and dedicated teachers
and that, *given Mr. O'Bama's desire to be of service to his country, he
should be given a chance, perhaps on a one-year basis.*

This was it, I thought to myself. My inheritance. I rearranged the
letters in a neat stack and set them under the registry book. Then I
went out into the backyard. Standing before the two graves, I felt
everything around me—the cornfields, the mango tree, the sky—
closing in, until I was left with only a series of mental images,
Granny's stories come to life.

I see my grandfather, standing before his father's hut, a wiry, grim-
faced boy, almost ridiculous in his oversized trousers and his button-
less shirt. I watch his father turn away from him and hear his brothers
laugh. I feel the heat pour down his brow, the knots forming in his
limbs, the sudden jump in his heart. And as his figure turns and starts
back down the road of red earth, I know that for him the path of his
life is now altered irreversibly, completely.

He will have to reinvent himself in this arid, solitary place.
Through force of will, he will create a life out of the scraps of an
unknown world, and the memories of a world rendered obsolete.
And yet, as he sits alone in a freshly scrubbed hut, an old man now
with milky eyes, I know that he still hears his father and brothers
laughing behind him. He still hears the clipped voice of a British captain, explaining for the third and last time the correct proportion of
tonic to gin. The nerves in the old man's neck tighten, the rage
builds—he grabs his stick to hit at something, anything. Until finally

his grip weakens with the realization that for all the power in his hands and the force of his will, the laughter, the rebukes, will outlast him. His body goes slack in the chair. He knows that he will not out-live a mocking fate. He waits to die, alone.

The picture fades, replaced by the image of a nine-year-old boy—my father. He's hungry, tired, clinging to his sister's hand, searching for the mother he's lost. The hunger is too much for him, the exhaustion too great; until finally the slender line that holds him to his mother snaps, sending her image to float down, down into the emptiness. The boy starts to cry; he shakes off his sister's hand. He wants to go home, he shouts, back to his father's house. He will find a new mother. He will lose himself in games and learn the power of his mind.

But he won't forget the desperation of that day. Twelve years later, at his narrow desk, he will glance up from a stack of forms toward the restless sky and feel that same panic return. He, too, will have to invent himself. His boss is out of the office; he sets the forms aside and from an old file cabinet pulls out a list of addresses. He yanks the typewriter toward him and begins to type, letter after letter after let-ter, typing the envelopes, sealing the letters like messages in bottles that will drop through a post office slot into a vast ocean and perhaps allow him to escape the island of his father's shame.

How lucky he must have felt when his ship came sailing in! He must have known, when that letter came from Hawaii, that he had been chosen after all; that he possessed the grace of his name, the *baraka*, the blessings of God. With the degree, the ascot, the Ameri-can wife, the car, the words, the figures, the wallet, the proper pro-portion of tonic to gin, the polish, the panache, the entire thing seamless and natural, without the cobbled-together, haphazard qual-ity of an earlier time—what could stand in his way?

He had almost succeeded, in a way his own father could never have hoped for. And then, after seeming to travel so far, to discover that he had not escaped after all! To discover that he remained trapped on his father's island, with its fissures of anger and doubt and defeat, the emotions still visible beneath the surface, hot and molten and alive, like a wicked, yawning mouth, and his mother gone, gone, away. . . .

I dropped to the ground and swept my hand across the smooth yellow tile. Oh, Father, I cried. There was no shame in your confusion. Just as there had been no shame in your father's before you. No shame in the fear, or in the fear of his father before him. There was only shame in the silence fear had produced. It was the silence that betrayed us. If it weren't for that silence, your grandfather might have told your father that he could never escape himself, or re-create himself alone. Your father might have taught those same lessons to you. And you, the son, might have taught your father that this new world that was beckoning all of you involved more than just railroads and indoor toilets and irrigation ditches and gramophones, lifeless instruments that could be absorbed into the old ways. You might have told him that these instruments carried with them a dangerous power, that they demanded a different way of seeing the world. That this power could be absorbed only alongside a faith born out of hardship, a faith that wasn't new, that wasn't black or white or Christian or Muslim but that pulsed in the heart of the first African village and the first Kansas homestead—a faith in other people.

The silence killed your faith. And for lack of faith you clung to both too much and too little of your past. Too much of its rigidness, its suspicions, its male cruelties. Too little of the laughter in Granny's voice, the pleasures of company while herding the goats, the murmur of the market, the stories around the fire. The loyalty that could make up for a lack of airplanes or rifles. Words of encouragement. An embrace. A strong, true love. For all your gifts—the quick mind, the powers of concentration, the charm—you could never forge yourself into a whole man by leaving those things behind. . . .

For a long time I sat between the two graves and wept. When my tears were finally spent, I felt a calmness wash over me. I felt the circle finally close. I realized that who I was, what I cared about, was no longer just a matter of intellect or obligation, no longer a construct of words. I saw that my life in America—the black life, the white life, the sense of abandonment I'd felt as a boy, the frustration and hope I'd witnessed in Chicago—all of it was connected with this small plot of earth an ocean away, connected by more than the accident of a name or the color of my skin. The pain I felt was my father's pain. My questions were my brothers' questions. Their struggle, my birthright.

A light rain began to fall, the drops tapping on the leaves above. I was about to light a cigarette when I felt a hand on my arm. I turned to find Bernard squatting beside me, trying to fit the two of us under a bent-up old umbrella.

"They wanted me to see if you were okay," he said.

I smiled. "Yeah. I'm okay."

He nodded, his eyes squinting at the clouds. He turned back to me, and said "Why don't you let me have a cigarette, and I will sit and smoke with you."

I looked at his smooth, dark face, and put the cigarette back in the box. "I need to quit," I said. "Come on, let's take a walk instead."

We stood up and started toward the entrance to the compound. The young boy, Godfrey, was standing beside the cooking hut, one leg propped like a crane's against the mud wall. He looked at us and offered a tentative smile.

"Come on," Bernard said, waving to the boy. "You can walk with us." And so the three of us made our way over the widening dirt road, picking at leaves that grew along the way, watching the rain blow down across the several valleys.

EPILOGUE

··

I REMAINED IN KENYA FOR two more weeks. We all returned
to Nairobi and there were more dinners, more arguments, more
stories. Granny stayed in Auma's apartment, and each night I fell
asleep to their whispering voices. One day we gathered at a photography studio for a family portrait, and all the women wore flowing
African gowns of bright greens and yellows and blues, and the men
were all tall and shaven and neatly pressed, and the photographer, a
slight Indian man with bushy eyebrows, remarked on what a handsome picture we made.

Roy flew back to Washington, D.C., shortly after that; Granny
returned to Home Squared. The days suddenly became very quiet, and
a certain melancholy settled over Auma and me, as if we were coming
out of a dream. And maybe it was the sense that we, too, would soon
be returning to our other lives, once again separate and apart, that
made us decide one day to go to see George, our father's last child.

It turned out to be a painful affair, arranged hastily and without the
mother's knowledge: we simply drove with Zeituni to a neat, single-
story schoolhouse, where a group of schoolchildren were playing in
a wide, grassy field. After a brief conversation with the teacher super-
vising the recess, Zeituni led one of the children over to us. He was

a handsome, roundheaded boy with a wary gaze. Zeituni leaned down and pointed at Auma and me.

"This is your sister," she said to the boy, "who used to play with you on her knee. This is your brother, who has come all the way from America to see you."

The boy shook our hands bravely but kept glancing back at games he'd just left. I realized then that we'd made a mistake. Soon the principal of the school emerged from her office to say that unless we had the mother's permission, we would have to leave. Zeituni began to argue with the woman, but Auma said, "No, Auntie, she's right. We should go." From the car, we watched George return to his friends, quickly indistinguishable from the others with round heads and knobby knees who were chasing a scuffed football through the grass. I found myself suddenly remembering then my first meeting with the Old Man, the fear and discomfort that his presence had caused me, forcing me for the first time to consider the mystery of my own life. And I took comfort in the fact that perhaps one day, when he was older, George, too, might want to know who his father had been, and who his brothers and sisters were, and that if he ever came to me I would be there for him, to tell him the story I knew.

That evening, I asked Auma if she knew of any good books on the Luo, and she suggested we go visit a former history teacher of hers, a tall, willowy woman named Dr. Rukia Odero, who had been a friend of the Old Man's. When we arrived at her house, Dr. Odero was about to sit down for dinner, and she insisted that we join her. Over a meal of tilapia and *ugali*, the professor insisted I call her Rukia, then asked me about my impressions of the country. Had I been disappointed? she wondered. I told her that I hadn't, although I was leaving with as many questions as answers.

"That's good," Rukia said, pushing her glasses up the bridge of her nose. "That's how we historians make a living, you know. All day long we sit, trying to find new questions. It can be very tiresome, actually.

It requires a temperament for mischief. You know, young black Americans tend to romanticize Africa so. When your father and I were young, it was just the opposite—we expected to find all the answers in America. Harlem. Chicago. Langston Hughes and James Baldwin. That's where we drew our inspiration. And the Kennedys—they were very popular. The chance to study in America was very important. A hopeful time. Of course, when we returned we realized that our education did not always serve us so well. Or the people who had sent us. There was all this messy history to deal with."

I asked her why she thought black Americans were prone to disappointment when they visited Africa. She shook her head and smiled. "Because they come here looking for the authentic," she said. "That is bound to disappoint a person. Look at this meal we are eating. Many people will tell you that the Luo are a fish-eating people. But that was not true for all Luo. Only those who lived by the lake. And even for those Luo, it was not always true. Before they settled around the lake, they were pastoralists, like the Masai. Now, if you and your sister behave yourself and eat a proper share of this food, I will offer you tea. Kenyans are very boastful about the quality of their tea, you notice. But of course we got this habit from the English. Our ancestors did not drink such a thing. Then there's the spices we used to cook this fish. They originally came from India, or Indonesia. So even in this simple meal, you will find it very difficult to be authentic—although the meal is certainly African."

Rukia rolled a ball of *ugali* in her hand and dipped it into her stew. "You can hardly blame black Americans, of course, for wanting an unblemished past. After the cruelties they've suffered—still suffer, from what I read in the newspapers. They're not unique in this desire. The European wants the same thing. The Germans, the English . . . they all claim Athens and Rome as their own, when, in fact, their ancestors helped destroy classical culture. But that happened so long ago, so their task is easier. In their schools, you rarely hear about the misery of European peasants throughout most of recorded history. The corruption and exploitation of the Industrial Revolution, the senseless tribal wars—it's shameful how the Europeans treated their own, much less colored peoples. So this idea about a golden age in Africa, before the white man came, seems only natural."

"A corrective," Auma said.

"Truth is usually the best corrective," Rukia said with a smile. "You know, sometimes I think the worst thing that colonialism did was cloud our view of our past. Without the white man, we might be able to make better use of our history. We might look at some of our former practices and decide they are worth preserving. Others, we might grow out of. Unfortunately, the white man has made us very defensive. We end up clinging to all sorts of things that have outlived their usefulness. Polygamy. Collective land ownership. These things worked well in their time, but now they most often become tools for abuse. By men. By governments. And yet, if you say these things, you have been infected by Western ideology."

"So how should we adapt?" Auma said.

Rukia shrugged. "I leave such answers up to policy makers. I'm only a historian. But I suspect that we can't pretend that the contradictions of our situation don't exist. All we can do is choose. For example, female circumcision is an important Kikuyu custom. With the Masai also. To a modern sensibility, it is barbaric. Perhaps we could arrange to have all these operations performed in hospitals and cut down on the death rate. Keep the bleeding to a minimum. But you cannot really have half a circumcision. This leaves no one satisfied. So we must choose. The same is true of the rule of law, the notion of independent inquiry—these things may conflict with tribal loyalties. You cannot have rule of law and then exempt certain members of your clan. What to do? Again you choose. If you make the wrong choice, then you learn from your mistakes. You see what works."

I licked my fingers and washed my hands. "But isn't there anything left that is truly African?"

"Ah, that's the thing, isn't it?" Rukia said. "There does seem to be something different about this place. I don't know what it is. Perhaps the African, having traveled so far so fast, has a unique perspective on time. Or maybe it is that we have known more suffering than most. Maybe it's just the land. I don't know. Maybe I am also the romantic. I know that I cannot stay away from here too long. People still talk to each other here. When I visit the States, it seems a very lonely place—"

Suddenly, all the lights in the house went out. Rukia sighed—blackouts were becoming more common, she said—and I handed her my lighter to light the candles she kept on the mantelpiece. Sitting in the darkness, I remembered the stories Zeituni had told us, and remarked that the night runners must be out. Rukia lit the candles, their glow shaping her face into a mask of laughter.

"You know about the night runners, then! Yes, they are very powerful in the darkness. There used to be many in our area, back home. It was said they walked with the hippos at night. I remember once—"

As suddenly as they had died, the light bulbs popped back on. Rukia blew out the candles and shook her head. "Alas, in the city the lights do come on eventually. My daughter, she has no use for night runners. You know, her first language is not Luo. Not even Swahili. It is English. When I listen to her talk with her friends, it sounds like gibberish to me. They take bits and pieces of everything—English, Swahili, German, Luo. Sometimes, I get fed up with this. Learn to speak one language properly, I tell them." Rukia laughed to herself. "But I am beginning to resign myself—there's nothing really to do. They live in a mixed-up world. It's just as well, I suppose. In the end, I'm less interested in a daughter who's authentically African than one who is authentically herself."

It was getting late; we thanked Rukia for her hospitality and went on our way. But her words would stay with me, bringing into focus my own memories, my own lingering questions. On the last weekend of my stay, Auma and I took the train to the coast and stayed at an old beachfront hotel in Mombasa that had once been a favorite of the Old Man's. It was a modest, clean place, in August filled mostly with German tourists and American sailors on shore leave. We didn't do much, just read and swam and walked along the beach, watching pale crabs scurry like ghosts into their sandy holes. The following day we visited Mombasa's Old Town and climbed the worn stairs of Fort Jesus, first built by the Portuguese to consolidate control of trade routes along the Indian Ocean, later overrun by the swift Omani fleets, later still a beachhead for the British as they moved inland in search of ivory and gold, now an empty casing of stone, its massive walls peeling like papier-mâché in strips of pale orange and green and rose, its dormant cannons pointing out to a tranquil sea where a lone fisherman cast out his net.

On the way back to Nairobi, Auma and I decided to splurge, buying tickets on a bus line that actually assigned seats. The feeling of luxury was short-lived; my knees were pinched by a passenger who wanted his money's worth from the reclining seats, and a sudden rainstorm sent water streaming through leaks in the roof, which we tried—unsuccessfully—to plug up with tissue.

Eventually, the rain stopped, and we found ourselves looking on a barren landscape of gravel and shrub and the occasional baobab tree, its naked, searching branches decorated with the weaver bird's spherical nests. I remembered reading somewhere that the baobab could go for years without flowering, surviving on the sparsest of rainfall; and seeing the trees there in the hazy afternoon light, I understood why men believed they possessed a special power—that they housed ancestral spirits and demons, that humankind first appeared under such a tree. It wasn't merely the oddness of their shape, their almost prehistoric outline against the stripped-down sky. "They look as if each one could tell a story," Auma said, and it was true, each tree seemed to possess a character, a character neither benevolent nor cruel but simply enduring, with secrets whose depths I would never plumb, a wisdom I would never pierce. They both disturbed and comforted me, those trees that looked as if they might uproot themselves and simply walk away, were it not for the knowledge that on this earth one place is not so different from another—the knowledge that one moment carries within it all that's gone on before.

It's been six years since that first trip to Kenya, and much in the world has changed.

For me, it's been a relatively quiet period, less a time of discovery than of consolidation, of doing the things that we tell ourselves we finally must do to grow up. I went to Harvard Law School, spending most of three years in poorly lit libraries, poring through cases and statutes. The study of law can be disappointing at times, a matter of applying narrow rules and arcane procedure to an uncooperative reality; a sort of glorified accounting that serves to regulate the affairs of those who have power—and that all too often seeks to explain, to those who do not, the ultimate wisdom and justness of their condition.

But that's not all the law is. The law is also memory; the law also records a long-running conversation, a nation arguing with its conscience.

We hold these truths to be self-evident. In those words, I hear the spirit of Douglass and Delany, as well as Jefferson and Lincoln; the struggles of Martin and Malcolm and unheralded marchers to bring these words to life. I hear the voices of Japanese families interned behind barbed wire; young Russian Jews cutting patterns in Lower East Side sweatshops; dust-bowl farmers loading up their trucks with the remains of shattered lives. I hear the voices of the people in Altgeld Gardens, and the voices of those who stand outside this country's borders, the weary, hungry bands crossing the Rio Grande. I hear all of these voices clamoring for recognition, all of them asking the very same questions that have come to shape my life, the same questions that I sometimes, late at night, find myself asking the Old Man. What is our community, and how might that community be reconciled with our freedom? How far do our obligations reach? How do we transform mere power into justice, mere sentiment into love? The answers I find in law books don't always satisfy me—for every *Brown* v. *Board of Education* I find a score of cases where conscience is sacrificed to expedience or greed. And yet, in the conversation itself, in the joining of voices, I find myself modestly encouraged, believing that so long as the questions are still being asked, what binds us together might somehow, ultimately, prevail.

That faith, so different from innocence, can sometimes be hard to sustain. Upon my return to Chicago, I would find the signs of decay accelerated throughout the South Side—the neighborhoods shabbier, the children edgier and less restrained, more middle-class families heading out to the suburbs, the jails bursting with glowering youth, my brothers without prospects. All too rarely do I hear people asking just what it is that we've done to make so many children's hearts so hard, or what collectively we might do to right their moral compass—what values *we* must live by. Instead I see us doing what we've always done—pretending that these children are somehow not our own.

I try to do my small part in reversing this tide. In my legal practice, I work mostly with churches and community groups, men and women who quietly build grocery stores and health clinics in the inner city, and housing for the poor. Every so often I'll find myself working on a discrimination case, representing clients who show up at my law firm's office with stories that we like to tell ourselves should no longer exist. Most of these clients are slightly embarrassed by what's happened to them, as are the white co-workers who agree to testify on their behalf; no one wants to be known as a troublemaker. And yet at some point both plaintiff and witness decide that a principle is at stake, that despite everything that has happened, those words put to paper over two hundred years ago must mean something after all. Black and white, they make their claim on this community we call America. They choose our better history.

I think I've learned to be more patient these past few years, with others as well as myself. If so, it's one of several improvements in my character that I attribute to my wife, Michelle. She's a daughter of the South Side, raised in one of those bungalow-style houses that I spent so many hours visiting during my first year in Chicago. She doesn't always know what to make of me; she worries that, like Gramps and the Old Man, I am something of a dreamer. Indeed, in her eminent practicality and midwestern attitudes, she reminds me not a little of Toot. I remember how, the first time I took her back to Hawaii, Gramps nudged my ribs and said Michelle was quite "a looker." Toot, on the other hand, described my bride-to-be as "a very sensible girl"—which Michelle understood to be my grandmother's highest form of praise.

After our engagement, I took Michelle to Kenya to meet the other half of my family. She was an immediate success there as well, in part because the number of Luo words in her vocabulary very soon surpassed mine. We had a fine time in Alego, helping Auma on a film project of hers, listening to more of Granny's stories, meeting relatives I'd missed the first time around. Away from the countryside, though, life in Kenya seemed to have gotten harder. The economy had worsened, with a corresponding rise in corruption and street crime. The case of the Old Man's inheritance remained unresolved, and Sarah and Kezia were still not on speaking terms. Neither Bernard, nor Abo, nor Sayid had yet found steady work, although they remained hopeful—they were talking about learning how to drive, perhaps purchasing a used *matatu* together. We tried again to see George, our youngest brother, and were again unsuccessful. And Billy, the robust, gregarious cousin I'd first met in Kendu Bay, had been stricken with AIDS.

He was emaciated when I saw him, prone to nodding off in the middle of conversations. He seemed calm, though, and happy to see me, and asked that I send him a photograph of the two of us during better days. He died in his sleep before I could send it.

There were other deaths that year. Michelle's father, as good and decent a man as I've ever known, died before he could give his daughter away. Gramps died a few months later, after a prolonged bout with prostate cancer. As a World War II veteran, he was entitled to be interred at Punchbowl National Cemetery, on a hill overlooking Honolulu. It was a small ceremony with a few of his bridge and golf partners in attendance, a three-gun salute, and a bugle playing taps.

Despite these heartaches, Michelle and I decided to go ahead with our wedding plans. Reverend Jeremiah A. Wright, Jr., performed the service in the sanctuary of Trinity United Church of Christ, on Ninety-fifth and Parnell. Everyone looked very fine at the reception, my new aunts admiring the cake, my new uncles admiring themselves in their rented tuxedos. Johnnie was there, sharing a laugh with Jeff and Scott, my old friends from Hawaii and Hasan, my roommate from college. So were Angela, Shirley, and Mona, who told my mother what a fine job she'd done raising me. ("You don't know the half of it," my mother replied with a laugh.) I watched Maya politely fending off the advances of some brothers who thought they were slick but who were, in fact, much too old for her and should have known better, but when I started to grumble, Michelle told me to relax, my little sister could handle herself. She was right, of course; I looked at my baby sister and saw a full-grown woman, beautiful and wise and looking like a Latin countess with her olive skin and long black hair and black bridesmaid's gown. Auma was standing beside her, looking just as lovely, although her eyes were a little puffy—to my surprise she was the only one who cried during the ceremony. When the band started to play, the two of them sought out the protection of Michelle's five- and six-year-old cousins, who impressively served as our official ring-bearers. Watching the boys somberly lead my sisters out onto the dance floor, I thought they looked like young African princes in their little kente-cloth caps and matching cumberbunds and wilted bow ties.

The person who made me proudest of all, though, was Roy. Actually, now we call him Abongo, his Luo name, for two years ago he decided to reassert his African heritage. He converted to Islam, and has sworn off pork and tobacco and alcohol. He still works at his accounting firm, but talks about moving back to Kenya once he has enough money. In fact, when we saw each other in Home Squared, he was busy building a hut for himself and his mother, away from our grandfather's compound, in accordance with Luo tradition. He told me then that he had moved forward with his import business and hoped it would soon pay enough to employ Bernard and Abo full-time. And when we went together to stand by the Old Man's grave, I noticed there was finally a plaque where the bare cement had been.

Abongo's new lifestyle has left him lean and clear-eyed, and at the wedding, he looked so dignified in his black African gown with white trim and matching cap that some of our guests mistook him for my father. He was certainly the older brother that day, talking me through prenuptial jitters, patiently telling me for the fifth and sixth time that yes, he still had the ring, nudging me out the door with the observation that if I spent any more time in front of the mirror it wouldn't matter how I looked because we were sure to be late.

Not that the changes in him are without tension. He's prone to make lengthy pronouncements on the need for the black man to liberate himself from the poisoning influences of European culture, and scolds Auma for what he calls her European ways. The words he speaks are not fully his own, and in his transition he can sometimes sound stilted and dogmatic. But the magic of his laughter remains, and we can disagree without rancor. His conversion has given him solid ground to stand on, a pride in his place in the world. From that base I see his confidence building; he begins to venture out and ask harder questions; he starts to slough off the formulas and slogans and decides what works best for him. He can't help himself in this process, for his heart is too generous and full of good humor, his attitude toward people too gentle and forgiving, to find simple solutions to the puzzle of being a black man.

Toward the end of the wedding, I watched him grinning widely for the video camera, his long arms draped over the shoulders of my mother and Toot, whose heads barely reached the height of his chest. "Eh, brother," he said to me as I walked up to the three of them. "It looks like I have two new mothers now." Toot patted him on the back. "And we have a new son," she said, although when she tried to say "Abongo" her Kansas tongue mangled it hopelessly. My mother's chin started to tremble again, and Abongo lifted up his glass of fruit punch for a toast.

"To those who are not here with us," he said.

"And to a happy ending," I said.

We dribbled our drinks onto the checkered-tile floor. And for that moment, at least, I felt like the luckiest man alive.

BARACK OBAMA is the junior U.S. senator from Illinois. He began his career as a community organizer in some of Chicago's poorest communities and then attended Harvard Law School, where he was elected the first African-American president of the Harvard Law Review. In 1992, he directed Illinois Project VOTE, which registered 150,000 new voters. From 1997 to 2004, he served as a three-term state senator from Chicago's South Side. In addition to his legislative duties, he has been a senior lecturer in constitutional law at the University of Chicago Law School, practiced civil rights law, and served on the board of directors of various charitable organizations.

Obama lives in Chicago's Hyde Park neighborhood with his wife, Michelle, and daughters, Malia and Sasha.